BEING KNOWN

Being Known

CHRISTOPHER PEACOCKE

CLARENDON PRESS · OXFORD
1999

Oxford University Press, Great Clarendon Street, Oxford OX2 6DP

Oxford New York

Athens Auckland Bangkok Bogotá Buenos Aires Calcutta
Cape Town Chennai Dar es Salaam Delhi Florence Hong Kong Istanbul
Karachi Kuala Lumpur Madrid Melbourne Mexico City Mumbai
Nairobi Paris São Paulo Singapore Taipei Tokyo Toronto Warsaw
and associated companies in
Berlin Ibadan

Oxford is a registered trade mark of Oxford University Press

Published in the United States by
Oxford University Press Inc., New York

British Library Cataloguing in Publication Data
Data available

Library of Congress Cataloging in Publication Data
Peacocke, Christopher.
Being known / Christopher Peacocke.
Includes bibliographical references.
1. Knowledge, Theory of. 2. Metaphysics. I. Title.
BD 161.P38 1999 121—dc21 98–45921
ISBN 0–19–823859–2
ISBN 0–19–823860–6 (Pbk.)

1 3 5 7 9 10 8 6 4 2

Typeset by Invisible Ink
Printed in Great Britain
on acid-free paper by
Biddles Ltd., Guildford and King's Lynn

PREFACE

The impetus for the main ideas of this book came from some reflection on my previous work. In the summer of 1994, in reviewing the preceding year's work, I was struck that the same issues about the relations between metaphysics and epistemology were arising again and again, in one area after another. Though one could certainly address these issues as best one could in any specific area, it became irresistible to ask broader questions. What are the constraints one ought to respect when attempting to resolve some tension between the metaphysics and the epistemology of a given subject matter? Can we identify principles which can guide us in the selection and development of one kind of resolution rather than another in a given area? How more generally should we conceive of the relations between metaphysics and epistemology?

These questions are immensely general. Therein lies both their attraction and their danger. If one can get something right at this level, it will have wide application. Yet any claim at this level will also be potentially refutable by points about almost any domain of thought. I am very conscious that this book is at best a beginning: an attempt to detail a few parts, and to outline a few broad contours, of what is really a vast and rich landscape. Not only have I unavoidably restricted myself to certain selected areas in which the issue of the relation between metaphysics and epistemology is particularly pressing. Even in the discussion of general, domain-independent principles, I am conscious of many large-scale issues which the discussion has generated in passing, and with which it has not been possible to engage without diverting attention from the argument. I have tried to indicate these points as they arise; and I express the hope that others may be encouraged to pursue them.

This book would certainly not exist without the quite extraordinary support of a Research Professorship from the Leverhulme Trust. I am deeply grateful for the appointment. It has allowed me to work on topics that I thought I might never reach. I thank Mark Sainsbury for first drawing my attention to the existence of the Research Professorships; the Board of the Faculty of Literae Humaniores and the General Board of Oxford University for allowing me to apply for one; Dorothy Edgington for taking up a Professorship at Oxford created for the period of my research leave; and Magdalen College for continuing support. The support of these individuals and institutions for this research leave has meant a great deal to me.

The referees commissioned by Oxford University Press to review and comment on a draft of this book were Stephen Schiffer and Timothy Williamson. Rarely if ever have I received commissioned comments of such perceptiveness and value. They have made me rethink many an argument. Even in cases in which I have ended up with the position I originally held, my understanding of the best route to the conclusion has been substantially altered. Uncommissioned, Derek Parfit also offered forceful and detailed comments on every chapter. When he was in Oxford for Trinity Term 1998, Wolfgang Künne was also able to advise me on what are now the first three chapters. I am extremely grateful to these four philosophers, both for the philosophy and for much wise editorial and expository advice.

Support from the Leverhulme Trust has also permitted me to discuss philosophy much more frequently than would otherwise have been possible with Tyler Burge of the University of California at Los Angeles. These stimulating discussions, ranging over the years across many parts of philosophy, have been immensely valuable to me.

It has been my privilege recently to be a Visiting Professor for a half-semester each year at New York University's outstanding Philosophy Department. Although these visits were arranged long before the Leverhulme Professorship was on the horizon, the combination of the two allowed me to develop a cycle of working on the material in this book for most of the year, and then presenting the results in a research seminar at NYU. I am especially grateful to Paul Boghossian, Chair of the NYU Philosophy Department, for proposing and bringing about this arrangement. Much of the present material has been honed in seminars and discussions at NYU, where I have benefited substantially from the comments of Ned Block, Paul Boghossian, Susan Carey, Hartry Field, Barry Loewer, Thomas Nagel, and Stephen Schiffer.

Early versions of this material were also presented to various other discussion groups, colloquia, conferences, and seminars. A version of Chapters 1 and 2 formed the first Weatherhead Lecture at Tulane

University, New Orleans, in the spring of 1998. For comments at presentations which have influenced me I thank Akeel Bilgrami, Bill Brewer, John Campbell, John Collins, Donald Davidson, Martin Davies, Michael Dummett, Dorothy Edgington, Graeme Forbes, Paul Horwich, Michael Martin, Barry Stroud, Bernard Williams, Timothy Williamson, and David Wiggins. Some parts of this book also draw upon, develop, and sometimes correct material in papers previously published ('First-Person Reference, Representational Independence, and Self-Knowledge', 'Entitlement, Self-Knowledge and Conceptual Redeployment', 'Conscious Attitudes, Attention and Self-Knowledge', 'Metaphysical Necessity: Understanding, Truth, and Epistemology', and 'The Modality of Freedom'; full details can be found in the Bibliography). For comments on that earlier work, I repeat my thanks to David Bell, Paul Boghossian, Bill Brewer, Tyler Burge, John Campbell, Mark Crimmins, Michael Dummett, Hartry Field, Jerry Fodor, James Higginbotham, Paul Horwich, Kirstie Laird, Michael Martin, Ruth Millikan, Thomas Nagel, Derek Parfit, John Perry, Mark Sainsbury, Stephen Schiffer, Paul Snowdon, Jason Stanley, David Wiggins, Timothy Williamson, Crispin Wright, Takashi Yagisawa, and Eddy Zemach. The reliable and far-sighted help of my secretary, Jo Cartmell, has also been of special value whilst I was working on this book.

I also wish to thank my editor at Oxford University Press, Peter Momtchiloff, for support, encouragement, and exemplary efficiency in all aspects of the handling of my manuscript. I have also been helped by the very experienced copy-editing of Angela Blackburn, of Invisible Ink. Her suggestions have improved the exposition on many pages.

Finally I thank my wife, Teresa, who suggested the title of this book ('Don't put another book in the world with a title of the form "X and Y", or "X, Y, and Z"!' was her prefatory remark). I was surprised, on checking through various databases, not to find books for which this title had already been used. The closest any other title came to it is that of the book *Being Informed*. That book apparently contains practical advice for metropolitan police forces on how to manage their networks of informers. I hope there is little danger of confusion of that topic with my own.

Magdalen College, Oxford   C.A.B.P.
24 September 1998

CONTENTS

I

The Integration Challenge

In a number of diverse areas of philosophy, we face a common problem. The problem is one of reconciliation. We have to reconcile a plausible account of what is involved in the truth of statements of a given kind with a credible account of how we can know those statements, when we do know them.

The problem of reconciliation may take various forms. We may have a clear conception of the means by which we ordinarily come to know the statements in question. Yet at the same time we may be unable to provide any plausible account of truth conditions knowledge of whose fulfilment could be obtained by these means. Alternatively we may have a clear conception of what is involved in the statements' truth, but be unable to see how our actual methods of forming beliefs about their subject matter can be sufficient for knowing their truth. In some cases we may be unclear on both counts. I call the general task of providing, for a given area, a simultaneously acceptable metaphysics and epistemology, and showing them to be so, the *Integration Challenge* for that area.

The Integration Challenge is the generalization, to an arbitrary subject matter, of the challenge which Paul Benacerraf so sharply identified and discussed for mathematical truth in his paper of that name.[1] Benacerraf wrote that 'the concept of mathematical truth, as explicated, must fit into an over-all account of knowledge in a way that makes it intelligible how we have the mathematical knowledge that we have' (409). While the Integration Challenge for mathematics certainly has its own distinctive features, what Benacerraf here asserts about mathematical truth applies to any subject matter. The concept of truth, as it is explicated for any given subject matter, must

---

[1] P. Benacerraf, 'Mathematical Truth', *Journal of Philosophy* 70 (1973), 661–80, repr. in P. Benacerraf and H. Putnam (eds.), *Philosophy of Mathematics: Selected Readings*, 2nd edn. (Cambridge: Cambridge University Press, 1983). Page references are to this reprinting.

fit into an over-all account of knowledge in a way that makes it intelligible how we have the knowledge in that domain that we do have.

In describing the task of meeting the Integration Challenge in any given area as that of integrating a metaphysics with an epistemology, I am, evidently, not meaning by 'metaphysics' an erroneous conception of the commitments of some class of judgements we make. No doubt that meaning has historical precedents. What I mean is a correct conception of what is, constitutively, involved in the truth of a given class of judgements.

There are several ways in which a metaphysics so conceived might proceed. It might, in a few exceptional cases, proceed by some reductive account of truth in the relevant domain. More commonly, a metaphysics will proceed by elaborating some general principles to which truth conforms in the particular class of judgements in question. Or it may elaborate various relations of dependence, independence, or interconnections between truth in the given domain and other matters—mental states, states of the non-mental world, or other classes of truth. The general conception of metaphysics I have in mind is then close to that of Peter Strawson's descriptive metaphysics, which aims 'to describe the actual structure of our thought about the world'.[2] Part of the actual structure of our thought about some particular domain is often implicit acceptance of certain principles about truth in that domain. For domains in which those principles are correct, the Integration Challenge for a given domain is quite properly described as characterizing a simultaneously acceptable descriptive metaphysics and an epistemology for statements about that domain.

It is of course a substantive question whether a plausible solution to the Integration Challenge in a given area could ever force us to think that the actual structure of our thought about that area involves incorrect principles. If there are areas for which that conclusion is forced, then metaphysics as conceived in the Integration Challenge, and descriptive metaphysics as conceived by Strawson, can come apart. In fact, in all the areas I will be considering in a little more detail later it seems to me that the metaphysics I will be endorsing is revisionary only of false philosophical theories of the area in ques-

---

[2] P. Strawson, *Individuals: An Essay in Descriptive Metaphysics* (London: Methuen, 1959), 9.

tion. It is not revisionary of the actual structure of our thought, when correctly characterized.[3]

In its most general and abstract form, the Integration Challenge is not dependent on any very contentious philosophical doctrines. The challenge does not arise only for someone who has some prior, domain-independent, general theory about truth, be it anti-realistic or of any other kind. Nor does the challenge arise only for someone with a prior general theory of understanding or epistemology, such as a neo-Wittgensteinian criterial theory. The challenge can be generated in a given domain simply by reflecting on particular features of truth in that domain, and asking how what we normally take to be our methods of coming to know truths in that area are to be reconciled with those features of truth in that area. In such a case, the only background presupposition necessary to generating a challenge is the unexceptionable principle that anything which is a means of coming to know that p must be something which can make rational acceptance of all that is involved in the truth of p.

Probably the best way to substantiate this claim of the relative theory-independence of the Integration Challenge is to move straight to some examples. The Integration Challenge of course needs to be addressed for every subject matter. There is probably no area for which we have a full philosophical understanding of how to meet it. All the same, the challenge is more pressing in some areas than in others, in particular in those in which the even the most general outlines of an integrationist solution remain obscure to us. So here are three areas in which the Integration Challenge arises in a particularly sharp form.

(a) *Necessity.* We naturally think of statements about what is necessary, and what is contingent, as objective. The most developed metaphysical account of modal truth, however, has been Lewis's modal realism, which treats other possible worlds as things of the same kind as the universe around you.[4] This modal realism arguably makes modal truth radically inaccessible. It must be tempting to give less exotic theories of the nature of modal truth. But many previous attempts at less exotic treatments have either relied on notions of

---

[3] No doubt we should, however, always keep it in mind that Berkeley said exactly the same of his undoubtedly revisionary views of the physical world.

[4] D. Lewis, *On the Plurality of Worlds* (Oxford: Blackwell, 1986).

provability, and result in treatments which are not even extensionally correct; or else they have embraced equally implausible expressivist, conventionalist, or other mind-dependent treatments of modality. We need a metaphysical treatment of modal truth which retains the objectivity of modal claims, but not at the price of their epistemic inaccessibility. A good treatment of modal truth must ratify our basic methods of establishing modal truths as sound methods. Extant accounts of the metaphysical modalities have not met the Integration Challenge.

(b) *Knowledge of the Intentional Contents of our Own Mental States.* Thinkers ordinarily know the intentional contents of a vast range of their beliefs and other propositional attitudes, without inference or reasoning, and without checking on their environmental relations. It would also be widely (though not universally) agreed that the conceptual components of these intentional contents are individuated in part by the complex environmental relations in which a thinker must stand if he is to possess those concepts. So we have the phenomenon of a thinker's having non-inferential, non-observational knowledge of a property he possesses, a property which nevertheless constitutively requires that he stand in certain external environmental relations.

How is this possible? In this domain, the metaphysics of what is involved in the enjoyment of states with intentional content is relatively clear. We have a relatively good preliminary understanding of the explanatory role of these states. This understanding makes it entirely natural to expect external individuation of intentional content. Propositional attitudes characteristically explain properties of actions which involve the environment. What we do not have, as yet, is a developed epistemology which meshes satisfactorily with this metaphysics. There have been important attempts to appeal to the self-verifying nature of some psychological self-ascriptions to resolve this problem, but they treat only a special case.[5] A general solution is needed, one which squares with what we already know about externalism and about self-knowledge.

This second example also illustrates the way in which the Integration Challenge is to be distinguished from the general anti-

---

[5] For pioneering discussion, see T. Burge, 'Individualism and Self-Knowledge', *Journal of Philosophy* 85 (1988), 649–63.

realist challenge developed in the writings of Michael Dummett.[6] Meeting the anti-realist challenge is certainly one part of integrating metaphysics and epistemology for any given subject matter. If we think that truth can outrun knowability in a given subject matter, then it must be part of the Integration Challenge for us to explain how that is possible. The Integration Challenge is, however, more general than the anti-realist challenge. It can arise even for areas in which undecidability or unverifiability is not an issue. The contents of a thinker's own mental states illustrate just that point. The intentional contents of a thinker's mental states mentioned in this particular challenge are certainly knowable by her and others. In the presence of an externalist treatment of intentional content, it is precisely the distinctive nature of this knowability, rather than any variety of unknowability, which is generating this instance of the Integration Challenge.

(c) *The Past*. The past is perhaps the most intuitively compelling domain in which we seem to have a conception of a kind of statement which can be true though quite undiscoverably so. The truth of certain past-tense statements may be undiscoverable now and undiscoverable in the future. I will even be arguing in Chapter 2 that their truth may also have been undiscoverable at the time which the statements concern. The intuitive metaphysics for such statements is realistic. The question of how our past-tense thought can have a content which is capable of undiscoverable truth has still not, in my judgement, been fully answered. If we are to continue to be realists about the past, we need to develop a theory which answers this question. The theory must answer the question in a way which still ratifies our ordinary methods of finding out about the past as capable of delivering knowledge of states of affairs of a kind which can, on occasion, obtain unverifiably.

It is certainly true that for this particular domain of the past, anti-realist versions of the Integration Challenge have been theory-driven. They have often been motivated by the underlying idea that meaning is somehow fixed by certain kinds of confrontation with states of

---

[6] Amongst Dummett's many writings on the topic, see especially his 'What is a Theory of Meaning? (II)', in G. Evans and J. McDowell (eds.), *Truth and Meaning: Essays in Semantics* (Oxford: Oxford University Press, 1976).

affairs. A satisfying response to the Integration Challenge here must also say what is right and what is wrong with that underlying idea.

Some may question whether there is any real challenge presented by these or other examples. For, they may argue, if there genuinely is a concept here, there must be a class of basic methods for coming to know truths involving the concept. Such a doctrine might be supported in various ways. In fact, I agree with a qualified form of this doctrine, and I will be developing an argument for it later in this chapter. The doctrine cannot, however, show that the Integration Challenge does not need to be met. It is one thing to argue, as does this doctrine, that it must be possible to meet the challenge. It is another thing to say how to meet it. It is the how-question which the Integration Challenge is raising. Moreover, we must remember that little clause 'if there genuinely is a concept here' which entered the formulation of the doctrine. In a case in which integration proves particularly difficult to achieve, the option of denying that there is any concept of the kind commonly supposed in the case in question becomes more attractive. This has certainly been so for the case of metaphysical necessity, where the sceptical position will be that we really do not have a concept other than that of the obvious, of the logically true, of the definitional, or the like. The only fully satisfying way of answering such scepticism is actually to meet the Integration Challenge in detail, for the concept as it is commonly supposed to be.

Contextualist theories of knowledge will not make the Integration Challenge disappear. Contextualist theories claim that certain puzzles about knowledge arise only because of a failure to appreciate a shift in epistemic standards, or in a class of relevant alternatives. The shift is said to be induced by a conversational or other contextual event. What might be the standard of which it is true that when we adopt it unshiftingly, the puzzles posed by the examples (a) through (c) then disappear? I doubt that there is any such standard, or at least any that we could accept. The puzzles do not depend on shifting standards. The puzzles will disappear only if the Integration Challenge is met in detail. But if we can meet the Integration Challenge in detail, we will not need to appeal to shifting contexts. This is not to denigrate the study of shifting standards and contextual phenomena. They are interesting in themselves, and have to be understood for a clear view of many examples. The present point is just that puzzles such as (a) through (c) do not seem to depend on shifting contexts.

We can distinguish at least seven possible kinds of response to the Integration Challenge in any given area. In attempting to meet the challenge in a given domain, we need to consider the following options, options to which I will be alluding throughout this book.

(1) We may reconceive our metaphysics of the domain in such a way as to integrate our view of truth in that domain with the epistemology appropriate to that domain. This is the course I will be recommending in a little more detail later for the case of metaphysical necessity.

(2) We may achieve integration by reconceiving the epistemology for the statements that led to a problem of integration. This seems to me the right course for the case of the knowledge each one of us has of the externally individuated intentional contents of many of his own mental states (and also arguably for our knowledge of the states that have those contents). This is the option which will tempt anyone who thinks that externalism about intentional content is so firmly grounded in the nature of the rational explanation of thought and action, and in the epistemology of ordinary non-psychological subject matters, that revising the externalist metaphysics of such states is not a live option.

Certain ways of reconceiving the metaphysics will also necessarily have repercussions for the epistemology. For instance, consider a theorist who revises some initially internalist conception of the metaphysics of certain mental events and states. These mental events may include conscious judgements and perceptions, and these are events of a kind which stand in justifying relations to other events and states. The theorist's revision will then have consequences for what can be counted as justified by those states. It may thus open the door to integrationist solutions which would not otherwise be available.

(3) A third option is for us to reconceive the relations between our existing metaphysics and epistemology in such a way that any appearance of incompatibility, or of unexplained gaps between them, is removed. Solutions of this kind will often fall into one of the first two kinds as well, for some questionable background theory about the metaphysics or the epistemology may be the source of an erroneous impression of incompatibility. But it is also possible that such an incorrect impression may result from some background theory of

the relations between metaphysics and epistemology. I believe that the proper resolution of the integrationist challenge about the past falls under this third case.

In general, a proposed response to the Integration Challenge may fall into more than one, and possibly all, of these first three kinds. A solution of any one of these first three kinds may need innovative thought. There is, however, also a sense in which any such solution can be classified as a conservative solution. What it conserves is the idea that there is a truth condition for the problematic statements which can be integrated with an acceptable epistemology.

The other four types of option are, by contrast, revisionary. They reject the idea that there is a truth condition of the sort the problematic statements are commonly thought to possess, and for which the Integration Challenge can be met. The following four revisionary options are, then, exclusive of the first three kinds. They are also mutually exclusive.

(4) One kind of revisionary option does not reject the notion of a truth condition altogether, but offers some kind of slimmed-down truth conditions which are said to capture some but not all of the intuitive content of the problematic sentences. The claim of theorists of this fourth kind is that the Integration Challenge can be met for their slimmed-down contents. They will say that the apparently insuperable problems are all traceable back to the excess, and perhaps spurious, content which these theorists intentionally cut away. For example, theorists who think that all legitimate statements about the infinite can be explained in terms of the potential infinite may agree that they do not capture everything that others have meant, or thought they meant, by the actual infinite. These theorists, if they adopt this fourth option, will say that the Integration Challenge is insoluble for the actual infinite. That does not mean, they will add, that we can never make true positive statements about infinity: we must acknowledge only the slimmed-down truth condition. Similarly, some theorists, when faced with the problem of the freedom of the will, may also be tempted to say that they cannot capture everything that many people think is meant by 'could have done otherwise'. They may, though, be prepared to offer some truth conditions for 'he acted freely' which can be fulfilled, and for which there is some integration of the metaphysics and epistemology.

(5) We may become sceptical that there really are, for some given problematic class of statements, any truth conditions—even slimmed-down ones—of which in suitable circumstances we can come to know that they are fulfilled. Instead of aiming for integration of assigned truth conditions with epistemology, under this option we give a theory which assigns those statements a certain role in our thought and action, a role which explains their importance for us. David Hilbert's treatment of the infinite is one example of this strategy, and Hartry Field's view of all apparent talk about numbers is another.[7] This fifth option is sometimes labelled the 'non-factualist' option. Peter Strawson's treatment of statements about freedom in his essay 'Freedom and Resentment' is very likely a non-factualist treatment of statements about freedom and responsibility.[8] An explicitly non-factual development of statements about freedom and responsibility is given by Christine Korsgaard in the title essay of her collection *Creating the Kingdom of Ends*.[9] It is no accident that all the areas treated by these various thinkers are ones in which the integration problem is acute.

The label 'non-factualist' for this fifth option is tendentious if applied to all theories which adopt its main idea. It would have to be accompanied by some qualifications if it is to be applied fairly to Simon Blackburn's quasi-realism.[10] Precisely what distinguishes Blackburn's quasi-realism about a given area is its intended combination of an explanation of contents in that area in terms of a certain kind of role (the expression of attitudes on his treatment of the modal and moral cases) whilst also allowing talk of the truth of these con-

---

[7] D. Hilbert, 'On the Infinite', trans. E. Putnam and G. Massey, repr. in P. Benaceraff and H. Putnam (eds.), *Philosophy of Mathematics: Selected Readings*, 2nd edn. (Cambridge: Cambridge University Press, 1983), esp. 192 ff.; H. Field, *Science Without Numbers: A Defence of Nominalism* (Oxford: Blackwell, 1980). Field does assign truth conditions to numerical statements such as '1 + 1 = 2', but he thinks that such truth conditions are not fulfilled, since, according to Field, there are no numbers to which their singular terms can refer. That is, the truth conditions he does assign are not ones for which he would say the Integration Challenge can be met in a way which explains their epistemic value for us.

[8] P. Strawson, 'Freedom and Resentment', repr. in his *Freedom and Resentment and Other Essays* (London: Methuen, 1974).

[9] C. Korsgaard, 'Creating the Kingdom of Ends: Reciprocity and Responsibility in Personal Relations', in her *Creating the Kingdom of Ends* (Cambridge: Cambridge University Press, 1996).

[10] S. Blackburn, *Essays in Quasi-Realism* (New York: Oxford University Press, 1993).

tents. If 'non-factual' means 'lacking truth', Blackburn's quasi-realist could fairly protest that his position is not non-factualist in that sense. It would be better to characterize the fifth option as one on which the significance and epistemic value for us of the statements in question is explained in terms of some favoured role in thought or action, rather than in terms of any ineliminable truth conditions (if any) which are assigned to the statements by the theorist of this fifth option.

An important pair of questions arises about the fifth option. What is the location of the boundary between those cases in which the fifth option is intelligible, and those cases in which it is not? Is the fifth option intelligible only against a background of sentences or contents for which a factualist position is correct? That these are prima facie live issues can be shown by a simple example. Suppose someone introduces us to what he says is a new expression, a logical constant, but insists that its meaning is to be given in accordance with this fifth option. Its meaning, says this theorist, is not given by its contributions to truth conditions, but by its role in certain inferences, a role which this theorist spells out to us in detail. In the case of a proposed logical constant, it seems always to be a substantive question whether there is a contribution to truth conditions for which the offered inferential rules are correct. If there is such a contribution to truth conditions, then this treatment of the new logical constant is not really an instance of the fifth option after all. If on the other hand there is no such contribution to truth conditions, it is a question whether we really know what this new expression means.[11]

Though these are matters of great controversy, my own view is that even for the simplest logical constants, we have some conception of a truth condition to which our ordinary rules are answerable, at least when those constants are ones which can be embedded in arbitrary operators. For some expressions for which arbitrary embedding is not so clearly significant, such as the indicative conditional, non-factualist accounts have been developed. It is then a major question whether a conditional explained, say, in terms of subjective conditional probability is possible only because at some level there are contents with genuine truth conditions. I will not pursue these issues

[11] Cp. my 'Understanding Logical Constants: A Realist's Account', *Proceedings of the British Academy* 73 (1987), 153–200, and 'Proof and Truth', in J. Haldane and C. Wright (eds.), *Reality, Representation and Projection* (New York: Oxford University Press, 1993).

further now, except to note that for a full understanding of the fifth option, these questions must be addressed.

The final two options in this enumeration are the most radical.

(6) The sixth option is that of the sceptic. The sceptic holds that there is no possibility of interesting knowledge in the domain in question. If he is right, there is no Integration Challenge to address. According to the sceptic, there are no interesting cases of knowledge which stand in tension with our conception of truth for the domain in question. Scepticism indeed often flows in part from a vivid appreciation of the demands of truth. Whilst I will not be tackling scepticism head-on in this work, if one of the forms of solution I propose is right, then possessing concepts of certain subject matters involves at least the possibility of knowledge of propositions about that subject matter. It has always been a good question to the sceptic how, by his lights, understanding of the notion of truth is possible at all. This book will propose some answers to how such understanding is possible, and how it is related to rational, knowledgeable judgement.

(7) The seventh option is the most radically revisionary. This option declares the whole alleged domain for which integration is in question spurious and based on illusions of such a depth of misconception that not even the options (4), (5), and (6) are available to us. On this seventh option, even to be a sceptic is to underappreciate the problem. The problem is not merely one of the unattainability of interesting knowledge. There is not even a coherent account of truth in the domain in question. Some have said that we are forced to occupy this seventh position in the case of any notion of a free action which could underwrite desert-implying attributions of responsibility. Galen Strawson has held that view in print,[12] and Derek Parfit has expressed it in conversation. It is also a common reaction to Roderick Chisholm's notion of agent causation.[13] Certain extreme doctrines of absolute space also arguably involve a notion of location for which not even the fourth to sixth options are available.

---

[12] G. Strawson, 'The Impossibility of Moral Responsibility', *Philosophical Studies* 75 (1994), 5–24.

[13] R. Chisholm, 'Human Freedom and the Self', repr. in G. Watson (ed.), *Free Will* (Oxford: Oxford University Press, 1982).

With these seven types of option before us, the following general questions arise:

How should we proceed in trying to achieve integration in any given area?

What are the general principles which determine, for any given area, the right type of solution for that area?

These are the questions for the next chapter. Then, in the remainder of the book, I go on to discuss ways of meeting the Integration Challenge in a series of domains, in accordance with the approach and constraints outlined in the course of addressing these questions.

2

Truth, Content, and the Epistemic

The overview in the previous chapter leaves us in need of some general and elaborated conception of the relations in which the metaphysics and the epistemology of some domain should stand to one another. Lacking any such conception, we are ill equipped to address the Integration Challenge in any given domain. This chapter aims to take some steps towards meeting the need.

2.1 THE LINKING THESIS

The first step I take in this attempt to meet the need is to propound a thesis linking the theory of intentional content with the theory of knowledge. After stating and defending the thesis, I will go on to consider its significance for the task of integrating metaphysics with epistemology.

The thesis states that there is a class of concepts each member of which can be individuated, partly or wholly, in terms of the conditions for a thinker's knowing certain contents containing those concepts; and that every concept is either such a concept, or is individuated ultimately in part by its relations to such concepts. I call this whole claim the 'Linking Thesis'.

Several approaches to the theory of intentional content attempt to individuate concepts in terms of certain conditions under which contents containing a target concept are accepted or judged. What is distinctive of the Linking Thesis is the claim that there is a class of concepts for which the theory of individuation can proceed not just in terms of acceptance or judgement, but in terms of knowledge. According to the Linking Thesis, a concept in this class can be individuated in part as the one for which satisfaction of certain conditions by the thinker suffices for knowledge of given contents containing the concept. If the Linking Thesis is right, the individuation of such a concept involves not just some canonical role in the formation of judgements, but a canonical role in the acquisition of knowledge. I call such concepts *epistemically individuated*.

The Linking Thesis can serve all comers—virtually anyone who uses the notion of a concept at all. For someone who holds that it is important to view concepts as given by the conceptual role of their corresponding expressions in a language of thought, there will be a version of the Linking Thesis available to them. For such a theorist, the roles characterized at the level of the language of thought will sometimes involve certain expressions being written in what Stephen Schiffer would call the 'belief-box'. The Linking Thesis is a thesis about the propositional attitudes, with intentional contents, which correspond to the inscription in the belief-box of sentences in the language of thought. The Linking Thesis can be accepted (or rejected, for that matter) without commitment to a specific one of the theories of concepts recently in circulation.

Not all concepts are epistemically individuated. Even when there are agreed ways of coming to know the truth or falsity of certain contents containing a given concept, the existence of those ways is not enough to establish that the concept is epistemically *individuated*. The existence of such ways of coming to know will be insufficient for epistemic individuation unless they are constitutive of possession of the concept in question. There are agreed ways of coming to know truths about atoms, electrons, and quarks which involve the results of cloud-chamber experiments, or displays on the screens at an accelerator complex like CERN or SLAC. There is no plausibility in the view that these ways of coming to know are constitutive of our way of thinking of atoms, electrons, and quarks. Understanding of these notions came first, and it was a substantial, and subsequent, intellectual achievement to work out how one might come to know the truth of certain contents containing these notions. That entities thought of in theoretical ways can be known about as the result of such-and-such experimental arrangements and results can be informative—just as, in a different kind of case, it can be informative to be told of a means of discovering whether the place 10^{30} metres from here in such-and-such direction is cold. So theoretical explanatory concepts of the empirical sciences are commonly not epistemically individuated.

There are of course often theoretical roles associated with theoretical concepts. These attributed roles are famously revisable without abandoning the theoretical concept in question. One cannot plausibly say that it is a condition for possession of a theoretical concept of an empirical science that anyone who possesses it must be willing to judge that something falling under the concept has a certain highly specific theoretical role. If on the other hand we make the role unspecific, it can hardly be individuative of the theoretical concept. Such roles as theoretical concepts have are not constitutive of those concepts.

An illustration of a rather different kind of concept which is not epistemically individuated is that of probability. Consider the judgement that the probability of the occurrence of an event of a given kind in specified circumstances is (say) one-third. This judgement is not one which is rationally required given certain frequencies or other evidence not involving the notion of probability. Frequencies and such other evidence are always compatible with the probability not being one-third. Perhaps one might develop a theory on which possession of the concept of probability involves some sensitivity of the thinker to how likely it is that the probability is so-and-so, given frequencies or other evidence. But that then is not a theory which is elucidating possession of the concept in terms of outright judgements of probability, but in terms of their likelihood (grasp of which would also have to be explained, of course). The conditions for possessing the concept of probability involve neither knowledge nor even outright judgements of probability in specified circumstances.

Someone questioning the Linking Thesis might ask: why does every concept which is not epistemically individuated have to be individuated ultimately by its relations to concepts which are epistemically individuated? Why cannot the model of inference to the best explanation, which is the basic way of coming to make rational judgements involving non-epistemically individuated concepts, apply all the way down?

The answer to this question is that if knowledge is to be possible at all, not everything can be known by inference to the best explanation. An inference to the best explanation can yield knowledge only if the propositions to be explained in the explanation are themselves already known. If they are not already known, the explanatory hypothesis in question, however impressive, cannot by that means acquire the status of knowledge. It follows that if knowledge is to be attainable in some cases by inference to the best explanation, there must be some knowledge which is not so attained.

The point is no more than a particular application to the case of inference to the best explanation of the principle that not everything can be known by inference. It is knowledge of contents containing epistemically individuated concepts which ultimately makes possible knowledge attained by inference to the best explanation.

So far, our characterization of the class of epistemically individuated concepts has been highly abstract. A first step towards characterizing the class of epistemically individuated concepts in more detail is to consider examples. A possession condition for an observational concept F plausibly entails that a thinker who possesses that concept will be prepared to judge that something is F when he has an experience of a certain kind, and is taking experience at face value. If the thinker is indeed perceiving properly, has an experience of the appropriate kind, and is taking experience at face value, and there are no other reasons for doubt, he does not merely believe, but knows, a content of the form 'That is F'. To take another case, if a thinker has the concept of conjunction, he must find the transition from the two premises p and q to the conjunction $p\&q$ compelling; and similarly for each of the two transitions from $p\&q$ to each of p and q as conclusions. If our thinker knows the premises of any one of these transitions, and comes to judge the corresponding conclusion by making the inference, the judgement of the resulting conclusion amounts to knowledge. It is intrinsic to the concept of conjunction that knowledge of $p\&q$ is attained when that conclusion is inferred from known premise p and known premise q; and that knowledge of each of p and q separately is attained when each is inferred from the known premise $p\&q$.[1] And so on: one could continue to look at credible philosophical accounts of the possession of various concepts, and case by case one could endeavour to confirm that these accounts could be transformed into accounts which speak of knowledge of certain contents containing the target concept. One could, case by case, build up a specification of a class of concepts of which it is true that its members are epistemically individuated.

Pursuit of this approach will, however, yield rather limited philo-

---

[1] R. Nozick's account of knowledge in his *Philosophical Explanations* (Cambridge, Mass.: Harvard University Press, 1981) famously commits him to denying this, but it is hard not to regard that as a problem for his account. There is further discussion of this and related issues in Saul Kripke's regrettably still unpublished lectures on Nozick's account, and in my *Thoughts: An Essay on Content* (Oxford: Blackwell, 1986), ch. 7.

sophical illumination. If there is a class of concepts which conforms to the first part of the Linking Thesis, we should want more than merely an enumerative characterization of its members. It would be good to have some more fundamental characterization which explains why any given concept which is epistemically individuated is so.

I suggest that any concept which can be individuated in terms of the conditions for accepting or judging outright certain contents containing the concept will also be an epistemically individuated concept. (A similar thesis arguably applies to concepts individuated in terms of outright non-probabilistic inference, but to keep things simple I will consider just the case of concepts individuated in terms of the conditions for making outright judgements of certain contents containing the concept.) The following four-step argument is an explanation for why this generalization holds. Here are the steps of the argument first, before I try to elaborate and justify them. In this argument, and throughout what follows, I use the expression 'possession condition' for any correct philosophical account of what it is to possess a given concept, without any proprietary restriction to some favoured type or form of account. The argument then runs thus:

(1) Take a target concept which is individuated in terms of its role in outright judgement. Then consider the judgements mentioned in the concept's possession condition, as judgements a thinker must be willing to make in specified circumstances. These judgements must be ones which are rationally required of the thinker, in those circumstances, if she makes any judgement on the matter at all. They must be rationally non-discretionary judgements.

(2) Rationally non-discretionary judgements aim at knowledge.

(3) So, if the suitably attained presuppositions of the thinker when making a rationally non-discretionary judgement are fulfilled, and any beliefs on which she is relying in making it are knowledge, and any faculties on which she is relying are operating properly, the rationally non-discretionary judgement will be knowledge.

(4) Hence the target concept could be individuated in part in the following way: as that concept which, when certain judgements

involving it are made by specified methods, and the properly
made presuppositions are fulfilled, and any beliefs on which
the thinker is relying are knowledge, and any faculties on
which she is relying are operating properly, then the judgements so reached involving the concept are knowledge. That
is, it will often explain the difference between two epistemically individuated concepts that they differ in respect of the
ways in which a thinker can come to know certain contents
containing those concepts, where these are ways which contribute to the individuation of the concepts in question.

So much by way of dogmatic statement: now I will attempt to justify
the steps of the argument.

Premise (1) just draws out part of what is involved in the idea of a
possession condition for a concept which is individuated in terms of
its role in outright judgement or acceptance. A possession condition
formulated in terms of outright judgement or acceptance says what
a thinker has to be willing to judge, in specified circumstances, if she
is to possess the concept. If, in given circumstances, a content is one
on which a rational thinker can intelligibly withhold judgement, consistently with her possession of the concepts involved, then judging
that content in those circumstances cannot be part of the possession
condition for any of the concepts composing the content. This is why,
for instance, there is no number of positive instances such that the
possession condition for an open-ended universal quantifier requires
acceptance of an open-ended generalization containing it once the
thinker has accepted that number of positive instances (and no negative instances). The inductive sceptic, who refuses to accept an open-
ended quantification on such a basis, understands open-ended
universal quantification only too well. Only those judgements which
a possessor of the concept must, rationally, be willing to make, in
specified circumstances, can be mentioned in the possession condition. In the particular case of universal quantification, those judgements would include acceptance of the negation of the universal
quantification once a negative instance is accepted.

The case for premise (1) connects something normative—the
rationally non-discretionary—with a descriptive condition which
states what it is for a thinker to possess a given concept. The case does
not confuse the normative and with constitutive description. Rather,
it connects the two. The case for premise (1) does make a tacit

assumption, the unexceptionable assumption that a thinker can do what rationality permits. Spelled out more fully, the case for (1) would run as follows. If rationality permits a thinker to withhold judgement on a content containing a given concept, in specified circumstances, while continuing to possess that concept, then it is possible for a thinker to withhold such judgement while possessing the concept. It follows that willingness to make such a judgement cannot be part of the possession condition for the concept in question. The judgement cannot, in the specified circumstances, be rationally non-discretionary. By contraposition, any outright judgements mentioned in the possession condition for a concept must, in the circumstances mentioned in the possession condition, be rationally non-discretionary.

To say that a judgement is rationally non-discretionary in given circumstances is not to say that the thinker is not free not to make it. Judgements are actions, normally made for reasons.[2] More specifically, a judgement is an accepting, an accepting as correct of the content of the judgement. Since acceptings do not have duration, this incidentally explains why a judgement—in contrast with an utterance—does not have a duration.[3] Psychological compulsions and the like aside, an agent is normally free to make a judgement and free not to make it. When I say that a judgement is rationally non-discretionary, all that I mean is that any failure to make the judgement, when the question arises, is a failure to do what rationality requires.

To say that judgements are actions is not to imply that the subject could rationally withhold judgement, or could rationally judge the opposite. It is too strong to demand, for something to be an action, that the subject could rationally do otherwise. That would be too strong even outside the realm of mental actions. The subject who steps aside to avoid being hit by a bicycle could not, given his desire to be uninjured, rationally do otherwise. His stepping aside is none the less an action. Having some real scope for the exercise of rational discretion is not a necessary condition for something to be an action. In some cases, exercising one's freedom to do otherwise than perform a certain action may unavoidably involve irrationality.

A further necessary element in a defence of the thesis that judgements are actions is the observation that not every case of coming to

---

[2] That judgements are acts was emphasized by P. Geach, *Mental Acts* (London: Routledge & Kegan Paul, 1957), 9.

[3] Hence I am in agreement with the point Geach is making when he writes that a judgement, unlike an utterance, is 'a non-successive unity' (*Mental Acts*, 105).

believe something is an action. We operate with a default practice of taking perceptual experience and the deliverances of memory at face value in a wide range of circumstances, without, impractically, stopping to endorse them in judgement case by case. We come to believe some of the contents of perceptual experience—or some of the conceptual contents which correspond to those contents—automatically. These are cases of coming to believe something which are not mental actions. Not every case of coming to accept something is a case of making a judgement.

The remainder of this book is written from the standpoint of one who accepts that judgements are actions. My own view is that the nature of belief, judgement, and intentional content cannot be properly elucidated unless we recognize that judgements are actions. It is, however, not strictly necessary for the treatment of the Integration Challenge in what follows to hold the thesis that judgements are actions. The claims I will be making can be modified into a form which is neutral on that thesis, and I ask readers who need to, to do so. When I talk of certain reasons making a judgement of a given content a rational act, these readers can construe me as saying that such a judgement would be a rational response to those reasons. (For my part, however, I cannot see why a response made for a reason is not also something done for a reason.)

I now turn to premise (2) of the argument. All judgements aim at truth, including those which are rationally discretionary. A rationally discretionary judgement is based on evidence which is inconclusive, even given the thinker's own other attitudes and presuppositions. It will be obvious to the thinker herself that it cannot amount to knowledge.

Judgements which are rationally non-discretionary are very different. That they aim at knowledge is shown by the conditions under which they will be withdrawn. Suppose you judge 'That's a coin' on the basis of your perceptual state. Suppose that this judgement is, given your other beliefs and presuppositions, rationally non-discretionary. If you are then told, and rationally accept, that there are many coin holograms in the vicinity, you must at the very least rationally reassess your acceptance of the content 'That's a coin'. It is no longer rational for you in these circumstances simply to take perceptual experiences as of coins at face value. If you decide to continue to accept 'That's a coin', that would rationally have to be the result of a new assessment, with new grounds. (You might, for instance, think it unlikely that a hologram of such detail could be created.) Your experience by itself no longer rationally sustains acceptance of the content 'That's a coin'. This point applies even if you are never told that the particular object you are seeing is not a coin.

It may be objected: 'All I'm initially relying on in such a case is the veridicality of my actual experiences. The fact that I could easily have had others which are not reliable, had I been looking in a different direction at another apparent coin, does not undermine that.' This objection substantially undercharacterizes the nature of the normal practice of taking perceptual experience at face value. The method the thinker is using is one she would equally have used had she been looking at something else. It was not dependent on her looking at this particular object, or in this particular direction, at this particular time. (If it had been, it would not have been a straightforward case of perceptual belief.) The rationality of taking perceptual experience at face value is undermined if the thinker comes to accept that something in these same circumstances, something at which she is not in fact looking, is not a coin even though it would produce the same subjective type of perceptual experience.

The kind of reliability which is needed here should not be characterized in statistical terms. It is better described in terms of counterfactuals: the subject would not have had the experience as of it's being the case that p had it not been the case that p, and this counterfactual holds too in circumstances which could easily have come about. A corresponding kind of reliability is presupposed in judgements based on personal memory, on propositional ('semantic') memory, and on testimony.[4]

I have been considering examples in which the thinker, in making a rationally non-discretionary judgement of a content, is relying on the deliverances of some faculty or social mechanism which operates to produce an event which represents that content as correct. The points I have been making seem to me to apply also to rationally non-discretionary judgements in general. That is, information implying that the judgement is not knowledge is by itself sufficient to require

[4] It is well known that there are examples in which an experience is a genuine perception, but if things had been only slightly different a backup mechanism would have intervened to produce the same kind of experience, regardless of whether it is veridical or not. These are, however, not cases in which the perception can yield perceptual knowledge. Nor is it rational for a thinker to take perceptual experience at face value if he has reason to believe that he may be in circumstances like this.

rational reassessment of such a judgement. If, for instance, a thinker's inferentially reached judgement that *p&q* is rationally non-discretionary, and the thinker then comes to learn that she does not know one of the premises *p*, say, from which the conjunction was inferred, rationality requires her to reassess her acceptance of the conjunction.

Such are the considerations in support of premise (2) of the argument. Now I turn to premise (3).

Suppose it is granted that a rationally non-discretionary judgement aims at knowledge. How does it follow, as (3) claims, that when the presuppositions in making such a judgement are properly fulfilled, the relevant faculties and mechanisms are working properly, and any beliefs relied upon are knowledge, the judgement will be knowledge? The argument is just that if they could all be fulfilled and yet the judgement still not be knowledge, then the judgement would not after all be rationally non-discretionary. Appreciation of the insufficiency for knowledge of the correctness of everything properly presupposed and relied upon in reaching such a judgement could lead the thinker rationally to withhold judgement of the content. For, once again, when a thinker makes a judgement which is rationally non-discretionary she is committed to thinking of her judgement as knowledge. Even if there are cases in which it is not decidable whether, in given circumstances, a judgement of a given content would be knowledge, that can only contribute to the intelligibility of a thinker withholding judgement in those same circumstances.

I have been oversimplifying a little (perhaps more). There are important further points about presuppositions. They must come to be held in a way which is reliably connected with their fulfilment, if fulfilment of the presuppositions, in the presence of the fulfilment of the other clauses of a possession condition, is to lead to knowledge of the corresponding content. Consider, for example, a thinker who works in Universal Studios and so is often surrounded by mere building façades not backed up by any real building. If he encounters some new construction on the lot, he cannot gain knowledge that it is an office building, even if it looks just like one and he is perceiving properly, simply by presupposing that this façade has a rear. The presupposition would not be appropriately made in his particular circumstances. Thus the earlier paragraphs were peppered with the qualifications 'suitably presupposed' and 'properly presupposed'.

It is also significant that this requirement about how the presuppositions come to be held cannot be dispensed with simply by enriching the content of the presuppositions. However rich the content of a presupposition, we can always conceive of it being reached by an inadequate route. When a presupposition comes to be held by an inadequate route, its fulfilment cannot help to sustain knowledge, however rich its content.

It is also important to distinguish sharply between presuppositions and what I will call 'informational conditions'. The operation of some faculty or mechanism may result in the occurrence of some event which represents a certain content p as being correct. The event may be a perceptual experience; or it may be a personal or 'semantic' (non-personal) memory; or it may be an utterance of a sentence. The informational conditions for a perceptual faculty are those which it has to meet to yield a genuine perception that p; the informational conditions for a memory faculty are those which it has to meet to yield a genuine memory that p; the informational conditions for a social mechanism are those which it has to meet for an utterance produced by the mechanism, and in which it is said that p, to be an utterance transmitting the information that p. (Here 'transmitting the information that p' is understood factively, to imply the truth of p.) The nature of the informational conditions is partly an a priori matter, and evidently also partly a matter requiring empirical investigation. Some of these faculties and mechanisms obviously embed others amongst these faculties and mechanisms. Personal memory can embed perception. Testimony can embed both. In such cases, the informational conditions for one faculty or mechanism may embed the informational conditions of another; and so on. For any given faculty or mechanism, the nature of the informational conditions, both in their a priori and in their empirical aspects, are not fully known and in some respects remain controversial. All that matters for present purposes is the point, which ought to be uncontroversial, that there are some such informational conditions.

The holding of informational conditions should not be assimilated to the fulfilment of a certain kind of presupposition. By this, I do not mean that a sophisticated thinker may not on occasion presuppose that she is perceiving, and even do so appropriately. (She obviously may do so.) What I mean is that in general the holding of an informational condition does not consist in the fulfilment of a certain presupposition made by a perceiver, rememberer, or language perceiver. The perceptual and memory faculties of a young child or a non-human animal may meet the informational conditions without the child or animal even having the concepts of perception or memory. Children and animals can gain knowledge by the use of perception and memory, when the informational conditions are fulfilled, by taking their deliverances at face value. An enthusiast for assimilating informational conditions to fulfilled presuppositions might at this juncture stretch. She might reach for the idea that there are presuppositions a thinker may make which are not conceptualized by her, and do not even feature in the content of any of her personal-level states. This move is in danger of separating presuppositions from reasons and the conditions for rational withdrawal of judgements and beliefs. It is also hard to see what would properly ground such attributions of presuppositions, if it is cut off from the level of reasons. I will continue to be taking it that the presuppositions of a thinker in making a judgement have contents which are accessible to her at the personal, conscious, reason-giving level.

Mature humans, young children, and some animals can share, that is can have exactly the same, simple observational concepts, such as observational concepts of shape and colour. Suppose we were to attempt to write it into the possession condition of any such simple concept that one who possesses it must be willing to apply it when having an experience of a certain kind, and when he is presupposing that he is perceiving properly. Since young children and animals cannot make any such presuppositions, we would have a theory which leaves it unexplained how it is that we mature humans share some simple observational concepts with children and some animals. The possession conditions for observational concepts must make reference to perceptual experience, and the possibility of knowing that an object falls under an observational concept involves the fulfilment of the informational conditions for perception. It does not need to involve conceptualization, presupposition, or knowledge of the holding of those informational conditions. We need both the notion of an informational condition and the notion of a presupposition in characterizing much of our more elementary knowledge about our environment.

We also need to use the notion of something being rationally non-discretionary for someone who is operating in the mode of taking perceptual experience (or memory, or testimony) at face value. An observational judgement may be rationally non-discretionary for a thinker who has a certain kind of perceptual experience and who is operating in the mode of taking perceptual experience at face value. The observational judgement is not absolutely rationally non-discretionary. It is not absolutely rationally non-discretionary, not even for one who has that experience, since a reflective thinker may question whether his experience is veridical.

This relative notion, of what is rationally non-discretionary for a thinker who is taking experience at face value, can be used in individuating certain concepts. Similarly, we may also use the notion of what is rationally non-discretionary for a thinker who accepts certain premises in individuating certain concepts which are fixed by their role in inference.

These points should help to dispel the impression that rationally non-discretionary judgement is something very strong, and in the nature of the case a rare occurrence. On the contrary, I think it is commonplace. In a wide range of cases, judgements made on the basis of evidence or reasons which may seem inconclusive, and so may seem rationally discretionary, are in fact cases in which, when one takes into account the thinker's presuppositions and the mode in which he is operating, the judgement is rationally non-discretionary. Visual experience as of a phone in front of you certainly does not by itself make your judgement 'That's a phone' rationally non-discretionary. But in ordinary circumstances, the thinker is operating in the mode of taking his visual experience at face value; he presupposes that objects which have one side like that of a phone have the remainder of the shape and material properties of a phone; he presupposes that objects of a certain shape and set of material properties have the function of permitting long-distance conversation by a certain means. In the presence of these presuppositions on the part of the thinker who is taking perceptual experience at face value, the judgement 'That's a phone' becomes rationally non-discretionary. That each of these is indeed a presupposition is evidenced in part by the fact that the thinker would be rationally obliged to reassess his judgement 'That's a phone' were he to come to believe that any one of them failed to hold. As before, similar points apply to judgements based on the deliverances of experiential memory, of non-personal memory, and of testimony.

There are also requirements for the status of being rationally non-discretionary which operate recursively. If a belief is inferred from a set of other beliefs, the inferred belief is rationally non-discretionary only if every member of the set from which it is inferred is rationally non-discretionary. If the set of beliefs involves beliefs resulting from the operation of some faculty like memory, the thinker must be taking the deliverances of that faculty at face value if any belief based on inference from that set is to be rationally non-discretionary.

Informational conditions and presuppositions both raise many issues which are important and interesting in their own right. Informational conditions have close links with what Tyler Burge calls 'entitlements'.[5] A thinker may be in a state which entitles him to form a certain belief or make a judgement, even though the state may be of a kind which is not conceptualized by an unsophisticated thinker. For each type of entitling event which presents a content p as true, there are certain conditions which, if met by that event, imply that its content is correct. These include the informational conditions I have been talking about. When the informational conditions are met (and also if there is no background reason for doubt), the occurrence of one of these entitling events can lead not only to true belief but also to knowledge. Informational conditions, entitlement, and knowledge are interrelated.

The conception of an event which represents a content p as holding, to a thinker who is taking the state and others of its general kind at face value, is somewhat different from the model of mere reliability offered by pure reliabilist approaches to epistemology. Pure reliability theories of knowledge have always had problems excluding the reliable but non-rational methods of reaching beliefs. By contrast, the thinker who has an experience as of its being the case that p when he is, legitimately, taking the experience at face value is a thinker who is rational in thereby coming to hold that p.

This observation carries argumentative weight, however, only to the extent that one can give some account of why it is rational to take certain events with representational content at face value which does not amount to a purely reliabilist account. It would take us some way off course to pursue this huge topic; but I would like to make one observation about a direction which could be pursued. The nature of the representational content in the fundamental case of perception is crucial in developing a view which is not exclusively reliabilist and which captures the required element of rationality. The account of what it is for a perceptual experience to have a representational con-

---

[5] T. Burge, 'Content Preservation', *Philosophical Review* 102 (1993), 457–88, at 458–9.

tent must advert to its membership of a kind some members of which possess correct contents in certain basic circumstances in which the subject of experience is, or was once, situated. I conjecture that this should be the starting point for an explanation of how it can be rational to take perceptual experience at face value. This starting point has the potential for explaining the rational legitimacy of taking perceptual experience at face value, without opening the floodgates to a pure, undiscriminating reliabilism.

To return to the main topic: if the general thrust of these points is correct, we are in a position to justify step (4) of the argument. A possession condition which mentions judgements can be transformed into one mentioning knowledge, as follows. We argued that judgements of the sort mentioned in the possession condition for the target concept F will be rationally non-discretionary. Let us fix on a judgement of a given content, the content $\Sigma(F)$, say, mentioned in F's possession condition. In the general case, the circumstances mentioned in this possession condition may include requirements such as these: that the rationally non-discretionary judgement be made when the thinker is operating in a certain mode M (such as that of taking perceptual experience at face value); that it be made with certain presuppositions, Prsp; that it is inferred from certain premises, Prem; and the judgement is made because the thinker is in some mental state, or is enjoying a certain mental event, E. We can now write the required knowledge-involving clause for a possession condition for the target concept F as follows, using these materials from the possession condition involving judgement.

Take the informational conditions, call them Inf, corresponding to the mode M in which the thinker is operating. In the case in which, for instance, the target concept is an observational concept, the informational conditions Inf would be the conditions for an experience to be a genuine perception. If what I have argued is correct, then the following conditional holds for an arbitrary concept F, where Prsp, Prem, and the rest are taken from the judgement-involving possession condition.

If:
  the informational conditions Inf are fulfilled;
  everything in the presupposition set Prsp is adequately reached
    and true, and all the premises in Prem are known;
  the thinker is in the mental state or enjoying the mental event E,

and judges that $\Sigma(F)$ because he is so, and because he accepts the members of Prem, and because he is making the presuppositions Prsp, and because of the mode in which he is operating;

then:

his judgement that $\Sigma(F)$ is knowledge.

This Kiplingesque formulation is just the generalization of the point I was making when I said that rationally non-discretionary judgements are knowledge when their various properly attained presuppositions are fulfilled, their premises are knowledge, and the relevant faculties or mechanisms are functioning properly.

The Kiplingesque conditional displayed in the preceding paragraph is cast in terms of knowledge. The Kiplingesque conditional can therefore function as one clause of a possession condition for the target concept F. We can similarly transform any other such judgement-involving clauses of a possession condition for F into clauses involving knowledge.

We need to be clear on the conclusion of the reasoning so far. The conclusion is not that there is, for concepts individuated in terms of outright judgement, a layer of epistemic requirements in addition to those formulated in terms of judgements. The argument is rather that when we appreciate the rationally non-discretionary nature of the judgements mentioned in such possession conditions, we are in a position to develop an argument that there are requirements for the possession of such concepts which can equally be formulated in terms of knowledge. The point is not that the formulation of the possession condition in terms of judgement is in some way incorrect. It is not. The point is rather that the formulation in terms of knowledge is equally correct.

We can distinguish between a concept's being epistemically individuated and its being *exclusively* epistemically individuated. A concept is exclusively epistemically individuated if it can be individuated in such a way that every clause of a judgement-involving possession condition for it can be replaced by one involving knowledge. The argument so far in this chapter, if sound, shows that concepts whose possession conditions are given in terms of outright judgement are epistemically individuated. It does not show that they are exclusively epistemically individuated. If that is true, it needs further argument to show it. I have dealt only with those clauses of a judgement-involving possession condition which take the form of requiring that a thinker should be willing to make a certain judgement in certain circumstances. Not every clause of a judgement-involving possession condition need take this form. A clause might, for instance, take the form of saying that to possess a certain concept F, the thinker must be unwilling to make certain judgements in certain circumstances. It is highly plausible that we sometimes need such clauses. A possession condition for negation will either write in, or entail, that if a thinker judges $\neg p$, then he must not be willing to judge that p. I mention this point just to signal my awareness of the issue of whether there exists a class of concepts which are exclusively epistemically individuated. I will not pursue it here, because it will be sufficient for the argument of this book that there is a significant class of epistemically individuated concepts, whether or not they are exclusively so.

Consider a clause of the possession condition for an epistemically individuated concept which says that a thinker must be willing to make a certain judgement in specified circumstances. To each such clause there corresponds a condition for knowing the content of that judgement. A single clause of a possession condition will often mention more than one specific concept or type of concept. To take just one example, observational concepts and perceptual demonstratives—such ways of thinking as are expressed by 'that cup', made available by the subject's perception as of a cup—are plausibly simultaneously individuated. They form part of a local holism. To possess a given observational concept G and a perceptual demonstrative concept *that F*, a thinker's judgements of the form *that F is G* must be suitably sensitive to what she takes to be her perceptions. The conditions for knowledge supported by this clause of the possession condition will be conditions for knowledge that equally concern both the perceptual-demonstrative and the observational concept. In some cases, the supported conditions for knowledge will also concern negations of contents containing the given concept, as the earlier example of universal quantification shows.

Now consider an arbitrary propositional content p built up from concepts $C_1, \ldots, C_n$, where each of the constituents C_i is epistemically individuated. For each constituent concept C_i there is some propositional content containing the constituent C_i which will, in certain circumstances, be known. It does not follow that there are some circumstances in which the content p itself will be known. None of the contents which verify the status of each individual constituent as epistemically individuated need be the same as the propositional content *p*. Nor is there any motivation for holding that, if the conceptual constituents of a content are epistemically individuated, there must be some content-fixing condition for knowing that whole content. A structured complex is grasped by a thinker provided only that the thinker grasps its constituents and their mode of combination in that complex. Nothing else is required for grasp of the complex concept. Even within the class of true propositional contents, the property of being knowable by the thinker under certain circumstances is not one which is preserved under the formation of complex contents. It can be that the content *A* is knowable by the thinker in certain circumstances, and that the content *B* is knowable by the thinker in certain circumstances. It does not follow that the content *A&B* is knowable by the thinker in certain circumstances. The position into which the thinker may need to get himself in order to know *A* may exclude his getting himself into the position to know *B*. In short, there is nothing in the Linking Thesis which tends to the conclusion that any true propositional content must be knowable by the thinker, not even in principle.

How can an epistemically individuated concept also occur in atomic contents which are not knowable by the thinker? The answer to this question is that the possession condition for a concept may involve a thinker latching on to a relation which extends far beyond the accessible. A good statement of the possession condition for the concepts *x is after y*, or *x is one kilometre from y*, will (together with the world) determine an extension for these concepts which goes far beyond the accessible times, places, objects, and events. A possession condition for an epistemically individuated atomic concept will involve a condition which can be formulated in terms of knowledge. It by no means follows that every instance of that concept is one which can be known about.

There is of course a philosophical obligation, in the case of any particular concept, to explain why its extension goes beyond the accessible. In the case of spatial and temporal concepts and concepts of matter, it seems to be involved in the very notion of an objective spatio-temporal world that the same properties and relations which explain our perceptions of them are also ones which can have inaccessible instances. The inaccessible instances can be thought about by iteration of operations applicable also to accessible instances, by the use of such phrases as 'the place 10^{30} metres from here in such-and-such direction'. The atomic propositional content 'The place 10^{30} metres from here in such-and-such direction is cold' is built up from atomic conceptual constituents which are arguably epistemically individuated. It does not follow that the understanding of that propositional content is to be given by reference to the conditions under which the thinker would know *it*. Once again, it is understood as soon as its constituents and their mode of combination are both grasped.[6]

A linguistically unstructured expression may express, on the lips of a given speaker, a complex concept. The claim that a concept is epistemically individuated applies to the conceptually atomic, and not necessarily to the linguistically atomic. So there is room for the possibility of the existence of words which are linguistically atomic, and which express complex concepts composed from epistemically individuated concepts, and for which there are no concept-individuating ways of coming to know *any* atomic contents involving the concept expressed by the word. The word 'tomorrow' is one plausible example. It is linguistically atomic. The word 'tomorrow' is not, in present-day English, composed of meaningful sub-expressions. The concept it expresses is, however, complex. It is the concept *the day immediately after today*. The constituents of this complex concept are plausibly epistemically individuated. There are ways of coming to know contents containing the concept *today* which are plausibly individuative of that concept; there are ways of coming to know contents containing the concept *x is after y* which are plausibly individuative of the concept; and so forth. That is all that is required by the status of the constituents as epistemically individuated. It is not required that there be concept-individuating ways of coming to know about tomorrow which are peculiar to the concept *tomorrow*. There are none.

Nothing I have said implies that knowledge of a content is impossible if it contains concepts which are not epistemically individuated. It had better not, for we can know that the family of quarks has a certain structure; or that the probability of an atom of uranium decaying in a given time is such-and-such. All that follows from the arguments so far is that the means by which we come to know these contents are not ones founded in knowledge-yielding methods involved in the very nature of the concepts in the contents. The means

---

[6] I return to some of these issues about objective thought in Chapter 3.

by which we come to know them will involve such methods as are rationally applicable to any contents, such as inference to the best explanation.

2.2 CONSEQUENCES OF THE ARGUMENT FOR THE LINKING THESIS

The Linking Thesis and the argument for it have several consequences for topics besides the Integration Challenge. Some of these consequences are independently plausible, and so give indirect support for the thesis. In this section, I consider some of these consequences, before returning to the main theme of the Integration Challenge in the next section.

(i) There is a striking fact about the examples commonly offered when an explanation is being given of the notion of the distinctness of a pair of singular senses *a* and *b*. The examples are offered as cases in which a thinker can rationally judge something of the form $F(a)$ without judging $F(b)$. Thus, the thinker can rationally judge that Hesperus is shining brightly this evening without judging that Phosphorus is shining brightly this evening; he can judge that it is raining now without judging that it is raining at 3 o'clock; and so forth. The striking fact is that all of these, and all of the other examples commonly used to establish the distinctness of senses, and indeed to introduce the notion of sense, are also cases in which the thinker can *know* that $F(a)$ without knowing that $F(b)$. The thinker can know that Hesperus is shining brightly this evening without knowing that Phosphorus is; the thinker can know that it is raining now, without knowing that it is raining at 3 o'clock; and so forth. To generalize: it seems to slice these senses no more finely, and to explain their identity equally well, if instead of speaking of rational judgement, we speak of knowledge.

This phenomenon is not merely an instance of Leibniz's Law, the law that if *x* and *y* are identical, they have the same properties. It is indeed an immediate consequence of Leibniz's Law that *a* and *b* are distinct senses if there are possible circumstances in which one can know some content $F(a)$ without knowing the corresponding content $F(b)$. I am concerned not just with distinctness, but with the fundamental ground of distinctness—with what *makes* these senses distinct. In the examples we mentioned, it seems to be possible to use the concept of knowledge in explaining what it is for senses *a* and *b* to be distinct, in explaining the fundamental ground of distinctness of such senses. This goes far beyond anything derivable just from Leibniz's Law.

The striking phenomenon can be explained as a consequence of the claim that the senses in these examples are epistemically individuated. Any one of these senses *a* is individuated in part at least in terms of the conditions under which certain contents containing it can be known by the thinker. So stating the fundamental ground of difference of a sense *b* from the sense *a* can consist in doing the following: citing circumstances, mentioned in individuating conditions for *a*, in which some content $F(a)$ can be known, but which are not sufficient for $F(b)$ to be known. For epistemically individuated senses it is not just an accident of the examples that we could have used the concept of knowledge in introducing and explaining the notion of sense.[7]

(ii) Writers who have favoured 'criterial' theories of meaning have sometimes included, in their criterial conditions for understanding a given predicate, a certain feature. They have required, for understanding, some appreciation of the conditions under which prima facie evidence in favour of sentences containing the predicate should be regarded as overturned. 'That's spherical' can no longer be accepted on the basis of experience if the subject turns out to be hallucinating, or involved, unbeknownst to him, in a psychological experiment. It does seem right that ordinary understanders have some such appreciation of the conditions which make earlier evidence an insufficient basis for acceptance. There must be many philosophers who would want to grant this point, but not to adopt a criterial theory of meaning. Can this tension in their position be resolved?

The above treatment of the Linking Thesis allows us to acknowledge the point about withdrawing judgements without any commitment to criterial theories of meaning. If rationally non-discretionary judgement aims at knowledge, then anything which shows that the thinker does not have knowledge makes withdrawal of such a judgement rationally obligatory. The point is entirely consistent with

---

[7] If there is a non-empty class of exclusively epistemically individuated senses, then for any distinct senses *a* and *b* in that class we can make the stronger claim that there must be some content or other $F(a)$, and some conditions or other, of which it is true that in those conditions the thinker knows $F(a)$ without knowing $F(b)$.

truth-conditional theories of meaning. In fact this explanation of the phenomenon does not involve a commitment to any one particular theory of meaning or content.

(iii) Consider a belief which is rationally non-discretionary for a thinker, but which is mere belief, because one or more of the following conditions holds: the informational conditions for the faculty and/or social mechanisms on which the thinker is relying are not met; or some premise on which the thinker is relying does not have the status of knowledge; or one or more of his presuppositions in making the judgement is not fulfilled. The treatment I have offered vindicates the description of any such mere belief as failed knowledge.[8] Indeed, for these beliefs, knowledge is fundamental in the explanation of their nature, for it is knowledge at which they aim. This is one of several points at which my treatment intersects with that of Timothy Williamson.[9]

Since some beliefs are rationally discretionary, we cannot say that all beliefs which are not knowledge are failed knowledge. They cannot be failed knowledge when we are not even attempting to acquire knowledge. Yet even in a case in which a thinker makes a judgement on the basis of evidence which is clearly inconclusive, still in cases in which the content of the judgement is built up solely from epistemically individuated concepts, there remains a respect in which the case in which the aim is knowledge is explanatorily more fundamental. Judgement of a content on inconclusive grounds is possible only if the thinker has some grasp of the content to be judged. We have argued that the possession conditions for such concepts will concern only rationally non-discretionary judgements, that is, those whose aim is knowledge.

(iv) These considerations also offer further support for Peter Unger's principle that in asserting something, a speaker represents himself as knowing it.[10] If a judgement is, given the speaker's presuppositions

---

[8] The point is evidently closely related to Bernard Williams's insight that the search for truth cannot but be a search for knowledge: see his *Descartes: The Project of Pure Enquiry* (Harmondsworth: Penguin, 1978), 39–45.

[9] T. Williamson, 'Is Knowing a State of Mind?', *Mind* 104 (1995), 533–65.

[10] P. Unger, *Ignorance: A Case for Scepticism* (Oxford: Oxford University Press, 1975), 253 ff. For further considerations, and an important discussion very congenial to the position I have been defending, see T. Williamson, 'Knowing and Asserting', *Philosophical Review* 105 (1996), 489–523.

and other beliefs, merely rationally discretionary, then he should not assert its content outright, without qualification or elaboration. To do so would be misleading. But if a judgement is rationally non-discretionary for the speaker, he is committed to regarding it as knowledge. So inevitably he represents himself as knowing what he asserts. There could not be a general public practice of representing oneself as rationally non-discretionarily judging something which is not also a practice of representing oneself as also knowing it.

(v) The Linking Thesis seems to me to be an important component in an explanation of the point and interest of the concept of knowledge. Consider someone who knows something composed only of epistemically individuated concepts, and who knows it because he has judged in accordance with the possession conditions for the concepts in the content judged. If this thinker's properly held presuppositions are fulfilled, his premises known, and the relevant informational conditions met, then his judgement will have a crucial combination of properties. It will be both rational and guaranteed as a matter of the theory of content to be correct. This combination of rationality and success is naturally to be valued.

Now obviously not all cases of knowledge—not even all cases of knowledge of a content built up from epistemically individuated concepts—are reached by judging in accordance with the methods mentioned in the possession conditions for the contents judged. I conjecture, though, that cases of knowledge not so reached count as knowledge because of their relations to cases in which knowledge is so reached. Methods ranging from the acquisition of knowledge by indirect mathematical proof to acquisition of knowledge by testimony are capable of yielding knowledge only because, in their various different ways, they give some rational assurance that the truth condition fixed by the possession conditions for the concepts in the content in question is a content which is fulfilled. (Note that I do not say: they give some assurance that the content could have been known in a more direct manner, corresponding to the clauses of possession conditions for concepts in the content. That is too strong, as is shown by cases of set-ups which alter when observed; we will return to the matter in Chapter 3.)

On Edward Craig's treatment of knowledge, social elements are fundamental in an account of the point and importance of knowledge. He writes: 'any community may be presumed to have an interest in evaluating sources of information; and in connection with that interest certain concepts will be in use. The hypothesis I wish to try out is that the concept of knowledge is one of them. To put it briefly and roughly, the concept of knowledge is used to flag approved sources of information.'[11] By contrast, if what I have said is correct, social elements are not fundamental in an account of the point and importance of knowledge. Knowledge as something which involves a relation of the sort I just outlined to judgements which are both rational and successful is something which is already of value and importance to us. That value can be elucidated, and indeed exists for the individual thinker considered in isolation, without mentioning the importance for us of saying that someone else knows something.

It is, certainly, important for us to have a device in the language for saying of certain other people something which implies that they attain, in a given subject matter, their beliefs by methods which are both rational and success-yielding. But this social dimension is present only because knowledge has a point which can be explained in terms which are not intrinsically social. For the case of knowledge, the social dimension is not fully explicable without mentioning the individual dimension. In trying to attain first-order information about the world, the beliefs of others about the world will be of use to us only in so far as they are formed by a suitable relation to methods which are both rational and successful.

2.3 THE LINKING THESIS AND THE INTEGRATION CHALLENGE

Even if the Linking Thesis is true, so that there is a class of concepts whose possession conditions can be written in terms of certain specific conditions for knowledge, what is the importance of this fact? I am going to argue that the Linking Thesis opens the door at least to the form of a solution to the Integration Challenge in cases in which two conditions are met. The first condition is that the solution still uses the notion of a truth condition. That is, the solution falls into cases (1)–(4) in the taxonomy of Chapter 1 above. The second condi-

[11] E. Craig, *Knowledge and the State of Nature: An Essay in Conceptual Synthesis* (Oxford: Oxford University Press, 1990), 11. There are of course many other possible arguments that knowledge, as a constitutive matter, has a social dimension.

tion is that the concepts for which the Integration Challenge in question is formulated are epistemically individuated concepts.

There are a few preliminaries before I can state the significance of the Linking Thesis for the Integration Challenge when these two conditions are met. I will be working within the scope of the background supposition that a substantive theory of intentional content must determine an attribution of truth conditions to such contents, at least in fundamental cases. Under this supposition, a theory of a specific concept will determine a contribution to the truth conditions of the complete intentional contents in which it features.

Intentional contents are here conceived as lying at the level of sense. Under our background supposition, though, the level of sense is inextricably and fundamentally involved with the level of reference. Senses fix truth conditions, which must be characterized via the level of reference. If senses fix truth conditions, it must be possible to individuate a sense by giving the condition for something to be its reference.[12]

Several different kinds of substantive theory of a given sense or concept can each, in their own way, succeed in determining an assignment of truth conditions. A conceptual-role theory can do so, if it relates semantic assignments to its conceptual roles. It may, for instance, hold that the reference of a sense or concept is the one which makes certain specified kinds of judgements involving the concept always true. It may, alternatively, say that the reference is the assignment which makes certain transitions always truth-preserving, where these judgements and transitions are the ones mentioned in its meaning-fixing conceptual roles. Another kind of substantive theory which succeeds in assigning truth conditions is one which claims that someone who grasps a given concept has implicit knowledge which specifies that concept's contributions to the truth conditions of contents in which it occurs. In this case, the assignment of truth conditions will be given immediately by the content of the implicit knowledge (if we prescind from any individual/social divergence).[13] Yet another kind

---

[12] This principle differs only in respects not relevant here from one Dummett has long emphasized: see, for instance, his *Origins of Analytical Philosophy* (Cambridge, Mass.: Harvard University Press, 1993). The difference is that between formulations which do, and formulations which do not, give philosophical priority to language.

[13] If we do not so prescind, the content of the implicit conception gives only the way the thinker understands an expression, which may not be the concept it conventionally expresses in the public language.

of case is given by some information-based semantic theories. An information-based theorist will say that in certain fundamental cases, a person's application of (say) a predicative concept stands in some lawlike relation to the instantiation of some property which explains his application. This theorist could go on to add that the contribution to truth conditions made by the concept proceeds, at the level of reference, via the extension of that property. Many variants are possible on all of these three styles of theory, and the elements of each are more plausible for certain sorts of concepts than for others.

Much more is of course involved in the determination of truth conditions by a substantive theory of content. In particular, it needs to be shown that every case in which a particular content is true is also one in which it is counted as true by the truth conditions determined by the favoured substantive theory of the concepts from which that content is composed (together with the way the world is). Any substantive theory of a particular set of concepts must be shown to meet that adequacy condition.

So much for preliminaries. The significance of the Linking Thesis for the integration of metaphysics and epistemology, in cases which meet the two conditions at the start of this section, is now as follows. When those two conditions are met, we can meet the Integration Challenge for a given domain by supplying a substantive theory of content for the concepts of that domain. According to the Linking Thesis, the theory of intentional content can be framed in terms of knowledge, in the way we described above. The Integration Challenge is that of showing how the methods by which we normally think we come to know contents of a given kind really do ensure the holding of the truth conditions of those contents. When those methods are mentioned in the possession condition for the problematic concept, the challenge is answered head-on if we can develop a theory of the concepts of the domain under which rationally non-discretionary judgements involved in possession of the concept must both be true and have the status of knowledge.

A good theory of content will then, if the Linking Thesis is correct, close the apparent gap that led to the Integration Challenge in cases meeting the following three conditions.

(a) The solution relies fundamentally on truth conditions, that is, it embraces one of the options (1)–(4) in section 2.1 above.
(b) The relevant problematic concepts of the domain are epistemically individuated.

(c) All of the methods for which the Integration Challenge arises are either mentioned in the possession conditions for the problematic concepts, or are ratifiable as sound by reference to their relations to methods which are so mentioned.

As I anticipated back in section 2.1, we need for this argument only the existence of epistemically individuated concepts, and not the existence of exclusively epistemically individuated concepts. It suffices for addressing the Integration Challenge in cases meeting (a)–(c) that a method for coming to make a rationally non-discretionary judgement which is mentioned in a clause of a possession condition can be transformed into a method which, in specified circumstances, is also capable of yielding knowledge.

This general claim about the significance of the Linking Thesis for the Integration Challenge does not involve some horrible, illegitimate slide from the level of sense to the level of reference and metaphysics. A substantive theory of a concept is indeed something concerned with the level of sense. But if a theory of concepts or sense must determine an assignment of truth conditions, we already have a connection with the level of reference. On the position for which I have argued, the theory of grasp of the concept can be formulated partly or wholly in terms of the conditions for knowing certain contents. Knowledge of the correctness of a content also requires the world to be a certain way. So there is no illegitimate slide. Rather, there is in these cases a general connection between the conceptual, the epistemic, and the metaphysical.

On this strategy for addressing the Integration Challenge in the cases meeting conditions (a)–(c), the Janus-faced character of the theory of understanding is pivotal. The theory of understanding has both a metaphysical aspect, in being a theory of grasp of truth conditions, and an epistemic aspect, having to do with rationality of judgement. This epistemic aspect, when we are concerned with epistemically individuated concepts, has to do not only with justification, but with knowledge. To have a rift between our epistemology and our metaphysics is, in these cases, necessarily to have some fragmentation in our theory of understanding and concept possession.

This formulation of the significance of the Linking Thesis should make it very clear that the importance of the Linking Thesis lies in determining *what* has to be done to meet the Integration Challenge in any given area. What we have to do is to provide a substantive theory of concepts from that area; the theory has to be cast in terms of conditions for knowing certain contents involving those concepts; and the means of coming to know contents which it acknowledges have to be suitably connected with the ordinary methods of forming beliefs which give rise to the Integration Challenge in the area in question. The formulation I gave of the significance of the Linking Thesis does not specify *how* to do any of this in the philosophically interesting cases. The hard work remains to be done. We have specified the form of a solution, but not yet its content.

Much of the rest of this book will be concerned with moving towards substantive solutions in this specified form in cases in which the conditions (a)–(c) are met. I do not mean at all to imply that when these conditions are not met, the Integration Challenge does not arise, or is not important. On the contrary: there is evidently a live instance of the Integration Challenge in one of the examples I gave of a concept which is not epistemically individuated, that of probability. It is certainly also arguable that there are still unresolved aspects of the Integration Challenge for theoretical explanatory concepts too. I shall not, however, be discussing these particular instances of the Integration Challenge in this book. This is partly for the practical reason that we have quite enough on our plate when the conditions (a)–(c) are met. It is also partly for the more theoretical reason that the case of epistemically individuated concepts is, as I argued earlier, basic. No instance of the Integration Challenge is solved unless we can solve it for the case of epistemically individuated concepts.

2.4 THREE INDICATORS FOR SOLUTIONS

How then are we to make progress in identifying what kind of substantive solution to the integration problem might be appropriate for a given area of discourse meeting conditions (a)–(c)? We can start by asking: are there any features of truth in a given area which can provide guidance about the kind of theory of content for that area which would help us to meet the Integration Challenge?

We can proceed by developing a set of indicators. An indicator is a property whose instantiation, or non-instantiation, by statements of the area in question ought prima facie to be explained by a good integrationist solution. The presence or absence of an indicator in a given area constrains philosophical treatments of that area, and thereby offers some guidance in constructing integrationist solutions.

An indicator might be thought of as a light which is either on or off for a given area. To fix ideas, I will consider indicators which are particularly pertinent to the modal and temporal cases, and discuss their application in those areas. The indicators do, though, also apply to other areas.

The first indicator is given in the question:

(1) Do true statements in the area have an a priori source?

By 'having an a priori source', I mean the following. In the modal case, we know from Saul Kripke's and David Kaplan's work that not all true statements of metaphysical necessity are a priori.[14] 'Necessarily, if Hesperus exists, Hesperus is Phosphorus' and 'Necessarily, water is constituted by H_2O' are familiar examples. But in both of these cases, the true a posteriori necessities are consequences of two premises, neither of which is both modal and a posteriori. One of the two premises is modal but also a priori. The other premise is, though a posteriori, also non-modal. In the case of 'Necessarily, if Hesperus exists, Hesperus is Phosphorus', the a priori premise is the necessity of identity. The a posteriori, non-modal premise is that Hesperus is Phosphorus. In the case of the statement about water, we have a similar division into the a priori premise that necessarily, water has its actual constitution, and the a posteriori non-modal premise that water is constituted by two parts of hydrogen and one of oxygen. I suggest that such a tracing back to a priori sources is always possible. Any a posteriori necessity rests, it seems, ultimately on principles each of which is either modal and a priori, or a posteriori and also non-modal.[15] If correct, this is something which should be explained by any integrationist solution.

This is in sharp contrast with the case of the past. Consider the statement 'It rained in Los Angeles yesterday'. It is quite implausible to suggest that this statement involving the past is a consequence of two other statements, one involving the past but a priori true, and the other not involving the past at all. True statements about the past are not somehow determined as true on the basis of some a priori principle or principles which, when taken in conjunction with other

---

[14] S. Kripke, *Naming and Necessity* (Oxford: Blackwell, 1980); D. Kaplan, 'Demonstratives: An Essay on the Semantics, Logic, Metaphysics, and Epistemology of Demonstratives and Other Indexicals', in J. Almog, J. Perry, and H. Wettstein (eds.), *Themes from Kaplan* (New York: Oxford University Press, 1989).

[15] The matter is discussed further below in Chapter 3, sect. 5.

past-free a posteriori statements, fix the truth values of statements about the past. Statements about what was the case at particular past times are just brute truths or brute falsehoods. There is no a priori determination of past-tense truths by other truths not about the past. A solution to the integration problem for the past must explain how we have such an understanding of the past, and why the case is so different from that of modality.

The second indicator involves causation, and is given in this question:

(2) Is some role in causal explanation essential either to the truth of statements in the area in question, or to our having our concepts of that area?

The answer to both parts of the question is negative in the modal case. Only what is actually so can causally explain something. The fact that something is necessarily so, or possibly so, never causally explains anything. Apparent counterexamples to this principle are cases in which it is someone's propositional attitudes to modality, or proofs about modality, or more generally some operator concerned only with what is the case in the actual world, which is involved in the causal explanation.

The same point seems to apply also to such modals as counterfactuals. Consider a person's belief that if he were to remove a particular card in a house of cards, the house of cards would fall down. Can we say that this belief is explained by the truth of the counterfactual which he believes? It seems that it is rather explained by his belief or perception that the cards have a certain spatial arrangement, together with his belief in the instability of this arrangement. That the cards have that spatial arrangement is a truth about how things actually are, rather than something modal. What actually explains belief in or knowledge of a counterfactual need not be something which is the categorical ground of that very counterfactual. It can suffice if what actually explains the belief is known to be suitably correlated with whatever is the categorical ground of truth of the counterfactual in question. A television engineer can know that, if he were to touch a certain shiny box with a certain shape and size inside a television set, he would receive an electric shock. The actual explanation of his belief is the box's being shiny and having a certain shape and size, together with his belief or knowledge about what such boxes are. The box's being shiny and having that shape and size is not, however, the ground of the truth of the counterfactual that if he were to touch it, he would receive a shock.

This second indicator in the modal case can also serve to illustrate the point we made earlier, that the Integration Challenge can also be formulated as a problem about the nature of understanding. It is very tempting to say that operators like 'necessarily' and 'possibly' should be treated as primitive. This is certainly attractive when we compare the position with that of the modal realist who takes these operators as quantifiers over worlds of the same kind as the actual world around you. Taking the operators as primitive, however, should be accompanied by some account of what it is to understand these primitive operators. In other cases where we have primitive predicates which are understood, such as observational predicates, the account of understanding involves some causal interaction between instances of the property picked out by the predicate and the understander's use of the predicate. The second indicator in the modal case implies, correctly, that this account of understanding a primitive predicate or operator is not available in the modal case.

I would argue that, in contrast with the modal case, the capacity of temporal relations to enter causal explanations is an essential component of an account of our mastery of temporal relations, including our capacity to think about the past. I will return to this when I sketch a response to the integration challenge for discourse about the past. For the moment, I want to note two points about this second indicator.

We should expect certain answers to the question defining the second indicator to go together with certain answers to the question defining the first indicator. When an area is involved in causal explanation, faculties or devices which are causally sensitive to states of affairs in that area will provide a means of obtaining knowledge of some of the truths about that area. Knowledge obtained in that way will not be a priori. So, for a given area, a positive answer to our second question about a constitutive role for causality will naturally be accompanied by a negative answer to our first question about the a priori. Conversely, a positive answer to the first question for a given area should be expected to imply a negative answer to the second question. If all knowledge in the domain in question can be obtained by a priori methods, causal interaction with the domain cannot be essential to thought or knowledge about it. So the two indicator lights fixed by the first questions are, for a given area, both on together, or both off together.

The other point to note concerns the talk in the second indicator of whether a role in causal explanation is essential to the domain, or to our thought about it. This reference to what is essential is itself essential. There are, perhaps surprisingly, examples of areas of which it is, or at least could be, just a contingent fact that there is causal explanation by its truths. An illustration is provided by certain infinitary statements, statements which would be classified by philosophers of mathematics as statements about the actual infinite. Consider the statement that there are infinitely many stars. This not only could be true, but in the context of a suitable physical theory, could be causally explanatory. The physical theory could entail that if there were only finitely many stars, gravitational forces would pull them together to make all the matter in the universe move towards its centre of gravity. If there were infinitely many stars, of suitable size and distribution, this would not happen. An actual argument of the same kind was reportedly given by Kepler, who argued against the universe containing an infinite number of stars on the ground that it would imply that the night sky would be everywhere bright, every line of sight eventually terminating at a star.[16] The intelligibility of these arguments seems to me to undermine some forms of the view that only the potential infinite can ever be necessary in describing nature.[17] None the less, such causal explanation by infinitary statements would seem to me to be an entirely contingent matter, were it to obtain. It is also not something that is necessary for our understanding of infinitary statements. We do not understand infinitary statements because of our ability to recognize their causal effects, if any. There may not be any such effects; and when there are, our ability to learn infinitary truths by their means seems to be consequential upon some understanding of infinitary statements which is not given in causal terms.

The third indicator I want to mention involves an identity of property, and is given in this question:

(3) Are statements in the problematic area predications of a property which also features in predications outside the problem-

---

[16] There is a brief history of the idea in the entry for 'Olbers' Paradox' in the 1998 CD-ROM edition of *Encyclopaedia Britannica*.

[17] For such a view of the potential infinite, see Adrian Moore, *The Infinite* (London: Routledge, 1990), and his paper 'A Note on Kant's First Antinomy', *Philosophical Quarterly* 42 (1992), 480–5.

atic area? If so, does grasp of this identity of properties play some role in understanding statements in the problematic area?

If the answer to the first of the two sub-questions in (3) is affirmative, and we also have some understanding of mention of the property outside the problematic area, this understanding can provide some constraints on both the metaphysics and the epistemology of statements in the problematic area.

In the case of the past, there are such identities of properties which support a positive answer to the first sub-question in (3). For instance, we can truly say this:

(PI/past): A thought (or utterance) 'Yesterday it rained' is true if and only if yesterday had the same property as today is required to have for a present-tense thought (or utterance) 'It is now raining' to be true.

We could equally have written 'if and only if yesterday had the same property as any arbitrary day is required to have for a present-tense thought (or sentence) "It is now raining" to be true with respect to that day'. If we were to be strict, we would with more precision say that the property yesterday is required to have for 'Yesterday it rained' to be true is that of having at some time or other within yesterday the same property as the present time is required to have for 'It is now raining' to be true. I will be sufficiently loose as to take this stricter, and correct, elaboration for granted in what follows without repeating it every time.

If the language uses unreduced temporal operators, rather than any ontology of times, the issue of whether there is a property identity needs to be framed differently if it is not to be trivialized. Consider a theorist who rejects for times and intervals the view which Arthur Prior canvassed as 'Platonism about instants', a rejection to which Prior himself was sympathetic.[18] This theorist will insist that

[18] For some statements of the view, see A. Prior, *Papers on Time and Tense* (Oxford: Oxford University Press, 1968), esp. 122–3, 132–3. At 138, Prior writes: 'For we can identify an instant with a tensed proposition, namely with the conjunction of everything which would ordinarily be said to be true *at* that instant; or alternatively, with something which would ordinarily be said to be true at that instant only. We can then interpret being true at an instant as being necessarily or omnitemporally implied by that instant (considered as a proposition), and one instant's being earlier than another as the futurity of the latter being true "at" the former . . .' I do not at all endorse the view which Prior here suggests. It involves many problems, and the fact that, as Prior emphasizes, one can formulate parallel views for apparent

temporal operators are not to be construed as quantifiers over times. We do not want this theorist to be entitled to answer the question we intended in the first sub-question in (3) in the negative, on the simple ground that on his view there are no times which could have properties. An alternative way of meeting the need would be to expand the identities in question to include not only properties, but also the identity of the way it has to be today for 'Today ——' to be true with the way it had to be yesterday for 'Yesterday ——' to be true.

Appreciation of the displayed property identity (PI/past) clearly cannot amount by itself to a full account of what is involved in understanding 'yesterday'. The right-hand side of (PI/past) simply uses the past tense, so any kind of appreciation of the biconditional must presuppose some possession of the concept *yesterday*. None the less, this property identity is a very substantial constraint upon the metaphysics and epistemology of the past. No account which is inconsistent with it can be acceptable; and we ought to aim for some account which explains why it is true. The property identity also has some explanatory power. Suppose yesterday you learned something which you would then have expressed by saying 'It is now raining', and that you store what you have learned in memory. If, today, you want to express what you learned yesterday, saying 'Yesterday it rained' is quite sufficient: you do *not* have to realign or readjust the predicate which was yesterday combined with the word 'now'. The property identity explains why not. You learned that 'Now it is raining' was true with respect to ('w.r.t.') yesterday; there is a uniform property any time must have for 'Now it is raining' to be true w.r.t. it; so yesterday had the same property as today has to have for 'Now it is raining' to be true w.r.t. it. So, by the property-identity link, 'Yesterday, it rained' is true.

Property identities are far from being trivialities. When we consider the first part of this third indicator in relation to the modal case, there are examples in which there is a failure of corresponding property identities. Suppose the actual world is conceived in the way David Lewis conceives of it, as (roughly) you and all your surroundings.[19] Then consider this biconditional:

quantification over places and over persons seems to me to count against it. See also Chapter 3, n. 32, below. Here I am concerned only with the significance of such a position for the correct formulation of what is intended in question (3).

[19] 'Maybe, as I myself think, the world is a big physical object; or maybe some parts of it are entelechies or spirits or auras or deities or other things unknown to

(PI/poss): The thought 'It is raining in Oxford at the start of the twentieth century' is true with respect to a given possible world if and only if that world has the same property the actual world, conceived on Lewisian lines, is required to have for the thought 'It is raining in Oxford at the start of the twentieth century' to be true.

This biconditional (PI/past) will be acceptable to a Lewisian modal realist. If, though, a possible world is conceived of as a set of propositions, or sentences, or suppositions, while the actual world is not so conceived, we must reject the biconditional. On that combination of conceptions, the property the actual world has when it is raining in Oxford at the start of the twentieth century is one which it is impossible for a possible world, so conceived, to have at all. The property of having rain falling in one of its spatio-temporal regions is not a property a set of propositions, or sentences, or suppositions, could ever have. What such a set can have is the property of being such that *according to it*, it is raining in Oxford then. But the property

x represents rain as occurring in a certain spatio-temporal region

is to be distinguished from the property

x has rain occurring in a certain one of x's spatio-temporal regions.

The actual world need of course not be conceived in a Lewisian way. It can be conceived of as some set of sentences or propositions, namely, just those which are true. Then there will be property identities of the sort in question in the first part of indicator question (3). The actual world will then also be a thing of the same kind as possible worlds also conceived of as sets of sentences or propositions. On such a conception of actual and possible worlds, (PI/poss) will be true. It is important, however, that on that combination of conceptions the answer to the second subquestion in (3), the question of whether grasp of such property identities plays a role in the explanation of understanding, is negative. Not all sets of sentences or propositions are (or correspond to) genuine possible worlds, but only those

physics. But nothing is so alien in kind as not to be part of our world, provided only that it does exist at some distance and direction from here, or at some time before or after or simultaneous with now.' Lewis, *On the Plurality of Worlds*, 1.

which are jointly possible. To understand the conception of possible worlds as sets of sentences or propositions, a thinker must have some grasp of possibility. It is precisely that grasp which we need to elucidate in an account of understanding. In the temporal case, part of the account of understanding the past will involve the causal impact of temporal relations and properties of particular events on the thinker's mental states. No form of causal interaction is correspondingly available in the modal case. So it seems that in the modal case a property-identity principle like (PI/poss) is either false, or true only in a form which cannot be of help in advancing the theory of understanding. I discuss the disanalogies between the modal and temporal cases, and some solutions to the generated problems about understanding, in Chapters 3 and 4.

This third indicator is also closely linked to the second. If we have a causal epistemology for a certain area, and properties in that area are identical with those predicated in the problematic area in question, it would be quite puzzling if there were not a causal epistemology in the problematic area. Similarly, contraposing, we would not expect there to be property identities between one problematic area whose epistemology is non-causal and another whose epistemology is causal. I also noted that the second and first indicators can be expected to be both on or both off for a given area. So we now have reason to expect that for any given area, these three indicator lights are all on together for that area, or all off together (where in the case of indicator (3), for its light to be on is for there both to be true property identities of the kind it mentions, and for them to be involved in understanding). If what I have been saying so far about the modal and temporal cases is right, they both conform to this expectation of correlation between the indicators.

2.5 A LOOK AHEAD: TWO STYLES OF SOLUTION

I now turn to outlining two radically different models of ways in which integration may be achieved. Each model is capable of explaining a pattern of indicator lights. The two models will be elaborated in more detail in Chapters 3 and 4, for the case of the past tense and of metaphysical necessity. The models are just two of several integrationist models which must exist. Certainly some other subject matters must be treated rather differently from those which do fit the two models I will be discussing. The two models do, though, serve to illustrate two paradigmatically different ways in which the Integration Challenge can be met.

The first model can be called *the model of constitutively causally sensitive conceptions*. The outlines of this model are already strongly suggested by cases in which the indicator of constitutive causal connections is lit up. It is this model which I will apply to the case of past-tense thought. On this model, one part of an account of grasp of temporal concepts such as *earlier than* is a causal sensitivity of certain judgements involving it to instances of that very relational concept. Instances of this model embrace a form of externalism about certain temporal concepts. Such a causal sensitivity must also be embedded in a conception of the past as the past. The model can be developed in a form which embraces the view that one who understands the past tense has implicit knowledge of the temporal property identities we noted earlier. Part of the task of the next chapter is to explain how this aspect of understanding is intertwined with the externalism.

The model needs elaboration in detail. Even from this briefest of descriptions, however, it appears that the model of constitutively causally sensitive conceptions promises an explanation of the pattern of indicator lights displayed by the case of thought about the past. Truths about the past can hardly be fundamentally a priori if the basic way of coming to know them involves the exercise of faculties causally sensitive to temporal relations and properties. Grasp of the property identities is also part of the model, as I just described it. That is, the same identities which are involved in the truth of a past-tense thought are also involved in grasping it. (This is a feature we will find in other models too.) I will also be arguing that appreciation of the import of these identities rules out any constructivist or evidential account of past-tense truth.

The other model is the model of *implicitly known principles*, and it seems to me the appropriate model for meeting the Integration Challenge in the case of metaphysical necessity. What makes a set of sentences, or propositions, or thoughts into a genuine possibility? The model of implicitly known principles, as I would develop it for the modal case, claims that there is a set of principles, 'principles of possibility', which any set of sentences, thoughts, or propositions must satisfy if it is to represent a genuine possibility. To understand modal discourse is to have implicit knowledge of these principles of possibility, and to deploy them in evaluating modal sentences. One of the tasks of a philosophical theory of modality is to identify and elaborate these principles.

If these principles of possibility are a priori, and they succeed, in combination with non-modal truths, in fixing modal truth, then we would have an explanation of why modal truth has, in the sense identified earlier, a fundamentally a priori character. On the model of implicitly known principles, no causal contact with some modal realm is required for understanding. Nor, on this model, does modal truth involve any realm of worlds of the same kind as the actual universe, conceived of as you and all your surroundings. The failure of the property-identity principle for the case of metaphysical necessity (when the actual world is construed in Lewis's way) is implicit in the background framework, since that framework treats non-actual possible worlds as sets of sentences, propositions, or thoughts—that is, not as things of the same kind as the actual world, on the Lewisian conception thereof. In these ways, the model of implicitly known principles is capable of explaining the pattern of indicator lights for the case of metaphysical necessity.

Our emerging plan is now as follows. As I said, I turn to the task of trying to substantiate these claims about the temporal case in Chapter 3, and the modal case in Chapter 4. The two models developed in those chapters—the models of constitutively causally sensitive conceptions and of implicitly known principles—no doubt generalize to some other cases too. They cannot, however, possibly cover all the cases in which the Integration Challenge arises. In other areas, different ideas are needed. In Chapter 5, I discuss thinkers' knowledge of their own intentional states, a case in which we need to develop a better conception not just of the epistemology of the problematic domain, but of reason-giving explanation more generally, if we are to meet the Integration Challenge. In Chapter 6, I consider a case of a different type, the case of the persistent philosophical arguments in support of a Transcendental Subject of experience and thought. Here genuine epistemological insights about certain aspects of first-person thought have been given an inappropriate metaphysical expression. They have thereby generated, rather than solved, integration problems. Finally, the topic of the freedom of the will—a case *par excellence* in which the metaphysics of the domain, its epistemology, and their interrelations, are all problematic—is addressed in

Chapter 7. For readers who are still with me, I will conclude the book with some brief retrospective and prospective reflections.

APPENDIX

Factive Reasons and Taking a Representational State at Face Value

I wrote in section 2.1 of a thinker's operating in the mode of taking the deliverances of a given informational system—perception, memory, testimony—at face value. It is in the nature of such modes of operation that they have both an objective and a subjective dimension involving reliability. On the objective side, the judgements made because the subject is operating in the given mode, and because she is in a representational state within the scope of that mode of operation, are knowledge only if the corresponding informational conditions are met. The informational conditions demand a form of reliability. Whether the informational conditions are met or not is in general an external matter, depending on the world around the thinker, and on what could easily have been the case.

Reference to the thinker's mode of operation, in the sense I described, is quite essential in characterizing basic cases of knowledge made available by the correct functioning of these informational systems. In particular, it is not sufficient for knowledge of (say) an observational content that p that the informational conditions for perception should be met, and the thinker should have an experience as of its being the case that p, and that the occurrence of this experience should be part of the (reason-involving) explanation of her belief that p. That is not sufficient, because that combination of conditions is consistent with her not operating in the mode of taking perceptual experience at face value, but rather with her attempting to reach knowledge that p inferentially. She might be starting with some premises which include one to the effect that it looks to her that p. If this inference, however it goes, involves hypotheses which are not known, the final belief that p will not be knowledge. It would, though, still be knowledge if it were reached simply by taking perceptual experience at face value under those same conditions (assuming there are no grounds for reasonable doubt).

On the subjective side, there are also requirements concerning reliability for any reflective thinker who has some conception of these informational systems. If such a thinker comes to think that the informational conditions for the system whose deliverances she has been taking at face value are no longer fulfilled, she can no longer rationally rely on representational states. So, unless she has independent reasons for it, she must withdraw the judgement.

This subjective aspect of reliability is inextricable from the objective aspect. A mode of operation could not have only subjective aspects, and lack objective aspects. The subjective presupposition of reliability is made by the reflective thinker only because of some appreciation of the fact that the judgement in question would not *be* knowledge if the informational conditions were not fulfilled.

On this approach, then, a certain kind of reliability is, and is necessarily, both an external and (for thinkers of moderate conceptual sophistication) an internal requirement for a judgement to be knowledge when it results from the occurrence of a representational state of a kind a thinker is legitimately taking at face value. We should not accept any treatment of knowledge which casts reliability, for sophisticated thinkers, in only one out of the external and the internal roles.

The question now arises: is the treatment I have given incompatible with the idea that only a factive state, with a content that *p*, can lead to a thinker's having knowledge that *p*, in the case in which she is endorsing the content of a representational state? Let us call that idea 'the factive view'. It has been argued for, in somewhat different forms, by John McDowell and Timothy Williamson.[20] It seems to me that there is no incompatibility between the factive view and the position developed in this chapter and its Appendix. Indeed, it would be surprising if there were, since I have been promoting a position on which knowledge has a position which is explanatorily at least as fundamental as belief. The natural way of developing such a position is that knowledge is a state which can be reached by means of certain factive states such as perceiving that *p*, remembering that *p*, learning

---

[20] J. McDowell, 'Knowledge and the Internal', *Philosophy and Phenomenological Research* 55 (1995), 877–93; T. Williamson, 'Is Knowing a State of Mind?'

that *p*, and the like. If the informational conditions are met for the mode of taking the representational states from a given system at face value, those representational states will have correct contents. The present treatment will not be counting any cases as cases of knowledge obtained in the most basic way from the operation of these faculties which would not also be counted as knowledge by those applying such a factive requirement.

There is, though, also a puzzle about combining the factive view with what I have said. The principal original argument for the factive view was that if we fail to adopt it, then, to quote McDowell's formulation, '[T]wo subjects can be alike in respect of the satisfactoriness of their standing in the space of reasons, although only one of them is a knower, because only in her case is what she takes to be so actually so. . . . Its being so is conceived as external to the only thing that is supposed to be epistemologically significant about the knower herself, her satisfactory standing in the space of reasons.'[21] I did not, apparently, use any factive notions essentially in explaining how knowledge could be acquired by taking certain representational states at face value. So it may seem that we are after all going to be forced to admit to the possibility of a pair of cases of the following kind: in one of the cases the subject knows, and in the other not, the only difference between them being the fulfilment of some non-factive state or condition, without any difference in the space of reasons. Is the combination of the factive view with the present approach not then committed to some sort of objectionable interiorization of the space of reasons?

To enjoy an experience as of its being the case that *p* is not to enjoy a state which is factive in respect of *p*; nor is the conjunction of that state with that of being in the mode of taking experience at face value. But the combination of experiencing a state which represents *p* as the case, while being in circumstances in which the informational conditions for states of that kind are fulfilled, *is* a factive state in respect of the content *p*. So a simple response to the puzzle of the preceding paragraph, a response which I label the 'Impossibility Response', is to note that in every case in which an informational condition fails, it is also the case that some other state on which the thinker relies in making his judgement is not factive. There is a range of cases for which this Impossibility Response is very plausible. If the

21 'Knowledge and the Internal', 884.

informational conditions for perception fail to hold, then certainly the subject is not in a factive perceptual state. If the informational conditions for a given kind of memory fail, then certainly the subject is not in a factive memory state of that kind; and so forth. According to this Impossibility Response, then, it is not a consequence of acknowledging the role of informational conditions in knowledge that there could be two cases differing *only* in that in one of them the informational conditions fail, and in the other they do not, without any corresponding difference in factive states. Given the way informational conditions were introduced, there could not but also be a difference in factive states.

The Impossibility Response is very satisfying in the cases in which it clearly applies. Further work, however, would be needed to make it fully convincing. A question may be raised not just about informational conditions, but about presuppositions. Are they all of the sort they would have to be for the Impossibility Response to apply quite generally? Consider a perceptually based recognitional judgement 'That's Bill Clinton'. The thinker presupposes in making such a judgement that there is not more than one person who has the kind of face and body Bill Clinton has. Now suppose there were a Clinton lookalike in the vicinity. Would a person who sees the lookalike, and mistakenly judges 'That's Bill Clinton', be making a *perceptual* error? Our questioner may insist that that is not so clear. The question raised here about perceptual recognition of individuals could also be raised for the recognition of types. Is it a perceptual error which is involved in falsely judging, of something which looks and feels just like a television, but is merely a stage-prop, that it is a television? I think it must be agreed that there is some limited sense in which in these cases the subject's perceptual processing may be in order. (Nor is there much future in trying to press the incorrect idea that lookalikes can never really look like the real thing.) What, however, may give encouragement to the idea that we can consistently combine the factive view with the role of presuppositions is the point that these cases are not ones in which the subject *sees that* that man is Clinton, or *sees that* that device is a television. If the presuppositions concern these factive states, these cases are ones in which the Impossibility Response continues to apply. The presuppositions fail only when the subject is not in a state of seeing that that man is Clinton, or the like.

These are obviously not the final moves in the discussion, but they do support the conjecture that the approach of this chapter, and the factive approach, may be systems of equivalent descriptions of the network of relations between knowledge, reasons, truth and entitlement.

3

The Past

What is it to understand a statement about the past? How are the truth conditions of past-tense statements related to this understanding? And how are the conditions for knowledge of past-tense statements related to that same understanding? These are the aspects of the Integration Challenge I will be addressing in this chapter.

Quite apart from the intrinsic interest of questions about time, the past is a subject matter where realist intuitions are at their strongest. So one of the background motivations for pursuing the issues about understanding statements of the past is the hope that in doing so, we may be able to construct a working account of at least one kind of realistic understanding. Examination of such an account ought to give us some insight into some of the conditions which make possible a realistic attitude to thought about a particular domain, if indeed there are such conditions.

In accordance with the general style of approach to the Integration Challenge outlined in the preceding chapter, I will propose a theory of understanding of the past tense, a theory which has the required links both to the metaphysics and the epistemology of the past. I will proceed by first offering an identification of one element in our understanding of the past tense. Then I will move on to the metaphysics of the past tense. I believe that there is a principle in this area which seems like, and perhaps is, a truism, but which also has significant metaphysical consequences. The principle is also one which is involved in our understanding of the past. Then I will go on to identify a second, externalist element in temporal thought, and discuss its relations to the metaphysics and epistemology of this domain. The position which emerges permits the formulation of a case for realism about the past which is rather different from those it has received hitherto.

As will be evident even from this briefest overview, metaphysics and the theory of understanding will be intertwined in this discussion. It is a discussion which points to some more general conclusions about the relations, in this area at least, between metaphysics and the theory of meaning and content.

3.1 THE PROPERTY-IDENTITY LINK AND ITS ROLE IN UNDERSTANDING

I begin by proposing a hypothesis about the role of a certain property-identity link in our thought about the past. The link I have in mind is the link identified towards the end of Chapter 2. It is the link which is the natural generalization of such instances as this:

> A thought (utterance) 'Yesterday it rained' is true if and only if yesterday had the same property as today is required to have for a present-tense thought (utterance) 'It is now raining' to be true when evaluated with respect to today.[1]

The property-identity link generalizes what is here said about the thoughts (and utterances) 'Yesterday it rained' and 'It is now raining' to all corresponding thoughts (and utterances) of the form 'Yesterday it was the case that A' and 'It is now the case that A'. I call this generalization 'the property-identity link'.[2]

The property-identity link is closely related to one of the principles which goes under the name of 'the truth-value link' in the literature. This is the principle which has such instances as

---

[1] Both this and the truth-value link given further below are to be distinguished from the biconditional with the same left-hand side, and which continues: 'if and only if an utterance yesterday of "It is now raining" would have been true'. That does not generalize correctly, as one discovers if one tries it for 'Yesterday no one uttered anything', or (for the case of thought) 'Yesterday no one thought anything about the rain'. The temporal property-identity link is also neutral on the question of whether it is an objective feature of reality that something is happening now in a way which cannot be captured by broadly token-reflexive treatments of indexicals.

[2] In this chapter I try to follow the notational convention of using 'p' as a schematic letter to be replaced by sentences which are truth-evaluable outright, and 'A' as a schematic letter to be replaced by something which determines merely a function from times to truth values, and so requires a time specification to fix a truth value outright. Those who prefer an ontology of thoughts can use the difference of notation to mark the corresponding difference between thoughts which are truth-evaluable outright, and those entities in the third realm which have a truth value only relative to a time.

A thought (utterance) 'Yesterday it rained' is true iff the sentence-type (thought-type) 'It is now raining' is true when evaluated with respect to yesterday.

The property-identity link is equivalent to the truth-value link, under the supposition of Uniformity:

For any temporally open sentence A (or corresponding thought-content), there is a property such that for any time t, 'Now A' is true when evaluated with respect to t iff t has that property.

The property-identity link also entails the truth-value link outright. The converse, however, is less clear. It is not obvious that the truth-value link involves commitment to an ontology of properties.

My reason for concentrating on the property-identity version is not that there is a real possibility of divergence from the truth-value link. It is rather a question of focus. We have very clear and robust intuitions about what properties something must have for a present-tense predication of it to be true. If the property-identity principle is correct, those intuitions constrain any account of what is involved in the truth of corresponding past-tense predications. Later on, I will be arguing that some extant accounts violate this constraint.

Almost everyone will agree that the biconditionals which are examples of the property-identity link are true biconditionals. But to agree that they are true leaves much else undecided. First, it leaves open the question of whether their truth is derivative from something else, or whether their truth has a primitive status. Second, it leaves open the question of whether the property-identity link itself explains anything, and if so, what. Third, if the property-identity link does explain some aspects of linguistic understanding and of concept possession, the nature of the explanation also needs elucidation.

Theorists who hope to make explanatory use of the property-identity link might have one of several quite different goals. One goal might be that of trying to explain the capacity to think about past times at all. This we could call a 'domain-explaining' use of the property-identity link. Trying to pursue that goal solely by citing some kind of mastery of the property-identity links is a distinctly unpromising enterprise. The right-hand side of the biconditionals which are instances of the link simply use past-tense ways of thinking, in the way that the displayed biconditional simply uses 'yesterday' on its right-hand side. The link itself does not connect up mastery of 'yesterday' with anything else. If there is a question about what it is to be capable of such past-tense thoughts, citing some favoured kind of grasp of the property-identity link cannot be the whole of the answer.

A goal of domain-explaining is not, though, the only explanatory goal which reference to the property-identity links might serve. A second goal is simply that of saying something about what, constitutively, is involved in the understanding or grasp of past-tense predications. It can contribute to the attainment of this second goal to mention the property-identity link in stating part of what is involved in a thinker's understanding of what it is for it to have been raining (say) yesterday. This I call a *bridging* use of the property-identity link.

The particular bridging use I want to consider is the claim that a thinker's understanding of the sentence 'Yesterday it rained' consists in part by his having precisely the information given in the property-identity link. The claim is that his understanding involves his having the information that that past-tense thought is true just in case yesterday had the same property that today has to have for it to be true that it is raining today. In saying that the understanding involves the thinker's 'having' this information I mean that the thinker has implicit knowledge of this piece of information, and that this implicit knowledge contributes systematically to the explanation of his past-tense judgments and his evaluation of certain past-tense claims. Henceforth I will understand the bridging claim to be this explanatory claim about understanding, taken as suitably generalized to other past-tense ways of thinking, and to other properties of times besides that of being rainy.[3]

The bridging claim is neither committed to, nor does it preclude, the possibility of further elaborating grasp of the past tense in a way that conforms to the A(C) form of *A Study of Concepts*.[4] The content

[3] For more on implicit knowledge, and the way in which it can explain judgements, see my paper 'Implicit Conceptions, Understanding and Rationality', in a Festschrift for Tyler Burge, ed. M. Hahn and B. Ramberg (Cambridge, Mass.: MIT Press, forthcoming); also in E. Villaneuva (ed.), *Philosophical Issues* 8: *Concepts* (1998) (Atascadero, Calif.: Ridgeview).

[4] Cambridge, Mass.: MIT Press, 1992. According to that work, a concept *F* is individuated by a possession condition of the form 'Concept *F* is that unique concept *C* to possess which a thinker must meet condition A(C)', where the material in A( ) may itself use the concept *F* outside the scope of the description of the thinker's psychological attitudes (pp. 6, 9). The idea was that the condition A( ) should specify a concept-individuating conceptual role.

of the informational state to which the bridging claim appeals itself contains the past tense. There will be other components in a good account of grasp of the past tense, and I will discuss some of them later in this chapter. Perhaps, taken together, the bridging claim and those other components permit us to frame something in the A(C) form. The formulation would have to be of such a kind that the occurrence of the past tense in instances of the property-identity link can be replaced by a variable 'C', and a distinctive kind of conceptual role for the past tense framed in the manner of *A Study of Concepts*. Or perhaps such a reductive framing is impossible. The issue is one on which the bridging claim itself is neutral. The bridging claim says just that implicit knowledge of the property-identity link is something constitutively involved in grasp of the past tense. That is something which can hold with or without reduction of grasp to something of the A(C) form.

The bridging claim is also not a claim about the nature of the evidence for past-tense statements, or about the manifestation of understanding, even though of course both topics have to be addressed by any theory which includes the bridging claim. The bridging claim itself aims to say something about the nature of a thinker's understanding of predications in the past tense. I want to start by discussing the attractions, obligations and commitments of the bridging claim.

The bridging claim has two important initial attractions. The first attraction is that the bridging claim entails, and if true it gives an explanation of, the following datum: that if someone understands 'yesterday', and also understands 'Today it is the case that *A*', then he is in a position to understand 'Yesterday it was the case that *A*'. The datum holds for any past-tense operator, and also holds correlatively in the realm of thoughts and concepts. If someone has the concept *yesterday*, and knows what it is for a thought *Today it is the case that A* to be true, then he is in a position to know what it is for *Yesterday it was the case that A* to be true. These data hold for arbitrary contents *A*, be they observational, theoretical, or of any other kind appropriate for embedding in temporal operators. According to the bridging claim, the explanation of the datum in the linguistic case is this. If someone understands 'Today it is the case that *A*', he must know what property today has to have for it to be the case that *A* on that day; the property-identity link entails that that property is the one required to have held of yesterday for 'Yesterday it was the case that *A*' to be true; and knowing (via this means) what property yesterday had to have for that past-tense sentence to be true is precisely what is involved in understanding it.

A second attraction of the bridging claim is that in itself it leaves entirely open, as it should, what sort of evidence might establish the truth of a thought of the form *Yesterday it was the case that A*. It can often take hard thought to work out what, if anything, could establish the truth of a past-tense thought such as *Yesterday there was a strong magnetic field in the garden*. In many cases it is a partially empirical matter what would establish such a past-tense claim. A good theory must explain how and why this is so. At the moment, the point to be emphasized is that the bridging claim does not at all proceed by trying to explain grasp of *Yesterday it was the case that A* by determining evidence conditions for it from either evidence or truth conditions for the present-tense content *Today it is the case that A*. (This makes it a little strange that some discussants have envisaged the truth-value link which corresponds to the property-identity link as something which might be offered by a theorist as by itself an answer to evidential and manifestation challenges.)

A realist may be tempted to add that there is a third attraction of the bridging claim: that it allows a past-tense thought to be true even though there is not, nor will ever be, any evidence for it. Some anti-realists, however, have insisted that they are entitled to certain forms of truth-value links, Crispin Wright being prominent amongst them.[5] One would expect them, if clear-headed, to insist that they are entitled to the property-identity link too. I myself think that, on the contrary, the bridging claim does require a form of realism. To argue the case, we need a distinction I will develop a few paragraphs hence. I will return to the whole issue of realism further on, when we have more pieces on the board. At this stage, I just want to note that the question of whether a theorist who makes the bridging claim is also making the truth of past-tense contents always, or possibly, or sometimes, inaccessible to us is an issue which cannot be assessed without looking at the theorist's attendant account of the metaphysics, and his fuller account of the mastery, of temporal concepts.

The commitments of the bridging claim are substantial. The notion of a property as it is used in the property-identity link is to be taken

---

[5] See especially his essay 'Anti-Realism, Timeless Truth and *Nineteen Eighty-Four*', repr. in his *Realism, Meaning and Truth*, 2nd edn. (Oxford: Blackwell, 1993). Later page references in the present chapter to Wright's work are to this collection.

seriously. If the present time and some past time can have the same property, that of being a time at which rain occurs, there must be some level of description of kinds at which they are things of the same kind. Similarly, its raining now and its having rained yesterday are, at some level of description, states of affairs of the same kind. Corresponding points apply if spatial and interpersonal property-identity links are used in the explanation of thought about other places or other persons. By contrast, as we argued in section 2.4, such property identities do not, for instance, hold in the modal case if the actual world is conceived of as 'you and all your surroundings' while merely possible worlds are conceived of as sets of sentences, propositions, or thoughts.

I will not investigate in detail here what notion of property is required in the proper formulation of the property-identity link, because the main concerns of the present argument can go through without settling that question. We will need certain intuitive judgements about the identity and distinctness of certain properties in order for the argument to proceed. We will also need to make use of the idea that a time's having a certain property can feature in certain sorts of causal explanation. Further determinations which must be made by a philosophical theory of properties will not matter for my argument. I do note, though, that any notion of property which will serve the needs of the property-identity link must be quite general, since almost any content, with almost any subject matter, can be embedded in the past tense. In basic cases, some generalization of the notion of a property identified by Putnam and elaborated by Shoemaker, on which properties are individuated by their causal potentialities, will serve the purposes of the bridging theorist.[6] Certainly the causal potentialities of a time's having a certain property—for instance, the property of being a time at which it is raining—will play an important part in what follows. It is clear, though, that much substantive work remains to be done in metaphysics to develop a theory of properties which has the required generality.

The bridging claim need not and should not be accompanied by the thesis that someone could be capable of thinking about the pre-

---

[6] H. Putnam, 'On Properties', repr. in his *Mathematics, Matter and Method: Philosophical Papers*, vol. ii (Cambridge: Cambridge University Press, 1975); and S. Shoemaker, 'Causality and Properties' and 'Identity, Properties and Causality', repr. in his *Identity, Cause and Mind: Philosophical Essays* (Cambridge: Cambridge University Press, 1984), esp. 248 ff.

sent whilst not yet having the capacity to think about the past. A thinker who is capable of objective thought about the present must, it seems, also be capable of past-tense thought. Even the simplest present-tense observationally made judgement of an observational property must be subject to rejection if perception of the perceived object from a different position undermines the original observational judgement. Without such a sensitivity, this would not be a case of thought about mind-independent objects. This sensitivity involves mastery of the past tense. It requires the ability to think 'This object is the same as the one I saw from over there'; or at least to think 'This object is the same as the one to which I previously stood in such-and-such a relation'; and these both involve past-tense descriptions. The ability must be present, even if on occasion circumstances are unfavourable for exercising it in a way which yields knowledge (if, say, everything is changing too fast, or if the subject is suffering from lapses of memory or attention). Even if the subject is thinking objectively only about events, rather than continuant objects, the objectivity of thought, and its connection with correction from other standpoints, seems at least to involve the identifiability of particular places over time. This again involves the use of past-tense ways of thinking. The same consideration can be applied to Strawsonian 'feature-placing' sentences, when understood—as they are in Strawson— as placing objective features in an objective world.[7] The objectivity of the features requires the potential correction of such judgements from other points of view, which again involves the identification of a place at which the thinker currently perceives something with some place at which something was encountered earlier.

So on the view of the property-identity link I am pressing, there is no commitment to conceptual independence of thought about the present from thought about the past. The bridging conception is proposing a constitutive link between understanding of predications about the present and understanding of predications about the past. It is consistent with the existence of this link that present and past be coordinate notions, with no conceptual priority of either over the other. We have here another example of a local holism.

It may be helpful at this point to compare the use of the property-identity link in elucidating thought about the past with corresponding links we could use in elucidating thought about other places.

---

[7] *Individuals*, 202 ff.

There is an equally good case to be made that implicit knowledge of the following is partially constitutive of grasp of thought about other places:

> A thought or utterance 'Ten miles to the east it is raining' is true if and only if the place ten miles to the east has the same property as here is required to have for the thought or utterance 'Here it is raining' to be true.

It is not a tempting position to hold that there is some conceptual independence of the idea of one's current location from the idea of other locations. In the nature of the case, the idea of one's current location and that of others are simultaneously grasped, or else neither is grasped. Consistently with that point, the property-identity link is still available in the spatial case for the explanation of our understanding of predications of other places.

It is also possible to endorse the bridging use of the property-identity links in both the temporal and the spatial cases without giving some explanatory priority to the thinker's current location—that is, to the very particular place itself—or to the very time at which he is thinking or speaking. The most defensible use of the property-identity link is one in which understanding of predications of other places and times involves an explanatory link, not with a particular time or place, but rather with a type of way of thinking of a place or time—the present-tense type or the *here* type. To move from an agreed explanatory priority of these types of ways of thinking of places and times to some kind of alleged priority of the particular place or time, thought of in a way of one of these two types, would involve an illicit shift. It would involve an illicit shift from a thesis about the level of sense to a thesis about the level of reference.

Once we accept that the bridging thesis is really a thesis about sense and understanding, rather than the level of reference, we had better improve our official formulation of the property-identity links. Our initial illustrative formulation of the link contains the word 'today'—the word is simply used in the initial formulation. If your understanding of past-tense predications does involve the property-identity link, it must be possible to explain how your understanding, today, of past-tense predications involves the *same* property-identity link as your understanding, yesterday, of the past-tense predications did then. Similarly, it must be possible to explain a sense in which your understanding of a predication of some location other than your then location remains constant as you move around in space. A formulation which meets these needs would be this. The information drawn upon by someone in their understanding of predications of times given in a way δ other than as the present can be illustrated thus:

> For any time t and utterance or thought u occurring at t of 'It rains at δ', u is true iff the time referred to by δ at t has the same property as any time has to have for an utterance of 'It is now raining' to be true with respect to that time t.[8]

This is a constant principle which can be used without ambiguity at different times. Its spatial analogue can similarly be used at different places. The move to explaining the property-identity principle in terms of types which may in principle be employed anywhere in space and time serves further to emphasize the way in which the whole spatio-temporal framework is presupposed in the property-identity principle.

It would be fair at this point for someone to press the question of what it means to say that grasp of the property-identity links is partially constitutive of understanding. Perhaps, it may be said, it would not be hard to accept the claim that it is constitutive if present-tense thought were possible without past-tense thought, for then a philosophically prior understanding of the present tense would be drawn upon in the thinker's understanding of past-tense predications. But I have precisely denied such modal independence. And there is a further worry about the constitutive claim. I said it is an advantage of the bridging claim that it explains why, if someone understands 'It is now raining', and also understands 'yesterday', then he will be in a position to understand 'Yesterday it rained'. Yet it is equally a truth that if someone understands 'Yesterday it rained', and also understands 'today', then he will be in a position to understand 'Today it is raining'. So where, it may be asked, is the evidence for any asym-

---

[8] The very relaxed use of inverted commas here is to be understood as follows. In the case in which we are concerned with an utterance, ' "It rains at δ" ' is to be understood as referring to an expression-type consisting of 'It rains at' followed by an expression whose sense is δ. In the case in which we are concerned with a thought, ' "It rains at δ" ' is to be understood as referring to the thought thinkable at time t of the type consisting of the sense *It rains at* in combination with the sense-type δ.

metry which must necessarily be present if the claim of constitutive status for grasp of the property-identity links is to be correct?

On any view, such as I would want to hold, that understanding consists in some specified kind of grasp of truth conditions, the claim that implicit knowledge of the property-identity links is partially constitutive of understanding the past tense must unfold into the claim that there are features of the grasp of truth conditions of which the links are explanatory. So any good case for the bridging claim must cite some data involving understanding, and develop the position that the bridging claim provides the best explanation of those data. The explanatory claim is crucial. It may be that some understanders, when presented with the bridging claim, are immediately struck by its plausibility as an explanation of their understanding of past-tense predications. But its so striking them cannot make it so (nor does any failure to strike them so make it false). It is the explanatory claim itself which it is important for the defender of the bridging claim to make good.

I will consider some other points in support of the bridging claim later in this chapter. Here I will outline one broadly structural respect in which it seems superior to a competing hypothesis (or more strictly, a competing class of hypotheses), and which supports the asymmetry to which we noted the bridging claim is committed. On these competing hypotheses, someone who understands past-tense predications has some information about what it is for any given temporal predicate he understands to be true of an arbitrary time. On these competing hypotheses, this information, unlike the bridging claim, gives no special explanatory position to the present-tense way of thinking of a time. Rather, there is some informational state which can be applied indifferently to any time which is thought about, whether the time is given as present, as past, or in a way which leaves open its relation to the present. We can call this 'the indifference hypothesis'. The indifference hypothesis has no dispute with the correctness of what is strictly stated in the property-identity link itself. After all, the defender of the indifference hypothesis will say, the fact that this biconditional is true,

> 'Yesterday it rained' is true iff yesterday had the same property today has to have for 'Today it is raining' to be true,

is simply a consequence of the generalized condition of Uniformity we identified earlier, i.e.

There is a single property which is the property an arbitrary time *t* must have for the tenseless 'It rains' to be true of *t*.

The problem for the indifference hypothesis lies in saying exactly what the content of its postulated informational state could possibly be. It has to be something which, together with the correct account of perceptual demonstratives and observational vocabulary, entails a certain truth condition for an utterance of the present-tense sentence 'That piece of paper is roughly rectangular'. Let us take it (i) that the truth of this present-tense content requires the fulfilment of a range of commitments about how the paper looks from other angles (amongst other things); (ii) that checking that some of these commitments are fulfilled involves essentially practical capacities, including those involved in the ability to move to look at it from other positions, or at least the capacity, when one is so moved, to tell whether the commitment is fulfilled, in the context of suitable auxiliary information (and indeed to check, in so far as one can, that it is a piece of paper); and (iii) that understanding this content involves some sensitivity to the fact that its acceptance involves a commitment to the fulfilment of these commitments, a sensitivity possible only for someone able, in suitable circumstances, to check on the fulfilment of any one of the commitments.

The question then arises: what content of an informational state, within the terms required by the indifference hypothesis, could possibly entail this condition of understanding for the present-tense 'That piece of paper is roughly rectangular', and also entail a condition of understanding for its past-tense variants? What could the entailed truth conditions for those variants be? It is not credible that understanding of a past-tense predication of shape, say, consists in possessing an unexercisable capacity, that of being able to check that the commitments were fulfilled yesterday if only one could travel back in time. And in any case, if one could travel back in time, what one would then be checking would be, at that past time, present-tense thoughts.

To these remarks, the defender of the indifference hypothesis may find himself tempted to reply that even if that is not a credible account of understanding, then at least the past-tense predication involves the object of the predication in question having the same property whose presence is ensured by the fulfilment of the range of commitments in the present-tense case. The temptation to give that reply is, however, one to which the defender of the indifference hypothesis cannot consistently yield. Yielding to that temptation is just to adopt the bridging use of the property-identity link after all.

Perhaps instead it may be proposed that the informational content needed by the indifference hypothesis has the following character. It is one which—for our sample content—requires the truth of a range of counterfactuals at the time mentioned in the content. Perceptual checks can show that some of these are fulfilled when the time mentioned is the present. But when it is a past time that is in question, the present memories of a thinker who was suitably placed at the past time in question can also establish the fulfilment of some of the commitments. However, I am in the next section just about to make a case that

(a) the counterfactuals are neither necessary nor sufficient for the truth of the past-tense content; and

(b) when they do coincide with the truth value of the content, they do so only because a condition best explained by the bridging claim is also met.

If this is correct, counterfactuals and memory will not provide resources which will allow the indifference hypothesis to meet the challenge. So once those arguments are developed, our provisional conclusion should be that the bridging claim has a structural advantage over the indifference hypothesis. The special status the bridging claim gives to *now*-thoughts in the elucidation of understanding allows us to reconcile the practical elements in the understanding of a present-tense thought 'It is now raining' with the existence of a uniform condition for 'It rains' to hold of an arbitrary time. The special practical elements in the understanding of the present tense, which do not exist for the other tenses, provide the asymmetrical data which justify the special place of now-thoughts in the bridging claim.

3.2 PAST-TENSE TRUTH: SOME METAPHYSICS

I now turn to develop some points about the nature of the truth conditions—about the metaphysics, if you will—of past-tense statements and thoughts. Then, in section 3.3, I return to the question of accounts of understanding which integrate properly with the emerging metaphysics.

A past-tense statement 'Yesterday it was the case that *A*' resists reduction to counterfactuals in the same way, and for the same reasons, that its present-tense counterpart 'It is the case that *A*' also does. 'Yesterday at such-and-such place an event of kind *F* occurred' cannot ever be explained as meaning 'If someone had been at that place, he would have discovered (or would have been able to discover) an event of kind *F* occurring there'. There are two reasons they are not equivalent. First, if the presence of a person would affect whether an event of that kind occurs, the proposed equivalence fails. The counterfactual could be true and the past-tense statement false; and conversely. This problem is not circumvented by adding the qualification 'If someone had been there, and if his presence were not to have affected whether or not an event of kind *F* occurs there, then . . . '. The newly added clause 'and if his presence were not to have affected whether . . . ' has not itself been explained in counterfactual terms. To attempt to explain it in terms of the counterfactual results of someone's investigating whether there is any mechanism linking the presence of a person at the place and the occurrence of *F*-events would be open to the same objection again. In general, when counterfactuals fail to ensure that some condition holds in the actual world, it is not a good idea to try to circumvent the problem by adding more counterfactuals. All these points apply equally to present- and to past-tense statements.

The other reason that any such proposed equivalence fails is that even when there is no interaction between the presence of an investigator and the holding of some condition, the coincidence in truth value between a past-tense statement and a proposed counterfactual elaboration of it still leaves a major difference between the two. The truth of the past-tense statement contributes to an explanation of why the counterfactual is true, when it is true. This by itself precludes analysing the past-tense statement as a counterfactual.

It would not be quite right to capture these points by saying outright that the past-tense statements are categorical. The present-tense counterpart of a past-tense statement may be highly dispositional, and if it is, its past-tense counterpart will also be highly dispositional. So one would better summarize the present set of points by saying that a past-tense statement or thought is *equi-categorical* with its present-tense counterpart. I am, then, endorsing the *equi-categorical thesis*, which states that past-tense statements are equi-categorical with their present-tense counterparts.

The equi-categorical thesis is not an isolated phenomenon, unconnected with our earlier reflections. On the contrary, it follows from
them. The equi-categorical thesis follows from the property-identity
link. If a present-tense statement is not to be given a counterfactual
analysis, then it follows from the property-identity link that the past-
tense counterpart is not to be given the corresponding counterfactual
analysis either. If it were, then in making the past-tense statement we
would not be attributing the very same property to the past time in
question as we are to the present time in accepting the present-tense
version.

Contrapositively, we can equally say that a theorist who insists
upon the counterfactual analysis for the past-tense statement will be
committed to denying the property-identity links if the present-tense
version is not to be analysed in terms of counterfactuals. It is worth
noting here that these points do not actually require the full strength
of the bridging claim, which is an account of understanding. They
require only the correctness of the principle—regardless of whether
it is crucial to the elucidation of understanding—that the truth of a
past-tense statement about a particular time requires that time to
have the same property that its present-tense counterpart requires of
the present time.

If our understanding of past-tense statements is elucidated along
the lines of the bridging claim, then it is also explained why we find
the possibility of an investigator's presence affecting whether an event
occurs at a certain place and time quite coherent. Consider a case in
which there would be such an effect, for instance, the statement that
there was a squirrel on this wall yesterday at noon. The truth of this
statement is still understood as requiring yesterday to have had the
same property as today has to have for there to be a squirrel on the
same wall today at noon. Yesterday still had that property even if it
is true that no squirrel would have appeared had there been an
observer around. Our intuitive judgements about the possibility of
such examples is well explained by the hypothesis that we have
implicit knowledge of the property-identity link.

Implicit knowledge of the property-identity link and its consequences unifies various characteristics of our understanding of the
past. If we have implicit knowledge whose content entails that past-
tense statements are equi-categorical with their present-tense counterparts, we are in a position to appreciate, as in fact we do, that the
holding in the past of categorical conditions can explain the past per-

ceptions of other persons too, and thereby determine the content of their present memories, and can also leave non-psychological traces. Correspondingly we are in a position to appreciate that effects of either of these two sorts can correct our own apparent memories. The possibility of these other effects of past states of affairs, and their potential role in the correction of our own memories, are not conventional elements in our conception of the past which could easily be deleted whilst leaving something coherent behind. Rather, these possibilities are already implicit in the conception of the past which conforms to the property-identity link.

The simple points illustrated in the example of the squirrel seem to me to undermine not just all forms of phenomenalism, but all species of verificationism, idealism, and anti-realism about the meaning of statements about the past. Some such verificationist views can claim distinguished parents. In the *Critique of Pure Reason*, Kant wrote: 'That there could be inhabitants of the moon, even though no human being has ever perceived them, must of course be admitted; but this means only that in the possible progress of experience we could encounter them' (A493/B521).[9] At greater length, and a little further on, Kant writes:

Thus one can say: The real things of past time are given in the transcendental object of experience, but for me they are objects and real in past time only insofar as I represent to myself that, in accordance with empirical laws, or in other words, the course of the world, a regressive series of possible perceptions (whether under the guidance of history or in the footsteps of causes and effects) leads to a time-series that has elapsed as a condition of the present time, which is then represented as real only in connection with a possible experience and not in itself; so that all those events which have elapsed from an inconceivable past time prior to my own existence signify nothing but the possibility of prolonging the chain of experience, starting with the present perception, upward to the conditions which determine it in time.

If, accordingly, I represent all together all existing objects of sense in all time and all spaces, I do not posit them as being there in space and time prior to experience, but rather this representation is nothing other than the thought of a possible experience in its absolute completeness. In it alone are

[9] My thanks to Ralph Walker for drawing this passage to my attention, as a clearer statement than some other passages I had previously selected. The translation, like those of other passages quoted from the first *Critique* elsewhere in this book, is that of the excellent edition of P. Guyer and A. Wood, the Cambridge edition of the works of Immanuel Kant (Cambridge: Cambridge University Press, 1998).

those objects (which are nothing but mere representations) given. But to say that they exist prior to all my experience means only that they are encountered in the part of experience to which I, starting with the perception, must first of all progress. (A495–6/B523–4)

Again, he says:

It is all the same to the outcome whether I say that in the empirical progress in space I could encounter stars that are a hundred times farther from me than the most distant ones I see, or whether I say that perhaps they are there to be encountered in world-space even if no human being has ever perceived them or ever will perceive them. (A496/B524)

There are many things going on in these passage, and some of them could consistently be endorsed on the conception I am developing. For instance, the idea that there is some form of connection between the intelligibility of past-tense statements and what Kant would call 'possible experience' would be enthusiastically endorsed by someone who accepts the property-identity link, and who also insists on links between the intelligibility of present-tense predications and possible experience. But some of Kant's claims in these passages go far beyond such a position. To claim that existence 'prior to all my experience' amounts to no more than what would be met with in certain investigations is incompatible with acknowledgement of the conjunction of the property-identity link and the categorical character of many present-tense statements. Here and in the passage about the distant stars Kant apparently commits himself to the existence of conditional equivalents of the categoricals.

The irreducibility of the categorical to the conditional, when taken together with the equi-categorical thesis, also bears negatively on the versions of temporal anti-realism elaborated in some detail by Crispin Wright. One of the versions receives the intuitive formulation that 'The facts . . . are always as they would have been determined to be if the opportunity to test them had been taken'.[10] This is what Wright calls the 'In principle/Sometime' ('I/S') version. In cases in which the presence of the investigator affects what he finds, this anti-realist account of truth or 'the facts' gives the wrong extension to the truth predicate. What would have been determined to be the case if the opportunity to investigate had been taken is not what would have been the case had the opportunity not been taken. For similar reasons,

---

[10] 'Anti-Realism, Timeless Truth and *Nineteen Eighty-Four*', 181.

the irreducibility to counterfactuals of present-tense statements about other places correspondingly undermines the 'In principle/ Now' and 'In principle/Now or Future' versions of the doctrine. Once again, the property-identity link would not be respected on these anti-realist accounts if the present-tense truth conditions for statements about currently perceived objects are given correctly but the past, and present-tense predications of objects at other places, are explained in terms of counterfactuals.

Wright's anti-realist ends up endorsing a version of the truth-value links, in an account with double-indexing.[11] My own variety of realism will not provoke any need for double-indexing. But the point I want to emphasize here is that even for someone who is happy to use double-indexing, those principles, however intuitively obvious, must both be justified, and shown to be consistent with the rest of one's theory. That issue of consistency is pressing. Once you have fixed a plausible meaning for a present-tense utterance or thought, occurring at any given time, and you have also fixed some favoured account of the meaning of a past-tense utterance, you need then to show that these fixings of meanings entail whatever formulation of the truth-value links is favoured. If you have a certain kind of meaning for present-tense utterances, and go on to specify a kind of meaning for past-tense utterances, and then also want to hold on to a truth-value link relating the two, you need to show that doing all those three things in the particular way proposed is consistent. Otherwise, you will in effect have put forward three equations in two variables.

By contrast, the bridging account as I gave it guarantees these links. The property-identity link, which entails the truth-value link, is the fundamental statement of what it is for a past-tense predication to be true. There is no other explication of the truth of past-tense predications, in terms of possible verification, with which the link must square or from which it must be derived.

The equi-categorical character of past-tense statements and their present-tense counterparts is also a necessary condition for another phenomenon. This is the general phenomenon of the perspective-independence of truths about causation and explanation. Suppose you ask me why there is a cloud of steam in the air, and I answer, pointing to a metal container, 'Because that boiler is leaking'. We then walk around to the other side of the same boiler, and I add, 'But the

---

[11] His principles A*–D*, ibid. 195.

cloud isn't there because that boiler is leaking', whilst manifestly pointing to the same boiler. You would rightly be totally baffled. You would insist that what does the explaining is at the level of reference, not the level of sense, so that a true explanatory statement is insensitive to which modes of presentation are used to pick out the objects, events, properties, and relations being talked about.[12] The same holds for the various ways of thinking of a time. If we can truly say now that a certain event is explained by the present time's having a certain property F, an utterance tomorrow of the sentence 'That event occurred because yesterday was F' will also be true. The truth value of explanation statements made today about the explanatory powers of the properties of yesterday are similarly related to explanations given yesterday about the then-present day. The equi-categorical character of past-tense statements with their present-tense counterparts is a necessary condition for such perspective-independence, since if the equi-categorical thesis failed, the door would be open to dependence of explanation statements on temporal location.

We could imagine someone saying that temporal modes of presentation are an exception to the perspective-independence of causal and explanatory statements which holds for all other modes of presentation. Such a position would face three challenges.

First, it would have to explain the fact that our practices in thought do not at all square with that position. At a later time, we will of course have to adjust the way we are thinking of a particular day if we want to store properly the information we gain now in seeing that it is sunny today—the issues of a cognitive dynamics. But once those necessary adjustments are made, we do not also have to revise our beliefs about what caused what, and what explains what, simply in virtue of our thinking about the same matter at a later time.

Second, one could make considerable mischief for this temporal form of perspective-dependence of explanation by pressing for the nature of its response to relativity theory. Whether one event is earlier than another is relative to a frame of reference, according to that theory. Can we really accept the apparent consequence of the proposed position, that causal and explanatory relations are relative to a frame of reference? On the proposed position of perspective-dependence, there would apparently be no obstacle to the following

---

[12] Here I am in agreement with Elizabeth Anscombe's incisive discussion in her paper 'Causality and Extensionality', *Journal of Philosophy* 66 (1969), 152–9.

holding. Two thinkers think of a single particular event e in two different ways m_1 and m_2, where to employ m_1 is to think of e in a present-tense way, and to use m_2 is to think of e in a past-tense way. On the position in question, the first thinker can think 'The occurrence of m_1 causes it to be the case that p', the second thinker can think 'The occurrence of m_2 did not cause it to be the case that p', and both could be correct. Prima facie, such relativizations seem to undercut the very notions of causation and explanation. (Is it, or is it not, the case that had e not occurred, then p would not have been the case?) To have a relativity of simultaneity to a frame of reference is not thereby to have a relativity of causation and explanation. Relativity is a problem for the position being criticized, rather than a support for it.

Third, the defender of this position has to say something positive about how and why causation and explanation are relative to modes of presentation of times, and about the principles according to which there is variation with the temporal mode of presentation. It is not at all clear to me how he could do this, nor how such variation could be squared with the property-identity link and the equi-categorical character of present- and past-tense statements.

The equi-categorical character of past-tense statements with their present-tense counterparts entails that no qualitative present-tense conditions are ever constitutively and conclusively sufficient for the occurrence of an event of a certain kind at some particular place at some past time. Here the caveat 'qualitative' is just to exclude present-tense conditions which write in requirements whose present satisfaction requires the world earlier to have been a certain way, such as 'fossil', 'footprint', and 'genuine (as opposed to merely apparent) memory'. The equi-categorical principle ensures that present-tense qualitative conditions are never so sufficient because, in the case of a present-tense statement that an event of the given kind occurs at a particular place, we can see only too clearly how it could, on this particular occasion, be false even though conditions obtain which are, in other cases, its effects. Conversely, there is no difficulty in seeing how the present-tense version could be true without having its normal effects, since any causal process can be blocked.

It should not be inferred from these points that the equi-categorical claim makes statements about the past epistemologically more problematic. On the contrary, the equi-categorical principle is a necessary condition of treating statements about the past as verifiable by personal experiential memory, in a way closely analogous to, and in fact involving, the way in which perception allows the verification of certain present-tense statements about the perceptible world. We need to be able to conceive of past states of affairs as having had the causal powers to produce experiences which themselves produce later experiential memories (or at least conceive that the past state of affairs had causal powers to produce states in the subject which were the common cause both of the earlier perceptual experience and of the later experiential memory). Such verification of past-tense statements is possible, of course, only with a substantial cognitive apparatus already in place, including all that is involved in the capacity for objective thought and first-person thought. A substantial cognitive apparatus must of course equally be present in the case of perceptual verification.

Here I again diverge from Crispin Wright, who holds that 'at least some observation-statements' are capable of actual verification, whilst statements about the past are not.[13] 'Certainly we do not want to regard statements about the past, for example, as susceptible to verification.'[14] Wright's conception of actual verification is that of a procedure which, in a case in which it is carried out and gives grounds for a statement, has a certain distinctive property. It has the property that if the statement is nevertheless false when asserted on the basis of the outcome of the procedure, this can only be because some or other of the commitments involved in accepting that the procedure has been properly carried out are false (where the commitments in question are those which are independent of the correctness of the statement whose verification is in question). So the idea is that when you come to believe a universal contingent generalization on the basis of a wide variety of true instances, you could be wrong just because some uninvestigated instance is false. But, Wright says, when you engage in a simple arithmetical computation, or make an observation statement on the basis of a suitable experience, you could be wrong only because the procedure has not been properly carried out, in certain ways specifiable independently of the truth or falsity of the original statement in question. In brief: grounds for questioning a statement made in this way must also be grounds for questioning its pedigree, as Wright says. To include observational statements, this

[13] 'Strict Finitism', repr. in his *Realism, Meaning and Truth*, at 120.
[14] Ibid. 115.

criterion must allow that when a perceptual system is producing experiences which do not correctly represent the subject's environment, the commitments of one who accepts a statement on the basis of the procedure are commitments which are not fulfilled.

Wright's criterion for actual verification seems to me to capture important aspects of the notion. It is, however, very hard to see why, if it is accepted, this criterion does not also allow for the actual verification of statements about the past by the use of experiential memory. Wright says of 'generalizations of natural science, statements concerning the past, statements concerning the still remote future, most subjunctive conditionals, and most types of descriptions of others' mental states' that 'in each of these kinds of case, all admissible grounds for belief can be overturned simply by *enrichments* of our total state of information quite consistent with our rationally retaining belief' in each of the statements we are committed to in accepting a statement on the basis of use of a given procedure.[15] I cannot see that this is correct for a statement about the past such as 'I once swam from a yacht', made, let us suppose, by you on the basis of your experiential memory as of swimming from a yacht. If that statement about the past is overturned, as in some sense it could be, that would indeed require you to think that there is something wrong with your memory or perceptual mechanisms.

There is a danger of applying Wright's criterion in a way which begs the question. For instance, in the course of a discussion of McDowell's views, in which Wright appeals to his account of actual verification, Wright asks,

[C]an any plausible account be produced of the *province* . . . on which one who wished, supposing such a thing were ever possible, directly to verify a statement about the past would have to concentrate? . . . What is the species of presently accessible states of affairs such that an agent who in a sufficiently attentive, comprehending and perceptual-error free way observes enough such states of affairs cannot arrive at a mistaken view about a putative state of affairs which antedated them all?[16]

Wright implies that the question is unanswerable, that there are no such presently accessible states of affairs. If, however, experiential memory is causally sensitive to a person's past situations, and if we

---

[15] Ibid. 120.
[16] 'Realism, Truth-Value Links, Other Minds and the Past', repr. in his *Realism, Meaning and Truth*, at 99.

are not to beg the question, Wright's question should concern not just
an agent who proceeds in a 'perceptual-error free way', but one who
proceeds in a 'perceptual- and memory-error free way'. The revised
question is then easily answered. Experiential memory can itself give
the required ground for your judgement that you once swam from a
yacht. Here 'ground' means reason, and is not restricted to something
which supplies, or is mentioned in, a premise of an inference. Of the
phrase 'presently accessible state of affairs', a critic of Wright is likely
to remark that a presently accessible state of affairs is not necessarily a present state of affairs which is also accessible. Experiential
memory gives present access to states of affairs which are not present
states of affairs.

Wright's differential treatment of perception and experiential
memory also raises a more general question about understanding.
What account of our understanding of the past-tense could be given
which would mesh with Wright's idea that the way in which past-
tense statements can be overturned by later enrichments of the evidence precludes the possibility of genuine verification of past-tense
statements? In the cases of other kinds of statement for which such
enrichments preclude verification, we have a very clear idea of what
it is about the nature of their meaning that accounts for this state of
affairs. In the case of unrestricted universal generalizations, there is
an evident open-ended commitment to the truth of a range of singular instances, and some form of sensitivity to that commitment is
necessary to understanding universal quantifications. A somewhat
analogous point applies in another kind of case, that of the application of a predicate which is fundamentally understood as having a
certain role in a particular kind of theory. The consequences of the
predicate's applying to an object will be given by the theory, and in
the general case no finite process of checking will be available to
ensure that all the consequences of its applying to the object are fulfilled.[17]

But statements about the past seem to be different. It is not at all

---

[17] Note that propositional-attitude ascriptions are *not* like this if the simulation
model is fundamentally correct as an account of our understanding of them. The
defender of the simulation account may say that when ascribing on the basis of imagining the other's situation leads to a false ascription, that is because the conditions
for proper application of the method have not been fulfilled. So it is an open question whether simulation-involving approaches may not be able to make something
of the idea that other-ascriptions of propositional attitudes are verifiable if that
notion is construed roughly along Wright-like lines.

easy to think of any kind of commitment about later conditions which meets all three of the following conditions. First, it is found in any past-tense statement, simply in virtue of its being a past-tense statement. Second, appreciation of its presence is constitutive of understanding of the past tense. Third—since I am emphasizing the appropriateness of genuine verification for some past-tense statements via experiential memory—the commitment is not just to the availability of memories to observers appropriately equipped and situated in relation to the way the world was. (The motivation for this third clause is that such memories are not commitments of the sort which are in question, since whether something is a memory will depend on its relations to what was really so in the past.) I suggest that there are no such memory-independent commitments. There are plausibly commitments about later times when the past-tense statement involves continuant objects, or properties whose instantiation involves a certain characteristic course of development over time, and so forth. These are all cases in which the commitment is present because of special features of the content to which an operator such as 'in the past', or 'yesterday', is applied. What are the memory-independent commitments for later times of the truth of the past-tense utterance 'It was quiet in the garden yesterday afternoon'? It seems to me that this is a wholly empirical matter, not settled at all just by the meaning of the utterance in question. Of course any empirical consequences we are able to work out, in the presence of other information, are not worked out from a starting point of nothing at all. But it seems to me that our starting point is just what is given in the property-identity link, in the form employed in the bridging claim. Our starting point is just that that past-tense utterance is true if yesterday had the same property today has to have for it to be true that it is quiet in the garden today. We then have to investigate empirically what might be the present consequences of yesterday's having had that property.

Certainly enrichments of your state of information can overturn your past-tense beliefs, including those based on apparent memories. Your apparent experiential memory of flying in a jumbo jet as a child no longer leads you to accept that you did so when you learn that there were no jumbo jets in existence in your childhood. These are cases in which the new information which overturns the past-tense belief also overturns your belief that your memory was functioning properly in this instance. Such examples lend no support to the view

that there is some further commitment, in the acceptance of a past-
tense statement, to what is later the case, beyond what is supported
by experiential memory when it *is* working properly. If indeed there
are no such further commitments, it must be tempting to conclude
that someone who also says that experiential memory does not verify past-tense statements is not actually left with any account of how
we understand the past tense at all.

   The question arises why thinkers have been attracted to verificationist and counterfactual accounts of the meaning of present- and
past-tense statements about the natural world. There may be two,
possibly related, reasons. One motivation may be a particular way of
reading Dummett's manifestation challenge. Meaning must determine and be exhaustively determined by use, according to this view,
and so for any particular meaning we attribute to an expression, we
ought to be able to give a philosophical account of the use which
legitimates that attribution of meaning. The manifestation challenge
comes in several strengths and varieties. I am not going to question
that there are forms of the manifestation challenge which need to be
addressed, provided that the challenge is framed in a way which
allows the use of intentional vocabulary in describing what is
involved in someone's employing one concept rather than another.
The particular form of the manifestation challenge most pertinent to
the case of understanding the past tense is one which holds that
meaning and content being must be fundamentally determined by a
thinker's intentional responses to observable, or decidable, conditions.[18] Once the manifestation challenge is thought to have that consequence, one can see how a theorist might be led towards a
verificationist and counterfactual theory. Even that remark may be as
much a matter of explanation of a line of thought rather than a justification for it. As we in effect noted in considering Wright's discussion of McDowell, even as formulated the challenge leaves open the

   [18] Dummett does sometimes lean towards the particular construal of the challenge which I am questioning. In 'The Philosophical Basis of Intuitionistic Logic', he
says this of the argument for intuitionism which starts from the premise that use
must fully determine meaning: 'The argument told in favour of replacing, as the central notion for the theory of meaning, the condition under which a statement is true,
whether we know or can know when that condition obtains, by the condition under
which we acknowledge the statement as conclusively established, a condition which
we must, by the nature of the case, be capable of effectively recognizing whenever it
obtains.' M. Dummett, *Truth and Other Enigmas* (London: Duckworth, 1978), 227.

possibility of present access to past states of affairs. But more fundamentally, meaning does not have to be determined from actual and
certain possible reactions to decidable circumstances for the manifestation challenge to be met. The commitment account of universal
quantification, of the sort I have in *Thoughts*, does not depend on
intentional responses to decidable circumstances in which the quantification holds.[19] Closer to home, the account I will be giving in the
next section on understanding the past tense does not depend upon
it either. It also seems to me that we have a relatively clear grasp of
what sorts of patterns of judgement implicit knowledge of the property-identity link would make rational. Those judgements would
include acceptance of the intelligibility of interference by the observer
on what conditions hold in the natural world of a kind incompatible
with verificationist or counterfactual analyses of past-tense thought.

Actually, even if a theorist does insist that intentional responses to
decidable circumstances must play a central, even if not exclusive,
part in the individuation of meaning and concepts, there would still
be a *non sequitur* in moving from that point to a counterfactual
theory. We can agree that the statement that a certain material object
is *F* can be verified by your being at its location and perceiving it to
be *F*. It by no means follows that what it is for it to be true that the
object is *F* when you are not there is for it to be the case that if you
or anyone else were there, it would be perceived to be *F*. Your being
there and perceiving it to be *F* may verify the original statement
because it establishes that some categorical condition is met by the
object.

If that is why it is so verified, it is also the case that nothing follows about what would be the case when neither you, nor anyone
else, is there. What categorical conditions would hold if you were not
there is not settled by that information.

Thinkers tempted to a counterfactual analysis may also have been
impressed by the idea that a verificationist account of understanding
is the right way of generalizing to the empirical world from the case
of decidable arithmetical equations. For decidable arithmetical equations, understanding does seem inseparable from grasp of a decision
procedure, whether the procedure is executed in a particular case or
not. In the nature of the case, performing a computation cannot
affect what the outcome of the computation is, in the way in which

---

[19] *Thoughts: An Essay on Content* (Oxford: Blackwell, 1986).

going there can affect what happens at a place. This fact encourages the verificationist account for the arithmetical case, but makes it the wrong model for the empirical case. The difference between the cases is a by-product of the underlying difference between a procedure which is a computation, and a procedure which consists in getting into the right position and state to be causally affected by a temporal state of affairs. One highly problematic variety of Platonism in the philosophy of mathematics seems to me to result in part from the attempt to assimilate arithmetical knowledge to the case of knowledge explained by contact with a categorical and temporally explanatory state of affairs.

I now turn to the question of the relation between realism, in Dummett's sense, about the past and the conception with which I have been elaborating the bridging claim. There is a highly intuitive argument, which I suspect articulates widespread realist intuitions, from that conception to such a realism about the past. The intuitive argument has three steps.

(Step 1). We can set up—or at least there could be—a present state of affairs of such a kind that all its effects, other than those involved in producing our perceptual states, do not distinguish between the state of affairs we have actually set up and some different kind. We shield off any such discriminating effects. So, for instance, a sealed, opaque incinerator may contain a wooden cube which, when burned, leaves a certain mass of ashes. We could set up things in such a way that a block of a different shape but the same mass would leave exactly the same mass and pattern of ashes of the same kind after incineration.

(Step 2). Such a state of affairs could exist even if we were not present and had no perceptual states to give us information that it obtains.

(Step 3). A state of affairs of exactly the same sort as is mentioned in Step 2 could have obtained in the past. In the nature of the case, this would be a state of affairs which could exist without our now being able to know that it did—since by hypothesis its effects to do not distinguish it from other states of affairs which could have obtained.

Now the transition here from Step 2 to Step 3 relies on the property-identity link being understood as it is formulated in the bridging claim. It is a legitimate transition if we are employing a notion of sameness of property, and endorsing the equi-categorical claim. It would *not* be a valid transition if truth were understood in either of the two anti-realist ways that Wright calls the I/N (In principle/Now) or I/NF (In principle/Now or Future). On the I/N conception, we may have evidence now that a certain state of affairs exists, and there is no evident reason not to allow that conception the modal claim that it would exist even if we were not aware of it. But the transition to Step 3 would be quite illegitimate on that conception. The transition involves the possibility of the existence of a state of affairs of which we have no present evidence, and need not have any in the future. A similar point applies to establish the illegitimacy of the transition for the I/NF (In principle/Now or Future) variant of anti-realism.[20]

It seems to me that the transition from Step 2 to Step 3 is not simply an instance of begging the question against the anti-realist.[21] It is an instance of a kind of non-philosophical reasoning found not only in ordinary thought, but in the work of any historian, or archaeologist, or other empirical scientist. It is simply the principle that a state of affairs of a given kind which could exist at one place and time, could, prima facie, exist at any other. We use such a principle frequently when thinking through how some known end result might have come about, as when an archaeologist investigates, using current sequences of events, whether a find of objects close together indicates that they were used close together, or that they have just settled there together from different locations. The principle needs the prima facie qualification. The apparent possibility it mentions may be successfully rebutted by all sorts of more specific considerations about the region of the spatio-temporal universe to which its application is in question. What does not seem to be the case is that there is any general pretheoretical restriction on its application having to do with verifiability or evidence. The defender of the bridging claim who reflects on this prima facie general principle will be unsurprised that

---

[20] I am not pressing the point for I/S anti-realism, for anti-realists like Wright are surely correct in doubting whether, by their own lights, that is a legitimate variant. In any case, even if it were, it would still be problematic to appeal to it to support the transition from Step 2 to Step 3. It would involve the counterfactual analysis that we have questioned. The I/N and I/NF versions do not have this problem, at least for actually encountered states of affairs, which is what the possibility in Step 1 involves.

[21] As Wright implies, 'Anti-Realism, Timeless Truth, and *Nineteen Eighty-Four*', 186–7.

there is no restriction concerning evidential relations. The idea that it is the same properties whose instantiation is in question as in present-tense instances is enough, in the presence of the equi-categorical claim, to make such investigations as that of the archaeologist reasonable.

These points suggest some reflections on the very delicate question of the proper account of the relation between truth-value links and realism, in Dummett's sense, about the past. In his original discussion of these issues, Dummett represents the realist as claiming that 'by stipulating the validity of the truth-value link, we thereby provide that from which a realist conception of truth and falsity for these statements can be derived'.[22] As we have in effect noted, some anti-realists have said they are entitled to certain formulations of the truth-value links, and their position may make one wonder whether there is any connection between those links and realism. But when one looks in detail at anti-realist approaches to content, it seems very doubtful that they really are preserving truth-value links between, for instance, present-tense predications and those in other tenses, when they go on to explain the past tense in counterfactual terms. The explication of the links that we do have, in the bridging claim, seem to validate fundamentally realistic forms of reasoning. The argument formulated in Steps 1–3 does not rely on very special features of some particular example. On the contrary, it seems to go through whenever we have the possibility of later evidence not discriminating between two competing hypotheses about some temporal state of affairs. So there may yet be some internal connection between realism and the truth-value links in their most defensible form after all. The explanation of why there is some internal connection has to allude to the equi-categorical character of past-tense statements with their present-tense counterparts, and to the ramifications of this fact. It is only when the truth-value link is placed in this context that one has the resources to explain why there is a connection between the truth-value link, properly explicated, and realism in Dummett's sense.

I turn now to consider very briefly the relations between the metaphysical position developed in this section and some earlier writings. Readers who want to continue immediately with the main thread of the argument should move straight to the start of the next section.

[22] 'The Reality of the Past', repr. in his *Truth and Other Enigmas*, at 364.

The defender of a verificationist and counterfactual theory of the meaning of statements about the past and about other places, of the sort I have been criticizing, need not be any kind of phenomenalist. He may maintain a staunchly anti-phenomenalistic line, and insist that the counterfactuals which he takes (mistakenly, if I am right) to be meaning-giving are about the perception of mind-independent material objects and events, in various hypothetical circumstances. So this sort of verificationist will be immune to some of the criticisms which were so damaging to phenomenalism. None the less, it seems to me that the most insightful critics of phenomenalism developed objections which were not merely objections to phenomenalism, but were—though their authors did not always appreciate the point—objections to any counterfactual, verificationist treatment of statements about the past or about other places.

The deepest critiques of phenomenalism drew upon a more positive conception of our thought about the empirical, public, spatio-temporal world—'objective thought', as I will call it. I would single out in particular the exceptionally acute contribution by Isaiah Berlin, in his paper 'Empirical Propositions and Hypothetical Statements'.[23] Berlin gave a description of objective thought which seems to me completely accurate, both in outline and in detail. Berlin's position can be summarized in three theses (I)–(III), which I will label respectively the theses of Irreducibility, of Uniformity, and of the Holism of the Objective.

Thesis (I), of Irreducibility, states, in Berlin's own words, that 'no direct translation from categoricals into hypotheticals is, as a general rule, and as our language is ordinarily used, a correct analysis of, or substitute for them' (43). Phenomenalism attempted to translate propositions about material objects into some favoured kinds of statements about sense experience. Berlin wrote that according to the phenomenalist,

Categorical propositions about material objects are replaced by unfulfilled 'counterfactual' hypothetical propositions about observers, and what troubles the plain man is the thought that if the hypotheticals are unfulfilled, if no observers were in fact observing . . . there was—in a sense datum sense—nothing at all, and, moreover, that this sense of 'existence' is basic: because

---

[23] Originally published in *Mind* 59 (1950), 289–312, and repr. in his *Concepts and Categories: Philosophical Essays*, ed. H. Hardy (Oxford: Oxford University Press, 1980). Page references are to the latter reprinting.

the alleged material object sense in which the non-existence of actual sense data nevertheless can be 'translated into' the existence of material objects, is not a sense in which the word 'exist' is commonly understood. (39)

Berlin's point that categorical character is never exhausted by hypotheticals seems to me to stand, and to draw on essentially the same metaphysical conception as I have been presenting. Berlin does not offer the arguments from interference, or from explanation of the hypothetical in the cases in which it is true. Those arguments are, though, simply further elaborations of the irreducibility of categoricals to hypotheticals. Further, as Berlin adds towards the end of the article, the conditionals which phenomenalists have sometimes offered as analyses of material object sentences have imported presuppositions which really have nothing to do with the meaning of the sentence being analysed. The phenomenalist may be tempted to say that 'There is a brown table in the next room' means something about what would be experienced by someone who went next door to investigate. But, Berlin notes, '[T]he question of when, or for how long, the table next door is coloured brown need not in principle ever affect the answer to the question "What do I mean when I say 'There is a brown table next door'?"'(54). This is an example of the general point that it is only with further empirical information that one can infer, from the statement that an object is a particular way at a given time, something about what will be so at some other place or time. The inference is not guaranteed purely by the meaning of the statement.

Thesis (II), the thesis of Uniformity, is illustrated by Berlin's remark that 'there is no logical difference dividing sentences which describe things in my field of vision from those which describe things beyond the horizon' (46). As we might put it now: in the sentences 'There is a table here' and 'There is a table on the opposite side of the world', the words 'There is a table' have exactly the same meaning. It seems clear from his paper 'Verification' that Berlin would say exactly the same about times as he says about places.[24] The Uniformity thesis seems to me to be a critical component of any good account of objective thought. Indeed, if the property-identity link and the bridging claim are true, the Uniformity thesis will also be true. The property-

[24] 'Verification', *Proceedings of the Aristotelian Society* 39 (1938–9), 225–48; also repr. in his *Concepts and Categories*; see in particular pp. 15–16 of the reprint.

identity link and the bridging claim consitute the beginnings of an explanation of Uniformity. (It is only a beginning, because we have not yet given the full account of understanding the past tense.)

Berlin also notes an apparent corollary of Uniformity: '[T]o describe the conditions in which alone I should be inclined to enunciate a sentence is certainly not equivalent to giving its meaning' (44). He attributes some of the odder consequences of phenomenalism to 'the confounding of the meaning of what we are saying with the varying conditions under which we feel inclined to say it' (51). This too is a point we would make once we insist that it is commonly a categorical property which is required for the truth of a judgement whose content contains a given observational concept. The categorical property required for truth is constant across the varying conditions which may make it reasonable to judge that an object falls under that concept.

Thesis (III), which I label the Holism of the Objective, is given in Berlin's statement that 'The meaning of such "basic" words as "here", "now", "observed", depends on the existence of an equally "basic" use for "not here", "not now", "not observed", in contrast with which alone the meanings of "here", "now" etc. can be established' (52). There could hardly be a better summary of some of the conclusions for which I have argued (and some still to come). In fact, the Holism of the Objective was already present at the point at which we noted (in section 1 of this chapter) that the whole spatio-temporal framework is presupposed in the proper formulation of the property-identity link.

Berlin adds that 'such comparatively primitive notions as "not now", or "beyond the horizon", cannot be "constructed" without circularity out of sense fields occurring in "specious presents"; but without such notions classification, and therefore language, in the ordinary sense, is demonstrably impossible' (52). I am afraid that Berlin does not actually supply the demonstration of this impossibility. For the moment, let us just note the close relation of the Holism of the Objective to Berlin's first two theses. If the Holism of the Objective were false, then it seems that there would be a possibility of a thinker's grasping here-thoughts without so much as conceiving of the existence of places elsewhere. If this were genuinely his situation, it seems that there would be a way of grasping the thought 'There is a table here' which did not presuppose the thinker's capacity to grasp 'There is a table elsewhere'. So, contraposing, Uniformity seems to require the Holism of the Objective. Further, it is very hard to see what the kind of uniform meaning common to 'There is a table here' and 'There is a table in the next room' could be, unless it were of a categorical kind.

Berlin's position thus seems to me both to result from a true conception of the relations between truth and verification in this area, and to be true in its detailed claims. Much of this chapter could be regarded as an attempt to work out part of a theory of meaning and understanding which would validate Berlin's position.

I also wish to note briefly the relation of the present treatment of the metaphysics of past-tense statements to the account in chapter 5 of my earlier book *Thoughts: An Essay on Content*. There I proposed a 'three-tier' account of thought about the inaccessible. At the first tier is the set of canonical commitments of a present-tense judgement about some observed object. The second tier contains the truth condition determined by these commitments and various features of our thought about the inaccessible. At the third tier are the truth conditions of statements about inaccessibles—determined, I said, by the contents of the second tier. In *Thoughts* I wrote that the three-tier account gives 'that in virtue of which those [truth-value] links hold' (82). I now think that that is the reverse of the truth. A three-tier account actually *relies* upon the property-identity links. The canonical commitments of a present-tense thought like 'That block is cubic' have to determine a property which can hold of the perceived block, and of things elsewhere, and of things in the past and future. I do not think that there is a satisfactory explanation of the link between tier two and tier three unless we rely on an explanatory property-identity link (and its consequence, a truth-value link). In *Thoughts*, I did get as far as realizing that counterfactual explanations of categoricals do not work (see 82–3). What I missed was that we need the property-identity link to explain how we do conceive of the truth conditions of categoricals. I suspect that in *Thoughts* I neglected the level of properties, and was also too influenced by the position, common to some anti-realists and to some realists, that the truth-value links cannot subserve a certain substantive kind of explanation of understanding.

3.3 EXTERNALIST ELEMENTS IN UNDERSTANDING THE PAST TENSE

Not only conditions which held in the past, but also the particular temporal relations which hold between past events and past or present states of affairs can be causally explanatory. The fact that the wet summer immediately preceded the dry one can explain the current spatial relation between the wide and the narrow rings in the cross-section of the tree. Particular temporal relations can equally be explanatory of facts in the mental realm. Your impression that a certain person left the room a certain interval of time ago, an interval which is, in fact, about ten minutes, can be explained by that person's having left about ten minutes ago. That this temporal relation between an event and the present can be causally explanatory is not any more problematic as a matter of general principle than is the fact that the spatial relation of some event to you now can explain your impression that it stands in that spatial relation to you now.

I have just been mentioning examples in which the content of the temporal or spatial impression is specific as to which (egocentrically identified) time or place it represents as being a particular way. But even when a genuine memory impression, for instance, is not specific in its content as to the temporal relation between the events it represents and the present, it is still true to say that you have an experiential memory of (say) having swum from a yacht because at some past time you did so.

The claim that certain mental states are causally sensitive to temporal facts would not carry much weight if we had no idea how underlying sub-personal mechanisms could be sensitive to such facts. We do, though, have some idea. Computational mechanisms which are sensitive to the passage of time and which have been discussed empirically in some detail include mechanisms which are sensitive to the state attained by some regular oscillatory process, or to the state of something which acts as an accumulator.[25] The fact that an oscillator is at a given time in a certain state, or that an accumulator has reached a certain level, are each of them causally explained in part by the fact that the given time is a certain interval of time after some other event. The nature of the sub-personal mechanism is, evidently,

---

[25] For an illuminating critical overview, see C. Gallistel, *The Organization of Learning* (Cambridge, Mass.: MIT Press, 1990), chs. 7–9.

an empirical matter. There may be a good a priori case that any being capable of temporal thought must possess some such mechanism or other. There is, though, no a priori argument, of any particular mechanism, that it must be possessed.

To possess a sub-personal mechanism which is, when functioning properly, thus temporally sensitive is of course not yet to have mastered temporal thought. Here again it can help to consider a spatial parallel. It is equally the case that to possess a sub-personal mechanism which is, when functioning properly, sensitive to spatial facts is not yet to have mastered spatial thought. I will return shortly to the question of what conditions are sufficient. At present, I want to emphasize that in both the temporal and the spatial cases, the presence of such sub-personal mechanisms is a necessary condition of mastery. Without such sensitive mechanisms, a person's thought would not be latching on to space or time at all. A philosophical account of temporal thought must have externalist elements just as our models of spatial and other kinds of thought do. Correlatively, an account of the manifestation of the meaning of temporal vocabulary must involve, amongst other elements, a sensitivity to temporal relations themselves.

The mechanisms which are sensitive to temporal conditions do not have to be perfect by any means. It is a commonplace that emotional states, ranging from fascination to boredom, will affect one's impression of the length of time which has elapsed since some specified event. Equally, perception of size can be distorted by expectations, or better, possession of sub-personal information, about the usual shapes and sizes of familiar kinds of objects. None of these phenomena show that we do not have faculties whose states are causally explained by temporal and spatial phenomena respectively. They show only that our temporal and spatial impressions are not a function solely of the output of these faculties, but are subject to other causal influences too. They do not show that there are no temporal and spatial faculties.

The examples I have given so far concern a thinker's impressions of the temporal relations of some remembered event to the present time. The cases in which temporal facts explain temporal impressions range much more widely than that. Consider an episodic memory of some particular event in which you participated. Even if you know when the event occurred, we can always make sense of the idea that we might be mislocating in time an event remembered in this way.

Equally, you may be remembering the event in this way, and wondering just when it did occur. Was it this year, or last year; here or in another continent? Now even if you do not currently have any beliefs about when it occurred, you can still raise the questions: what happened next? And what led up to this event? Memory will sometimes serve up further episodic memories which answer these questions. It will sometimes serve up answers in which the events remembered in the new episodic memories are remembered as occurring a certain length of time before, or after, the initially remembered events. Again, these temporal impressions are explained, when all is working properly, by those newly remembered events standing in just those temporal relations to the initially remembered events.[26]

What is the difference between being merely responsive to the temporal interval which has elapsed since a particular event occurred, and taking it as a temporal interval? In the latter case, the event at the far end of the temporal interval is assigned a position in one's own history, and, correlatively, in the history of the world. The difference is analogous to that found in the spatial case. One similarly goes beyond simply being causally sensitive to an instance of a spatial magnitude in assigning some perceived event or object a location on one's spatial cognitive map. In both the temporal and the spatial cases, what more specific consequences flow from the subject's appreciation of the event or object as having an objective character will depend on what other objective beliefs, inclinations, or projects the individual may have. There may be some general a priori connections between the capacity for objective thought and first-person thought. For a creature with an objective conception of the world, many of his actions will be explained under objective and first-personal descriptions. Such explanations will sustain counterfactuals which would not be supported for the actions of a creature whose psychology does not involve any grasp of the objective. If you want to shake hands

---

[26] Note that the newly remembered events are temporally identified just by their remembered temporal relations to the initially remembered events. So we have a phenomenon of event-relative temporal identification. There are many ramifications of this point which would take us too far off course here. One is that mode of access to a past event can determine the particular temporal identification one has of it. My own view is that reflection on the case suggests that not all episodic memories are accessed by their being mentally indexed by the time at which they are (represented as) occurring. For a contrasting view, see Gallistel, *The Organization of Learning*, ch. 15.

with that man you perceive, you will move towards him. If he had been in a different location, you would have moved to that location; and so forth.[27] It is important to note, though, consistently with these points, that attribution of an objective conception may be necessary to making sense of the subject's actions and mental life, without there being any simple correlation of behavioural effects with particular objective assignments. On this, I am entirely at one with Gallistel when he writes, 'Representational approaches make a much sharper or consequential distinction between what has been learned . . . and the effects that the existence of this representation may have on diverse behaviors. Representational approaches assume that these effects will be as diverse as are the computational mechanisms brought to bear on the represented information by different behavioral readout systems'.[28] Indeed, creatures with very different behavioural repertoires, at one level of description, may both be capable of states with objective representational contents.

There are several consequences of the presence of externalist elements in a philosophical account of temporal thought. One of them can be brought out by reflection on a passage from Russell. The first, but not the second, sentence of this passage is well known. Russell wrote:

There is no logically necessary connection between events at different times; therefore nothing that is happening now or will happen in the future can disprove the hypothesis that the world began five minutes ago. Hence the occurrences which are *called* knowledge of the past are logically independent of the past; they are wholly analysable into present contents which might, theoretically, be just what they are even if no past had existed.[29]

What interests me for present purposes is not the sceptical hypothesis, but rather what immediately follows Russell's 'Hence' in the second sentence of this passage, and whether the 'Hence' is justified. If we accept the existence of externalist elements in an account of what makes something an impression that a certain event happened a certain length of time ago, we will want to distinguish between two notions of independence. They can be brought out by considering a spatial analogue of Russell's argument.

---

[27] There is more on this and related themes in my paper 'Externalist Explanation', *Proceedings of the Aristotelian Society* 93 (1993), 203–30.

[28] Gallistel, *The Organization of Learning*, 257.

[29] B. Russell, *The Analysis of Mind* (London: George Allen & Unwin, 1968), 159–60.

There is no logically necessary connection between events at different places; therefore nothing that is happening here (at the location of a perceiver) can disprove the hypothesis that there is nothing anywhere else. Hence the occurrences which are *called* knowledge of what is happening elsewhere are logically independent of what is happening elsewhere; they are wholly analysable into contents about the location of the perceiver, which might, theoretically, be just what they are even there were nothing anywhere else.[30]

Presented with this argument about space, I think we would be inclined to distinguish at least two kinds of independence. Even if what is happening at one place, or what objects are located there, has no necessary connection with what is happening at any other particular place, that specific independence does not entail that one could give an account of what it is to be capable of having thoughts and perceptions of other places which do not mention the complex relations of those thoughts and perceptions to other places themselves. What I am concerned with here is not the issue of whether the representational content of, say, an individual spatial experience is correct. I am concerned rather with the issue of what makes it an experience with a certain specific spatial content, as one which represents objects or events as being at such-and-such distances and directions from the subject. It seems to me that there is no hope of giving an account of what it is for experiences and thoughts to represent certain things or events as being at certain distances and directions from the subject without at some point mentioning the role of those experiences and thoughts in explaining the various complex capacities the subject of the experiences has in relation to the places at those represented distances and directions. It would be an interesting and fruitful task to elaborate these complex capacities in more detail. The elaboration would certainly have to take into account the role of specific spatial contents concerning distance and direction in explaining, in the presence of a suitable background, the subject's actions in relation to places in those same directions and distances (whether he moves to them or is moved to them). But however the elaboration runs, if this point is sound, then there is at least one reading of the conclusion of this spatial analogue of Russell's reasoning on which it is an incorrect conclusion. An account of what it is for a perceiver at a given location to have experiences with a spatial representational content cannot

---

[30] Or should I conclude the spatial version, 'even if no other place existed'? Russell's intentions are not wholly clear.

be given without mentioning his complex relations to other locations, even if on this occasion, and perhaps on many others, his experiences misrepresent what is the case at those other locations. There would be no question of, in Russell's terms, 'wholly analysing the occurrences which are *called*' knowledge of other places without making at least some reference to other places.

The analogous point seems to me to hold in the temporal case. It is hard to see how one could give an account of what it is to have an impression that something happened a certain period of time ago— a period which is about five minutes, say—without mentioning that person's ability, in suitable circumstances, to track and mark out temporal intervals of roughly that length. The thinker must have an ability to be sensitive to the passages of certain-sized intervals of time themselves. Even if a thinker is wholly mistaken about what happened to him about five minutes ago, none the less an account of what makes it the case that it is about five minutes ago that it seems the events occurred is one which undermines one reading of Russell's conclusion. Thought about the past involves past-tense contents, and the fundamental abilities involved in having the capacity for past-tense thought cannot be explained in purely present-tense terms. In fact it is noteworthy that we understand the sceptical hypothesis of Russell's premise as describing a case in which the initial illusory impressions of what was the case more than five minutes ago—say, about half an hour ago—are of the same subjective kind as those later impressions with similar temporal contents which *do* track the passage of time, and track the (apparent) state of the world at later times.

The presence of externalist elements in a philosophical account of temporal thought has not only constitutive, but also epistemological, aspects. It is only if a temporal impression has an externally individuated content—in this case, a content individuated by its relations to the passage of time itself—that it can yield, in appropriate circumstances, non-inferential knowledge with a temporal content. The way a mental state represents the world as being must be a way which is externally individuated, if taking it at face value is to be capable of yielding knowledge that the world is that way. Here, taking an experience at face value is simply judging that things are as—or are in one of the ways—the state represents them as being, and because it so represents them (see Chapter 2 and its Appendix for further discussion). More precisely, we can formulate the principle as stating that the representational content of a mental state must be individuated by its relations to objects, properties, or events of a given kind if a thinker's taking it at face value is to be capable of yielding non-inferential knowledge about objects, properties, or events of that kind. If it were not so individuated, any knowledge about objects, properties, or events of that kind obtained by being in the state would be at most inferential.

This principle seems to me also to be correct for ordinary perceptually-based knowledge of current states of affairs. It also seems to explain why perceptual knowledge of the external world could never be accounted for were perceptual judgements regarded merely as responses to sensational, non-representational properties of experience, if such there be. Though the principle surely merits independent discussion in epistemology and the theory of content, I mention it here as a plausible additional element in the case for treating temporal impressions as externally individuated. If the principle is correct, it also poses a further problem for constructivist, anti-realistic accounts of temporal content. According to the principle, temporal content must be externally individuated if memory is to give a thinker non-inferential knowledge of the past. But the external individuation seems to proceed by reference to temporal relations between events and states of affairs of such a kind that these events and states of affairs could still exist in circumstances in which all causal paths which would lead to later evidence for them are blocked.

In epistemology, as elsewhere, we ought always to respect a threefold partition between (a) an entitlement; (b) a norm; and (c) a philosophical explanation of the existence of a norm. This is a natural series of distinctions to make once we acknowledge the importance of a Burge-like notion of entitlement, and follow Burge's important discussion of these topics.[31] A particular entitlement to judge a given content on a certain occasion will exist because such a judgement meets certain norms. The norms can be given a general formulation which covers judgements made on other occasions. It is a philosophical task to formulate the general norms correctly, and it is another philosophical task to give a philosophical explanation of why they exist. This threefold partition applies equally to temporal contents. A temporal impression entitles the thinker to make a corresponding temporal judgement. The norm which underlies the entitlement is the more general one of the legitimacy of taking perceptual impressions

[31] See Burge, 'Content Preservation'.

at face value, in the absence of positive reasons for doubt. The philo-sophical explanation of the norm is evidently a vexed issue. It is cer-tainly reasonable to expect that any account which explains the entitlement of a thinker to take spatial experience at face value will, other things equal, apply also to temporal experience. I will not attempt to tackle that whole issue here. For the present, it suffices that, whatever the full philosophical explanation of the existence of the norm, the distinction between entitlement and the norm is already sufficient to explain how temporal impressions can lead to temporal knowledge without the subject's having the concept of temporal impressions or temporal experience. The temporal impressions them-selves are entitling, regardless of whether the subject has the concept of temporal impressions.

In the previous section, I already argued that in general under-standing of, for instance, 'Yesterday it was the case that A' does not involve any kind of appreciation that any particular qualitative, purely present-tense conditions are evidence for its having been the case yesterday that A. What such evidence might be is always some-thing which has to be worked out empirically in the general case. The most recent points about externalism underwrite the point that the possibility of experiential memory as itself evidence is no counter-example to this general principle about evidence. If what makes an experiential memory a memory state with a certain temporal content cannot in general itself be elucidated without alluding to the relations of states of that kind to what happened to their subjects in the past, then experiential memories are not purely qualitative traces concern-ing only the present. If it is insisted that 'purely qualitative' here should mean only that any particular apparent memory does not require any particular conditions to hold at earlier times in the his-tory of the actual world, then the point must be agreed. But since apparent experiential memories are evidently not conclusive, they cannot give an account of a thinker's knowledge of *what it is* for a particular past-tense condition to hold. The content of that know-ledge must rather be specified in part by citing the property-identity link.

3.4 MEMORY AND THE PROPERTY-IDENTITY LINK

A pivotal question about understanding now arises. On the account I have given, grasp of the property-identity link and some form of memory faculty are both involved in the capacity for thought about the past. What is the relation between them? We did note that any kind of grasp of the property-identity link presupposed some mastery of the past elucidated in some way additional to the property-identity link, and externally individuated memory is serving that additional function in the account I am outlining. There is, however, more that needs to be understood about this apparently simple division of labour. In particular, there are two pressing questions. The first is as follows:

(1) If the property-identity link and an externally individuated memory capacity are both present in an account of thought about the past, must there not be some danger of overdetermination, perhaps even divergent determination, of the conditions for the correctness of a past-tense content? If there are not two independent sufficient conditions for the correctness of a past-tense content, what is the explanation of this fact?

The second question is prompted by the combination of the realistic position I have been endorsing with acknowledgment of a constitutive role for memory in understanding the past. In the nature of the case, apparently, truths delivered by means of memory are knowable truths about the past. So the other question is:

(2) How can an account of understanding the past tense which essentially involves a capacity for learning knowable truths about the past reach as far as legitimizing the intelligibility of unknowable truths about the past?

I will address this second question first, since it seems to me that a good answer to it contains the resources and approach for answering the first question. The issues involved in addressing the second question have been elaborated in some detail by Wright, who summarizes one of his own critical discussions of the issue thus: '[T]he evident problem is to make out how *experience* can teach us that the occurrence of certain factors within our experience reliably indicates the character of states of affairs beyond it'.[32] It should be agreed that a

---

[32] 'Second Thoughts about Criteria', repr. in his *Realism, Meaning and Truth*, at 394 (Wright's italics).

model under which we have to investigate empirically, and then discover that in fact some favoured 'decidable' class of statements is correlated with verification-transcendent ones, is incoherent. The realist
can, however, do much better than offering that unsatisfactory
response. A much better response asserts that the alleged problem is
only formulable on a highly questionable conception of what is
involved in the capacity to have experiential memories in the first
place.

Suppose we consider an analogous issue, this time not about experiential memory, but once again about perception. Imagine someone
asking, 'How can anything in our perception of the world teach us
that the states of affairs we perceive are also capable of existing
unperceived?' That is not, it seems to me, a good question, despite
the fact that it was in effect the question also asked by Bishop
Berkeley. Nothing can be a perception unless it is of objects, events,
or states of affairs which could exist without being perceived. The
possibility of unperceived existence is integral to the nature of perception itself. So it is not coherent to accept that one is perceiving,
and then to wonder whether or not what one is perceiving is something that could exist unperceived. Similarly, if you are thinking of
objects, events or states of affairs in ways made available by perception of them—if, for example, you are thinking of them by using perceptual demonstratives—what is thus thought about must be capable
of existing unperceived. A commitment to the existence of things
which could exist unperceived is not, then, something to which one
is entitled to make only because one's perceptions take a certain particular course. The commitment is already made in taking perceptions at their face value, whatever their detailed course.

The general point here is constitutive, not epistemological. Of
course a person may on occasion be enjoying something which seems
to be a perception, but is not in fact so. Yet even to enjoy something
which seems to be a perception, a thinker must be capable of mental
states which employ the ways the apparent perception represents the
world as being. The correctness conditions of even the apparent
perception must already concern perception-independent objects,
events, or states of affairs.

This feature of perception, that it has objects which can exist independently of being perceived, is not a mere add-on, something which
could be stripped away to leave a wider concept of equal philosophical significance. Stripping off this feature would not result in some-

thing of equal philosophical interest. The significance of the feature is multiple. I mention just two points, from epistemology and the philosophy of action respectively. It is only if perception is of perception-independent entities that it can yield non-inferential knowledge of a world whose existence is independent of being perceived. It is hard to see how any concept resulting from the stripping away of the feature—if indeed any concept remains—could possibly sustain such non-inferential knowledge. The feature is also crucial to the role of perception in the explanation of action. Actions are explained under descriptions which relate them to the objects, properties, and relations of the objective world. An action may be explained as, say, a reaching out to a particular object. As we noted earlier, the counterfactuals defeasibly supported by such an explanation correspondingly concern the objective world.[33] If the object had been in a somewhat different location, then *ceteris paribus* the agent would have reached out to a different location, for the agent would have perceived that object at that different location; and so forth. Stripping away the objective aspect of perception would yield (if anything) a kind of mental event incapable of playing the role in the explanation of action under environmental descriptions which is actually played by perception.

The inextricability of the idea of experience-independent existence is further emphasized if the spatial property-identity link is endorsed as explanatory of our understanding of spatial contents (or indeed merely as correct for spatial contents). Suppose it is true that for some other place to be F is for it to have the same property as this place here has to have if it is to be F here. If this is correct, then the condition that one's current location has to satisfy for 'Here it is F' to be true is one it could have met even if one had not been perceiving it. Indeed, if a corresponding bridging claim is correct in the spatial case, an understanding of what it is for an arbitrary place to be F is inextricably involved in possession of one's capacity to perceive one's current location to be F.

These points may elicit the following reply. Although these considerations show that the idea of the possibility of unperceived existence must be an inextricable part of the idea of genuine perception, that does not take us as far as the idea of unperceiv*able* states of affairs of the same kind as those which are actually perceived. It is

---

[33] See my 'Externalist Explanation'.

hard to see, however, how we can avoid commitment to the intelligibility of that idea too, given the position we have built up so far. Once we have the conception of perceived states of affairs as categorical, whose existence is not to be explained in counterfactual terms, it seems that it must always in principle be possible for some such state of affairs somewhere to be surrounded by arrangements of such a kind that anyone investigating it would be unable to discriminate between the existence of one, rather than another, specific state of affairs there. The possibility of detectors which, when observations are attempted, destroy any traces of evidence that one rather than the other state of affairs existed is something which is conceptually unproblematic.

What has just been argued in outline for perception holds broadly analogously for memory (though with an extra layer of structure). Genuine experiential memory of an event or state of affairs must be memory of something which could have existed without having been remembered at all.

In the memory case, we can further distinguish two sub-species of possibility of unknowable truth which seem inseparable from the conception of memory as giving, via some form of storage, information about past states of affairs.

(i) The first sub-species is already instanced by the examples of two paragraphs back. Suppose it is agreed that a currently perceived state of affairs is of a kind which could now obtain unknowably elsewhere. Suppose, too, that we accept the equicategorical claim. It follows that in remembering, in experiential memory, perceiving some state of affairs, one is remembering a state of affairs of a kind which could have held unknowably somewhere else in the past.

(ii) The second sub-species of cases are those specific to memory, and do not just ride on the back of present-tense possibilities. What is remembered is a state of affairs which could exist without being remembered, and which causally explains the remembering when it is experientially remembered. So, once again, it must in principle be possible for a state of the remembered kind to have occurred, while the subject is in some state which results in the failure of operation of the causal mechanisms needed for the formation of a memory trace. This sort of possibility, unlike sub-species (i), arises not only for memories of objective states of affairs, but also for memories of the subject's own pains and other subjective states.

After this discussion, the answer to our question (1) above should now be apparent. There is no possibility, even in principle, of the truth conditions fixed by the property-identity link coming apart from those made available by an understanding which involves an externally individuated memory capacity. A properly functioning experiential memory capacity is sensitive to whether, at some earlier time, a truth condition of the form 'It is *now* the case that A' obtained with respect to the earlier time. When functioning properly, it delivers later the information 'It was the case that A'. That is, it relies on Uniformity (section 3.1) and the property-identity link: on this point, I am completely in agreement with John Campbell's discussion.[34] It follows that, given Uniformity, there cannot be a case in which memory is functioning properly, and conveys the present information that it was the case that A, and yet the past-tense statement is not true by the criterion of the property-identity link. It is precisely the condition required by the property-identity link that memory confirms to be true. I conjecture that the use of experiential memory and grasp of the most primitive instances of the property-identity link for the past tense are necessarily coeval.

Past-tense concepts made available by personal (episodic) memory are epistemically constrained in the sense of Chapter 2, section 1. Consider, for instance, a thought 'That tree was in blossom', where the demonstrative 'that tree' is a way of thinking of a particular tree made available by an experiential memory of a tree. If a thinker has a personal experiential apparent memory as of the tree in blossom, and is taking the memory state at face value, the judgement 'That tree was in blossom' is rationally non-discretionary for him. The judgement will also be knowledge if the informational conditions for perception and experiential memory are met (and any presuppositions correct and properly attained). Somewhat analogous remarks could be made for a similarly based judgement 'I was once in front of a tree in blossom'. On the conception developed here, for these informational conditions to be fulfilled involves explanation by past states of affairs themselves, and appropriate preservation of the content through time (nothing about evidence). In particular, given the equi-

[34] J. Campbell, *Past, Space and Self* (Cambridge, Mass.: MIT Press, 1994), final chapter.

categorical claim, the past state of affairs which explains the memory
is one which could have obtained unknowably, had it been appropriately sealed off causally. There could have been other states of
affairs of the same kind, actually sealed off, and consequently now
(and possibly then) unknowable. As in other cases, the status of these
past-tense ways of thinking as epistemically constrained is compatible with a realistic attitude to past-tense truth.

In his paper 'On "The Reality of the Past"', John McDowell
writes, 'A realist who thinks he needs to appeal to a truth-value link,
in order to meet the anti-realist challenge shows—unless he is confused—that he pictures the truth conditions of the problematic sorts
of sentence not merely as not being always accessible but rather as
being always inaccessible'.[35] McDowell also argues, concerning realists of a certain kind, that 'Truth-value links are actually impotent to
do what realists of this kind want them to do' (132). He is not advocating the rejection of the truth-value links: 'In fact room must surely
be found for them in any acceptable position. The point is just that
they cannot serve to answer the anti-realist challenge' (133).

The property-identity links, and the corresponding truth-value
links, have played a major role in the account of understanding I have
offered. Besides constituting the content of the implicit knowledge
which underlies understanding of the past tense, I have argued that
we need to appeal to them at five junctures. To summarize: first, they
can be used to explain various structural facts about the understanding of past-tense sentences (section 3.1). Second, they permit reconciliation between the uniformity principle—that there is a single
property which any arbitrary time must possess for 'It is raining' (for
instance) to be true of that time—with the special role of the present
tense in the understanding of many predicates (also in section 3.1).
Third, in entailing the equi-categorical thesis, they help to explain
why past-tense truths resist any kind of reduction to counterfacuals
or conditionals (3.2). Fourth, their implication, in the presence of
other theses, of the categorical character of many past-tense statements permits the truth of the latter to enter explanations of later
states of affairs, including memories. Finally, as we just saw, the
property-identity links underlie the possibility of obtaining non-
inferential knowledge of the past by memory.

---

[35] 'On "The Reality of the Past"', in C. Hookway and P. Pettit (eds.), *Action and
Interpretation* (Cambridge: Cambridge University Press, 1978), at 131. The title of
McDowell's paper is a reference to Dummett's paper of the same name.

The position for which I have been arguing is one which combines a major role for the truth-value links whilst also insisting that the holding of a past-tense truth can on occasion be made available by memory. The externalist account of the grasp of temporal relations I offered requires mental states sensitive to temporal properties and relations themselves, and any mental faculty which underlies such a sensitivity must be some form or other of memory faculty. I am, then, committed to disagreeing with McDowell's statement that a realist who thinks he needs to appeal to the truth-value links must be conceiving of past-tense truth as always inaccessible.

In fact McDowell's principal target in his discussion of the truth-value links is a much more specific kind of truth-value-link realist. His target is a truth-value-link realist who thinks he can, in an account of understanding, simply 'bypass' any mention of the circumstances under which 'past-tensed sentences are *themselves* correctly assertible' (130). McDowell indeed envisages his target as holding that the point of an appeal to the truth-value links is precisely to effect such a bypassing (130). Now the theory I have offered is certainly not this species of bypass-realism. In giving the externalist account of the understanding of temporal relations, I have been driving straight to the centre of the destination that this targeted theorist is trying to bypass. (Indeed, I agree with McDowell's principal criticisms of the bypass theorist.)

McDowell complains that Dummett's own classic discussion of these issues does not recognize a third option, 'a realism which meets the anti-realist challenge in the way I distinguished [regarding memory as giving access to the holding of past-tense truth conditions— CP] . . . from appeal to a truth-value link' (135). On the view I have been proposing, there are good appeals and there are bad appeals to truth-value links. The good appeals should certainly not be regarded as in tension with theories which give a significant the role to memory, for as we have noted, memory relies in more than one way on the truth-value link. We need, then, to recognize not just a McDowellian third, but also a fourth, option in the field: a position which is realistic, and which gives an important constitutive role in understanding the past to the truth-value links, but which is not any form of bypass realism.

3.5 'THE EXPLANATION BY MEANS OF *IDENTITY* DOES NOT WORK HERE': WHEN AND HOW IT DOES

The bridging claim is a partial explanation of meaning in terms of identity, a property identity. Wittgenstein famously criticized certain explanations of meaning which involve appeal to some application of the identity relation. Of one such explanation, he wrote that it

> gets us no farther. It is as if I were to say: 'You surely know what "It is 5 o'clock here" means; so you also know what "It's 5 o'clock on the sun" means. It means simply that it is just the same time there as it is here when it is 5 o'clock.'—The explanation by means of *identity* does not work here. For I know well enough that one can call 5 o'clock here and 5 o'clock there 'the same time', but what I do not know is in what cases one is to speak of its being the same time here and there.[36]

It is not clear that Wittgenstein is objecting to all explanations in terms of identity. He says only that the explanation in terms of identity does not work 'here'. But his remarks do prompt these questions:

> What are the conditions which distinguish the legitimate from the illegitimate explanations of meaning in terms of identity?

> In so far as Wittgenstein raises objections to explanations in terms of identity, to what class of cases do they generalize? If they do not generalize to all cases, what are the limits of their application?

> Is the temporal property-identity link on the legitimate side of the line once we have considered the Wittgensteinian objections?

It will be helpful to have a terminology which is applicable to any proposed explanation in terms of identity. We can distinguish between the *base case* and the *linked case*. In the temporal property-identity link as I have been considering it, the thought or sentence 'It is now *F*' is the base case, and the past-tense thought or sentence, such as 'Yesterday it was *F*', is the linked case—explained from the base case by use of the notion of identity of property. For the proposed

---

[36] L. Wittgenstein, *Philosophical Investigations*, trans. G. E. M. Anscombe, 2nd edn. (Oxford: Blackwell, 1958), § 350.

spatial property-identity link, the base case is 'It is F here', the linked case is 'It is F at such-and-such place elsewhere'; and so on.

Wittgenstein's own critical comments on explanations in terms of identity fall into two sorts.

(i) He gives examples in which it would be widely agreed that an attempted explanation in terms of identity does not succeed. The example of the time on the sun is one such; another occurs in this passage, which starts off with a remark by his imagined interlocutor: 'But surely "I believed" must tell of just the same thing in the past as "I believe" in the present!'—Surely $\sqrt{-1}$ must mean just the same thing in relation to -1, as $\sqrt{1}$ means in relation to 1! This means nothing at all.'[37]

(ii) Wittgenstein's second criticism develops a positive theory of what does allow one to speak of identity in the cases where an explanation by means of identity does not work. The theory—no doubt he would hate the word, but it is a little theory—is that identity of predication justifies the acceptance of an identity, and not vice versa, and that this is so for reasons having to do with meaning. This claim is already in the passage about the sun, when he wrote in the passage quoted at the start of this section that 'I know well enough that one can call 5 o'clock here and 5 o'clock there "the same time"'. He also makes the point explicitly about the topic for which he was using the example of the time on the sun as a foil: 'For *that* part of the grammar is quite clear to me: that is, that one will say that the stove has the same experience as I, *if* one says: it is in pain and I am in pain.'[38]

(iii) There is also a third line of critical thought one might also imagine a Wittgensteinian giving, one drawing upon ideas more prominent in the *Remarks on the Foundations of Mathematics* than in the *Investigations*.[39] This line of thought attempts to appeal to his views on rule-following. Wittgenstein is opposed to the idea that 'going on in the same way' can be an explication of what is involved in following a particular rule, given an initial set of examples of correct application of the rule, if going on in the same way is understood as something which is independent of human reactions to new examples. When we are following a rule, we look at what we do 'from the point of view: *always the same*'.[40] This form of words is, though,

[37] Ibid. p. 190.   [38] Ibid. § 350.
[39] L. Wittgenstein, *Remarks on the Foundations of Mathematics*, trans. G. E. M. Anscombe, 3rd edn. (Oxford: Blackwell, 1978).
[40] Ibid. 419.

merely a typical expression of one who finds it natural to go on in one way rather than another. It is not a description of anything that can guide a rule-follower independently of the rule-follower's reactions to new cases.[41] So one might imagine a Wittgensteinian arguing that an identity relation can enter an explanation of meaning only if one improperly overlooks the role of human reactions in fixing concepts, rules, and meaning. (It should be noted, though, that were this argument to be sound, it would be a general argument against explanations in terms of identity. I do not know of any reason for attributing it to Wittgenstein himself.)

There is a fundamental necessary condition for an explanation of understanding or meaning in terms of identity to be legitimate. The requirement has the form of an existentially quantified conjunction. It states that (a) we must have some conception of the entity mentioned in the base case and of the entity mentioned in the linked case which classifies them as things of the same kind, and (b) this kind must permit legitimate application to them of the more specific sameness relation mentioned in the proposed property-identity link. This requirement is met in the case of, for instance, a bridging explanation of predications of other locations. Consider, for instance, predications of observational shape concepts. Perception can give a thinker a reason for judging, knowledgeably, 'This thing here is square'. The spatial property picked out by the concept *square* is in the nature of the case something instantiable by space-occupying things, whether located here or elsewhere, whether perceived or not. Using the relation of sameness of shape in an account of grasp of the concept *square* meets the requirement given in (a) and (b).

It is because that requirement is not met in Wittgenstein's example of the time on the sun that no one should be tempted to offer an identity explanation there. What makes it five o'clock at a particular time and place is the angle the sun bears to that place then. Perhaps the place in question must be on or close to the surface of the earth; or perhaps we can make sense of it being five o'clock on some other planet in the solar system were that other planet to take twenty-four hours to rotate; we are in the realms of some indeterminacy here. It is clear, though, that the sun does not ever bear any angle to itself. So no identity explanation, nor any other, can be an explanation which

[41] See esp. ibid. 420–1.

succeeds in giving 'It's five o'clock on the sun' a truth condition which can be fulfilled.

From the example of the time on the sun, nothing follows about the possibility of explanations in terms of identity in cases where the fundamental necessary condition of explanation by means of identity is met. No general bar can be inferred from this example.

The case of $\sqrt{-1}$ must be very different, since '$\sqrt{-1}$' refers and is used in a well-established theory, that of the complex numbers. Wittgenstein's discussion is so brief as to lend itself to many different readings of his intentions (at least as many as the number of different people with whom I have discussed the passage). Perhaps his point is that the sign for the square root operation's 'meaning the same' is consistent with different detailed accounts of what is involved in something's being the square root in the non-complex and in the complex cases. Perhaps it matters that if one tried to explain some core notion *being the square root of*, its properties would underdetermine the character of the theory of complex numbers. Other readings are possible too. But whatever Wittgenstein's intentions, it seems to me that there is no non-question-begging use of the example against the bridging claim and the importance of the property-identity link for understanding the past tense. There is no distinction between a simpler and a more complex use of 'in the past', or 'yesterday', or any other past-tense operator, which corresponds to the distinction between applying the square root operation to positive numbers, and applying it to both positive and negative numbers. There is a single use, and we gave reasons in earlier sections for saying that its meaning is to be given in part in terms of a property-identity link. The case of $\sqrt{-1}$ shows that there is sometimes not complete uniformity underlying various cases in which we speak of 'same relation', 'same operation', or 'same property'. It does not show that there is never complete uniformity.

Wittgenstein's second criticism was, in a nutshell, that the predication of identity is to be explained in terms of identity of predication, and not conversely. The main challenge for this Wittgensteinian view is to avoid, in the cases under discussion, the charge of ambiguity of the predications without collapsing into the view to which it presented itself as an alternative. On the view I have been defending, there is no threat of ambiguity in a predicate F as between the base case, x is F, say, and the linked case y is F. The bridging claim entails precisely that for y to be F is for it to have the same property as x has to have for *x is F* to be true. Things stand very differently for the Wittgensteinian view. On his view, *y is F* must be explained independently of any relation to *x is F* if we are really being offered an alternative to the bridging claim. How then can the Wittgensteinian view meet the charge that the predicate 'is *F*' does not, on that view, have the same meaning when predicated of *x* and of *y*, given that understanding of the predicate in the base case does seem to have a special relation to *now*, *here*, or whatever way of thinking is involved in the base case? The Wittgensteinian must show how it is a consequence of his own account that *y is F* is true only if *y* has the same property *x* has to have for *x is F* to be true, whilst still presenting a genuine alternative to the bridging account. My own view is that this problem is apparent in Wittgenstein's own positive account of the relation between third- and first-person predications of sensation vocabulary.

The challenge to the Wittgensteinian view is compounded by the fact that in the examples in which the bridging account is plausible, it is also plausible that the meaning of the predicate in question has a special connection with the way of thinking of the object of predication which is mentioned in the base case. Thus observational predicates plausibly have a special connection with the present tense; and so forth. On the Wittgensteinian view, however, the predication in what his opponent calls the linked case is not (or not as a matter of the explanation of meaning) given any special connection with the base case. It is noteworthy that Wittgenstein's example of the time of day at a given place is precisely one where there is no special connection with the 'here' or 'now' ways of thinking. For it to be five o'clock at a given time and place is just for the sun to bear a certain angle to that place at that time.

Of course, there are other cases too in which the predication of identity is to be explained in terms of identity of predication. Virtual set theory, as elaborated by Quine, is one clear example, as are some other treatments of abstract objects. If we are concerned only with virtual set theory, the explication of

$$\{x: F(x)\} = \{x: G(x)\}$$

as

$$\forall x(F(x) \equiv G(x))$$

is unproblematic. It is also structurally quite different from the kind of case in which the bridging claim is meant to apply. In the case of virtual set theory, we are concerned with the introduction of new (apparent) singular terms, flanking an identity sign. The threat of ambiguity we noted is present rather in cases where our concern is with the same predicate applied to different things, where the understanding of the predicate as applied to one of the things—the base case of the bridging theorist—is not in question, and seems to have a special connection with the way of thinking mentioned in the base case. In the treatment of virtual abstract objects, we are not taking the meaning of one predication for granted and then addressing the issue of its relations to applications of the same predicate to different objects, as we are in the case of the temporal and spatial property-identity links.

The third argument we identified holds that the bridging conception must rest upon a mistake about rule-following. The argument as given seems to fail to draw a necessary distinction. To agree that thinkers' reactions to new cases—how they go on—must play some role in the determination of sense or meaning is not to deny that expressions have mind-independent references, nor in the case of predicative expressions, that they may refer to mind-independent properties and relations. Thinkers' reactions to examples can help to fix which property or relation it is which is being referred to. The property or relation thus fixed may be entirely mind-independent. It will be so in the case of expressions for primary qualities and relations (in the sense of Locke's classification), and indeed for identity itself. If we acknowledge that human reaction to examples helps fix which property is being referred to, we are already taking on board the Wittgensteinian point that sense or meaning is not independent of human reactions to new examples. We are already agreeing that 'going on the same way' does not give such a reaction- or judgement-independent account of sense or meaning. But once the point has been taken on board, there is no reason that one of the relations, fixed in part by human reactions, cannot be the relation of identity itself between properties. That is all the bridging claim needs. The defender of the bridging claim will say that ordinary thinkers' reactions to examples like that of section 3.2, the case in which it is true that there was a squirrel on the wall even though no investigator would have discovered that, provide evidence—clearly not independent of human reactions—that the property-identity link helps to explain what is meant by past-tense predications.

There must be more to say of a positive character about the conditions under which explanations by means of identity are legitimate. So far we have just given a rather minimal existentially quantified conjunction, put forward as a necessary condition of legitimacy. The second part of this conjunction stated that the thinker must have a conception of some kind which permits legitimate application of the sameness relation in question. We have to ask further: what does permit legitimate application of the sameness relation used in a proposed identity explanation?

One suggestion which seems to me promising is that an explanation of understanding in terms of identity is legitimate only if the following condition is met. The base case used in the putative explanation of the holding of a property already involves the thinker's having the conception of a range of things of which that property may or may not hold. This will be a range of times in the explanation of tensed predications, and a range of places if the spatial property-identity link is used in explanation of predications of other places. Back in section 1 of this chapter, I argued that this condition, that the base case involve the conception of such a range, is a condition which is met in both the temporal and the spatial cases. When the condition is met, the property-identity link serves simply to specify which property, out of the indefinitely many properties which may hold of another time or place, is the one which must hold for a certain predication to be true of another time or another place.[42]

It is a virtue of this suggestion that it supplies a reason why overstepping its limits risks illegitimacy. When the base case does not involve such a conception of a range of entities, the thinker need not have the conception of how other entities beyond the base case might have the property in question. Of course, there may be some other way of obtaining the conception of such a range. It would have to be supplied by materials other than those necessarily involved in grasping the base case. If there is no other way of obtaining the conception, illegitimacy threatens.

A second virtue of this suggestion is that it explains why the problem of other minds is so acute. Each one of us, both intuitively and upon philosophical reflection, naturally thinks that for someone else

---

[42] Note that this suggestion implies that an approach which suggests that one could have the concept of the present without that of the past—an extreme priority theory—could not coherently use the property-identity links in the explanation of meaning.

to be in pain is for that other person to have exactly the same property she herself has to have for it to be true that she herself is in pain. However, it is also part of our intuitive conception that when each one of us self-ascribes the property of being in pain, this is a rational response in thought to the experience of pain itself. But only the thinker's own pains can be so rationally responded to by her: only they are experienced as pains by her. So if we try to use a bridging explanation for the explanation of our understanding of the ascription of sensations to others, and combine it with the intuitive account of self-ascription, we come up against a roadblock. The base case does not, apparently, meet the necessary conditions we just identified. If self-ascriptions are made according to the intuitive model, then the case of self-ascription does not, seemingly at least, involve the conception of a range of other subjects, each of whom may or may not be in pain. Other-ascription is not, apparently, legitimate, *if* we are given only those resources in the description of the base case.

I am not going to attempt to take on this problem here. All I want to emphasize here is the nature of the problem, and its relation to general constraints on explanations by means of identity. The following seem to be the only possibilities. Either we are under an illusion that no more is involved in the first-person case and without that illusion we could come to see that the necessary conditions of identity explanations are met after all; or there is some other way of explaining what it is to have the conception of a range of subjects of experience, which has to be combined with the base case before any bridging explanation can begin; or a bridging explanation is the wrong way to proceed altogether. So, although I have been disagreeing with Wittgenstein on several points, I am in agreement with him that an explanation by means of identity in the sensation case, if it can be given at all, cannot take as simple a form as it does in the temporal and spatial cases. More complex forms may still be possible.

3.6 REALISM, METAPHYSICS, AND THE THEORY OF MEANING

I want now to consider the status and some of the philosophical implications of the position I have been developing, by comparing it with some other well-known positions.

Michael Dummett describes the realist who appeals to the truth-value link thus:

What the realist would like to do is to stand in thought outside the whole temporal process and describe the world from a point which has no temporal position at all, but surveys all temporal positions in a single glance: from this standpoint—the standpoint of the description which the realist wants to give—the different points of time have a relation of temporal precedence between themselves, but no temporal relation to the standpoint of the description—i.e. they are not considered as past, as present or as future. The anti-realist takes more seriously the fact that we are immersed in time: being so immersed, we cannot frame any description of the world as it would appear to one who was not in time, but we can only describe it as it is, i.e., as it is now.[43]

Is the bridging conception I have outlined committed to a realism of the sort Dummett describes here?

There is more than one question here, because of the many issues just below the surface of Dummett's characterization of the issues. Let me start by a drawing a distinction, which Dummett need not contest, but which is a first step in clarifying the commitments of the bridging conception.

We should distinguish the following two properties of a state of affairs. The first property is that of having an existence with causal powers of the sort implied by the equi-categorical claim. The realist who endorses the bridging conception as I have elaborated it is committed to saying that true past-tense statements involve the existence of states of affairs with this first property. This first property is to be distinguished from a second: that of being describable in ways that at no point rely on the thinker's relations to that state of affairs, or to others of the same kind.

The second property is not implied by the first. It would not be at all surprising that some ways of thinking of objects, properties, events, places, or times should be dependent upon the thinker's relations to them. The particular way in which we have elaborated a realism involving the bridging claim has involved an externalist approach to temporal thought, one which brings with it an irreducibly indexical way of thinking of particular past times. Whenever the passage of time itself explains a subject's temporal impression, the content of that impression will be in one way or another indexical. In some

---

[43] 'The Reality of the Past,' 369.

cases, the impression will be of the temporal relation of some event to the present. In the case of the memory-dependent impressions of intervals and ordering on which we touched in section 3.3, the indexicality will involve memory demonstratives, ways of thinking of events made available by the subject's having episodic memories of them. So an externalist conception embodying the bridging claim should say that the states of affairs described in true past-tense sentences have the first of the two properties we distinguished, but not the second. They are necessarily *not* thought about as from a point describable as 'nowhen'.

From the standpoint of some of the fundamental issues in the philosophy of time, however, drawing the distinction we have just made can be no more than a preliminary, a curtain-raiser. To draw this distinction between the two properties is to make a claim about ways of thinking, about modes of presentation, of times. The clear-headed defender of the more 'immersed' conception that Dummett sketches will say, much more radically, that his is a thesis about times and temporal relations themselves, not just ways of thinking of them. His thesis is that this domain of reference itself cannot be satisfactorily characterized without mention of the present, understood as the present. I will argue that, even after the curtain-raising issue has been set aside, there are two considerations which support the claim that the realist who endorses the bridging conception is not thereby committed to what Dummett describes.

The first consideration is specific to issues about time. It is that the bridging conception as I have described it is, as far as I can see, entirely consistent with the view that the future is open in a way the past is not. That is, the bridging conception is consistent with a view that adopts a certain kind of realism about the past and present which it does not apply in exactly the same way to the future. In fact, in the minds of some theorists, the bridging conception might positively encourage a view of the future as open. The bridging theorist can hardly deny that for the statement 'There will be a sea-battle at Salamis tomorrow' to be true, tomorrow must have the same property that today has to have for 'There is a sea-battle at Salamis today' to be true. Precisely what our discussions have been emphasizing is what a substantial property that is. This may simply encourage the believer in the open future. Whether or not he is right to be so encouraged, it seems clear that he could maintain his stance consistently with acceptance of the bridging claim about our understanding of statements about the past. But in that case, the bridging claim itself is consistent with attributing a very special status to the present, for that is what the believer in the open future must do. For him, what is open is substantially time-relative: not all of what was open last week is open today. If these views are indeed consistent, then the bridging claim is not committed even to an 'in principle' possibility of a description of the world from no particular temporal standpoint.

The bridging conception does not, incidentally, seem to me to be consistent with the view, adopted explicitly by Prior in his very late writings, that only the present is real.[44] Prior wrote, 'indeed on my view . . . the present simply is the real considered in relation to two particular species of unreality, namely the past and the future'.[45] I do not see how the view that only the present is real can be reconciled with the equi-categorical claim about past-tense predications, and with the role of the past in causal explanation of what is now the case. Prior's reason for saying that only the present is real is as follows:

I want to suggest that the reality of the present consists in what the reality of anything else consists in, namely the absence of a qualifying prefix. To say that Whitrow's lecture is past is to say that *it has been the case that* Whitrow is lecturing. To say that Scott's lecture is future is to say that *it will be the case that* Scott is lecturing. But to say that my lecture is present is just to say that *I am lecturing*—flat, no prefixes.[46]

By this reasoning, one could equally argue that rain elsewhere is unreal. For while rain here is reported in *It is raining*, without the need for any prefix, *In Paris it is the case that it is raining* has, and needs, the prefix. Prior's argument also seems to me much too heavily dependent upon contingent features of language to establish any metaphysical conclusion. Its premise would be lacking for a language in which one was always required to use such operators as 'It is now the case that ——' in making reports about one's immediate spatio-temporal environment.[47]

I promised a second consideration to support the claim that the realist who endorses the bridging conception is not thereby commit-

[44] 'The Notion of the Present', *Studium Generale* 23 (1970), 245–8.
[45] Ibid. 245.
[46] Ibid. 246–7.
[47] Parallel issues arise, as Prior was well aware, about the significance of impersonal forms such as 'There is pain', 'There is thinking'. For a position on this which parallels the position of the text above on time, see the later parts of Chapter 5, section 5, below.

ted to the possibility of thought at a standpoint outside the whole temporal process. Unlike the first, this second consideration is more general, and not specific to the temporal case. As against Dummett's description of the realist, it does not seem to me that a realist, even one who uses some form of property-identity or truth-value link in the explanation of understanding of some range of predications of a certain domain of entities, is thereby committed to the possibility 'in principle', or even to the intelligibility, of a being who is capable of surveying or perceiving that whole domain. Let us take very briefly the case of statements about places. I have equally endorsed a truth-value link in the explanation of understanding of statements about other places. The thesis that there is such an intelligible possibility of a being who can survey the totality of places is one that some thinkers have explicitly defended. Dummett writes,

We can, I think, describe an arrangement of objects in space although I do not myself have any position in that space. An example would be the space of my visual field. In that space there is no here or there, no near or far: I am not in that space. We can, I think, conceive, on the strength of this analogy, of a being who could perceive objects in our three-dimensional physical space although he occupied no position in that space.[48]

The space of my visual field must here be taken as something subjective, mind-dependent (as what makes possible what I called 'sensational shape properties' in *Sense and Content*).[49] The space of my visual field cannot, for the purposes of the argument Dummett is presenting, mean just 'that part of physical space which I see'—since that is part of a larger space in which I am located. But a space which is not anything objective, and in which it does not make sense to suppose that physical objects are located or physical events occur, seems to be an insufficient basis for analogical reasoning to the possibility of a being who can survey all of our physical space.[50] Mathematical

---

[48] 'A Defence of McTaggart's Proof of the Unreality of Time', repr. in *Truth and Other Enigmas*, at 354. See also J. Lucas, *The Future: An Essay on God, Temporality and Truth* (Oxford: Blackwell, 1989), 3.

[49] C. Peacocke, *Sense and Content: Experience, Thought, and their Relations* (Oxford: Oxford University Press, 1983), ch. 1.

[50] Also, even though I have no location in my visual field, thought about one's visual field still arguably requires the use of demonstrative ways of thinking of locations in it. We think of *that location, that relation, that shape in the visual field*. My not having a location in the visual field does not undermine the availability of these ways of thinking.

spaces seem even less suited to the task. What is motivating these proposed analogies is the underlying thought which Dummett identifies when he says that '[b]y contrast' with the case of time, 'the use of spatially token-reflexive expressions is not essential to the description of objects as being in a space'.[51] The property-identity-link realist about spatial predications should reply that it seems impossible to give an account of what it is to think of a genuine space which does not bring with it the capacity to think in indexical and demonstrative ways about locations in that space, or at least the capacity to think of it as something of the same kind as a space which can be so thought about (to accommodate those cosmological hypotheses according to which a black hole in a pre-existent universe gives rise to the big bang which is the origin of a new universe). Our property-identity-link realist should say that there is no commitment on his part to the intelligibility of statements about such a superior all-surveying being, except and unless they are construed as a colourful way of speaking of the determinacies of truth value explained independently of any appeal to such a being.

The property-identity-link realism defended here should not be accused of spatializing time. We already noted the consistency of this view with a treatment of the future as open, and that combination cannot be described as spatializing time. But even if that combination is not held, the charge of spatializing time seems to me far more appropriately lodged against a realist who does tie his flag to explanations which make reference to the possibility of a superior all-surveying being. When we do not make any commitment to the possibility of such explanations, and our account of mastery of temporal notions makes reference, amongst much other necessary material, to a sensitivity to temporal properties and relations themselves, then the charge of spatializing time does not seem to me to stick. The account may support certain parallels between temporal and spatial thought, but there is no assimilation to the spatial in the fundamental accounts of mastery.

I turn finally to one of the implications of this account for the correct way of conceiving of the relations between metaphysics and the theory of meaning and understanding. Dummett has written of this relation:

---

[51] Dummett, 'A Defence of McTaggart's Proof of the Unreality of Time', 354.

The task of constructing a meaning-theory can, in principle, be approached without metaphysical presuppositions or *arrières-pensées*: success is to be estimated according as the theory does or does not provide a workable account of a practice that agrees with that which we in fact observe. It thus provides us with a means of resolving the metaphysical disputes about realism: not an indirect means, but one which accords with their true nature, namely as disputes about the kind of meaning to be attached to various types of sentences.[52]

The account I have given does not accord with that description of the relation between the metaphysics and the theory of understanding. The bridging account has an essential background of the equi-categorical claim and the thesis that explanation is perspective-independent. These are metaphysical claims, and they were presupposed and drawn upon in the above externalist account of understanding past-tense predications. They did not fall out of the theory of understanding by itself.

Perhaps, though, it may be said that the opposition between the two accounts of the relation need not be so stark. Can we at least say that a metaphysics is to be tested by its capacity to dovetail with a good theory of understanding? Even if a theory of understanding has sometimes to draw on a metaphysics, still that is consistent with the position that the metaphysics is ratified by its ability to dovetail with the theory of understanding. However, the position I have been developing seems to me to be in tension also with this intermediate position. Presumably this intermediate position is saying more than just that a metaphysics must be consistent with a good theory of understanding. To say only that would be to give no special position to the theory of understanding. All the theories we accept had better be consistent with one another. The intermediate position is making the stronger claim that the fundamental source of ratification of metaphysical claims is their ability to dovetail with a theory of understanding. There is tension between the account developed here and this reading of the intermediate position, because the claims of the equi-categorical nature of past-tense statements with their present-tense counterparts, and of the perspective-independence of explanation, were illustrated and argued for not in connection with any phenomena having to do with meaning, thought, or understanding, but in connection with ordinary explanatory claims about the world. Examination of our explanatory practices outside the realm of thought and meaning can sometimes give a rational basis for accepting or rejecting metaphysical claims.

3.7 FINAL OBSERVATIONS ON THE TEMPORAL CASE

I have tried to elaborate the following three salient characteristics of thought about the past: the role of the property-identity link in understanding; its role in the metaphysics of time and in making a realistic conception philosophically explicable; and the constitutive presence of externalist elements in temporal thought. The elaboration I have given in effect tries to explain the presence and role of a particular combination of values of the indicators mentioned in Chapter 2. Though the framework I have offered does sustain various a priori claims (notably the property-identity links themselves), the discussion of the present chapter also offers a rationale for the intuitive view that there is no a priori determination of the truth value of particular past-tense statements from information which is not past-tensed. That there is no such determination is only to be expected from a view which makes possession of a faculty causally sensitive to temporal relations, and to what held at times past, constitutively necessary for temporal thought. The various arguments against constructivist and evidential theories of past-tense thought are, in one guise or another, just amplifications of the consequences of this point.

4

Necessity

4.1 PROBLEMS AND GOALS

The challenge of integrating the metaphysics of necessity with its epistemology is acute. The metaphysics of necessity seemingly shares with the philosophical problem of consciousness and some problems in the philosophy of mathematics this distinction: that there is practically no philosophical view of the matter so extraordinary that it has not been endorsed by someone or other. In recent years, all of the following views have been taken of a statement such as 'There could be a 500-floor skyscraper': that its truth involves the existence of a genuine material 500-floor skyscraper which is spatially unrelated to any actual objects; that its utterance is the expression of a certain kind of imaginability; and that its correctness is dependent upon what conventions are in force. It is natural to wonder whether some of these views have resulted from a concern with truth conditions insufficiently constrained by epistemology; or vice versa. In this chapter, I will be attempting to steer a middle course. I am going to be developing a treatment which does not regard statements of necessity or contingency as being made true by the mental states they express, or by any form of convention. But the account I propose does not buy the objectivity it claims at the price of postulating an inaccessible reality which determines the truth values of modal statements.

In accordance with the strategy outlined in Chapter 2 for addressing the Integration Challenge in a given area, I will be developing a theory of understanding for modal sentences. First, I will give an account of the truth conditions of modal sentences, of statements involving what is usually called 'metaphysical necessity' in the literature. These truth conditions will be suited to a theory of understanding: I will give a theory of understanding which determines the truth conditions given in this account as the ones possessed by modal sentences. Then I will go on to propose a corresponding epistemology of the modal. I will be arguing that the ordinary ways in which we acquire modal knowledge are appropriate for the truth conditions I propose.

In the past twenty years, significant advances have been made, particularly in the writings of Robert Adams and Robert Stalnaker, in elaborating a moderate view of modality which does not involve David Lewis's modal realism.[1] These elaborations can be regarded as ways of elaborating Kripke's own view of possible worlds, which is not that of a modal realist.[2] The detailed views of Adams and Stalnaker differ somewhat from one another. They do, though, agree in treating discourse about possible worlds as legitimate, and in explaining such discourse as talk, immediate or derived, about ways the world might have been. The possible worlds of their moderate view are, by David Lewis's standards, ersatz possible worlds. Their non-actual possible worlds are not things of the same kind as the actual spatio-temporal universe around you. These moderate views will acknowledge the existence of a particular way the spatio-temporal universe around you is. This particular way will be a thing of the same kind as the non-actual worlds. But the way in question is not to be confused with the thing that is that way, namely, the spatio-temporal universe around you.

Anyone who wants to follow the middle course I described will find one or another of such moderate views attractive. Does this moderate view also give us an answer to the question of what it is to understand discourse involving necessity? The moderate view in itself—as opposed to additional doctrines with which it might be combined—simply takes for granted the notion of something's being a consistent (metaphysically consistent) way the world might have been. Indeed, Stalnaker himself goes further, and says 'Lewis is right, I think, that if we reject modal realism, then we must give up on the project of providing a reductive analysis of modality'.[3] Even if that is a little strong, it is certainly fair to say that nothing in the usual expositions of the moderate view gives any clue about what a reductive analysis of modality would be like.

Now in other cases, the fact that an expression has to be treated as primitive is no bar to our stating what is involved in understand-

[1] R. Adams, 'Theories of Actuality', *Noûs* 8 (1974), 211–31; Lewis, *On the Plurality of Worlds*; R. Stalnaker, 'Possible Worlds', *Noûs* 10 (1976), 65–75, and Critical Notice of David Lewis, *On the Plurality of Worlds*, *Mind* 97 (1988), 117–28.
[2] Kripke, *Naming and Necessity*.
[3] Stalnaker, Critical Notice, 123.

ing it. The problem is rather that it is not at all apparent how any of the various extant accounts of understanding other primitive expressions provide a model which we could follow, if we are out to provide an accurate and credible treatment of the concept of necessity.

Some primitive concepts require for their possession that certain of the judgements involving them are, in favourable circumstances, appropriately caused by the holding of the content judged. Observational concepts, and possibly some others, fall in this class. It seems to be impossible to assimilate the concept of metaphysical necessity to this case. The making of judgements, like any other actual events or states, can be explained only by what is actually the case. As we noted in Chapter 2, the fact that something is necessarily the case is never part of the causal explanation for some temporal state of affairs. That is what is right in a quasi-Humean principle that there is no impression from which the idea of metaphysical necessity could be derived. When the word 'of' bears a partially causal sense, an impression—something impressed by the way the world is—cannot be *of* a metaphysical necessity. Any concept individuated in part by the fact that certain judgements involving it are responses to its instantiation would, it seems, fall short of being the concept of metaphysical necessity. The distinctively modal character of the concept could not have its source in that sort of causal role.[4]

A second kind of model for understanding a primitive expression is provided by the logical constants. The condition for understanding a logical constant is plausibly given by alluding to some kind of grasp of certain introduction and/or elimination rules involving it. If, though, we take the inferential rules for necessity in some specific modal system, such as K or T, they are far from uniquely satisfied by the pretheoretic concept of metaphysical necessity. They will for instance equally hold for certain notions of provability.[5] Now it is

---

[4] My position on metaphysical modality is thus the modal analogue of those who claim that moral truths do not play a causal-explanatory role. For development of that position, the arguments for which at many points parallel those for the modal point, see C. Wright, *Truth and Objectivity* (Cambridge, Mass.: Harvard University Press, 1992), on the absence of a 'wide cosmological role' for moral truths, and the position of J. J. Thomson in her contribution to G. Harman and J. Thomson, *Moral Relativism and Moral Objectivity* (Oxford: Blackwell, 1996), and in her 'Reply to Critics', *Philosophy and Phenomenological Research* 58 (1998), 215–22.

[5] G. Boolos, *The Unprovability of Consistency* (Cambridge: Cambridge University Press, 1979), and in particular the references therein to Kripke's early thoughts on the matter.

true that various notions of provability will have their own distinctive axioms which distinguish them from metaphysical necessity. So could we perhaps develop an approach under which metaphysical necessity is characterized as the weakest operator meeting certain conditions? To this, though, there are three objections.

First, if we are really to capture the concept of metaphysical necessity, we will have to include such celebrated Kripkean principles as those of the necessity of origin and of constitution. These Kripkean principles look much less like anything of a broadly logical character. We also seem to have some general understanding of metaphysical necessity upon which we can draw to work out that the Kripkean principles are correct. The class of true general principles of metaphysical necessity is potentially open-ended.

Second, the point just made about the Kripkean principles actually applies to the more 'logical' ones like 'From the premises necessarily *p* and necessarily if *p* then *q*, it follows that necessarily *q*'. It seems that we have some understanding of metaphysical necessity from which it can be worked out that this is a valid principle of inference. If that is so, the principle should not just be stipulated as a primitive rule, part of an implicit definition. The principle should rather be derived from whatever is involved in our more fundamental understanding of metaphysical necessity, from whatever it is which allows us to work out the correctness of the principle. The same applies to other modal axioms which contain essentially only the operator for metaphysical modality and logical constants. Our fundamental grasp of this class of axioms is not given simply by a list.

Third, even if (perhaps *per impossibile*) we had a notion of provability which precisely coincided with that of metaphysical necessity, we would still not have fully answered the questions about understanding metaphysical necessity. It is one thing to say that a proposition is provable; it is another to say that it is necessary. Saying that the proposition is provable is not yet to say that it holds in other possible worlds. It is only to say that its actual truth is establishable in a special way. There must always be a further task of showing that establishability in the special way ensures necessity. In carrying out that further task, we must be drawing on some feature of our understanding of necessity which in the nature of the case goes beyond anything in our understanding of provability.

Given that necessity operators behave somewhat like universal quantifiers, it may also be tempting to elucidate the understanding of metaphysical necessity in a way which follows the pattern for universal quantifiers generally. The pattern for universal quantifiers I myself favour is one in which the distinctive feature of understanding a universal quantification is the range of commitments a thinker incurs in accepting the quantification. So one might say that metaphysical necessity is that operator O such that in judging Op a thinker incurs the commitment that in any possible state of affairs, p. These possible states of affairs do not need to be things of the same kind as the universe around you, so no Lewisian modal realism need be involved in this approach. It seems, though, that a thinker can satisfy the suggested condition for understanding only if he already has the concept of possibility. Only the failure of p to hold in a genuinely possible state of affairs should make a thinker give up his acceptance of 'Necessarily p'. The thinker must have some grasp of which specifications of states of affairs are relevant counterexamples to a claim of necessity, and which are irrelevant, if he is to possess the concept of necessity. But if we are taking grasp of possibility for granted, how is that to be explained without adverting back to something which involves the thinker's grasp of necessity? If we are allowed to take the thinker's grasp of possibility for granted, we might just as well have defined necessity in terms of possibility. To have the burden of explanation passed back and forth between the concepts of necessity and possibility is not answering the question of the nature of understanding in any explanatory fashion.

At this point, a theorist may object that what I am seeking is something it is not necessary to find. If we make optimal total sense of someone by interpreting him as meaning necessity by a given operator, then he has the concept of necessity, and we should not look for anything explanatorily more fundamental. Similarly, if another person's beliefs about necessities are reached by methods we recognize as ones which, when applied by us, yield us knowledge of necessities, then the other person knows the necessities in question too. Why should we ask for more?

I make two points in response. First, it seems to be in order to ask 'Are our methods of reaching modal beliefs enough to entitle us to belief in their contents, and if so, why?' The question is neglected by the objector when he says that we should not ask for more. It makes a difference to answering this question whether modal realism, or some form of non-cognitivism, or some other treatment altogether, is correct. In asking this question, we are asking questions of a kind which we can legitimately raise and address for any kind of content.

Second, I should emphasize that the tasks of explaining the understanding and epistemology of necessity do not presuppose some reductive account of meaning and content. It is true that for someone who believes that a concept is individuated by its possession condition, in the (somewhat) reductive sense of 'possession condition' I employed in *A Study of Concepts*, the issues could be formulated as ones concerning the nature of the possession condition for necessity and its bearing upon the epistemology of modality. But that position on concept individuation is not compulsory for the present enterprise. Even if the account of the role of a concept in thought can never exhaust what is involved in its identity, one can still raise this question: 'What would be the nature of a non-reductive account of what is involved in understanding necessity discourse? What account of truth for modal statements would mesh with this account? And how would modal knowledge be possible on the correct account?' Here I am indeed making the substantive presupposition that there is a connection between what are, a priori, good reasons for judging a content, and what is involved in understanding a sentence expressing that content. But this substantive presupposition does not involve even the weakest reductionism.

The substantive presupposition that a theory of understanding is relevant to addressing these questions is one which ought to be congenial to anyone who accepts that understanding is a matter of grasping truth conditions. For something to give an entitlement, justification, or reason for judging a given content, it must be favourably related to that content's holding, to its truth condition's obtaining. If that is so, these normative relations must be related to the nature of understanding, on truth-conditional theories of understanding.

The plan for this longish chapter is as follows. In the next two sections, 4.2 and 4.3, I build up the promised account of the truth conditions of modal sentences and Thoughts. (Throughout, I use 'Thoughts' with the initial capital for truth-evaluable contents built up from Fregean senses.) This account of truth conditions involves neither modal realism nor thinker-dependence. I go on to discuss the relations between this account and modalism (4.4). Section 4.5 outlines an epistemology for modal contents which aims to dovetail with the positive account of their truth conditions. I contrast my approach in detail with that of thinker-dependent treatments in section 4.6.

There are important neo-Wittgensteinian challenges to 'fact-stating' treatments of modal discourse which need to be addressed, and I do so in section 4.7.

A treatment of the truth conditions of modal statements must speak to the question of which modal logical principles it validates. The question is important, and answering it in detail can bring out otherwise hidden aspects of a conception of modal truth. The question is, however, somewhat more technical than the rest of the subject matter of this book, and so it is addressed an Appendix to this chapter. The same applies to the question of the effect of relaxing some of the simplifying assumptions in my discussion.

4.2 ADMISSIBILITY, THE PRINCIPLES OF POSSIBILITY, AND THE MODAL EXTENSION PRINCIPLE

Let us return to the commitment model of understanding necessity. The problem we noted was that it presupposed the thinker's grasp of a distinction between those states of affairs which are possible, and those which are not. Suppose we could give a substantive account of what is involved in a state of affairs being possible. We might then argue that understanding a necessity operator involves some grasp of this substantive account of possibility. The problem we noted would then be overcome. That will be my strategy. I will try to state conditions which must be met if a specification of a state of affairs is to be a specification of a genuine possibility.

I call these conditions the 'Principles of Possibility'. The approach aims to identify a set of substantive principles of which it is true that a specification represents a genuine possibility only if it respects these principles.

These specifications are similar to the 'ways for the world to be' discussed by moderate modalists.[6] There are ways the world might be, there are ways the world is, and there are ways the world could not be. My claim is that someone who understands modal discourse has a form of implicit knowledge of the Principles of Possibility. It is this implicit knowledge that allows him to discriminate between those ways which are ways the world might be, and those ways or

---

[6] Stalnaker, 'Possible Worlds', and N. Salmon, 'The Logic of What Might Have Been', *Philosophical Review* 98 (1989), 3–34, esp. 5–17.

specifications which are not. More generally, someone who understands modal discourse applies this knowledge of the Principles of Possibility in evaluating modal claims.

I begin by explaining in more detail two auxiliary notions I shall be using. These are the notions of an *assignment*, and that of an *admissible* assignment. The point of introducing the notion of admissibility is that it is a step towards the elucidation of genuine possibility. Genuine possibility and admissibility are, I propose, related thus:

> A specification is a genuine possibility iff there is some admissible assignment which counts all its members as true.

Here assignments are not assignments to uninterpreted schematic letters. Since specifications are either specifications given by sets of meaningful expressions, or by Thoughts, our concern cannot be just with the uninterpreted. We have a choice as to whether to proceed with assignments to meaningful linguistic expressions, or to concepts which are built up into Thoughts. I will consider assignments to concepts. The changes needed to treat expressions are straightforward. An assignment *s*, then, does the following:

(i) *s* assigns to each atomic concept—whether singular, predicative, an operator on thoughts, or a quantifier—a semantic value of the appropriate category. We will take the semantic values to be the kinds of entity Frege assigned as the level of reference. So *s* assigns an object to a singular concept; it assigns to a monadic predicative concept a function from objects to truth values; and so forth. Subject only to clause (iii) below, there are no restrictions on what the assignments may be, provided that the category is correct. We can call the assignment which *s* makes to an atomic concept *C*, *the semantic value of C according to s*, and write it

$$\text{val}(C, s).$$

(ii) An assignment has an associated domain of objects, which is the range of the quantifiers under that assignment.

For many purposes, these first two clauses are all we need in the notion of an assignment. They allow us, derivatively, to use the notion of *the semantic value, according to assignment s of a complete Thought*. A complete Thought is built up from atomic concepts. The semantic value, according to assignment *s*, of a complete Thought is determined in the standard way from the semantic values of that Thought's constituent atomic concepts. Since we have set things up in a Fregean fashion, the semantic evaluation of a complex Thought or concept from the semantic values of its constituents is just a matter of the application of a function to an argument (or n-tuple of arguments). If the semantic value, according to s, of the concept C is the function f, and the semantic value, according to s, of the singular concept m is the object x, then the semantic value of the Thought Cm according to s is just the value of the function f for the argument x. If we were in a mood for formal and explicit characterizations, we could give a general inductive definition of the semantic value, according to a given assignment, of a complete Thought.

For any given assignment, there is its *corresponding specification*. The specification corresponding to a given assignment is just the set of Thoughts it counts as true (maps to the truth value True). The notion of the specification corresponding to an assignment will play an important part in what follows.

Sometimes it is important to consider properties and relations of a sort which cannot be identified with anything at the level of Fregean semantic values. There are several good reasons for acknowledging properties and relations, understood as distinct both from concepts and from Fregean semantic values.[7] For example, the most convincing way to understand the role of an expression occupying the position of F in a true statement of the form 'The fact that x is F explains such-and-such' is as involving reference to a property. So we add:

(iii) An assignment may assign such properties and relations to atomic predicative and relational concepts respectively.

When there are such assignments, assignments must also specify the extensions of these properties and relations. So we need several additional pieces of notation. When we are considering assignments of properties and relations, let us continue to use 'val(C, s)' for the semantic value at the level of Fregean reference. This must be distinguished from *the property value of C according to s*, which we write

$$\mathrm{propval}(C, s).$$

The property value of a monadic concept according to an assignment

---

[7] For an early compelling statement, see Putnam, 'On Properties'.

must be a monadic property; for a binary concept it must be a binary property; and so forth. Finally we must also specify, for a given assignment *s*, *the extension of property P according to s* ('ext(*P*, *s*)'). For a monadic property, this will be a function from objects to truth values; for a binary property, it will be a function from ordered pairs of objects to truth values; and so forth. We also stipulate that assignments must be such that these three notions, of semantic value, property value, and extension under an assignment, be related in the intuitive way, namely, that the semantic value of a concept under a given assignment be the same as the extension of its property value under that assignment. That is, in distinctly un-Fregean notation: for any *C*, *s* and *f*, we have that

$$\text{val}(C, s) = f \text{ iff } \text{ext}(\text{propval}(C, s), s) = f.$$

When assignments do deal with properties and relations, we can correspondingly explain a notion of the truth value of a singular proposition, built up from a property and an object, according to a given assignment. The truth value of the singular proposition *Px* according to the assignment *s* is True iff the extension of *P* according to *s* maps *x* to the True. Similarly we can explain the notion of the truth value, according to an assignment, of a singular proposition consisting of an n-place relation and an n-tuple of objects. We can then also extend the notion of the specification corresponding to an assignment. We can allow this specification to include not only the Thoughts, but also the singular propositions, which the given assignment counts as true.

I am initially going to make two simplifying assumptions about assignments, solely for the purpose of allowing us to walk before we run. The first assumption is that the assignments are, for some presumed background range of concepts, properties and objects, *total*. Any given assignment, under this supposition, assigns a semantic value to every atomic concept in the background range. The reasons for wanting eventually to relax this assumption need not stem only from a questioning of bivalence. Even one not disposed to question it can still recognize that our ordinary talk of possibilities does not involve treating them as total at all—otherwise we would hardly talk, as we actually do, of *the* possibility that it will rain tomorrow.

The second initial simplifying assumption is that assignments are sufficiently comprehensive, in a sense I will explain at the point at which we need the assumption. I will also, to start with, make only a minimal use of property values. The issues involved in relaxing the first simplifying assumption, and also of making more extensive use of property values, are considered in Appendix B.

In the standard Kripke-style model-theoretic semantics for modal logic, as we noted, assignments are made to uninterpreted expressions. In making assignments to uninterpreted expressions, rather than exclusively to meaningful expressions or interpreted sentences, the standard semantics does not deal, even indirectly, with the question of which Thoughts are true at a given world. The standard model-theoretic semantics does not need to. There are good reasons for saying that it is unnecessary to use the notion of which Thoughts or interpreted sentences are true at a world, when one's fundamental concern is with the modal *validity* of a schematic formula. Since the atomic predicate letters and individual constants of the schema do not have a sense, there is no question of respecting any constraints flowing from the concepts they express. But when our concern is with modal truth, rather than modal validity, matters must stand very differently. We may be interested in the question of whether the sentence or Thought that all material objects have a certain property, or that all conscious beings are thus-and-so, or that all fair arrangements are such-and-such, are each of them necessary or not. When we are asking such questions, we cannot evade the issue of whether it is genuinely possible for the concepts in these thoughts to have certain extensions in given circumstances.

In the case of those expressions of a modal logic which are not schematic, i.e. the logical constants, it is particularly clear that the standard modal semantics takes for granted points which it must be the concern of a philosophical treatment to explain. For instance, standard modal semantics takes it for granted that if either A is true with respect to a possible world w, or B is true with respect to w, then the sentence 'A or B' is true with respect to w. There is no gainsaying the correctness of the principle. But its correctness is in no way explained by the model-theoretic semantics. The model-theoretic semantics simply writes that very same principle into the rules for evaluating complex formulae with respect to a world. If, however, someone came along and asked why that rule of evaluation is correct, for any arbitrary possible world, he would not find any answer within the modal semantics. A philosophical account must attempt to answer this questioner.

The question is not one which arises only for the logical constants.

It is a special case of the general question: what determines the restrictions on semantic values for given concepts and meaningful expressions at genuinely possible worlds? A correct answer to this general question should have as a special case an answer to what determines the conditions to be satisfied, at genuinely possible worlds, by the semantic values assigned to sentences and Thoughts containing the logical constants.

We will seek in vain for an answer to these questions—even for the restricted case of the logical constants—in the standard semantical theories of absolute truth, that is for truth not relativized to a model. If the theory or definition is concerned with absolute truth, rather than truth relativized to a model, then it is not in itself, without supplementation, speaking to the question of which models correspond to genuine possibilities. Some theories of absolute truth do, certainly, use modal notions, and have as axioms such principles as 'Necessarily, any sentence of the form "*A* or *B*" is true iff either *A* if true or *B* is true'. Our question, however, is why this principle is correct. We are looking for a rationale for the principle, not just a use of it.

On the other hand, if we do turn to the notion of a model which has been developed for the elaboration and investigation of logical consequence, we also draw a blank in attempting to answer our imagined questioner. It is indeed true that intuitive expositions of the notion of logical consequence employ modal notions. This is true of Tarski's own intuitive expositions, which use the word 'must'. For instance, Tarski says of a sentence *A* which 'follows in the usual sense' from a certain set of other sentences that 'Provided all these sentences are true, the sentence *A* must be true'.[8] However, the models used in discussing logical consequence are confined to those in which varying assignments are made *only* to the non-logical vocabulary. It is indeed the case that $A \lor B$ is true in any model iff either *A* is true in it or *B* is true in it; but this is simply a consequence of not varying the assignments to the logical vocabulary (or replacing them with variables, in the fashion of Tarski). The schema 'If *A*, then $A \lor B$' would not be true in all models if we varied assignments to '$\lor$', in the way we do with the non-logical vocabulary. Equally, if we varied even less, a wider class of schemata would be true in all models. If we had

---

[8] A. Tarski, *Logic, Semantics, Metamathematics: Papers from 1923 to 1938*, 2nd edn. (Indianapolis, Ind.: Hackett, 1983), at 411. The modal 'must' also features in his requirement (F) on the consequence relation at 415.

some additional reason for saying that the usual kind of models employed in the investigation of logical consequence correspond to precisely the genuine possibilities, we might then have a rationale for the usual principles for evaluating formulae at non-actual worlds. But that additional reason would then be doing all the work in explaining the bounds of genuine possibility.

When, following the work of Kripke and Kaplan, we sharply distinguish the a priori from the necessary, it becomes in any case much less plausible to try to explain aspects of metaphysical necessity by relating them to notions designed to elucidate validity.[9] We expect validity to be a relatively a priori matter. An inference such as 'From *p*, it follows that *Actually p*' is a priori. It is not necessarily truth-preserving. The demands of a theory of validity, then, are going to be rather different from those of a theory of metaphysical necessity. This makes model theory conceived as in the service of a theory of validity a less promising resource for the philosophical elucidation of necessity.

The positive strategy I said I would follow is that of trying to characterize the admissibility of an assignment in such a way that for each genuinely possible specification there is some admissible assignment which counts as true all the Thoughts (and propositions) in that specification. The goal, in characterizing admissibility, is to give some explanation of *why* an assignment which, for instance, assigns the classical truth function for conjunction to the concept of alternation is not an admissible assignment. If we can do this properly, we will have answered our imagined questioner about the model-theoretic rules for logical constants.

The first constraint on admissibility—my first Principle of Possibility—is one which is basic to my whole approach. It can be initially formulated as a two-part principle which I call the *Modal Extension Principle*. The name is doubly appropriate. First, the Modal Extension Principle constrains the extension a concept may receive from an assignment, if that assignment is to be admissible. That is, it gives a necessary condition for admissibility. Second, the Modal Extension Principle also extends to genuinely possible specifications the *way* the extension is fixed in the actual world. The

[9] Kripke, *Naming and Necessity*; D. Kaplan, 'Demonstratives: An Essay on the Semantics, Logic, Metaphysics, and Epistemology of Demonstratives and Other Indexicals', repr. in J. Almog, J. Perry, and H. Wettstein (eds.), *Themes from Kaplan* (New York: Oxford University Press, 1989).

intuitive idea behind the Modal Extension Principle starts from the point that for any given concept C there will be some rule R whose application determines the actual semantic value of C. The actual extension of C is determined by applying the rule R to the actual extensions of certain other concepts or properties. The notion of determination being used here is one involving an explanatory claim. The concept C has a certain extension because it is the output of R when R is applied to the actual extensions of certain other concepts or properties. The idea behind the Modal Extension Principle is then simply stated: if an assignment s is to be admissible, the semantic value it assigns to C must result from applying that same rule R to the semantic values which those certain other concept or properties have according to s.

Before I attempt a formal, general statement of the Principle, I give four examples to illustrate the intuitive idea.

As a first example, consider the hoary case of the concept *bachelor*. Let us take it that the rule R which fixes the actual semantic value of this concept is that it is the intersection of the actual extension of the concept *man* with the actual extension of the concept *unmarried*. The Modal Extension Principle implies that an assignment s is admissible only if the semantic value that s assigns to *bachelor* is the one obtained by taking the intersection of the extension that s assigns to *man* with the extension that s assigns to *unmarried*. If s assigns to either of the two concepts *man* and *unmarried* an extension different from its actual extension, an admissible assignment may assign to the concept *bachelor* an extension distinct from its actual extension.

Second, consider an assignment s which treats the concept of logical conjunction, &. Suppose s assigns to & a function which does not, when applied to the truth values True and False (say), taken in that order, yield the truth value False. Then s would not be assigning to & a semantic value which is the result of applying the same rule for determining the semantic value, according to s, of Thoughts containing & as is applied in determining the semantic value of Thoughts containing & in the actual world. Here I am taking it that the rule R applied in determining the actual truth value of conjunctions does not depend on the extensions of any other concepts or properties in the way in which the actual extension of *bachelor* does. For this reason, s would be counted as inadmissible by the Modal Extension Principle.

As a third example, take the case of a binary universal quantifier

$\forall x(Fx, Gx)$, meaning that all Fs are G. Suppose we have an assignment s with a domain which includes the three objects x, y, z. We further stipulate that s gives the concept *planet* a semantic value which maps just these three objects to the True. It also assigns to *spherical* a semantic value which maps these three objects to the True. Now consider the Thought *All planets are spherical*. Under these suppositions, s is admissible only if the function s assigns to this universal quantifier $\forall$ maps the pair of functions assigned to *planet* and to *spherical* respectively to the truth value True. If the assignment s were not to do so, it would not be applying the same rule in determining the semantic values, according to s, of Thoughts containing $\forall$ which is applied in determining the actual truth value of Thoughts containing $\forall$. That rule is just that the extension of F be included in that of G. So if s is as described, we would again have a violation of the Modal Extension Principle.

As a fourth illustration of the Principle, consider an assignment s which assigns to the concept F a function which maps only the particular object x, and nothing else, to the truth value True. Now consider the function which the same assignment s makes to the definite description operator ι. Suppose the function s assigns to ι is one which does not map the function it assigns to F to the unique object x. Then the assignment s would not, according to the Main Part of the Modal Extension Principle, be admissible. For the way in which the semantic value of a definite description $\iota x(Fx)$ is fixed in the actual world is by applying the rule that it refers to an object if that object is the unique thing which is F.

Now we can give a general, formal statement of the Modal Extension Principle. As I said, we can initially divide the Principle into two parts, and I take first the Main Part. This Main Part is concerned with concepts which are not, to extend the terminology of Kripke and McGinn, *de jure* rigid.[10] In cases of *de jure* rigidity, as Kripke explains the distinction, 'the reference of a designator is *stipulated* to be a single object, whether we are speaking of the actual world or of a counterfactual situation, and mere "*de facto*" rigidity, where a description "the x such that Fx" happens to use a predicate "F" that in each possible world is true of one and the same unique object (e.g. "the smallest prime" rigidly designates the number

[10] Kripke, *Naming and Necessity*; C. McGinn, 'Rigid Designation and Semantic Value', *Philosophical Quarterly* 32 (1982), 97–115.

two)'.[11] Kaplan's operator 'dthat' is another example of a *de jure* rigid expression, and so too would be the concept it expresses.[12] The distinction between what is *de jure* rigid and what is not begins to bite only for expressions or concepts for which variation of reference between possible specifications is in question.

We are at last in a position to formulate the Modal Extension Principle.

> **Modal Extension Principle, Main Part.** Take any concept C which is not *de jure* rigid. Suppose the actual semantic value of C is determined by applying a certain rule R to the actual semantic values of concepts $C_1, \ldots, C_n$. The following is then a necessary condition for the admissibility of s: that the semantic value of C according to s is the result of applying R to the semantic values of $C_1, \ldots, C_n$ according to s.

For brevity, I shall summarize the necessary condition stated here by saying that the semantic value of C according to s is the result of applying the same rule as is applied in the determination of the actual semantic value of C. In some cases the rule R may make the actual extension of C depend also on the actual extension of various properties. In such cases, the admissibility of s will require that the semantic value of C according to s is similarly dependent upon the extensions which those same properties have according to s.

What, in the general case, *is* the rule which determines the actual semantic value of a concept? On the theory I once offered, the rule is given by what I called the determination theory for the concept in question.[13] On that approach, the determination theory takes the material in the concept's possession condition, and says how something in the world has to stand to it if it is to be the concept's semantic value. In the case of an empirical concept, it will be an empirical condition something has to satisfy to be its semantic value. On a different theory, which is more plausible for certain concepts, the semantic value of a concept is determined by an implicit conception governing the concept, and the content of that implicit conception is what an assignment has to respect if it is to be admissible. But the

---

[11] *Naming and Necessity*, 21 n. 21.

[12] D. Kaplan, 'Dthat', in P. Cole (ed.), *Syntax and Semantics* (New York: Academic Press, 1978).

[13] *A Study of Concepts*, ch. 1.

details and general presuppositions of my own or any other particular approach to concepts are not at all required by the present treatment of possibility. Take whatever may be your favoured theory of how the actual semantic value of a concept is fixed: it can then be used in combination with the Main Part of the Modal Extension Principle, to formulate a constraint on the admissibility of an assignment. Provided that we can make some sense of the notion of the way the semantic value of a particular concept is fixed in the actual world, the Modal Extension Principle can get off the ground. I will return at the end of section 4.4 to consider whether this notion of a way in which the semantic value is fixed is a notion which is sufficiently independent of the thinker's understanding of modality to be used in its explanation.

The Main Part of the Modal Extension Principle can apply equally to atomic predicational concepts. Suppose, for the sake of illustration, that the actual extension of an atomic observational shape concept *diamond-shaped* consists of all objects which have the same shape as those which, as they actually are, would produce a certain kind of experience in a properly perceiving subject. That the concept's actual extension is so fixed does not require the concept to be taken as defined. Such a determination of its semantic value would on some theories be regarded as a consequence of the concept's possession condition, together with a theory of how the semantic value is fixed from that possession condition. Under these suppositions, an assignment *s* is then admissible only if *s* assigns to *diamond-shaped* an extension which includes precisely those objects which, according to *s*, are of the same shape as those which, as they actually are, would produce a certain kind of experience in a properly perceiving subject.

This, incidentally, illustrates the need for the assumption that the range of assignments we are considering is sufficiently comprehensive, in the following sense: they determine the extensions of all properties and relations on which the actual semantic value of a given atomic concept depends.

For someone who thinks that we can in fact make no sense of the idea that some particular rule contributes to the determination of the actual semantic value of a concept, the Main Part of the Modal Extension Principle does not formulate any substantial constraint on admissibility, nor, therefore, on possibility either. The apparatus and theses I am developing are, in the case of necessities involving concepts, dependent upon the applicability of such a notion of a rule, a

notion which involves the rule's explaining why a concept has the
extension it does. It is no accident that those who have been sceptical about the intelligibility of any such notion of a rule have also
tended to be sceptics of one stripe or another about the notion of
necessities involving concepts. Such rules and necessities sink or swim
together.

The other part of the Modal Extension Principle deals with concepts which are marked as rigid. This second part does not amount
to much more than an application of the definition of *de jure* rigidity.

> **Modal Extension Principle, Second Part.** For any concept C
> which is *de jure* rigid, and whose actual semantic value is A, and
> for any admissible assignment *s*, the semantic value of C accord-
> ing to *s* is A.

As before, both parts of the Principle should be understood as generalized to arbitrary categories of concept and their appropriate
kinds of semantic value. Of course, when we are considering the
Modal Extension Principle as formulated for expressions, and a particular expression is such that in the language only a semantic value
and not a concept is associated with it, only the Second Part of the
Modal Extension Principle can apply. It is no accident that proper
names are *de jure* rigid.

I have separated out the formulation of the Main Part and the
Second Part of the Modal Extension Principle for expository purposes. The separation should help to dispel any impression that some
illegitimate modal element is playing a part in the rule which formulates the way in which the actual semantic value of a concept is determined. But of course even in the case of a *de jure* rigid concept, it is
correct to say that (for instance) the rule which determines the actual
semantic value of 'dthat(the *F*)' is this: 'dthat(the *F*)' refers to
dthat(the *F*). Provided the rigidifying operator is present in the statement of the rule, we could, as Timothy Williamson remarked to me,
unify the two parts of the Modal Extension Principle. Indeed, using
the abbreviation I introduced above, we could make it as brief as this:

> **Unified Modal Extension Principle.** An assignment *s* is admissi-
> ble only if: for any concept *C*, the semantic value of *C* accord-
> ing to *s* is the result of applying the same rule as is applied in the
> determination of the actual semantic value of *C*.

In the case of a *de jure* rigid concept, the rule which is applied in the determination of the actual semantic value will either contain a rigidifying element, or will simply fix an object and no more. In either case, this will secure the effect of the Second Part of the Modal Extension Principle on the previous treatment.

Alarm bells will now have been ringing in the reader's mind for several paragraphs. If our aim is to give an account of the nature of genuine possibility, how can we help ourselves to the notion of rigidity or to rigidifying operators? Must not the notion of *de jure* rigidity directly or indirectly involve the notion of genuine possibility, either by way of the notion of a possible world, or via that of a counterfactual situation, or even via some notion of the truth conditions for sentences or Thoughts containing a operator for metaphysical necessity? I reply that I have alluded to the notion of *de jure* rigidity as a heuristic device for drawing attention to the class of concepts to which the Second Part of the Modal Extension Principle applies. My claim is that there is a class of concepts and expressions grasp or understanding of which involves some appreciation that in their case, an assignment is admissible only if it assigns to each one of them its actual semantic value. That a particular concept or expression is in this class is something which has to be learned either one by one for the concept or expression, as with Kaplan's 'dthat', or has to be learned by the concept's membership of a general class for which this constraint on admissibility holds, such as the classes of demonstratives, indexicals, and proper names.

If the reader is still worried that there may be a damaging circularity here in the use of *de jure* rigidity, perhaps it may alleviate the concern to think of the matter as follows. We can label two classes of expressions (and concepts), one class with the otherwise meaningless label 'A' and the second class with the otherwise meaningless label 'B'. Expressions and concepts in class A are such that an assignment to one of them is admissible only if the semantic value under that assignment is the result of applying the same rule as is applied in the determination of the actual semantic value of the concept or expression. Expressions and concepts in class B are such that an assignment to one of *them* is admissible only if the semantic value under that assignment is the same as its actual semantic value. One has to learn one by one which expressions and concepts are in class B. In this characterization, there is no damaging kind of circularity in the specification of the classes A and B. This characterization would equally have served our purposes. It could equally be adapted to the approach in which we use rigidifying operators in the statement of the rules themselves, and which permits the formulation of the Unified Modal Extension Principle.

What of the notion of admissibility—is it itself modal? Must it not mean '*can* be admitted'? I have chosen the label 'admissible' because of its intuitive resonance, as appropriate for those assignments which are admitted as determinants of genuine possibility. The meaning of 'admissible' in our common language is, however, quite inessential to the statement of the present theory of modality. For the purposes of the theory itself, admissibility can be taken to be defined by its role in the theory. That role is to summarize the constraints on those assignments which contribute to the determination of genuine possibility. The theory could equally proceed by claiming:

> A specification is a genuine possibility iff there is some assignment which meets the Modal Extension Principle and the other constraints detailed below and which counts all the members of that specification as true.

The conception I am in the course of outlining sits well with the view that the distinction between *de jure* rigid expressions and the rest can, in the general case at least, be elucidated only by reference to their differential behaviour in relation to modal evaluation. One way in which the difference between 'the capital of the United States' and the Kaplanian 'dthat (the capital of the United States)' shows up is their respective behaviours when embedded in modal operators. (That is a sufficient condition of difference, but, as Scott Soames has argued, modal operators do not always need to be in the language for differences in modal evaluation to show up.)[14] As their respective semantical clauses would lead one to expect, an account of what is involved in understanding Kaplan's 'dthat' or the word 'actual' can be given only simultaneously with, and not in advance of, the thinker's grasp of modal notions.

With this apparatus in place, we can return to doing some more substantial philosophy, and consider some very simple philosophical applications of the Modal Extension Principle.

(a) We can establish, without begging the question, the metaphysical necessity of, for instance, truths of propositional logic. Consider

---

[14] S. Soames, 'The Modal Argument: Wide Scope and Rigidified Descriptions', *Noûs* 32 (1998), 1–22.

the propositional logical constants. Suppose it granted that these constants have truth functions as their semantic values. Suppose also that you hold one of two theories. One theory is that the truth function for any given constant is fixed as the one which makes certain inferential principles always truth-preserving. These are the principles a theorist might say are mentioned in its understanding condition. Here 'always truth-preserving' does not mean something modal. It means 'truth-preserving under all assignments of truth values to schematic letters', in the way in which, for example, the classical truth function for conjunction is the only truth function which makes truth-preserving the classical introduction and elimination rules for conjunction. Or suppose, alternatively, you hold that understanding a logical constant involves having an implicit conception stating the truth conditions of Thoughts or sentences containing it in terms of the truth conditions of its constituents.

On each of these theories, the semantic value of a logical constant with respect to an admissible assignment will always be the same as its actual semantic value. Under the first of the two theories I mentioned, this point holds because a logical constant's semantic value under any admissible assignment must be the one which makes truth-preserving certain principles of inference. It will be the same semantic value that will make them truth-preserving whatever the nature of the assignment. So the principles mentioned, according to this first kind of theory, in the understanding-condition for the logical constant will be truth-preserving in any admissible assignment. It follows that the inferential principles which individuate the meaning of a logical constant, such as the introduction and elimination rules for conjunction, are metaphysically necessary.

The same result follows even more straightforwardly under the theory that the rule by which the semantic value of a logical constant is determined is given by the content of some implicit conception such as '*A* or *B* is true iff either *A* is true or *B* is true'. To assign a semantic value—a truth function—to *or* other than the one fixed by the content of this rule would thereby be to depart from the way the truth value of alternations is actually determined.[15]

---

[15] Both the inferential role account and the implicit conception account should aim to rule out deviant semantic values for the logical constants ultimately by appeal to the account of understanding which generates the semantic value. This is a substantive task, both in detail, and in the formulation of the constraints to which it is subject.

For the propositional logical constants, this is the answer I offer to our imagined questioner who asked how we could justify the usual principles for evaluating, at an arbitrary possible world, formulae containing propositional logical constants. The metaphysical necessity of such principles is a consequence of what is involved in a specification's being possible, when possibility is explained in terms of admissibility, and when the explication of possibility involves the Modal Extension Principle.[16]

It is crucial to note that this rationale neither explicitly, nor tacitly, relies on the premise that the relevant inferential principles, on the first theory, or the content of the implicit conceptions, on the second theory, are metaphysically necessary. That those principles are necessary is the conclusion of the argument, not its premise. In the rationale, reliance is rather being placed on the point that part of what makes an assignment admissible involves conformity to the Modal Extension Principle. Hence a respect for certain inferential principles, or alternatively the content of implicit conceptions, is guaranteed by the Modal Extension Principle. Conformity to the Modal Extension Principle helps, via the connection proposed between admissibility and possibility, to fix which specifications are genuinely possible. The Modal Extension Principle, and other Principles of Possibility are, on the conception I am offering, antecedent in the order of philosophical explanation to the determination of what is genuinely possible.

If we suppose that we have some conception of the genuinely possible specifications elucidated without reliance on the Modal Extension Principle, I think it will (rightly) seem to be an impossible task to explain why certain primitive logical principles are metaphysically necessary without some kind of question-begging. The impossibility of that task, according to the present approach, results from a wrong way of looking at the problem. We can explain why conformity to the primitive logical principles helps to fix which specifications are genuinely possible, rather than having some independently understood notion of possibility for which we then have to explain why genuine possibilities respect those logical principles.

Logical concepts contrast sharply, in respect of this first point, with

---

[16] With an eye on later epistemological issues, we can also note at this point that if the Modal Extension Principle is a priori, then principles whose necessity is deducible from it in the way illustrated are also a priori. I will return to the relations between necessity and the a priori in a later section.

many empirical concepts. In the case of the empirical concept *expensive*, say, nothing in the conditions on admissibility formulated so far, nor any to follow, excludes an admissible assignment *s* in which the concept *expensive* has an extension different from its actual extension. Such a difference in extension would be entirely in accordance with the Modal Extension Principle if *s* also assigns semantic values to other concepts—in particular those on which truths about relative prices depend.

(b) One of our introductory illustrations of violations of the Modal Extension Principle supported the claim that no admissible assignment will ever count anything of the form *a is a bachelor and a is married* as true. Hence, no specification corresponding to an admissible assignment will count such Thoughts (or their corresponding sentences) true. This places me in disagreement, by implication, with one of David Lewis's claims. He says that it is a serious objection to what he calls ersatz possible worlds—possible worlds which are not things of the same kind as the actual world—that an approach involving them must take modality as primitive.[17] In particular, he emphasizes that if a theorist who endorses ersatz possible worlds tries to explain them in terms of logically consistent sets of propositions, 'That would falsify the facts of modality by yielding allegedly consistent ersatz worlds according to which there are unmarried bachelors, numbers with more than one successor, and suchlike impossibilities'.[18] Using sets of propositions which are consistent in a strict logical sense, though, is not the only way of developing a treatment of modality with ersatz possible worlds. The worlds I have been speaking about are certainly ersatz worlds in Lewis's classification—they are nothing more than sets of Thoughts and/or propositions; and I noted earlier that the present approach does not need to be reductive of modality. But I have also just argued that the Main Part of the Modal Extension Principle does rule out the existence of possible worlds at which there are unmarried bachelors. Only by not applying the same rule which determines the actual extension of *bachelor* can an assignment count something of the form *a is a bachelor and a is married* as true. So we can meet part of David Lewis's objection to ersatz possible worlds if we accept the Modal Extension Principle. A theory employing ersatz

---

[17] *On the Plurality of Worlds*, 150 ff.
[18] Ibid. 153.

worlds can and must go beyond logical necessity in any strict or narrow sense having to do only with the logical vocabulary. More generally, I think we should also draw the conclusion that an account of what other worlds are possible must draw on information about how concepts come to have their semantic values in the actual world.

The Main Part of the Modal Extension Principle can be seen as an implementation and articulation of a widely held intuitive point, that we should not, when concerned with fundamental philosophical explanation, regard the one-place concept *x is happy* as just a special case of the two-place relativized concept *x is happy in world w*, namely, the special case in which *w* is assigned the actual world as its value. The two-place relativized predicate is not explanatorily prior. Rather, world-relativized concepts have a general relation to their unrelativized versions, and there is a general rule stating how the extension of the two-place *x is happy in w* is fixed from the rule determining the actual extension of the predicate *x is happy*. The Main Part of the Modal Extension Principle is just such a general rule.

Whether the meaning of the unrelativized predicates is absolutely prior must depend in part on the resolution of a metaphysical issue about the actual world: the issue of whether it is to be conceived in a fully non-modal fashion, or in a partially modal fashion. (There will be more on this in section 4.6 below.) The Main Part of the Modal Extension Principle does, however, exclude the hypothesis that understanding of the world-relativized concepts is absolutely prior to the unrelativized versions. It is, then, in apparent contrast with the view of Hintikka, who holds that for first-order languages '"meanings" are bound to be completely idle', and that 'in order to spell out the idea that the meaning of a term is the way in which its reference is determined we have to consider how the reference varies in different possible worlds, and therefore go beyond first-order languages'.[19] If the Modal Extension Principle is correct, the meanings for the expressions in the first-order language, far from being idle, actually serve to determine the world-relative extensions.

This brings us to the more general issue of the correct way to conceive of the relation between meaning and *de dicto* necessities. In some earlier work on the a priori, like many other writers, I rejected the applicability of the notion of truth purely in virtue of meaning. But I did defend the idea that meaning can explain the special status

---

[19] J. Hintikka, *Models for Modalities* (Dordrecht: Reidel, 1969), at 93.

of a priori truths.[20] I argued that a priori truths are ones whose truth in the actual world can be derived from the understanding conditions (and associated determination theories) for their constituent expressions. An analogous link between meaning and the a priori arguably still holds if we replace possession conditions with implicit conceptions. So the question arises: is there any analogous link between meaning and necessity?

The idea that meaning can explain the special status of necessary truths has certainly been found attractive historically. Not surprisingly, the temptation to succumb to that idea has been strong in times in which the notions of necessity, the a priori, and analyticity were not sharply distinguished. Carnap, for instance, in *Meaning and Necessity*, offered 'L-truth' as an explication of necessity. He wrote: 'A sentence σ is *L-true* in a semantical system S if and only if σ is true in S in such a way that its truth can be established on the basis of the semantical rules of the system S alone, without any reference to (extra-linguistic) facts.'[21] So can we give a qualified endorsement of the view that meaning plays a special role in the explanation of certain *de dicto* necessities, analogous to the way in which the treatment of the a priori gave some qualified endorsement of the view that meaning plays a special role in the explanation of the a priori?

The approach which I am developing already suggests a positive answer. I already noted that the necessity of certain *de dicto* sentences is derivable from the Modal Extension Principle for expressions, together with whatever feature of the meaning of those expressions determines their extensions. Just as the earlier treatment I endorsed of the a priori does not legitimate any application of the notion of truth-purely-in-virtue-of-meaning, so this explanation of *de dicto* necessities does not underwrite the applicability of the notion of necessity-purely-in-virtue-of-meaning. It would hardly be consistent to do so. Since necessity entails truth, any endorsement of necessity-purely-in-virtue-of-meaning would require endorsement of at least some cases of truth-purely-in-virtue-of-meaning. There is no endorsement in the present framework of the application of necessity-purely-in-virtue-of-meaning, because logic, the Modal Extension Principle

---

[20] For the rejection and the defence, see my 'How are A Priori Truths Possible?', *European Journal of Philosophy* 1 (1993), 175–99.

[21] R. Carnap, *Meaning and Necessity: A Study in Semantics and Modal Logic*, 2nd edn. (Chicago, Ill.: Chicago University Press, 1956), 10. I have altered the notation.

and other principles are used in the derivation of the necessity of a *de dicto* truth. Everything I have said is consistent with the principle that what makes a statement of the form *Necessarily A* true is just its disquoted truth condition. The substance of what I have said lies in giving some necessary and sufficient conditions for that disquoted truth condition to hold.

(c) The Modal Extension Principle does not count all a priori principles as metaphysically necessary. I mention two cases familiar from discussions in modal semantics.

Suppose that the whole set of Principles of Possibility ensures that there is a possible world—a genuinely possible specification—at which *p* is not true. Suppose also that 'actually', and equally the concept it expresses, is marked as a rigidifer. 'If actually *p*, then *p*' will be a priori. By the Second Part of the Modal Extension Principle, however, it is not necessary.

Another example, made familiar by David Kaplan's writings, is given by 'I am here now'. The Thought that I am here now is a priori but is not necessary. The present apparatus secures this result, given that 'now', 'here', and 'I' are *de jure* rigid, and given the Second Part of the Modal Extension Principle. Provided the whole set of Principles of Possibility ensures the existence of a world at which you are somewhere else now, your present thought 'I am here now' will be false with respect to some genuinely possible specification. As Kaplan insists, though, it has an a priori status (at least if preceded with the antecedent 'If this place here exists').

4.3 OTHER PRINCIPLES OF POSSIBILITY AND THE TRUTH CONDITIONS OF MODAL STATEMENTS

I turn now to a set of Principles of Possibility that can be called constitutive principles. I will deal with them briefly, because they are more familiar than the Modal Extension Principle. These constitutive principles concern not concepts and the level of sense, as the Modal Extension Principle does; they are rather about objects, properties, and relations. Intuitively each such principle states that an assignment is admissible only if it respects what is constitutive of the objects, properties and relations it mentions. Given the connection we have proposed between admissibility and possibility, this implies that a specification is possible only if it respects what is constitutive of the objects, properties, and relations it mentions.

One plausible constitutive principle concerns the fundamental kind of an object, where for instance your fundamental kind is the kind *human being* and the fundamental kind of New York is the kind *city*. This notion of an object's fundamental kind is the one David Wiggins aims to elucidate in saying that it is the highest sortal under which the object falls.[22] The plausible constitutive principle is this:

> If *P* is a property which is an object *x*'s fundamental kind, then an assignment is inadmissible if it counts the proposition *x is P* as false.

This principle is to be understood as universally quantified, as propounded for all properties and objects. I have formulated the principle in such a way that, even if the property *P* is *x*'s fundamental kind, the principle allows that an admissible assignment may make no pronouncement on the truth value of the proposition that *x is P*. This will be helpful when we come to allow that assignments need not be total. What the principle does require is that if an assignment pronounces on the truth value of the proposition *x is P* at all, it must count it as true.

Properties are essential to formulating this principle correctly. It is not a mode of presentation which is the fundamental kind of an object. The fundamental kind must be something at the level of reference, not of thoughts. Nor can the fundamental kind be merely a Fregean semantic value, a function from objects to truth values. The fundamental reason for this is the list-like character of such a function. The kind-essence of an object is supposed to contribute to a metaphysical (not an epistemological) account of what individuates the object. If the kind-essence is to succeed in doing that, the kind-essence cannot be something whose individuation involves the object itself, as the Fregean function does. The same point applies to sets and to Fregean courses of values.

Similarly, if there are individual essences, admissible assignments must respect them. Suppose, as is also plausible, that it is constitutive of person *a* that she originated in the particular sperm *b* and egg cell *c* from which she actually developed. Then this should be another of our constitutive principles:

---

[22] D. Wiggins, *Sameness and Substance* (Oxford: Blackwell, 1980).

An assignment is inadmissible if it both counts the proposition *a exists* as true and counts the proposition *a develops from b and c* as false.

More generally, in any case in which it is constitutive of the object *x* that it bear *R* to the object *y*, we should endorse the principle that

An assignment is inadmissible if it both counts as true the proposition *x exists* and counts the proposition *x bears R to y* as false.

There will also be constitutive principles for properties and relations, stating what is constitutive of them.

There is obviously an immense amount to be said about which constitutive principles are true, and why. My main concern here is not with which particular constitutive principles are true. It is rather to note the apparent existence of this class of Principles of Possibility, and their role in our understanding of possibility. It is a matter for further philosophical, metaphysical research whether, for instance, colour incompatibilities should be included amongst the constitutive properties of colours; or whether certain links between consciousness, explanation, and behaviour are constitutive of consciousness; and so forth. These issues all merit separate books in their own right. The present treatment of modality, in recognizing a category of constitutive principles, simply offers a framework in which any defensible constitutive claims emerging from such investigations can be formulated, and contribute to the determination of modal truth. We certainly cannot, though, totally bypass the issue of how the constitutive is related to the modal.

Some constitutive properties of objects have a life—that is, a significance—outside the sphere of the modal. The kind-essence of an object illustrates the case. The kind-essence of an object helps to determine the conditions under which a particular continuant object persists. If *F* is an object's fundamental kind, the object *x* persists from one time to another only if there is at the later time something which is the same *F* as *x*. The notion of the persistence condition of an object should be elucidated by saying that it is the condition which specifies *what it is* for the object to persist. If we omit the constitutive phrase 'what it is', we will not have excluded overlapping persistence conditions which happen, given the way the world is, to give the right answer, but which do not answer to the constitutive condition. Since, though, it is not at all obvious that the constitutive has to be explained in terms of the modal, this may still be an application of the notion of kind-essence which is not fundamentally modal—though it will of course have modal consequences.[23]

It is, however, much harder to see essence of origin as having applications outside the modal. On the contrary, the fundamental role of truths about the individual essence of an object seems to be that of constraining which genuinely possible states of affairs are ones in which the object exists. I am not sure whether truths about individual essence have any role beyond this. An objector may now say that this point threatens the whole project of elucidating modality in terms of a set of Principles of Possibility with a fatal circularity. This objector may say: 'It is one thing to try to elucidate our understanding of modality by stating the conditions required for a specification to be possible. But if those conditions themselves employ the notion of possibility, explicitly or implicitly, your whole approach is doomed to circularity.'

This may sound plausible, but it is a mistake to suppose that these points about essence of origin mean that the Principles of Possibility have themselves to use the notion of genuine possibility. They do not, and there is no circularity of that sort. The constitutive principle implied by a true statement of the individual essence of a particular object amounts simply to a further axiom placing a condition on what has to be the case for any given assignment to be admissible. We do not need to use the notion of possibility to state what that condition is: it is just that the assignment must not deny the object in question what are in fact its actual origins. Indeed, we could even formulate the constraint in accordance with the austere demands of the A(C) form of *A Study of Concepts*. We would say: possibility is that concept C, predicated of specifications, to possess which a thinker must have implicit knowledge of certain principles $P_1(C)$ . . . $P_n(C)$, where one of these principles states that any specification falls under C only if any continuant object which exists, according to that specification, has its actual origins. An account of possession of the concept of possibility along these lines does not take for granted that the thinker already possesses the concept.

---

[23] For the view that a theory of individuation should quite generally be given in non-modal terms, with modal propositions as consequential, see Wiggins, *Sameness and Substance*, ch. 4, sect. 1.

Still, even if that is granted, it may be objected that we have a circularity if we try to specify the general *class* of constraints to be included in the restrictions on admissible assignments, if individual essence has to be explained in terms of its connections with the modal. Whether this objection stands depends on whether we can make sense of what is constitutive of a particular object independently of the modal. There is some plausibility in the idea that constitutive matters are explanatorily prior in fixing which object is in question. They then contribute, via Principles of Possibility, to fixing what are genuine possibilities. Some of Kit Fine's work tends in this direction.[24] In the worst case, if it turns out that a notion of the constitutive which is explanatorily prior to the modal cannot be sustained, there may be still be a fall-back position in characterizing the class of constitutive principles. Graeme Forbes, for instance, has argued that there is an objectionable kind of bare identity which would have to be swallowed if necessity of origin were rejected.[25] So another option which might be explored as a fall-back position in characterizing the class of constitutive principles is that they are principles which can be justified in a certain fashion. But I will leave this fascinating diversion for now. All that matters at present is that constitutive principles must be included in the constraints upon the admissibility of an assignment.

So far, we have two kinds of Principles of Possibility: the Modal Extension Principle and the constitutive principles. Though the Modal Extension Principle and the constitutive principles have very different subject matters, they are not just arbitrarily slapped together. Both the Modal Extension Principle and the constitutive principles require that what holds according to a genuine possibility must respect what makes something what it is—whether it be a concept, an object, a property, or a relation. On any plausible theory of concepts, the identity of a concept depends on the rules which determine its semantic value in the actual world. The Modal Extension Principle then requires that what is involved in this identity be preserved in a certain way across genuinely possible worlds. So the Modal Extension Principle draws out the consequences of what is

[24] K. Fine, 'Essence and Modality', in J. Tomberlin (ed.), *Philosophical Perspectives*, 8: *Logic and Language* (Atascadero, Calif.: Ridgeview, 1994), 1–16.
[25] G. Forbes, *The Metaphysics of Modality* (Oxford: Oxford University Press, 1985), ch. 6, sects. 3–4.

individuative of a concept for what is genuinely possible, while the constitutive principles for objects, properties, and relations draw out the consequences of what is individuative of objects, properties, and relations.

A third kind of principle of possibility is a principle of plenitude, and it has, within the framework I am proposing, the effects of David Lewis's principle of recombination.[26] This principle of plenitude is a second-order principle. Unlike the Principles of Possibility given so far, this principle of plenitude makes reference to the other Principles of Possibility. This principle, unlike all the other conditions on admissibility, which to date have been only necessary conditions, formulates a sufficient condition on admissibility:

> **Principle of Constrained Recombination.** An assignment is admissible if it respects the set of conditions on admissibility given hitherto.

All sorts of recombination of properties and relations amongst individuals are allowed as possibilities, as long as they respect the full set of Principles of Possibility. Since we have said all along that a specification is genuinely possible iff there is some admissible assignment which counts all its members as true, this principle of plenitude implies that:

> A specification is possible iff it corresponds to some assignment which satisfies the set of constraints on admissibility formulated in the earlier paragraphs.

If 'respecting', as it occurs in the Principle of Constrained Recombination, meant the same as 'metaphysically consistent with', we would have a serious circularity problem. But it does not. The Modal Extension Principle and the constitutive principles each state necessary conditions for a specification to be possible. The recombination principle states that conformity to these principles—if indeed they do exhaust the Principles of Possibility—is sufficient for a specification to be possible. So all that a specification's 'respecting' the Principles of Possibility involves is its conforming to the conditions they lay down. In explaining what is involved in that, all that is involved is the notion of joint satisfaction of the conditions, period.

[26] *On the Plurality of Worlds*, 87–92.

It would indeed be open to a theorist to follow a different approach. He could introduce some notion of a canonical description of a specification. One could then raise the question of whether, under some consequence relation, it is a consequence of the Principles of Possibility that a specification so described is not possible. Finally, one could propose that a specification is possible if its impossibility is not such a consequence. Such an approach in effect takes the propositions and thoughts which are true according to a given specification, and then considers the consequence relations in which those propositions and thoughts (or their canonical specifications) stand. It seems unnecessarily roundabout as compared with the approach which considers simply whether a specification meets the Principles of Possibility. It is also not clear that our intuitive notion of possibility fixes on one particular relation out of the many consequence relations there are, and is to be individuated in terms of that one particular relation.

Now that we have explained a specification's being possible in terms of the Principles of Possibility, as formulated in terms of admissible assignments, we are in a position to state the contribution made to truth conditions by the standard modal operators:

> A Thought or proposition is possible iff it is true according to some admissible assignment.

> A Thought or proposition is necessary iff it is true according to all admissible assignments.

We call these two displayed biconditionals 'The Characterization of Possibility' and 'The Characterization of Necessity' (sometimes simply 'Chzn') respectively.

These truth conditions suggest a corresponding account of understanding. That account states that when we evaluate modal claims in our ordinary modal thought and reasoning, we draw on our implicit grasp of the body of information stated in the Principles of Possibility, understood as including the Characterizations of Possibility and Necessity. (I give this formulation to respect the point that one and the same body of information may be captured in many different axiomatizations.) To understand the metaphysical modalities is to have tacit knowledge of the above Principles of Possibility, and to draw on that knowledge in one's evaluation of modal sentences and Thoughts. It is also required for genuine understanding that this body of information which is drawn upon in evaluating the modal sentences and Thoughts is fundamental, rather than being derivative from some other condition. If a person possesses the body of misinformation that a sentence is necessary just in case its necessity follows from the principles listed in a certain book, or accepted by a certain community, or whatever, where these principles are in fact the Principles of Possibility, then that person does not properly understand modality.

Henceforth, I will call this conception the *principle-based conception* of metaphysical modality and our understanding thereof. The principle-based conception is an example of the model of implicitly known principles of the sort mentioned at the end of Chapter 2.

An important point about the Modal Extension Principle—one it took me some years to notice—is that it operates recursively. It is self-applicable; it applies to the concept which it helps to define. The Modal Extension Principle, when taken together with the other Principles of Possibility, fixes a rule for determining the actual extension of the concept *admissible*. The Modal Extension Principle can then be applied to the concept *admissible* itself.

This point has a twofold significance. First, it permits a treatment of the truth conditions of sentences and Thoughts containing iterated modalities. Iteration requires us to consider what is admissibly admissible. We will make use of recursive application of the Modal Extension Principle in Appendix A below, in discussing which logic is validated by the principle-based conception.

Second, recursive application of the Modal Extension Principle is crucial in solving a major and apparently formidable dilemma of a structural character which arises for the principle-based conception, and for any conception of a similar general kind. The principle-based conception gives a characterization of necessity: we just gave it in the form of a biconditional a few paragraphs back. Now is this characterization being said to be necessary, or is it not being said to be necessary? If it is not being said to be necessary, the theory will hardly carry much conviction. (We are not merely in the business of characterizing properties which happen to coincide with necessity.) And, once again, we will in any case require the necessity of any such characterization if we are properly to account for the truth conditions of iterated modalities. On the other hand, if we simply add to the principle-based conception the assertion that its characterization of necessity is itself necessary, will this not be a use of necessity which has not been explained in terms of the Principles of Possibility? The theory, and any theory like it—for the problem does not turn on the details of the characterization of necessity—seems to be stuck between a rock and a hard place.

Recursive application of the Modal Extension Principle solves the problem. Structurally, the way to solve the problem is to show that the necessity of the offered characterization follows from the non-modal biconditional, under the principle-based conception's *own* characterization of modality. This can be done by recursive application of the Modal Extension Principle. The Characterization of Necessity above gives the rule which determines the actual extension of 'necessarily'—that is, the propositions or Thoughts to which it can be truly prefixed. This rule uses the notion of admissibility, as constrained by the Modal Extension Principle, amongst others. The rule for determining the actual extension of 'necessarily' can then be taken as one of the objects of application of the Modal Extension Principle. When it is so taken, we see that it follows from the Modal Extension Principle that in any admissible assignment *s*, the semantic value of *necessarily* will include precisely those propositions or Thoughts which are true under all assignments which are admissible according to *s*. Hence, according to any admissible assignment, the above Characterization of Necessity will be true. But this is precisely what it is for it to be necessary, under the principle-based conception. So we have secured the desired result. The principle-based conception need not become stuck between a rock and a hard place provided it applies the Modal Extension Principle recursively.

Recursive self-application of the Modal Extension Principle is not merely a trick with no intuitive foundation. On the contrary, there are strong pretheoretical intuitions supporting the claim, implied by such self-application, that the Modal Extension Principle is itself necessary. It is hard to think of any merely contingent feature of the actual world upon which the truth of the Modal Extension Principle depends. Consider a possible world *w* at which—*per impossibile*—the semantic value of a concept *C* with respect to some possibly (from *w*) admissible assignment is not fixed in accordance with the rule which fixes its actual semantic value. (Here I am taking the Modal Extension Principle in its Unified version.) That is, the semantic value is not fixed by applying the same rule which, when applied to the actual world, yields its actual semantic value. There could not then be any good answer to the charge that we have lost touch with what is involved in making something a possibility for that very concept C. This is a piece of intuitive pretheoretical reasoning in support of the necessity of the Modal Extension Principle.

Similar reasoning seems to apply with equal force to any merely possibly possible world; and to any possibly possibly possible world; and so forth. For any such world, if the semantic value there of C were fixed by a different rule than is applied in the actual world, we would not really have the same concept any more. Again, if this intuitive reasoning is sound, we have arbitrary finite necessitations of the Modal Extension Principle—that is, it is necessary, necessarily necessary, necessarily necessarily necessary, ... The intuitive reasoning of this and the preceding paragraph is not strictly part of the principle-based conception, but is an articulation of the modal intuitions which support it.

The principle-based conception is an also actualist conception. Given our approach, it has to be. An unreduced notion of a merely possible object is not explicable in terms of a predicate of possibility which applies to our specifications, which are sets of Thoughts and propositions built up from actual object properties and relations. The actualist is not, however, committed to endorsing only model theories in which the domain of every possible world is a subset of the domain of the actual world. That would involve a commitment to endorsing the intuitively invalid Barcan formula, that if everything is necessarily F, then necessarily everything is F. The actualist can acknowledge the possibility of objects which do not actually exist, provided that these are constructed from the materials of the actual world. I resist the temptation to pursue an actualist programme here in more detail, and just note that the obligations and challenges faced by any actualist theory are equally faced by the principle-based conception as I have formulated it.

The principle-based conception is part of an attempt to meet the Integration Challenge which adopts the first of the six options outlined in Chapter 1, the option of reconceiving the metaphysics of the domain in question. It contrasts with approaches which adopt the fourth option identified there, that of offering slimmed-down truth conditions which do not purport to capture the full purported meaning of sentences about the area in question. In particular, the principle-based conception contrasts with those forms of fictionalism about the modal which pursue that fourth option. A particularly clear and illuminating statement of one fictionalist option has been given by Gideon Rosen.[27] The modal fictionalist treats talk of possible worlds as fiction. He regards modal discourse as answerable to what holds in the relevant piece of fiction. In Rosen's development, the modal fictionalist proceeds as follows. Let PW be a formulation of the modal realist's theory of possible worlds, such as is given by David Lewis in *On the Plurality of Worlds*. For any modal sentence P, let P^* be the translation of P into a non-modal sentence of the language of PW. In Rosen's treatment, the modal fictionalist asserts instances of the schema

P if and only if according to PW, P^*.[28]

Such pressure as there is towards the use of the modal realist's translations in an account of the meaning of modal sentences seems to me relieved if we can give an adequate account of the understanding, truth conditions, and epistemology of the modal using the Principles of Possibility and ersatz possible worlds. But, more particularly, I want to consider Rosen's response to the charge of fetishism which the modal fictionalist must face.

The charge of fetishism lodged against the modal fictionalist is that there is no saying what is so special about the theory PW of possible worlds which is mentioned in the schema asserted by the modal fictionalist. Since the fictionalist does not take the theory PW to be true, why should we be peculiarly interested in what follows from it, rather than from some other theory? Rosen considers as a potentially fruitful response the reply that 'PW derives its "authority" from being an explicit formulation of our own imaginative habits'.[29] I have two comments. First, it is not clear why our imaginative habits are not equally well captured by the Principles of Possibility. Those principles include the Principle of Constrained Recombination, which certainly plays an important part in imagining possibilities. It is hard to find anything in our pretheoretical imaginings which suggests that we may be going further, and employing a conception of a plurality of Lewisian concrete worlds. Second, the question arises of the connection between an accurate formulation of the procedures we follow in imagination, when thinking about possibilities, and the *correctness* of those procedures. On the treatment I have been offering, the connection is immediate, because the Principles of Possibility that I

---

[27] G. Rosen, 'Modal Fictionalism', *Mind* 99 (1990), 327–54.
[28] Ibid. 335.
[29] Ibid. 353.

would say are used in guiding our imaginings are the very same ones which contribute to the determination of the truth values of modal sentences in a quite specific way: a modal sentence is true only if it conforms to the Principles of Possibility. But the fictionalist cannot take exactly the same attitude to realistic possible-worlds theory, since he does not think it is true. Perhaps the fictionalist would say that the procedures used in imagination are correct, because the Principle of Plenitude is one of the principles of the theory *PW*. But this response reopens, rather than answers, the question of why *PW* rather than some other theory matters to us. The response appeals back to *PW*, rather than providing a source for the authority of *PW*. The charge of fetishism stands if that is the only answer that can be given. The problem is not specific to the choice of *PW*: it would arise whatever theory the fictionalist put in the place occupied by *PW* in Rosen's account. It begins to look as if it is only on a more radical theory, on which modal sentences are made true by our imaginings, or are, as a matter of meaning, expressive of them, that the appeal to imagination can do work in answering the charge of fetishism. This leads us into consideration of a rather different kind of theory of the modal, to which I return in section 4.6 below.

4.4 MODALISM, UNDERSTANDING, REDUCTION

What is the relation between the principle-based conception and what is sometimes called 'modalism'?

Modalism has received various non-equivalent characterizations, but one idea central to it is that we have some grasp of the notions of possibility and necessity which is explanatorily prior to any under-standing of possible worlds. At first blush, the principle-based con-ception, with its use of the Characterizations of Necessity and Possibility, may seem incompatible with modalism. For implicit knowledge of these characterizations is said to be partially explana-tory of understanding, and the characterizations explain modality by mentioning specifications which are possible. And are not these gen-uinely possible specifications—to all intents and purposes—possible worlds? They are not the Lewisian modal realist's possible worlds, to be sure, but they are fine 'ersatz' worlds.

Such a claim of incompatibility would, however, be superficial. A central motivation for modalism was the idea that there are constraints involving possibility and necessity that determine which worlds are possible: the possibility of a world is dependent upon its satisfaction of these constraints. The Principles of Possibility I have been outlining are precisely such constraints. They are just what is needed to make specific one central idea of modalism.

We should, then, distinguish between what we can call *constraint modalism* and *ontological modalism*. Constraint modalism is the doctrine that there are constraints involving the notion of possibility which are explanatorily prior to whether a world is possible or not. A supporter of constraint modalism can consistently quantify over possible worlds of an ersatz kind, and use such quantification in the explanation of modal discourse, so long as the possible worlds he so uses are conceived as derivative from the satisfaction of various constraints involving the notion of possibility. Ontological modalism, by contrast, states that possible worlds have no part to play in the elucidation and understanding of modal discourse. The ontological modalist will insist that 'necessarily' is never in any way to be understood as a quantifier. The letter of the principle-based conception I have presented is indeed in conflict with ontological modalism, for I have quantified over worlds, of a sort, in talking of the genuinely possible specifications. But the letter of the formulations could be altered. If we become convinced, for one reason or another, of the truth of ontological modalism, we could adapt the main ideas I have put forward to square with it. For instance, in assessing whether two propositions are compossible, we would have to ask whether they could both be true only in circumstances in which the semantic value of some concept is not fixed in the way it actually is; and so forth. In short, we could maintain the core ideas of the principle-based conception without quantifying over worlds at all.[30] Ontological modalism is really orthogonal to the main claims of this chapter. I do myself, though, think that, once we have an account of the understanding of possibility, it would be straining at a gnat to object to possible worlds set-theoretically constructed using the principle-based conception of possibility.

It cannot be said that all of the literature of the seventies and early eighties was completely clear on these matters (I certainly suspect that

[30] For an exchange which is primarily concerned with ontological modalism, see J. Melia, 'Against Modalism', *Philosophical Studies* 68 (1992), 35–56, and G. Forbes, 'Melia on Modalism', *Philosophical Studies* 68 (1992), 57–63.

I was confused myself). Disquotational truth theories for necessity were developed in that period by Martin Davies, Anil Gupta, and myself.[31] Some of the literature of that period reads as if these disquotational truth theories are all that is required by way of a theory of meaning and understanding for modality. I would now say that a disquotational truth theory can never by itself give us a full account of what is involved in understanding an expression, even though it is a necessary part of a full account, and constrains the additional parts of the required full account. The disquotational theory cannot by itself answer (for instance) the questions of section 4.1 above, the questions raised by the inapplicability to modality of models of understanding available and appropriate for other primitive expressions. The question then arises: from the perspective of the principle-based conception, how should we understand the relation between a truth theory for necessity and the substantive account of understanding involving implicit knowledge of the Principles of Possibility?

For any substantive account of understanding a particular expression, we should aim to give a dovetailing account of its contribution to truth conditions. If we do not succeed in that aim, we will not have explained how the expression, when understood in the way specified in the account of understanding, is also capable of occurring in truth-evaluable sentences. So it would be absurd to regard a substantive theory of understanding a particular expression as somehow in competition with a truth-conditional theory for it. The theory of understanding requires the existence of a dovetailing truth-conditional theory. What is involved in the relation of dovetailing is one of the central issues in the theory of intentional content. It must involve at least the kind of integration of epistemology with the truth conditions discussed as a desideratum back in Chapter 2, and in the first section of this chapter. For the principle-based account of understanding of necessity, the dovetailing takes a particular form. The conditions which are implicitly known in understanding necessity are just those which do determine the truth conditions of modal statements.

For any substantive account of understanding, issues of soundness

---

[31] M. Davies, 'Weak Necessity and Truth Theories', *Journal of Philosophical Logic* 7 (1978), 415–39; A. Gupta, 'Modal Logic and Truth', *Journal of Philosophical Logic* 7 (1978), 441–72; C. Peacocke, 'Necessity and Truth Theories', *Journal of Philosophical Logic* 7 (1978), 473–500.

and completeness also arise.[32] By soundness, as applied to this treatment of modality, I mean the following: every proposition, sentence, or Thought which is genuinely possible is true according to some admissible assignment. I hope this is plausible by inspection of the Principles of Possibility, taken collectively.

We should also aim for completeness: that any proposition, sentence, or Thought which is genuinely possible is true according to some admissible assignment. At the moment, I simply note this as an important commitment of the approach I am advocating. It will be crucial in section 4.5, when we come to discuss epistemological matters. The commitment is one which sharply differentiates the principle-based conception from Lewisian modal realism, under which it is not apparent why any such claim of completeness should be true.

This general treatment in terms of the Principles of Possibility which I have been offering is in itself neutral on the issue of whether there exists a genuinely reductive analysis of necessity and possibility. It would plausibly contribute to a reductive account if two further conditions were met. First, we would have to have a set of Principles of Possibility which we could reasonably believe to be exhaustive (for some background range of objects, properties, relations and concepts). Second, we would have to be convinced that none of the auxiliary concepts used either in formulating or in deploying the Principles of Possibility rely on modal notions. If these two further conditions were met, then an enthusiast for reduction could define a possible specification as one which respects the allegedly complete set of principles. This is a big 'if'. The Principles of Possibility include constitutive principles, and it takes hard philosophical thought to discover what is constitutive of a given property or relation. Who is ever in a position to say that there are not more constitutive principles to be discovered about the objects, properties, and relations in our ontology? It does not seem at all necessary to believe that both those two conditions are met in order to regard the principle-based conception as promising. Even someone who is sceptical of the possibility of reduction will still be making progress if he identifies certain central Principles of Possibility and argues that implicit knowledge of those principles is involved in our understanding and knowledge of modal truths. He can then go on to say that

---

[32] See my 'Sense, Truth and Understanding', written 1991, forthcoming in J. Higginbotham (ed.), *Language and Cognition* (Oxford: Blackwell).

our very general grasp of the notion of possibility involves some implicit grasp of the idea of a set of Principles of Possibility of which it may always be an open question whether it has completely captured the relevant constitutive principles.[33]

A more specific doubt that the principle-based conception can be reductive, one that might even be elevated into an objection of circularity, is that the notion of identity of rule, or of identity of concept, has to be explicated modally. For example, it may be objected that the only reason that we say the same rule is applied in determining the extension of *bachelor* as is applied in determining the extension of *unmarried man* is that it is necessary that all and only bachelors are unmarried men.

In this formulation, the objection misunderstands the principle-based conception. The identity of rules and concepts is fixed at a level having to do with informativeness and epistemic possibility, the level of sense. The position of the principle-based conception is that we do not in general (*de jure* rigid cases aside) need to appeal to the truth or falsity of object-language modal sentences to explain what is involved in someone's employing one concept rather than another, nor to explain the identity of concepts and rules.

A more persistent objector may say that even in the principle-based conception as here explicated, modality is in the wings. For in the classical neo-Fregean explication of identity of concepts *C* and *D*, do we not say that there is no *possible* circumstance in which a pair of thoughts *A*(*C*) and *A*(*D*) differ in cognitive significance? So the objection is that the very notion of concept we are employing, and the notion of a way of fixing a semantic value which goes with it, already involves the notion of metaphysical necessity. To this there are two responses. The first is that identity of concepts may be explained in constitutive terms, in terms of what it *is* to possess one concept rather than another. Modal facts about informativeness can then be regarded as consequential upon this constitutive level. That is the position to which I am most tempted.[34] It has to be granted, though, that we need a better understanding of the constitutive and the nature

---

[33] Reductive aspirations would also be unattainable if a conception of how things actually are could not be fully non-modal. For some further discussion, see section 4. 5 below.

[34] My own previous writings have not consistently stuck to the position endorsed here. In some of them, talk of the modal would be better replaced with talk of the constitutive.

of its links to the modal. Even if this first response were quite unavailable, however, there is a different response to the challenge. The use of modality in the identity condition for concepts is a use of modality by us as theorists. It is not a use by the thinker whose mastery of concepts is being characterized. The distinction is important. It means that the alleged circularity is no more objectionable than, for instance, our using logical vocabulary—as we can hardly avoid doing—in giving an account of a thinker's understanding of the logical constants. These uses of modality outside the scope of the thinker's own attitudes would not at all reduce the principle-based conception to vacuity. We have already seen how the principle-based conception can be used in the explanation of the truth of some necessities. The logical, epistemic, and understanding-theoretic uses to which I am about to put the principle-based conception equally do not require a definitional reduction of modality. They would not be undermined by our using modal operators in the metalanguage in our account of understanding.

4.5 THE EPISTEMOLOGY OF METAPHYSICAL NECESSITY

We can divide questions about the relations between modality and knowledge into two broad kinds. There are questions about how certain particular methods can succeed in producing knowledge of modal truths. There are also questions about the general relations between modal truth and knowability. Let us consider some issues about particular methods first. Here we are aiming to carry out the task of the kind we identified back in condition (c), in section 2.3 in Chapter 2. We are aiming to show that the methods for which the Integration Challenge arises in the modal case are ratifiable as sound, by reference to their relations to methods mentioned in the possession conditions for necessity and possibility proposed two sections back (4.3).

The Principles of Possibility fix the concept of possibility. Suppose that understanding modal discourse does involves implicit knowledge of these Principles of Possibility. We can then see why some common methods of establishing or refuting particular modal claims are appropriate to the content of those claims. 'Necessarily, p' is sometimes established by giving a proof of p. There may be an outright proof of *p*—a proof in which all premises are discharged—or *p* may be proved from other propositions whose necessity is already established. The following is a sufficient condition for proofs of each of these kinds to be sound methods of establishing a necessity: that each of the inferential principles relied upon in the proof, besides being valid, contains essentially only expressions whose semantic values are constant across admissible assignments. We argued that the propositional logical constants are just such expressions.

For quantifiers, our formulations must be adapted to take account of varying domains of existents for different specifications. Suppose an actual object *x* is not in the domain of admissible assignment *s*. The actual semantic value of *every* will map a first-level function *f* to the truth value True only if *f* maps *x* to the True. (For brevity, I ignore variable-binding apparatus in making the point.) But we cannot require that what *s* assigns to *every* be a second-level function mapping a first-level function to the True only if the function maps *x* to the True. The semantic value of *every* according to *s* is rather that function which maps a first-level function *f* to the True if and only if for every object *y* in the domain of *s*, *f* maps *y* to the True. This variation in semantic value of quantifiers over admissible assignments is in accord with what determines their actual semantic value. The semantic value of *every* according to an assignment depends on the domain of the assignment in just the way that the actual semantic value of *every* depends on what actually exists. The logical laws governing the quantifiers still hold under all admissible assignments.

When the inferential principles in a proof contain essentially only propositional logical constants or quantifiers, the validity of the inferential principles for the actual world will carry over to any other genuinely possible specification. So any such proof in which all premises are discharged, or there is antecedent reason for believing in the necessity of its premises, is a proof which justifies belief in the necessity of its conclusions.

This is only a sufficient condition for the success of those methods of establishing a necessity. It is not a necessary condition. There are cases in which the expressions occurring essentially in a proof's principles of inference do not have constant semantic values across admissible assignments, where the variation goes far beyond the quantifier-like case of mere variation with the domain of the assignment, and yet the proof can still establish a necessity. It is enough if the conditions fixing the semantic values of the expressions, together with the Modal Extension Principle, ensure that the principle of inference is truth-preserving in every admissible assignment, even when the semantic values vary across assignments radically (and not merely with the domain). Such is the humble case of the inference from *t is a bachelor* to *t is a man*. This kind of case, together with the other two outlined in the preceding paragraphs, between them cover a large part of the territory in which we establish a necessity by means of a demonstration.

When our concern is rather to refute a claim of necessity, we have to invoke more than the Modal Extension Principle. Suppose we are concerned with the a priori content 'I am here', and that we want to show that it is not necessary. Given that 'I' and 'here' are *de jure* rigid, the Second Part of the Modal Extension Principle applies. But the Modal Extension Principle by itself does not imply that there is a genuinely possible specification according to which the actual utterer of 'I' is located somewhere else. For that, we have to rely on the Principle of Constrained Recombination, that a specification is possible if it respects the full set of Principles of Possibility. This need to appeal to Constrained Recombination accords with our pretheoretical awareness that any claim of the existence of a genuinely possible specification according to which the actual utterer or thinker is somewhere else can always be defeated by showing that it violates some constraint on possibility.

If it is granted that implicit knowledge of the Principles of Possibility is appropriately employed in reaching a modal judgement, we can also see how the judgement so reached can be knowledge. Provided that any non-modal principles upon which she relies are known, a thinker's modal judgements reached by the proper use of the implicit knowledge of the Principles of Possibility will, in the nature of the case, be knowledge. This is not only a matter of reliability. The judgement of the modal truth is explained by the thinker's implicit grasp of principles which *make* the modal truth hold. It is a constitutive, and a priori, matter that judgements which come to be made by drawing upon this information will be true. By contrast, the familiar kinds of counterexamples to pure reliability theories of knowledge involve reliability which is by no means a priori or constitutive.

In the principle-based conception, knowledge of particular necessities and possibilities does not require dubiously intelligible faculties connecting the thinker with some modal realm. So it seems that we have objectivity of modal discourse and a means of knowing modal truths, without obscure faculties, and without being modal realists in Lewis's sense. This is how the principle-based conception of modality integrates its epistemology with its metaphysics.

This treatment of the Integration Challenge in the modal case both respects and relies on the Linking Thesis of Chapter 2. The materials above permit formulation of a theory of possession of the concept of metaphysical necessity in which the very Principles of Possibility which fix modal truth are also mentioned in an account of the conditions under which modal contents are known, by way of those principles being contents of the understander's tacit knowledge. It is because of this connection between truth, understanding, and knowledge that the ordinary means we take to establish modal truth do not fall short of reaching modal truth and genuine modal knowledge. In the case of a mathematical belief which is also knowledge, Benaceraff wrote that 'it must be possible to link up what it is for p to be true with my belief that p'.[35] In the case of a modal belief which is also knowledge, it is tacit knowledge of the Principles of Possibility which makes us able to link up what it is for p to be true with the belief that p.

I do not mean to imply that a thinker who understands modal operators cannot make mistakes. On the contrary, she evidently can. The apparatus I have introduced itself contains many points at which mistakes can be made, even by one who fully understands modality. One source of error is a mistakes about the nature of the rule which determines the extension of a given concept in the actual world. Someone who is in error about this may make an erroneous modal judgement, even though she has implicit knowledge of the Modal Extension Principle. Another possible source of error is mistakes about which properties give the kind-essence of an object. A third possible source of error comes in application of the principle of plenitude, the Principle of Constrained Recombination of section 4.3 above. One may err in thinking that an assignment respects all the other conditions on admissibility, and thus judge something to be possible when it is not so. Finally, non-modal errors, both factual and logical, may lead to erroneous modal judgements. There is, then, plenty of room for modal error, even on the part of one who fully understands modal notions.

Implicit knowledge of the Principles of Possibility seems to be

[35] Benaceraff, 'Mathematical Truth', 409.

rather closer to the operations of reason at the personal level than is the classic Chomskian case of tacit knowledge of the principles of grammar of our natural language. There are certainly respects in which the two cases are on a par, in particular in respect of their role in content-involving psychological explanation. But there are different subspecies of implicit knowledge. Your judgement that a string of words is grammatical does not result from conscious inference. If asked why a sentence that seems to you grammatical is so, you may or may not be able to come up with reasons. But even if you can, the reasons you come up with will not have been operative in the production of your initial perceptual impression of the grammaticality of the sentence. By contrast, when an ordinary thinker makes a judgement of possibility or necessity for himself, not on the basis of testimony, he will have reasons. In the case of a judgement of possibility, there will be some conception of a possible state of affairs in which the possibility obtains; in the case of a reasonable judgement of necessity, there will be some informal demonstration or proof of the proposition, or some reasonable belief that one exists. The ordinary user of modal notions cannot state the Principles of Possibility, but nevertheless the Principles of Possibility bear a much closer relation to his personal-level modal thought than do the principles of grammar to his thought about his own language. It is a question worth further thought what that relation is.

In some very unproblematic cases, an attribution of implicit knowledge is justified simply because it systematizes, and does no more than make explicit, the general principles of which a thinker has explicitly used instances, even if he has not stated the generalizations himself. Such would presumably be the case when we justifiably attribute implicit knowledge of the Peano axioms to nineteenth-century arithmeticians prior to their explicit formulation. Attribution of implicit knowledge of the Principles of Possibility certainly goes beyond that very simple case, since the Principles of Possibility employ concepts which are not simply generalizations of instances the thinker is already using at the personal level. The talk, for instance, of the way in which semantic value is fixed, in the Modal Extension Principle, goes far beyond such generalization. On the other hand, it is arguable that some inchoate appreciation of the Modal Extension Principle is responsible for our judgements that certain specifications are, or are not, genuine possibilities. As I said, those judgements seem to be based on reasons which go beyond a mere immediate impression that their content is correct. What explains the patterns of reasons we take as supporting or refuting modal claims is our implicit grasp of the Modal Extension Principle and the other Principles of Possibility. In order not to divert our attention too far from the topic of this section, the epistemology of modality, I will not pursue these important issues about implicit knowledge here. I confine myself to noting that to elaborate the nature of the implicit knowledge involved in modal understanding we will have to consider other areas where implicit knowledge interacts with reason-guided capacities. My own view is that implicit knowledge is a notion we need to use in explaining understanding in many other cases, including even understanding of the ordinary logical constants.[36]

I now turn to what seems to me to be the more difficult of the two epistemological questions distinguished at the start of this section, the question of the general relation between the metaphysical modalities and knowability. On this topic, I wish to propose three general theses. I will try to make the three theses plausible by consideration of examples. The theses are all principles whose truth would be explained if possibility is constrained by the Principles of Possibility I have formulated.

> **Thesis (I).** In every case in which a modal truth involving metaphysical necessity or possibility is unknowable by us, its unknowability is wholly explained either by the unknowability by us of some truth not involving metaphysical modalities, or by the unknowability by us of one of the Principles of Possibility.

Let me first illustrate Thesis (I) in various ways, before discussing its significance. Take Goldbach's Conjecture, that every even number is the sum of two primes. If this conjecture is true but unprovable, it is none the less necessary. Its necessity is unknowable (by us) if its truth is. The unknowability of its necessity, if it is unknowable, is wholly explained by the unknowability of its truth. The general principle that any truth of arithmetic is necessary is knowable and known. What we do not know is the totality of thoughts to which this known general principle can be applied.

A wide range of examples with empirical elements also falls

---

[36] For further discussion of implicit knowledge and understanding, see my 'Implicit Conceptions, Understanding and Rationality'.

straightforwardly within the ambit of Thesis (I). It may now be unknowable whether the colourless liquid in the bottle on the kitchen table two years ago was water or vinegar. Suppose it was water. Then, concerning the liquid in that bottle at that time, it was necessarily H_2O. 'Concerning the liquid in that bottle at that time, it was necessarily H_2O' is now unknowable, but its unknowability is wholly explained by the unknowability of whether it was water in the bottle.

It is worth noting at least three other subspecies of unknowability consistent with the present framework. First, there is no obvious guarantee that everything which is constitutively involved in possession of a particular concept, even one of our concepts, must be discoverable by us. Undiscovered features may, via the Modal Extension Principle, generate necessary truths.

Second, what has just been said of concepts applies to everything else. There is no obvious reason that we should be able to know the constitutive properties and relations of each item in our ontology. It takes hard philosophical investigation to discover them, and we may be intellectually limited in our ability to attain knowledge of them. Unknowable constitutive properties will equally generate unknowable necessities, via the constitutive Principles of Possibility.[37]

Third, it will be recalled that a specification of a genuine possibility was required to respect the Principles of Possibility. Whether a specification respects the full set of Principles of Possibility (even if they are all known to us) is not, outside specially restricted cases, a decidable relation. After all, the specification may mention propositions of mathematics, set theory, or of higher-order logic. So in some cases a genuinely possible specification cannot be known by us to be so. This too will generate modal truths which cannot be known by us. But the explanation of the unknowability involves a general logical phenomenon which applies to any subject matter whatever. It has nothing to do with the existence of any inaccessible modal realm.[38]

---

[37] The provision of a general theory of the constitutive, as opposed to the modal, seems to me to be an urgent task for philosophy. We certainly do not want all the initial puzzlement about modality simply to be transferred to the domain of the constitutive. Only a satisfactory general theory of the constitutive, and an attendant epistemology, can allay this concern.

[38] Suppose consistency is explained in model-theoretic terms which involve set theory. If set theory were itself to be explained in modal terms, then the unknowability of some instances of the relation of consistency would trace back after all to the unknowability of certain modal truths—thus contradicting Thesis (I). So either set theory is not to be understood in modal terms (or at least not those of 'meta-

If Thesis (I) is correct, it has a twofold importance. Its first important consequence is that the existence of unknowable modal truths cannot, without further argument, be used to support a position according to which modal truth goes beyond what is fixed by a set of Principles of Possibility of at least the general kind I have given. (I write 'general kind', because of course it is entirely possible that I have omitted some principles which ought to be included with the Principles of Possibility.) In particular, it is fallacious to argue from the fact that the particular Principles of Possibility I have suggested are knowable, together with the existence of some unknowable modal truths, to the conclusion that the present approach must be incorrect. The onus is rather on one of the other parties to this discussion, the Lewisian modal realist. If Thesis (I), or anything very close to it, is correct, it presents a problem for the Lewisian modal realist. How a modal realist could account for Thesis (I) or anything close to it I do not know. He cannot account for it by regarding his possible worlds as merely reflections of what is permitted by a set of Principles of Possibility. That would be to give up the modal realism. But if he does not so regard the possible worlds, Thesis (I) remains unexplained by the modal realist.

The other significant feature of Thesis (I) is the strong contrast it points up between modality and tense, despite the many well-known and undisputed formal parallels between them. We explained the existence of, for instance, unknowable arithmetical necessities by remarking that we know a priori that, if p is a true arithmetical content, then necessarily p. If Thesis (I) is correct, there will be similar conditionals for other domains about whose members there are unknowable truths. Absolutely nothing analogous holds for the past. There is no class of present-tense contingent a posteriori propositions p, not already about the past, for which we know a priori conditionals of the form: if p, then in the past p. What makes some thoughts about the past presently unknowable cannot be explained satisfactorily by citing the unknowability of some truths not about the past, which in turn are sufficient for truths about the past. Similarly, there is no set of a priori 'principles of the past', analogous to the Principles

---

physical' modality), or the relation of consistency is not to be understood in model-theoretic terms. If both of these alternatives are untenable, but the approach to understanding modality in terms of a set of principles of possibility is correct, then Thesis (I) will be false.

of Possibility, which collectively distinguish a past-tense operator from other operators, and grasp of which is fundamental to understanding past-tense discourse. No set of purely a priori principles can, together with purely present-tense truths, settle the truth value of a statement like 'Yesterday there was a place in Greenland with a temperature of −100° Celsius'.

The present unknowability of some statements about the past has a source which is different in kind from the two potential sources of unknowable modal truths, namely, unknowable non-modal truths and, perhaps, some unknowable Principles of Possibility. We can conceive of the truth of some past-tense statement being unknowable because we can conceive, in principle, of some past state of affairs leaving no traces now accessible to us which would identify it. By contrast, any unknowable modal truths are not such that, if only they were embedded in the world in such a way that they left the right traces accessible to us now, then we would be able to know them. On the contrary, even the known modal truths are not known about because of their causal interactions with us. The defence of the intelligibility of unknowable past-tense truths would also, correspondingly, draw on resources not present in the modal case.

I also suggest a second thesis.

> **Thesis (II).** In every case in which a content containing a metaphysical modality is known, any modal premises in the ultimate justification which underwrites the status of the belief as knowledge are a priori premises.

Thesis (II) implies that any a posteriori premises in the ultimate justification for a piece of modal knowledge will not themselves be modal. A paradigm, and maximally simple, example of Thesis (II) is knowledge of the necessity that Hesperus is Phosphorus. The justification for this belief consists of two parts. One part is the a posteriori, but non-modal, knowledge that Hesperus is Phosphorus. The other part is the modal, but a priori, general knowledge of the necessity of the identity relation, in cases in which it holds. There is an analogous division into two parts of our justification for believing in particular instances of Kripke's a posteriori necessities of constitution and of origin. Thesis (II) is, of course, wholly consistent with Kripke's famous discussion and treatment of his examples.

One of the substantive consequences of Thesis (II) is that principles of constitution and origin always have an a priori component in their ultimate justification. On the conception Thesis (II) is elaborating, though it is a posteriori that humans originate in sperm and egg cells, it can be known a priori that whatever the origins of any given individual human, they are essential to that individual. This implication of Thesis (II) deserves consideration in its own right. One of the attractions of Thesis (II) is its potential for making the epistemology of constitutive claims less problematic. A full defence of Thesis (II) would also need to draw some more distinctions involving the a priori. Some philosophers have held that horses necessarily descend from a certain stock of animals, and that animals with a physiology and genetics identical with that of ordinary horses, but descending from a different stock, would not be horses. Let us suppose that this is so. (If it is not so, consider a natural-kind concept for which the corresponding claim of necessity does hold, for, these theorists would claim, there could be such a concept and we can adapt the discussion accordingly.) It seems also that a particular thinker could have attitudes properly described as involving the concept *horse* without being in a position to know a priori that horses necessarily descend from a certain stock. This thinker may have seen many horses, and correctly apply the word to them. He may not know, though, that they are biological entities—to adapt a remark of Putnam's, he may even believe that they are remotely controlled devices. So this thinker is certainly not in a position to know a priori that horses necessarily descend from the stock from which they actually descend—he does not even know that they descend from some stock. How is the defender of Thesis (II) to respond to this challenge?

He might react by saying that we already know that merely partial understanding suffices for attribution of attitudes whose content involves the concept *horse*. The defender of Thesis (II) might, then, aim to use a notion of the a priori on which we can say that a Thought is a priori if someone—not necessarily every possessor of the concepts it involves—can know it a priori. Some merely partial understanders of the expression would not be in a position to reach such a priori knowledge, but full understanders would, on this view.

This reaction does not, though, seem to me entirely adequate to the nature and the extent of the phenomenon. Consider another Putnam-inspired example. We may explore the remains of a newly discovered ancient civilization, and come across brightly decorated objects we take to be ancient ornamental items attached to clothing. We may introduce a word for these objects. It may turn out later that these objects are actually a species of brightly coloured hibernating beetle. If they are so, then they necessarily come from the actual stock of beetles from which they are descended (or, if 'beetle' does not work like that, we can introduce some notion which does). It is quite implausible, though, to say just after the word was introduced and before the true nature of the objects was discovered that someone who fully understood the word would be in a position to know this modal truth. No one could have known a priori that these objects were descended from any stock at all, as opposed to having been designed by human beings. Learning that they are biological objects is simply an empirical discovery.

A better reaction is to note that even in this case, someone who holds that organisms of a given species necessarily come from the actual stock from which they are descended will also hold the following proposition to be a priori: that if some kind of organism is self-reproducing, members of that kind necessarily come from the stock they do. What is empirical, for these theorists, in this most recent example is that objects of the newly discovered sort are organisms of a kind which reproduce. The (claimed) modal and a priori proposition is just that organisms of kinds whose members reproduce necessarily come from the stock they do. Such, at any rate, would have to be the position of one who wants to defend those modal claims in the context of a principle-based treatment of modality.

Thesis (II) is a consequence of the treatment in terms of Principles of Possibility, if the Principles of Possibility are a priori. The particular Principles of Possibility I have suggested have an a priori status. It is true that I have drawn back from claiming that we know all the Principles of Possibility, so an argument from case-by-case enumeration of the Principles of Possibility actually cited will not establish that all are a priori. But I do suggest that we have no conception of how some being, intellectually more powerful than us and who knows Principles of Possibility which we could not, could know them in anything other than an a priori manner. If we agree that something's being necessarily the case cannot causally explain anything, we already have an explanation for the impossibility of such a posteriori knowledge. A posteriori methods can produce, and rationally produce, various beliefs in us, but they cannot by themselves produce knowledge that something is necessary. We cannot at this point apply the model of our knowledge of the a posteriori but necessary truth that Hesperus is Phosphorus. That model worked only because there was also a priori knowledge of the general principle of the necessity of identity. In the present case we are *ex hypothesi* concerned with fundamental Principles of Possibility, which are not inferred from anything else. If the fundamental principles were a posteriori, there would in the nature of the case be no further a priori principles to which we could back up in an account of justification, on pain of their not after all being fundamental.

If this line of thought is sound, we have prima facie reason to make a claim not merely about actual cases of modal knowledge, as Thesis (II) does, but about all possible cases. We can propose:

> **Thesis (III).** Thesis (II) is necessary, and holds for all possible knowers.[39]

Thesis (II), like the principle-based conception itself, has a highly Leibnizian flavour. What really matters to Leibniz in what he calls innateness is justifiability, possibly involving definitions, in terms of logical truths which can themselves be seen to be true given an understanding of the terms they contain, and thus are true a priori. In the *New Essays*, Leibniz's protagonist, Theophilus, is asked how he would respond to the challenge to provide some examples of innateness. Theophilus answers: 'I would name to him the propositions of arithmetic and geometry, which are all of that nature; and *among necessary truths no other kind is to be found*' (my italics).[40] Leibniz had, of course, a pre-Fregean conception of logic, and in pre-Kripkean fashion, he also did not sharply distinguish the a priori and the necessary. When we factor out these historical differences, there remains between Leibniz and the present position a core of agreement on the explanation and the epistemology of necessary truths, a core which involves Thesis (II) and the a priori status of the Principles of Possibility.

How would the present account respond to broadly neo-Humean or neo-Quinean problems about the concept of metaphysical necessity? Having said several times that necessity itself cannot be causally influential, I am not about to find after all a suitable impression of necessity from which the idea could be derived. Nor is there any need

---

[39] The conception articulated in these three theses, and the underlying motivations for them, can be used in support of the view of the relations between the a priori and necessity developed in Forbes, *The Metaphysics of Modality*.

[40] G. W. Leibniz, *New Essays on Human Understanding*, trans. and ed. P. Remnant and J. Bennett (Cambridge: Cambridge University Press, 1981), at 86.

to do so, on the principle-based account. The Principles of Possibility must be implicitly known by someone who possesses the concept of metaphysical necessity, but it is not at all required that this knowledge should result from some causal influence of modal facts. The principle-based account and its attendant theory of understanding are both consistent with the principle that there is no impression from which the idea of metaphysical necessity is derived.

A full answer to all the major sceptical doubts about the concept of metaphysical necessity would require defence of all the pieces of apparatus I have deployed. I will not take on that task here. I will, though, briefly consider what conception of the relations between the actual and the possible should go along with the principle-based account. There is, first, on the present account a systematic and general connection between necessary truths and thought about the actual world. The Principles of Possibility fix the truth values of modal contents by relating them to the conditions which individuate particular concepts, and the principles of individuation for the objects and properties we think about. These are the concepts employed, and the things thought about, in thought and discourse about the actual world that do not explicitly involve metaphysical necessity and possibility. The present treatment ties an account of the modal to these aspects of such thought about the actual world. In particular, the operators of metaphysical necessity and possibility, because of their relations to the Modal Extension Principle, can then be described as operators which are *dependent upon the individuation of concepts*. An operator or relation is dependent upon the individuation of concepts when its conditions of application are fixed, in the most fundamental cases, in part by the individuation conditions of the concepts which comprise the thought contents to which it applies, or which form one term of the relation. Besides the metaphysical modalities as applied to thoughts, another example of a concept which I would argue to be dependent upon the individuation of concepts is the relation of a priori justification of one content by another, or by suitable perception or thought.[41]

A question it is sometimes tempting to raise is this: 'Why do we need the concept of necessity at all? Why should we ever need to talk about anything other than the actual world?' One answer to this question is that it is certainly desirable to know of a class of principles

---

[41] See my 'Sense and Justification', *Mind* 101 (1992), 793–816.

which can be legitimately employed when reasoning within the scope of any counterfactual supposition whatever. These principles will be the necessary truths, and we must be able to identify some of them if reasoning within the scope of counterfactual suppositions is to proceed. Indeed, metaphysical necessity can be defined in terms of the counterfactual conditional, as David Lewis noted: 'necessarily p' is equivalent to 'If *not-p* were the case, then A & ¬A would be the case', where A is some arbitrarily selected contradiction.[42] Counterfactuals are also indispensable in practical reasoning. So we can expect some identification of necessary truths to be practically, as well as theoretically, indispensable.

That is a first-pass answer to the question. Whether we can then go on to say more depends in part on which of two metaphysical conceptions we adopt.

We can distinguish between a *fully non-modal conception* of the actual world and a *partially modal conception* thereof. The two conceptions are agreed on the central role of causal relations in the way the world actually is. Many properties are individuated by their causal powers—some have even defined identity of properties in terms of identity of causal powers. It is also arguable that the very idea of a material object is a causal one, perhaps for more than one reason. To be composed of matter is (at least) to stand in certain causal-explanatory relations to the magnitude of force. Material objects also have the property that their later states are explicable in part by their earlier states. If material objects necessarily involve causation, so too will all events individuated in part by their relations to material objects. We could continue in this vein at some length— we have not, for instance, even begun to talk about the role of causation in the mental realm. But these points should already be enough to make it overwhelmingly plausible that causal relations must be inextricably involved in any plausible account of the actual world. The fully non-modal conception and the partially modal conception diverge not on these agreed points, but rather on the nature of causation itself.

[42] See, for instance, D. Lewis, 'Counterfactuals and Comparative Possibility', repr. in his *Philosophical Papers*, vol. ii (New York: Oxford University Press, 1986), at 11. Timothy Williamson also remarked to me that, if counterfactuals with impossible antecedents are vacuously true, then the necessity of p is equivalent to the truth of the counterfactual 'If ¬p were the case, then p would be the case', which avoids the need for the arbitrarily chosen contradiction.

The divergence is over the issue of whether causation itself has to be explained in terms of counterfactuals or not. This need not involve divergence over whether there is a *link* between causation and counterfactuals. Both sides may accept that there is a link; but they will regard it very differently. For the partially modal theorist, the link is something written into the nature of causation, which cannot itself be properly elucidated without reference to counterfactuals. For the fully non-modal theorist, the truth conditions for counterfactuals must be elucidated in such a way that they involve conditions on causal relations whose nature is not dependent upon counterfactuals. Now the partially modal theorist will insist that we need to employ counterfactuals even in the description of the actual world. To try to describe the actual world without using counterfactuals would, for him, to be to try to describe it without making reference, direct or oblique, to causal relations; and that would be impossible.

It would take us too far from our principal topic of metaphysical modality to try to decide between the fully non-modal and the partially modal conceptions (even if I were capable of doing so). One could expect there to be many more rounds to the argument. The partially modal theorist may complain, with some historical justice, that those who have tried to employ a notion of the actual world which is purged of counterfactual notions have had to use devices which seem clearly inadequate. Nelson Goodman once wrote: 'The fictive accident to a given train under the hypothetical circumstance that a given rail was missing can be taken care of, for example, by saying that the train at that time was "accidentable", or, more fully, "rail-missing-accidentable".'[43] Such hyphenated predicates are a paradigm case for applying Davidson's demand that it should be explained how the meaning of the complex depends upon the meaning of its constituents.[44] The first-pass attempt to do so would reintroduce the counterfactual locution. That is a challenge to which the fully non-modal conception must respond if it is to be a viable option.

One challenge the fully non-modal theorist faces is that of giving an account of causal laws consistent with his general position. Important steps have been taken towards explaining counterfactuals

[43] N. Goodman, *Fact, Fiction and Forecast*, 2nd edn. (Indianapolis, Ind.: Bobbs-Merrill, 1965), at 54.

[44] D. Davidson, 'Theories of Meaning and Learnable Languages', repr. in his *Inquiries into Truth and Interpretation* (Oxford: Oxford University Press, 1984).

in terms of causation, notably by Frank Jackson.[45] But the developed and relevant explanations of counterfactuals known to me all employ the notion of a causal law, and whether this is a modal notion remains moot. The fully non-modal theorist must supply some account which treats the notion of a law non-modally. He has to do this for probabilistic as well as for deterministic laws. One might, at this juncture, distinguish two varieties of non-modal theorist. One variety declines this challenge for laws, and so confines non-modalism to the particular. The bolder variety aims to defend non-modalism without restriction.

If the partially modal conception is correct, one important consequence is that we could not regard grasp of contents that do not explicitly contain the concepts of metaphysical possibility and necessity as not tacitly involving any grasp of the notion of possibility. We could not then regard a person's understanding of apparently 'categorical' sentences as explanatorily wholly prior to any understanding of the concept of possibility. This point does not of course undermine the principle-based account of necessity, and its correlative theory of understanding. It means only that we have another example of a local holism. Possession of the concepts of necessity and possibility, and of a large family of 'categorical' concepts, can be eludicated only simultaneously. Neither is prior to the other in the order of philosophical explanation, if the partially modal conception is correct. The correctness of the partially modal conception would also pre-empt any attempt to view modal principles as giving just a conservative extension of non-modal discourse. If the partially modal conception is correct, there is no relevant non-modal segment of discourse of which modal principles might be a conservative extension.

If, on the other hand, the fully non-modal conception is defensible, then stronger claims are possible. We could then defend the view that the categorical is fully explanatorily prior to the counterfactual. Correlatively, we could sustain the claim that unrelativized predicates are wholly prior, in the order of explanation, to their world-relativized counterparts. This option remains attractive; but it clearly needs to be earned by further argument.

[45] F. Jackson, 'A Causal Theory of Counterfactuals', *Australasian Journal of Philosophy* 55 (1977), 3–21.

4.6 AGAINST THE THINKER-DEPENDENCE OF NECESSITY

A type of statement is thinker-dependent if true instances of the type are true in virtue of facts about thinkers. A concept is thinker-dependent if any truth involving it is true in virtue of facts about thinkers. These characterizations are almost as rough as can be, but they will serve for present purposes. The kinds of facts about thinkers mentioned by thinker-dependent theorists of necessity have included thinkers' policies in forming judgements, their powers of imagination, and their subscription to linguistic conventions. There is no bar to statements which are of a thinker-dependent type being true, nor to their being known. Since there is no such bar, it is not entirely happy to describe a theorist who says that statements of necessity are thinker-dependent as 'non-cognitivist'. The noncognitivist label has sometimes been so applied in the literature, though on occasion the intention has been the respectable one of attempting to characterize distinctively expressivist views, such as the view that the meaning of 'necessary' is to be explained in terms of its role in expressing a certain kind of unimaginability. I will be concerned in this section more specifically with those theorists who argue for the thinker-dependence of statements of necessity by appealing specifically to the phenomenon of unimaginability in their positive accounts of necessity.

It is natural to wonder whether this initially somewhat unintuitive position would ever have been found at all tempting had it not been for the problems thought to attach to the alternatives. In any case, as against the theory that saying that a proposition is necessary is fundamentally just an expression of the unimaginability of its negation, I will argue that:

(a) at least one alternative does not have the problems which have made the claim of thinker-dependence tempting;

(b) the notion of imaginability needed in thinker-dependent accounts cannot be elucidated independently of the Principles of Possibility; and

(c) some of the crucial arguments given in support of thinker-dependence have turned upon contentious characterizations of the location of the boundary between approaches which are thinker-dependent and those which are not.

I take these claims in turn.

(a) The principle-based conception of necessity I offered in the earlier sections is not in itself thinker-dependent. I tried to sketch the beginnings of an acceptable epistemology to accompany the principle-based conception. It is only a beginning, but it is enough to show that it is not given in advance that any rejection of thinker-dependence must involve epistemological inadequacy. So strong has been the presumption that it must that at one point Crispin Wright, for instance, describes a position as involving only a 'technical defeat' for thinker-dependence, on the ground that the position does not involve 'epistemological extravagance or epistemological head-burying'.[46] The core of the claim of the thinker-dependence of modal statements is given by the definition of thinker-dependence. All attributions of epistemological virtues or of defects associated with positions located on one side or the other of the boundary given by that definition have to be established by relating those virtues or defects to what defines that boundary.

(b) Edward Craig and Simon Blackburn have developed more detailed, original treatments of modality which treat it as thinker-dependent, and as linked in one way or another to unimaginability.[47] Their views are not identical. Craig holds that judging something to be necessary is a policy which a thinker 'adopts towards propositions when he finds their falsehood unimaginable'.[48] For Craig, there is a genuine step from the unimaginability of the falsehood of a proposition to the judgement of necessity. Of the policy he identifies, he remarks that 'it would be wrong to think that the non-cognitivist has to offer anything more about the "policy" we adopt than that it is the policy of believing the relevant propositions to be necessarily true'.[49]

   An immediate reaction to Craig's development of the position is to

---

[46] 'Necessity, Caution and Scepticism', *Proceedings of the Aristotelian Society* supp. vol. 63 (1989), 203–38, at 237.

[47] E. Craig, 'Arithmetic and Fact', in I. Hacking (ed.), *Exercises in Analysis* (Cambridge: Cambridge University Press, 1985); and S. Blackburn, 'Morals and Modals', repr. in his *Essays in Quasi-Realism* (New York: Oxford University Press, 1993).

[48] 'Arithmetic and Fact', 103.

[49] Ibid. 105. Craig's view is that we take this further step because we need reality to be intelligible to us, and the unimaginable is unintelligible.

wonder whether it will deliver not necessity, but only some notion of a distinctive kind of truth in the actual world. Craig considers the objection, and responds: 'If we do not take [something] to be *necessarily* true, how can we justify our a priori acceptance of it as regards the actual world; on what should we base our confidence that this world will not turn out to be one of those admittedly possible worlds in which it is false?'.[50] There is a danger that this involves the fallacious argument which aims to establish that anything that is a priori is necessary. The standard semantics for an 'Actually' operator makes it clear how one can know that something holds in the actual world, whatever is the actual world, without what is known being necessary. Any instance of the schema 'If *p*, then Actually *p*' is a priori. But it has some instances whose necessitations are false. This is one of many cases in which we can justify our a priori acceptance of something whilst also rationally accepting that it is not necessary.[51]

It would, though, be incorrect to take the argument just rejected as an essential part of Craig's view. That view can be considered independently of his explanation of the reasons we might have for adopting the policy he mentions. In any case, I myself argued in earlier sections for a connection, albeit looser than Craig's, between the a priori and necessity, and a sympathetic exposition of the core of Craig's position could make use of those ideas.

It is a question what, on Craig's view, the content of a belief in the necessity of a proposition can be. What is the correct account of grasp of the concept of necessity, which is a constituent of the beliefs formed in accordance with the policy Craig describes? A theorist of thinker-dependence is very exposed if he does not say something more about grasp of the concept of necessity. If the correct account does somehow fix a truth condition for necessity statements, the question is reopened of whether an epistemology on which they are discovered, rather than conferred, is really impossible. Blackburn takes a bolder and in many respects more thoroughgoing view which is not exposed in quite that way. He states that if we restrict our attention to a particularly strong kind of unimaginability, which he calls 'inconceivability', then there is no step from that sort of unimagin-

---

[50] Ibid. 108.
[51] For more on these cases, see M. Davies and L. Humberstone, 'Two Notions of Necessity', *Philosophical Studies* 38 (1980), 1–30.

ability to the commitment to necessity.[52] If there is no step, there is no onus on the theorist to elucidate what it might be a step to. On Blackburn's view, an account of possession of the concept of necessity should simply say that judgements of necessity are expressive of the appropriately strong kind of unimaginability.

There are indeed links between unimaginability and judgements of necessity, and a satisfactory theory should explain them. I have already noted that, on my own account, one natural but defeasible way of establishing a possibility, given the Principle of Constrained Recombination, is by the exercise of imagination. But the central problem for the current thinker-dependent views is that the sense of unimaginability on which the unimaginability of $\neg p$ suffices for the necessity of p is a sense which cannot have sufficient distance from the notion of necessity to be used in the explanation of the grasp of necessity. As Blackburn rightly emphasizes, 'imaginable' for the purposes of his theory must mean something weaker than 'visualizable' or 'experienceable', since not all possibilities are visualizable or experienceable. But 'imaginable' must also mean something stronger than merely 'supposable'—in the sense in which one argues from a set of suppositions. Now it seems to me that the same Modal Extension Principle which we employ when evaluating claims about possibilities is also applied in assessing the coherence of worlds which are imagined in this intermediate sense. It is indeed true that we cannot imagine a state of affairs in which everyone in the room is English and in which John is in the room and is not English. But the reason this is unimaginable is that the truth value with respect to an imagined world of the content 'Everyone in the room is English' depends on the way individuals in the imagined world are imagined to be. The dependence is essentially of the kind stated in the Modal Extension Principle. The truth value of the quantification with respect to the imagined world is fixed by applying the same rule to singular propositions true in that world as is applied to singular propositions true in the actual world, when evaluating the same quantification with respect to the actual world. (This is formulated in terms of worlds instead of assignments, but we can consider the worlds as specifications corresponding to assignments.) If, however, someone already has some implicit grasp of the Modal Extension Principle, and employs it in evaluating modal statements, we do not need to mention

---

[52] 'Morals and Modals', 68, 70.

imagination in an account of the way in which he reaches judgements of necessity.

This problem for the expressivist view of modality is strikingly analogous, structurally, to a problem for the expressivist view of moral concepts. It is a familiar problem for expressivist theories whether they can specify the attitudes expressed, the attitudes in terms of which they aim to explain the meaning of moral terms, without using such notions as *morally wrong*, *morally required*, and the like in describing the content of the relevant attitudes. Less specific attitudes, like that of approval, would be insufficient to the task; while more specific ones are in danger of either inducing circularity, or of making points which non-expressivist views could equally endorse. The points of the last few paragraphs suggest that something similar holds for modality. Mental states which are apparently modally untainted in the relevant respects, like visual imaginability, or imaginability in some sensory modality or other, would not be the right state to take as expressed in correct utterances of impossibility. Mere supposability is much too unspecific, as is approval in the moral case. To get the right content of the attitude expressed, the right kind of unimaginability, we seem to need to appeal to a notion which is subject to the same constraints as modality itself. Once a thinker has implicitly grasped those constraints, we have the resources we need to explain understanding of necessity without mentioning expression of attitudes. Modal attitudes are expressed in modal discourse, but that by itself can be accommodated by non-expressivist theories of the nature of modal concepts.

This is not to say that we do not employ a notion of unimaginability which is tied to necessity. We do employ such a notion, suitably constrained, and imagination can help us establish possibilities. It is consistent with this position that in particular domains, notably those of spatial reasoning and attribution of attitudes, imagination has a more fundamental role to play, a role constitutive of a certain kind of thought about that domain. It is also consistent with these points about the explanatory priority of the Modal Extension Principle that possession of the capacity to imagine is psychologically essential for acquiring and using the Principle of Constrained Recombination, for whatever domain may be in question.

Despite their extreme differences, there is one respect in which thinker-dependent views and modal realism are in agreement, and stand opposed to the principle-based conception. For very different reasons, the thinker-dependent theorist and the modal realist hold that satisfaction of the Principles of Possibility cannot be, at the most fundamental, constitutive level, what *makes* a specification a genuine possibility. A thinker-dependent theorist like Blackburn will say that some additional requirement relating to imaginability must be present in the constitutive account. The modal realist, even though he need have no dispute with the correctness of the Principles of Possibility, will still insist that a genuine possibility that p fundamentally requires the existence of something at which p holds, something which is of the same kind as the actual world around you. The theorist of the principle-based conception will say, though, that if something is counted as true by an admissible assignment, that is all there is to its being possible. Nothing more is required.

(c) I also said that I would take issue with some of the characterizations of thinker-dependence of modality employed by some of its advocates. Craig, for instance, says that the difference between what he calls cognitivism and non-cognitivism is shown in their differing answers to this question: '[I]s there a faculty by means of which we *recognise* necessity, or is belief in necessity a psychologically determined consequence of our recognition of facts of another type?'[53]

I am sceptical that this is the right way of distinguishing thinker-dependent views of necessity, and sceptical that acceptance of the second of the alternatives offered in this question involves commitment to thinker-dependence. From the fact that beliefs in necessities are psychologically determined consequences of the recognition of facts of some other type, it does not follow that necessity is, in Craig's phrase, 'conferred, not discovered'. Belief in existentially quantified propositions is a psychologically determined consequence of recognition of the truth of singular instances, at least in the sense that for someone who has the concept of existential quantification, the transition to the existentially-quantified conclusion from such a premise is psychologically compelling. Anyone who does not find the transition compelling does not fully understand existential quantification. It does not follow that the truth of existential quantifications is conferred rather than discovered. Nor does it follow that if we say the truth of existential quantifications is discovered, we are committed to postulating some mysterious faculty for discovering their truth.

[53] 'Arithmetic and Fact', 104–5.

Though the analogue for necessity is not part of Craig's view, it also does not follow that the truth conditions of necessity statements are really disguised statements about the mind. None of these conclusions follow, because an account of understanding the existential quantifier which mentions the psychological determination of certain beliefs involving the concept of existential quantification may also fix a truth condition for existential quantifications which makes talk of conferring, rather than discovering, existential quantifications quite inappropriate. If the account of understanding fixes, as it should, the classical contribution to truth conditions for the existential quantifier, the resulting truth conditions for existential quantifications are ones whose obtaining is a matter of discovery, not decision.

Of course the cases are not precisely parallel. If we regard knowledge of a given existential quantification as epistemologically unproblematic, that will be so in part because knowledge of the singular instance from which it is inferred is epistemologically unproblematic. In the modal case, when a thinker reaches a belief that a content is necessary by application of his implicit knowledge of the Modal Extension Principle, he is not making an inference from an explicitly known premise. He is, though, drawing on his implicit knowledge of something else: the Principles of Possibility (and whatever knowledge is needed in applying them). The similarity is one of structure. In both cases, a conclusion is reached from initial information, in accordance with a principle mentioned in a requirement for understanding. In neither case can we infer that conclusions so reached are thinker-dependent.

The kinds of thinker-dependence I have been discussing so far in this section have been global theories about modality in general. There are also more limited claims of thinker-dependence, applying just to certain restricted types of modal statement. These more limited claims would have to be considered case by case. But to illustrate the kind of stance on these more limited claims which could be developed consistently with the present approach to necessity, I will briefly consider one such limited claim of thinker-dependence. In the Introduction to *Realism, Mathematics and Modality*, Hartry Field says that we accept the identity of possible worlds isomorphic over their entire histories 'simply as a matter of convention'.[54] He speaks

---

[54] H. Field, *Realism, Mathematics and Modality* (Oxford: Blackwell, 1989), 40.

of certain modal statements as 'false by convention', such as this statement (DE):

> (DE) There exists a possible world distinct from ours, but qualitatively identical with it, in which the individual electron A and the individual electron B are switched throughout their entire history.

Field himself favours a convention under which (DE) is counted as false. But on the question of whether (DE) follows from some other premise, Field writes: 'My answer is that you can say what you like: these are just two alternative conventions for talking about possible worlds.'[55]

There are probably several different anti-conventionalist responses to this view, and I note two. The first is that if we assert (DE), we are committed to the truth of transworld identities of individuals which go quite beyond the principles we use in settling identities when engaging in counterfactual thought about the actual world. The principles for settling identities we use in such counterfactual reasoning fundamentally involve a branching conception of possible worlds, and an individual *a* described as featuring in one possible state of affairs is identical with an individual *b* described as in another only if *a* and *b* trace back, in the right kind of way, to the same origin, as Kripke emphasized in *Naming and Necessity*. Denying (DE) involves commitment to identities which are not so grounded in identity of origin. Indeed, if there are distinct worlds in which electrons A and B are switched throughout their histories, presumably there are equally distinct worlds in which A is switched with some third electron, C. So if there are *k* electrons in the universe, there are at least *k!* qualitatively indistinguishable possible worlds. This is before we start considering switching the members of other kinds of individual too. It seems to me doubtful that we really know what it would be for one rather than another of this vast array of allegedly possible worlds to be actual. This worry is of course quite distinct from the spurious worry about whether we know we are in the actual world.

It may be said that what this line of thought really shows is that identity of individuals between possible states of affairs determinately holds or fails to hold only when the possible worlds have a common initial segment of history. So, it may be concluded, identity

---

[55] Ibid.

claims across worlds without such a common initial segment should really be classified as neither true nor false. Actually, it seems to me more plausible to classify them as false. But if the position that they are neither true nor false is insisted upon, it is still not one that supports any form of conventionalism. If there are some cases of indeterminacy, it seems to me that we should follow the strategy which Field himself recommends elsewhere.[56] Only those modal statements should be counted as true outright which come out as true under any acceptable way of resolving the indeterminate cases. Under this approach, even if some indeterminate cases are acknowledged, (DE) will still not be true outright—and not for any reasons having to do with conventionalism.[57]

4.7 NEO-WITTGENSTEINIAN CHALLENGES

In the third part of his pioneering book *Wittgenstein on the Foundations of Mathematics*, Crispin Wright presents an extended discussion of necessity, and develops two important challenges to those, like me, who deny that statements of necessity are thinker-dependent.[58] The first of his challenges draws upon Wittgenstein's arguments about rule-following, as Wright reads them. His second challenge is one which could still be mounted without accepting the rule-following arguments Wright offers.

Wright speaks of the 'enormously destructive effect' of Wittgenstein's ideas on rule-following on a competing conception. That competing conception Wright describes thus:

[W]e want to describe ourselves as reflecting on the content of a sentence and *thereby* coming to see that it cannot but be true. In such cases necessity is recognised by *the light of* understanding, even if the way the understanding casts its light cannot be explained in terms of a premises/consequences model. We want to attribute to ourselves a capacity reflectively to apprehend

---

[56] H. Field, 'Quine and the Correspondence Theory', *Philosophical Review* 85 (1974), 200–28. Field's approach is also attractive if it should prove to be indeterminate which identities to accept even within a given world.

[57] Perhaps there are some individuals whose transworld identity is not grounded in identity of origins, and the branching conception applies only to certain kinds of individual. If so, it remains that the correctness of the branching conception for the kinds to which it does apply is not a merely conventional matter.

[58] C. Wright, *Wittgenstein on the Foundations of Mathematics* (London: Duckworth, 1980).

impositions and constraints which the manner in which we understand particular expressions places upon us.[59]

This description covers several anti-conventionalist views, but it is certainly squarely applicable to the view I have been developing. Do the arguments Wright attributes to Wittgenstein undermine the position I have been developing?

The reason, Wright says, that Wittgenstein's views have such a destructive effect, is that, according to Wittgenstein,

whatever sincere applications I make of a particular expression, when I have paid due heed to the situation, will seem to me to conform with my understanding of it. There is no scope for a distinction here between the fact of an application's seeming to me to conform with the way in which I understand it and the fact of its really doing so . . . [T]here is no possibility of an account of what the fact of the idiolectic correctness of my use of the expression consists in.[60]

More strictly, Wright says, objectivity of some alleged kind of fact requires 'that the facts do not *consist* in one's having a certain impression of them—that there is something for my impression to be an impression *of*'.[61] So on the view Wright attributes to Wittgenstein, there are no facts about the way in which a subject understands an expression of the kind needed by a theory of necessity that appeals at some point to the way in which expressions are understood. It is worth noting that if these considerations are sound, they would apply equally to any corresponding theory of the a priori.

On the account I have been presenting, the conformity of a thinker's use of a word with the way in which he understands it does not consist in the thinker's impression that it so conforms. It consists in the use being in accordance with the corresponding condition for possession of the concept expressed by the word. (If the word is one which is not associated in the language with a concept, but only with a reference, then correctness of use can involve only the weaker condition that the person's use of the word suitably draws upon his knowledge that it has a certain reference.) In cases in which we have a good philosophical understanding of the concept in question, we can actually specify what that condition is. The basic criterion of objectivity is met, on the account I have given, for the notion of the way in which an expression is understood.

---

[59] Ibid. 353–4.   [60] Ibid. 355.   [61] Ibid. 356.

It is very important to recognize that this basic objectivity is consistent with there being a limited sense in which, on any theory of concepts meeting two conditions, 'what seems to the thinker to be right will be right'. The first condition is that the account of possession of a given concept mentions what the thinker finds it compelling to judge, in specified circumstances. The second condition is that the account of possession has the consequence that judgements made in accordance with the conditions for possession are true. These two conditions have the following consequence. If someone possesses a concept, and applies it in circumstances which, according to the conditions for possession, he is required to apply it, then his application of the concept will be *correct*. In this respect, what seems to him right will indeed be right. But this is entirely consistent with the existence of the required minimal objectivity for the notion of the way in which an expression is understood, that a person's being right does not consist in its seeming to him that he is so.

The misapprehension that it is not so consistent may result from overlooking the possibility of incorporating into the conditions for possession of a concept some reference to the thinker's finding a content containing the concept compelling in certain circumstances. If one does not so incorporate the thinker's reactions, a problematic gap opens up between, on the one hand, all the facts about the thinker's willingness to apply a concept in various circumstances, and, on the other hand, what his understanding allegedly consists in. To espouse a theory which postulates such a gap is indeed to endorse a pre-Wittgensteinian account of understanding, and to fail to take into account what is best in the rule-following considerations. But if we do incorporate a thinker's reactions into the conditions for possessing a concept, we have, consistently with some Wittgensteinian insights, the resources for explaining how the way in which an expression is understood can contribute to fixing the status of contents containing it as necessary via the Modal Extension Principle.

As I said, the second challenge presented by Wright is quite independent of the rule-following considerations. This is the challenge posed by Wright's example of the Cautious Man. Wright characterizes the Cautious Man thus:

What he does is grant the apparent correctness of all the steps [of a proof]; grant that it is indeed imaginatively obscure how he might come to revise that assessment; grant that there is every reason to believe that whenever the proof is reproduced in a satisfying way, it will lead to the same outcome; *but* dispute that there is anything in all that which justifies him in claiming to have apprehended any essential connection between basis, process and outcome—in claiming, indeed, of any statement in the vicinity that it 'cannot but' be true.[62]

Wright argues that the Cautious Man's attitude does not involve any kind of misunderstanding or misapprehension of the circumstances.[63] Nothing distinguishes the Cautious Man from someone who just fails to participate in the convention of placing the prefix 'necessarily' in front of a statement for which we have a certain kind of ground.

The Cautious Man is not someone who holds that there is no intelligible concept of necessity. 'Cautious' would not be the right word to describe such a person. The conventionalist who offers the example of the Cautious Man is committed to thinking that there is an intelligible notion of necessity—of which he gives a conventionalist account. The coherence of the example of the Cautious Man undermines, Wright suggests, any 'recognitional' conception of necessity on which an assertion of necessity is a 'genuine (fact-stating) assertion'.[64] Wright holds that it is a criterion for something to be 'a (genuine) fact-stating assertion—something whose correctness is subject to discovery'—that 'the linguistic community acknowledges conditions of appropriate assent to it of such a sort that someone's sincere unwillingness to assent to it when those conditions obtain and he is in a position to appreciate as much will indicate either a misunderstanding or some sort of misapprehension of the character of the presented circumstances'.[65]

So Wright is here putting forward two theses: (a) that the Cautious Man is coherent in his attitudes, and (b) that if the example is coherent, statements of necessity are not 'fact-stating' discourse.

Is the Cautious Man coherent? What can he say about the Modal Extension Principle, if it is presented to him? Perhaps he thinks it is false, and has some alternative account of how contents are to be evaluated with respect to alternative possible circumstances. I do not know what such an alternative might be like. The epistemic possibility that there is an alternative is not to be gainsaid. Fallibility is an all-pervasive condition. But the mere epistemic possibility of the

---

[62] Ibid. 455. Wright has qualified his earlier views about the Cautious Man in his paper 'Necessity, Caution and Scepticism'. What I have to say here should be taken to engage with Wright's views as published in 1980.

[63] *Wittgenstein on the Foundations of Mathematics*, 459.   [64] Ibid.

[65] Ibid.

coherence of the Cautious Man is hardly enough to support conventionalism. If such epistemic possibility is all that part (a) of Wright's position were to involve, the conditional component (b) would not be plausible. If the conditional (b) is to be true, its antecedent must be understood to mean real coherence, and not just the epistemic possibility thereof. What is epistemically possible (in the sense in question here) depends upon our state of knowledge. What is fact-stating discourse cannot depend upon our state of knowledge.

Suppose, on the other hand, that the Cautious Man has no alternative to offer to the Modal Extension Principle. In this case, it must be doubtful whether his attitude is coherent. On the understanding condition I have tried to make plausible for necessity, a thinker's judgements involving necessity must be in accordance with the Modal Extension Principle. The Cautious Man refuses to move from, for instance, the existence of an outright proof in propositional calculus of the non-modal statement A to the conclusion that it is necessary that A. But such a proof—supposing we prescind from complications caused by indexicals or 'Actually' operators—is sufficient to establish the following: that given the semantic values assigned in the actual world to the logical constants in A, whatever the truth values of its atomic constituents, A will be true in the actual world. By the reasoning from the Modal Extension Principle we gave in section 4.2 above, A will be true with respect to any possible circumstance. So if the Modal Extension Principle is correct, the Cautious Man's attitude is not coherent after all.

It should be noted that in arguing this point we do not need to use modal notions in explaining what makes something a proof. What makes something a proof is that each of its steps is one which can be inferred to be truth-preserving given just the conditions for possession and conditions for determining the semantic value of each of the concepts involved in the inference.[66] 'Can be inferred' here does not need to involve anything modal—model-theoretic validity, for instance, would suffice for the account. Nor do we need to invoke a premise to the effect that it is *necessary* that when a proof is constructed in accordance with certain general principles, the last line will be of a certain form. Though that is true, I would argue it is a

---

[66] For further discussion of this account of proofs, developed within the framework of possession conditions for concepts, see sect. 5 of my paper 'How are A Priori Truths Possible?'

consequence of the fundamental explanation of what it is to be a proof, rather than something primitively written into the notion of a proof. All that is required for the development of these points about the Cautious Man is that a sequence of sentences in fact conforms to the non-modal principles which give a sufficient condition for it to be a proof.[67]

On the view I am defending, then, statements of necessity meet Wright's criterion for being 'fact-stating'. But it also remains true that it would be an overblown description of my position to say that it postulates, or is committed to, the existence of a 'necessity-sensitive faculty'. So if these views I am defending are correct, fulfilment by a class of statements of Wright's criterion for being 'fact-stating' is not sufficient to motivate the postulation of a faculty which, by some causal mechanism, detects the truth or falsity of statements in that class.

It seems that Wright's criterion can be fulfilled in at least two rather different kinds of way. In cases of the first kind, the sentence in question is one which consists of a present-tense predication of a concept which refers to a property to which those who understand the sentence must be causally sensitive. In this sort of case, when two people differ over whether the sentence should be accepted, then at least one of them either misunderstands the sentence, or has a partially defective faculty for detecting the property in question (or is in error on whether his faculty is misfunctioning!). But Wright's criterion will also be met in a second kind of case, one in which the condition for understanding the main operator of the sentence in question mentions its role in inference, either implicit or explicit. On the treatment of the concept of necessity I have been advocating, that concept should be classified in the second, not the first, of these two kinds of case. It is implicit inference from the semantic properties of its terms which helps to determine, for one who understands the expressions, whether a sentence containing 'necessarily' should be accepted. A theorist's treatment is committed to postulating a faculty causally sensitive to the presence of the property expressed by the concept only if the theorist incurs a further commitment: to the condition for possessing the concept requiring its possessor to be capable of being

---

[67] These remarks bear on Wright's elaboration of the Cautious Man's attitude, where he has the Cautious Man's caution apply to the necessity of the outcome of applying certain rules to certain premises.

causally influenced by the property to which it refers. This condition is not met by the present treatment of necessity, nor indeed by any plausible treatment of the logical constants, or of any other concepts which are individuated in terms of their role in one or another kind of inference.

In a later paper, Wright doubts the coherence of the Cautious Man for rather different reasons. That a proper application of an inference rule has only one outcome is, he says, 'an epistemically primitive feature of the concept'.[68] He says, too, that the epistemology of the necessity that an application of a given inference rule, with particular premises, has the outcome it does, is 'empirico-conventional'.[69] I would reply that epistemically primitive features of concepts generate a priori truths, in the first instance. To move, without fallacy, from its being a priori that correct application of a given inference rule has the outcome it does to any conclusion about necessity, one must appeal to something like the Modal Extension Principle, together with particular features of this case. The approach developed here also has no commitment to the existence of 'empirico-conventionalist' elements in the epistemology of a priori truths. The present treatment dovetails best with an account of the a priori which is not conventionalist.[70] There could perhaps be a middle position, which combines a conventionalist account of the a priori with some adaptation of the Modal Extension Principle—and the Principles of Possibility in general—as a means of building out to mastery of necessity from a conventionalist starting point. But the idea of a rule, dependent upon the identity of the concept, by which its semantic values are fixed in the actual world is part of the way in which the Modal Extension Principle fixes the semantic values of concepts in various possible worlds. Once we have that idea in place, we have the resources to explain the a priori without any need for conventionalism.

4.8 CONCLUSION AND PROSPECTS

The present chapter has aimed to meet the Integration Challenge for metaphysical necessity by developing an instance of what, back in

---

[68] 'Necessity, Caution and Scepticism', 236.   [69] Ibid. 238.
[70] Such as that in my 'How are A Priori Truths Possible?'.

Chapter 2, I called the model of implicitly known principles. On this way of attaining integration in the modal case, we can retain the objectivity of statements of necessity without accepting that they concern an inaccessible modal reality. We can also retain their knowability without regarding them as thinker-dependent. I am more wedded to the general approach by way of the articulation of the principles of possibility than to the particular development of it I have attempted here, and other, better developments in the same general style may be possible.

If the present version, or some variant, can be successfully defended, there are two kinds of area in which further investigation may prove fruitful.

The first such area is that of modalist treatments of at least the more elementary parts of mathematics, and possibly other domains of abstract objects. Modalist treatments of those areas have often run up against a cluster of objections to the effect that the metaphysics and epistemology of necessity are totally obscure, and that we do not really possess a genuine notion of necessity distinct from such tamer notions as logical truth. If this chapter is correct, those objections can be overcome.

The second area is defined by a very general question. Can the general features of the principle-based approach to modality be applied to other domains where we need to steer a middle way between a realism which involves inaccessibility, and a position which secures accessibility at too high a price? The domains of moral thought, and thought in all other domains which necessarily involve norms and the giving of reasons, are perhaps the most salient for which extensions or variants of the present approach merit further investigation.

APPENDIX A

Modal Logic and the Principle-Based Conception

Which modal logic does the principle-based conception underwrite as correct? Does it guarantee the absolutely minimal axioms and inference rules that should be delivered by anything which is recognizably an account of metaphysical necessity? And if so, how far beyond the minimal axioms does the principle-based conception go?

I begin by arguing that the principle-based conception of modality implies the correctness of the propositional modal system T, as it is called in Hughes and Cresswell.[71] This is the system called 'M' by Kripke in his well-known paper 'Semantical Considerations on Modal Logic'.[72] We follow essentially Kripke's concise formulation of the axiom schemata and rules for the system in question:

> A0 All truth-functional tautologies.
> A1 $NA \supset A$.
> A2 $N(A \supset B) \supset . NA \supset NB$.
> R1 From A, $A \supset B$, we can infer B.
> R2 If A is a theorem, so is NA.

I think it would be widely agreed that a philosophical account of modality which is unable to support the correctness of the principles of T would be unacceptable. (Constructivists will of course not accept A0, but when they replace it with something more restrictive, the remaining distinctively modal part of T should be uncontroversial for them. They will also have to give a separate treatment of possibility, since for them it can no longer be defined as $\neg N\neg$.) It must then be a task for the defender of the principle-based account to show that on his conception, the axioms, inference rule, and rule of proof in T are correct. The ground rule in carrying out this task is not to rely on any modal principles, however compelling and obvious, unless they can be justified from the Principles of Possibility. Any such reliance would mean that we have not relied only on the Principles of Possibility in showing that T is correct. We would not have established that the Principles of Possibility suffice, as an account of the modal, to establish the correctness of T.[73]

---

[71] G. Hughes and M. Cresswell, *A New Introduction to Modal Logic* (London: Routledge, 1996), ch. 2.

[72] S. Kripke, 'Semantical Considerations on Modal Logic', repr. in L. Linsky (ed.), *Reference and Modality* (Oxford: Oxford University Press, 1971). The label 'M' is used also in G. H. von Wright, *An Essay in Modal Logic* (Amsterdam: North-Holland, 1951).

[73] This appendix differs substantially in its argument, though not in its conclusions, from Appendix A of my paper 'Metaphysical Necessity: Understanding, Truth and Epistemology' in *Mind* 106 (1997), 521–74. The new, and much simpler, version results from an attempt to respond to Timothy Williamson's challenge to me to

In what follows I assume that we have fixed on a given background set of objects, properties, relations and concepts, and of expressions referring to these objects and expressing these concepts, so that we have a determinate background range of meaningful non-modal sentences.

I aim to establish the correctness of T under the principle-based conception by proving the following Metatheorem.

> **Metatheorem.** Every theorem of T is a schema the necessity of any instance of which, in the sense of the principle-based conception, follows from the Modal Extension Principle, the Characterization of Necessity, and the rules for determining the actual semantic values of the propositional logical constants.

This Metatheorem has the corollary that any instance of any theorem of T is true under the principle-based conception of modality.

Proof of Metatheorem

We proceed straightforwardly by induction on the length of the proof of a theorem of T. We take the three axiom-schemata first.

A0. Take any instance of a schema whose main connective is a propositional logical constant. The Modal Extension Principle implies that according to any admissible assignment s, the semantic value of this instance will be identical with the result of applying the same function to the semantic value (according to s) of its constituents as is applied in determining its actual semantic value. This implies that all truth-functional tautologies are true according to all admissible assignments. Hence they are necessary, by the Characterization of Necessity (Chzn). What we have just given is an argument for their necessity which takes as premises the Modal Extension Principle (MEP), Chzn, and the semantic rules for the logical constants. Hence instances of A0 have the property required by the Metatheorem.

A1. Suppose *NA*. Then by Chzn, *A* holds under all admissible assign-

develop the argument in a form which has no reliance at all on modal principles which cannot be justified from within the principle-based conception. The fact that the Modal Extension Principle is self-applicable and can be applied recursively to the concepts it helps to define is critical in meeting the challenge.

ments. Now to the way things actually are, there corresponds a certain assignment $s_@$. This is the assignment which assigns to each concept its actual semantic value, and to each property its actual extension. From this choice of $s_@$, we have that any sentence or Thought is true according to $s_@$ if and only if it is true (true outright, not relative to or according to anything). From MEP, it also follows that $s_@$ is admissible. Since A holds under all admissible assignments, and $s_@$ is admissible, A is true outright. Hence all instances of A1 are true.

Next we have to show that all instances of A1 are necessary, in the sense of the principle-based conception; and that this follows from the MEP, Chzn and the rules for fixing actual semantic values.

Now consider a second-level assignment s_2, by which I mean an assignment which assigns semantic values to the concepts *admissible* and *necessary* themselves. Assignment s_2 itself is admissible only if it respects the rules determining the actual semantic values of *admissible* and *necessary*. According to the principle-based conception, these rules are given in the MEP and Chzn themselves. (This is one of the crucial uses of recursion noted in advance in the main text, in section 4.3.) So under any admissible assignment, the MEP and Chzn will hold. But we showed two paragraphs back that all instances of A1 follow from the MEP and Chzn. The property of holding under an admissible assignment is one which is preserved by the relation of following-from, on pain of an assignment not assigning to some logical constant its actual semantic value, or not preserving the constitutive properties of assignments. Hence all instances of A1 hold under all admissible assignments: that is, they are necessary. The fact that they are has been shown to follow from the MEP and Chzn, and the actual semantic rules for various constants, which is what we were required to prove for the case of A1.

A2. Any admissible assignment assigns to ⊃ the classical truth function for the material conditional. So if the conditional $A \supset B$ holds in all admissible assignments, any admissible assignment in which A is true is also one in which B is true. Hence if A holds in all admissible assignments, so does B. This shows that the truth of all instances of A2 follows from MEP and Chzn. The argument that its necessity follows from MEP and Chzn is then precisely parallel to the last stage of the argument for the case of A1.

R1. Trivial.

R2. By induction. The induction hypothesis is that the necessity of *A* follows from the MEP, Chzn and rules for the actual semantic values of concepts and expressions. We are required to prove that the necessity of *NA* follows from the MEP, Chzn and rules for the actual semantic values of concepts and expressions. We noted in the proof for the case of A1 that the property of holding under a given admissible assignment is preserved by the following-from relation. Now under any admissible assignment, the MEP and Chzn hold, and we use the rules for assigning actual semantic values to concepts and expressions, and the induction hypothesis tells us that *NA* follows from the MEP, Chzn and the rules for assigning actual semantic values. Hence *NA* holds under any admissible assignment: that is, *NA* is necessary, and its necessity follows from MEP, Chzn, and the rules for assigning actual semantic values. This is what we were required to prove for the case of R2, and it completes the proof of the Metatheorem.

I close Appendix A with two comments on logical issues arising out of the principle-based conception.

(i) Does the principle-based conception validate something stronger than T? Does it validate S4?

Consider first the special case in which *NA* follows from the MEP, Chzn, and rules for the concepts in *A*. In such a case, the reasoning given in the Metatheorem can be used to establish that *NNA*. For such contents or sentences *A*, we thereby have an argument for the characteristic conditional of S4, $NA \supset NNA$. This is a special case, though an important one. It will include at least the valid formulae of the propositional and predicate calculus, and theorems of T.

None the less, it is a special case. If we ask whether the characteristic principle of S4 will hold in absolute generality, for any content or sentence, simply as a result of the principle-based conception itself, then the initial answer must be: only if all the Principles of Possibility themselves hold under every admissible assignment, and every admissibly admissible assignment, . . . and so forth. We have seen that the Modal Extension Principle and the Characterization of Necessity do have this property. But as far as I can see, nothing guarantees that all the Principles of Possibility which I have put under the label of 'Constitutive Principles' must have this property. Indeed there are some theorists who self-consciously adopt constitutive principles which they also hold to be contingent.

An example is provided by Nathan Salmon's discussion of the origins of artefacts. Take the statement that if a particular table in fact originally came from a certain particular quantity of matter m, then according to any genuinely admissible assignment according to which that table exists, the table originally came from a quantity of matter overlapping to some specified degree with that of m. Nathan Salmon observes that on this approach to the origins of artefacts, it can be very reasonable to claim that although a particular table could not actually have come from a certain quantity of matter m^* which differs too much from its actual origins, the following may be true: had the table had somewhat different origins, it could then have come from m^*.[74] Something is possibly possible for the table which is not actually possible for it. If we accept this, then the principle of possibility restricting the genuinely possible specifications to those in which the table in question comes from matter overlapping to a specified degree with m is, though true, not necessary. So S4 would not then be counted as correct by the approach in terms of the principles of possibility. Elsewhere, Salmon conjectures that T, and not S4, 'may well be the one and only (strongest) correct system of (first-order) propositional modal logic'.[75] What has emerged in this chapter and Appendix A offers some support for this conjecture.

In special cases, such as those in which we are considering only a restricted vocabulary, like that of arithmetic, it is relatively uncontroversial that we have arbitrary necessitations of the relevant constitutive principles amongst the Principles of Possibility. In those cases, we could give an argument for the principles of S4, as restricted to the bounds of that special case.[76]

---

[74] N. Salmon, *Reference and Essence* (Princeton, NJ: Princeton University Press, 1981), sect. 28.

[75] N. Salmon, 'The Logic of What Might Have Been', *Philosophical Review* 98 (1989), 4.

[76] At this particular point, too, I am in agreement with Salmon. See also his 'Modal Paradox', in P. French, T. Uehling, and H. Wettstein (eds.), *Midwest Studies in Philosophy* 11 (1986), 75–120, esp. bottom of p. 109. Salmon also holds (ibid., middle of p. 109) that his intransitive-accessibility account refutes Forbes's view of the relation between the necessary and the a priori, a view which I have said that my Thesis (II) supports. Salmon writes: 'The necessary *a posteriori* truth that table a is not formed from hunk h_m is thus a counterexample to Forbes's claim concerning the source of necessary *a posteriori* truths. Since the conditional proposition that if a is not formed from h_m then a is necessarily not thus formed is not *a priori*, it cannot be entailed by any conceptual *a priori* truth' (109). Much depends here on how the term 'h_m' is functioning. Suppose it is introduced in such a way that it is *a priori* that

We could also make all the corresponding points for S5. For instance, a sufficient condition for the characteristic principle of S5, that if it is possible that A, then it is necessarily possible that A (i.e. $PA \supset NPA$), to hold for a given range of sentences or Thoughts is this: that if an assignment s_1 (of the sort relevant to this range) is admissible, then any admissible second-level assignment s_2 is such that s_1 is in the extension of *admissible* according to s_2. This sufficient condition for S5 to hold requires that there are no constraints on admissibility—no Principles of Possibility—which, though they do not actually hold, would obtain if some contingency had been otherwise.

(ii) It may be found helpful to compare the argument one would offer for certain propositions involving iterated necessities within the framework of the principle-based conception with the model-theoretic arguments one would offer for the same propositions within the standard Kripke-style semantics. Take, for example, a proposition NNA, where A is a tautology of the propositional calculus. Within the Kripkean semantics, we would argue that NA holds at any world (and a fortiori, the actual world), from the rules for evaluating propositional calculus formulae at arbitrary worlds. We would then argue that for any world w accessible from the actual world, NA holds with respect to w; and so NNA holds at the actual world. This argument relies on the standard evaluation rules holding not just at possible worlds, but at possibly possible worlds. As we noted earlier, there is no gainsaying the claim that they do (for 'total' worlds, at least). It would be quite wrong to see the principle-based conception as in any way incompatible with the Kripke-style semantics. We can, however, recall the question of why the standard evaluation rules for complex formulae hold for possibly possible worlds. A plausible answer to the question would say that the Modal Extension Principle constrains the admissible assignments, and by

---

if h_m exists, then h_m is something from which it is not possible that a is formed, but from which a is possibly possibly formed. (Salmon's own subscripting notation at p. 101 might be thought to be such an introduction. He writes, 'Eventually, there is a scenario w_m that is not possible relative to the actual total scenario, i.e., that is not a genuinely possible scenario, but that might have been'.) When the term is so introduced, it is a priori that a is not possibly formed from h_m, and a priori that it is possibly possibly so formed. There will certainly also be other ways of thinking of that same hunk h_m for which these propositions are not a priori. But it suffices for Thesis (II) and for a Forbes-like position that there is some way of thinking of the hunk in question which supports the a priori claim.

application of the Modal Extension Principle to the concept of admissibility itself, it also constrains the semantic values which can admissibly be assigned to the concept *admissible*. The correctness of the standard evaluation rules for the possibly possible worlds follows from the Modal Extension Principle when it is self-applied and taken in conjunction with the Characterization of Necessity and the rules which determine the actual semantic values of the logical constants. If the Modal Extension Principle and the Characterization of Necessity are fundamental for the elucidation and understanding of modal truths, then, it seems to me, a derivation of *NNA* from these resources is a derivation from what is explanatorily more fundamental.

APPENDIX B

Relaxing the Assumptions

The first assumption that we need to relax is that of the completeness of assignments and specifications. This was the assumption that, for each of the Thoughts and propositions of the range in question, each admissible assignment counts the Thought or proposition as true or counts it as not true. As Martin Davies noted, this is at variance with our normal conception of 'ways the world might have been', if possible specifications are meant to be such ways. Davies's having straight hair is a way the world might have been, but this 'way' leaves open virtually everything else about the world.[77] So we should admit partial, genuinely possible specifications, if they are to capture the genuinely possible ways the world might be. When assignments and specifications are partial, however, we cannot hold on to the letter of the Modal Extension Principle.

The Modal Extension Principle implies, for instance, that at any admissible assignment which counts $A \lor B$ true must either count A as true or count B as true. The motivation for allowing partial specifi-

---

[77] The point was made in M. Davies, 'Singular Terms, Quantification and Modality', B.Phil. Thesis, Oxford University, 1975; quoted in L. Humberstone, 'From Worlds to Possibilities', *Journal of Philosophical Logic* 10 (1981), 313–39, at 314.

cations means that this consequence of the Modal Extension Principle cannot be required of partial assignments, for that would be to demand a form of determinacy after all. Let a refinement of *s* be any assignment *t* such that anything (Thought or proposition) counted true by *s* is also counted true by *t*. When we have partial assignments, all that we can require in respect of alternations is that if *s* is to be possible, and $A \lor B$ holds at *s*, then for any refinement *t* of *s*, there is a refinement at which *A* holds, or there is a refinement at which *B* holds. (We cannot require that any refinement of *s* distinct from *s* be one at which either *A* or *B* holds, since the refinement may consist in settling the values of thoughts or propositions other than *A* or *B*.)

What is needed is a qualification only of the letter of the Modal Extension Principle, and not of its spirit. The idea underlying the Modal Extension Principle can still be adapted to take account of the distinctive features of the framework of partial specifications. We can continue to illustrate with the example of alternation. Let us take it as granted that whatever our favoured theory of understanding alternation, it is constitutive of the concept of alternation that it fixes two conditions, each separately sufficient and jointly necessary, for the actual truth of $A \lor B$ (namely, the truth of *A* or of *B*). The appropriate clause in the partial framework then says that for $A \lor B$ to hold at a possible specification is for any refinement of this specification to have a refinement in which one or other of these two conditions holds. This clause is still anchored in the way the semantic value of an alternation is fixed in the actual world. It is just that it is modified in precisely the respect needed to accommodate the possibility of partial specifications.

In this treatment of partial specifications, I follow Humberstone, who has shown that the natural semantical clauses for partial specifications, with the natural conditions on the refinement relation between specifications, will validate the modal system K, and the modal system T if accessibility is reflexive. The natural conditions include what Humberstone calls 'Refinability': if a sentence is undefined at a specification *s*, there is a refinement of *s* according to which it is true, and another refinement of *s* according to which it is false.[78]

---

[78] There are also conditions linking the refinement relation and the accessibility relation: see Humberstone, 'From Worlds to Possibilities', 324–5.

The reader is urged to study Humberstone's paper for illuminating details.

The other assumption to be relaxed is that we have only concepts and Fregean semantic values in our semantical apparatus. The apparatus of this chapter as we have developed it so far must represent an unstable middle position. For we have properties featuring in propositions, and we also refer to them in the constitutive principles. If there are such properties, why should there not be atomic expressions which refer to them? But once these expressions are recognized, the Modal Extension Principle again needs further examination.

A theorist who treats predicates, and perhaps higher-level operators, as referring to properties may well doubt whether there are any non-rigid (atomic) expressions. When operating earlier within the Fregean framework, I classified as non-rigid a wide range of atomic predicates. The theorist who employs properties in his semantic theory will say that these allegedly non-rigid expressions are simply ones which always pick out the same property, and what varies from world to world is merely which things have that property. The precise nature of this theorist's approach will depend on many decisions, including decisions on whether a sense/reference distinction is to be recognized and used, on the nature of the properties treated as semantic values, on the handling of compositionality, and much else. But however these matters are resolved, it may seem that as long as the theory says that all atomic expressions are rigid, the Main Part, at least, of the linguistic version of the Modal Extension Principle never applies.

We must, however, be cautious. When properties are taken as semantic values, we have to distinguish between semantic value and extension. The Modal Extension Principle was formulated above in the context of a Fregean theory for which semantic value and extension coincide. But for theories on which they come apart, what matters to the Modal Extension Principle is a claim (as one might expect) about extensions. Even for a theory which treats a property as the semantic value of a predicate, there is an important and wide class of expressions and concepts for which it remains true that their *extension* according to any admissible assignment is determined by applying the same rule which determines its actual extension. For the theorist of properties, the rule which determines actual extension has to be formulated in (at least) two steps. First, something determines which property is the semantic value; and then the actual extension is determined by which things actually have that property. The extension of such an expression or concept with respect to an admissible assignment involves an application of the second step, from the property to the extension, under that assignment, of the property. The spirit of the Main Part of the Modal Extension Principle is then preserved for this class of expressions and concepts. The plausibility of the Main Part of the Modal Extension Principle for one class of cases is not proprietary to just one semantical framework.

There are, though, cases outside this class, and for which we need some analogue of the Second Part of the Modal Extension Principle. Let us first consider an example or two. Very roughly, the condition for something actually to have the property picked out by the word 'red' is for it either to be producing a certain kind of experience in a certain sort of person in normal circumstances, or to have a certain kind of physical quality which is the ground of the disposition to produce certain experiences in those circumstances. (The roughness here will not matter for the present point.) However, the following counterfactual seems true: if humans were not to have colour vision and were to see only in shades of grey, there would still be red things in the world. This counterfactual is true, because the extension of 'red' according to other admissible assignments is fixed by the following rule. Take the physical quality Q of surfaces and solids which is the actual ground of objects' disposition to produce a certain kind of experience of them in normal circumstances. Then an assignment s is admissible only if, in the terminology of section 3.2, an object is in the extension of the property value s assigns to 'red' iff it has the physical quality Q. If humans were to see only in shades of grey, there would still be objects having that quality Q. We can say that the concept *red*, and the predicate 'red', are *marked as tethered*. They are tethered to the quality Q, which is related in a certain way to what fixes the extension in the actual world. Other concepts are not marked as tethered. As is often noted, the concept *poisonous* is not: if our digestive systems were different, certain substances which are now poisonous would not then be poisonous. It seems clear that there can be two concepts or expressions which differ only in that one of them is marked as tethered, while the other is not. (There may of course be very good reasons in particular cases for operating with one of the concepts rather than the other.)

Does being marked as tethered coincide with being *de jure* rigid, at least within expressions which refer to properties? That depends

in part upon our treatment of terms which express higher-order properties. Consider the predicate 'poisonous' again. On one treatment,
this refers to a higher-order property of objects, namely, the property
of having some first-order physical property whose possession by an
ingested substance kills humans. Using lambda-notation for properties, we can say that under this treatment the predicate refers to the
property $\lambda x[\exists P(Px \ \& \ H(P)]$. Under that treatment, it could be held
that 'poisonous' is *de jure* rigid, referring rigidly to the higher-order
property. Alternatively, 'poisonous' may be taken to refer, at any
given world, to the physical first-order property which satisfies at that
world the condition $H(\ )$ on properties. Then the point of the preceding paragraph implies that on that alternative treatment, 'poisonous' is not seen as *de jure* rigid. Under the former treatment, being
de jure rigid comes apart from being marked as tethered: for the former treatment takes 'poisonous' as *de jure* rigid, though it is not tethered in the way 'red' is. Under the latter treatment, 'poisonous' is not
rigid at all. The choice between these treatments is analogous to that
which arises in the semantics of other terms in which higher-order
conditions are involved, functional terms and (according to some)
theoretical terms. David Lewis gives a classical discussion.[79]

When we are acknowledging properties and relations in our
semantical theories, the Second Part of the Extension Principle
should be revised to read thus, for the case of concepts:

> **Modal Extension Principle, Second Part.** For any concept C
> marked as tethered in a specified way to a property Q, any
> assignment s is admissible only if propval$(C,s) = Q$.

Once again, this can be seen as no more than a definition of what it
is for a concept to be marked as tethered.

---

[79] D. Lewis, 'How to Define Theoretical Terms', repr. in his *Philosophical Papers*,
vol. i (New York: Oxford University Press, 1983).

5

Self-Knowledge and Intentional Content

Many of the philosophical problems involving the first person and the self are, in one guise or another, instances of the challenge of integrating a metaphysics with an epistemology. This chapter concentrates on just one of them. It concentrates on the task of reconciling two apparent truths. The first apparent truth, an epistemological truth, is that thinkers are able to know the intentional contents of many of their own attitudes without first checking on their environmental relations. The other apparent truth, a truth of the metaphysics of mental states with intentional content, is that for a wide range of intentional contents, a thinker is, as a constitutive matter, able to have attitudes with those contents only if he stands in certain relations to an environment of a certain kind. A thinker is, it seems, able to know that he is in a state which requires certain environmental relations without first checking, or relying on anyone else's checking, that he stands in the requisite relations. How is this possible?

In this area, the option of revising the metaphysics is unattractive. The external individuation of intentional content arguably plays an important role in the possibility of acquiring knowledge by perception, and in the explanation of action by states with intentional content, to name but two. I will discuss later some of the problems which would arise if external individuation of intentional content were rejected. Anyone moved by these considerations will look for a reconciliation of our two apparent truths by reconceiving the epistemology of self-knowledge.

In any case, we have in advance a clue that rejecting externalism about intentional content cannot be the key to any solution here. The clue is that even when the content of an attitude is not externally individuated—as with the belief in a logical principle containing only logical constants essentially, or with an arithmetical belief like $7 + 5 = 12$—a thinker equally does not have to check on the *internal* relations of the conceptual constituents of her beliefs before coming to know what it is that she believes. This observation suggests that whole model of needing to check on content-fixing relations (whether internal or external) before you can know the contents of your own attitudes is mistaken. And if a different model is correct, may it not apply both to attitudes with internally individuated contents, and to attitudes with externally individuated contents? That is what I will be arguing.

The truth of externalism as a thesis about the metaphysics of the contents of intentional states does not imply that knowledge of those states and their contents can be obtained only by first checking that the relevant external relations obtain. On the other hand, we will simply not have addressed one aspect of the Integration Challenge in this area if we do not explain how our actual ways of coming to know the contents of our own mental states are ways appropriate for states with contents which are externally individuated.

One of the sources of the interest and the difficulty of the problem of a thinker's knowledge of the content of his mental states is that any solution has to lie in the intersection of three areas: the areas of epistemology, of the philosophy of mind, and of the theory of concepts. The problem is posed as a problem of epistemology. The philosophy of mind is germane, for it seems clear that the solution must have something to do with the nature of the relation between a thinker and his own mental states and their intentional content. There is no wholly general phenomenon of a thinker's knowing the relational properties of something without checking on those relations. Intentional content has also already entered the description of the problem; and there is a further respect in which the theory of concepts must also be germane to a solution. Consider someone who believes that summers are becoming hotter, and who self-ascribes the belief that summers are becoming hotter. In his belief about the summers, the concept *summers* is used to pick out a certain part of the year. In his belief about his belief, he is thinking about that concept *summers*. We identify the way in which he is thinking of that concept, in making the self-ascription, by using the very same word 'summers' again. There seems to be an identity between the concept picked out by the word 'summers' when we are describing how he thinks of his belief, and the very concept *summers* that he, and we, use to think about a certain part of the year. This identity seems to be essential to the status of ordinary self-ascriptions as knowledge. Someone who believes that summers are becoming hotter is not normally in a position to know that he believes the intentional content formed by predicationally combining (say) a certain poet's favourite concept with that of becoming hotter. It is a task of the theory of concepts to elucidate and explain the possibility of this identity between the concept employed in the first-order belief and the concept the thinker employs in specifying the content of the attitude when he self-ascribes it. The theory of concepts must elucidate the possibility of such an identity in a way which explains its importance for the status of self-ascriptions as knowledge.

I begin this chapter with an effort to clarify the notion of a conscious occurrent propositional attitude, for it plays an important part in this area. With the results of that discussion before us, we will be in a position to outline, in section 5.2, a solution to the problem of reconciling the two apparent truths we mentioned at the outset. I go on to contrast the suggested solution with other approaches (section 5.3). In these early sections of the chapter, the philosophy of mind dominates, intertwined with epistemology and the theory of concepts. A central section pursues epistemological issues raised by the approach (5.4). The final part offers further evidence for the position taken in the theory of concepts (5.5), and draws out some further consequences of this position (5.6).

5.1 CONSCIOUS ATTITUDES, SELF-ASCRIPTION, AND THE OCCUPATION OF ATTENTION

What is involved in the consciousness of a conscious, 'occurrent' propositional attitude, such as a thought, a sudden conjecture, or a conscious decision? And what is the relation of such consciousness to attention? These questions are of some intrinsic interest; but we will also not have a full understanding either of consciousness in general, nor of attention in general, until we have answers to them. I think there are constitutive features of these mental states and events which can be identified by broadly philosophical-cum-phenomenological investigation.

Perceptual experiences and sensations, on the one hand, and so-called 'occurrent' conscious propositional attitudes, on the other, differ in many respects. But there is one property they share. They both contribute to what, subjectively, it is like to have them for the person who enjoys them. A person may try to recall who was Prime Minister of Czechoslovakia when the Soviet Union invaded. It then occurs to this person that Dubček was the Prime Minister. Its so occurring to him contributes to the specification of what it is like for the person then. It would be subjectively different for the person if it occurred to him—falsely—that it was Husák; and subjectively different again if nothing comes to mind about who was Prime Minister. The same is true of other occurrent thoughts. It may suddenly strike you that you have left the kitchen tap (faucet) running: a full description of your subjective state of consciousness must mention the intentional content that you left the tap running. In these cases, your thought is not a conclusion inferred by you from other premises; but reasoned conclusions may be conscious in this familiar sense too. When, on an appointing committee, you conclude in thought 'On balance, Smith would be the best person', your so concluding can be a partial specification of what it is like for you then. On the general point that occurrent conscious propositional attitudes are often subjective states, I am in agreement with such writers as Owen Flanagan and Alvin Goldman.[1] It is important to note, though, that acceptance of this point does not require any internalist theory of conceptual content. I would want to defend the view that the intentional contents which, in each of these examples, contribute to the specification of what it is like for the thinker are composed of concepts which are in part externally individuated (and here I differ from Goldman). I will return to the issue in section 5.3.

When a thought occurs to you, or you make a conscious judgement, your attention is engaged. Your attention will often be shifted from whatever external events may have been the object of your attention at the time. The engagement of your attention in conscious thought is by no means confined to those moments at which thoughts occur to you or you make a judgement. Any one of the following can occupy your attention:

the very activity of trying to find a proof of a particular proposition;

trying to reach a conclusion on the basis of conflicting evidence;

[1] O. Flanagan, *Consciousness Regained* (Cambridge, Mass.: MIT Press, 1992), 214; A. Goldman, 'The Psychology of Folk Psychology', *Behavioral and Brain Sciences* 16 (1993), 15–28.

trying to remember something; or
trying to find evidence for a particular hypothesis.

Ryle, whose late writings on thinking do not contain the slightest hint of behaviourism, once considered an example involving a blind-folded chess-player. Ryle noted: '[W]hen, after struggling to remember the positions of the pieces, the chess-player does remember, then his seeing them in his mind's eye, if he does do this, is not something by means of which he gets himself to remember. It is the goal, not a vehicle, of his struggle to remember.'[2] Ryle is emphasizing that the occurrence of a memory image cannot be identified with, nor taken as the vehicle of, the thinking that led to the image. My present point is that this thinking, what Ryle calls 'the struggle to remember', is itself occupying the player's attention prior to any success he may have in that project.

If we are to describe correctly the relation between conscious thought and attention, we must respect the distinction between the *object* of attention and what is *occupying* attention. In a normal case of perceptual attention to some physical object, feature, or event, there is something to which the subject is attending. The object of attention is perceived: it causally affects the subject. No doubt we may want to say that there is, or can be, some sort of object of attention in a pure case of perceptual hallucination. But those cases are plausibly understood as parasitic on the central case of genuine perception. In the cases of pure hallucination, it is for the subject as if there were a genuine object of attention.

In conscious thought, by contrast, there is no object of attention, nor is it as if there is. The notion of an object of attention which is inapplicable in conscious thought is that of an *experienced* object, event, or state of affairs. In mental states other than those of conscious thought, a genuine object of one's attention might be a material object; or a continuing event; or the continuing or changing features of an object or event; or an object's changing relations to other objects or events. Having a sensation is also an experience. A pain, for instance, can equally be an object of attention. But thinking is not experiencing. There are objects of thought, but an object of thought is not thereby an experienced object, and is not an object of attention in the sense in question.

[2] G. Ryle, 'A Puzzling Element in the Notion of Thinking', *Collected Papers*, vol. ii: *Collected Essays 1929–1968* (London: Hutchinson, 1971), 398.

All the same, in conscious thought, your attention is still *occupied*—as it is also occupied in the perceptual cases, and in cases of imagination. It would be a crude *non sequitur* to move from the true point that there is no object of attention in conscious thought to the false conclusion that conscious thought does not involve attention.

It has to be said that those who have recognized the involvement of attention in conscious thought have not always been helpful to its best elaboration. It is a great virtue of William James's justly famous discussion of thought and attention that he recognizes a general category of what he calls 'intellectual attention'. But the effect is somewhat spoiled by his distinguishing the intellectual variety of attention by its alleged distinctive objects, which he says are '[i]deal or represented objects'.[3] It emerges from his other discussions that by 'ideal object' he means a certain kind of concept. But genuine objects of attention are, in the central cases, experienced objects. Correlatively, in central cases genuine objects of attention are also such that their continuing and changing properties at the time of the state involving attention causally contribute to the way those objects are given in the conscious state. Neither of the objects James proposes as objects of intellectual attention, concepts of a certain kind or the objects thought about (the 'represented objects'), need stand in that sort of relation to conscious thought. I suspect that it is not an accident that those, like James, who have supposed that there are objects of intellectual attention have also been drawn to perceptual models of knowledge of one's own mental states. It was James who wrote, in making the transition from the volume of the *Principles of Psychology* containing his famous chapters on the Stream of Thought, Attention, and Memory,[4] to the volume dealing with perception, 'After inner perception, outer perception!' (the first sentence of volume ii).

To believe in a single general kind of attention which is occupied both in cases of perceptual attention and in conscious thought is not to be committed to a perceptual model of thought, nor to a perceptual model of our knowledge of it. In addition to the applicability to both perceptual attention and conscious thought of a pretheoretical ordinary notion of there being something it is like for their subject, there are also some explanatory consequences of the hypothesis that

[3] Second paragraph of the section 'The Varieties of Attention' in the chapter 'Attention' of W. James, *The Principles of Psychology*, vol. i (Cambridge, Mass.: Harvard University Press, 1983).

[4] Ibid. 651.

there is a single general kind of attention of which perceptual and sensational attention, and conscious thought and imagination, are all subspecies. It is a familiar truth about attention that any one of these species of attention can interrupt any one of the others. Perceptual attention can be interrupted by conscious thought; conscious thought can be interrupted by external events which capture the thinker's attention; either of these two subspecies of the occupation of attention can be interrupted by imagination; and so on. What we have here is not merely some family resemblance between varieties of conscious states, but apparently some form of competition for the exclusive use of a limited single faculty of attention. The familiar facts about attention are explained if there is a single suitably high-level resource, drawn upon by perception, conscious thought, or imagination, a resource with access to some of its own recent states and to memory representations generated by its own previous states. I do not say that it is absolutely impossible to explain any one of these facts in some other way. I conjecture, though, that other explanations will be *ad hoc*, and unable to explain the full range of familiar facts. For instance, one might try to explain the facts about the interruption of the occupation of attention in thought by perceived events as follows. One might say that there are two radically different kinds of attention, drawing on quite different resources, but that there is some separate explanation altogether of why a normal thinker is subject to severe limitations in his ability to be in both kinds of state in parallel. There is, though, a real danger that any such theory will need to postulate some additional system which favours now one of the two alleged attentional systems, now the other, but cannot favour both. This additional system would appear to have just the features of the limited high-level resource to which this account was proposed as an alternative.

I now attempt some further analysis of the occupation of attention by conscious thought. When you have a thought, it does not normally come neat, unconnected with other thoughts and contents. Rather, in having a particular thought, you often appreciate certain of its relations to other thoughts and contents. You have a thought, and you may be aware that its content is a consequence, perhaps gratifying, perhaps alarming, of another conclusion you have just reached; or you may be aware that its content is evidence for some hypothesis that you have formulated; or that it is a counterexample to the hypothesis. Now when you think a particular thought, there is of course no intention in advance to think that particular thought. But there can be an intention to think a thought which stands in a certain relation to other thoughts or contents. It is thought carried out in accordance with such an intention that is directed, as opposed to idle, thought.

The relation that one intends one's subsequent thoughts to bear to one's earlier thoughts may be that of logical consequence; or that of being evidence for the earlier thought; or that of being an amusing observation about some event, or the like, if one is engaged in writing an after-dinner speech. As always, there is a distinction between the intended and the actual relation a later thought bears to earlier thoughts. On a particular occasion, there may in fact be no intended relation; but an actual thought appreciated as bearing certain relations to others may none the less occur to the thinker. Or there may be an intended relation, but one may be distracted from one's goal in thought by the occurrence of a thought bearing a relation different from the intended relation; or, as in the case of the uninspired drafter of the after-dinner speech, nothing bearing the intended relation may come to mind.

It is worth reflecting further on the striking fact about attention and consciousness that your attention can be occupied by your trying to do something in thought. Your state is subjectively different in the case in which you are trying, in thought, to achieve a particular kind of result from that in which you are casually drifting in thought. This can be so even if the same sequence of thoughts occurs to you in each of the two cases. Though striking, the point seems to be a special case of a more general phenomenon. In general, a subject's trying to do something (and what it is he is trying to do) contributes to what it is like for the subject. It does so in a way which goes beyond any occupation of attention by external events, sensations, or thoughts. The phenomenon can be illustrated, beyond the realm of conscious thought, in the first instance by some perceptual cases.

Consider an example in which doing something is occupying your attention. Your attention might be occupied by driving down a narrow street without scraping the cars parked on each side; or by getting the cursor from the top left-hand corner to the bottom right-hand corner of your computer's screen; or by getting someone with whom you are in conversation to decide to take a certain course of action without pressurizing them. Your attention's being occupied in such actions cannot be identified with your attending to the events in the external world which they involve. In the example of driving down the narrow street, you could attend to exactly the same external movements and objects without being the driver at all. Similarly, in the example of moving the cursor, your pattern of attention to motions and symbols on the screen could be exactly the same as when someone else is operating the mouse which controls the cursor. Nor can the action's occupying your attention be identified with attention to some further external events or perceptual states. In the driving example, it does not consist in your attending to the movements of the steering wheel, or to sensations of pressure on the wheels and pedals. The experienced driver will not be attending to such things when his attention is occupied with the action of driving down the narrow street. Nor, again, is the object of your attention any event of trying.

So it seems that the occupation of your attention by your doing something always goes beyond mere perceptual attention to particular events or objects. It follows that there could not be events or objects your mere perceptual attention to which constitutes the occupation of your attention by your doing something. There could not be so, because trying, in thought or action, to achieve a certain goal can on occasion be a subspecies of consciousness in its own right. When it is so, it is something additional to perceptual attention and the occupation of attention by occurrent thoughts. To make this point is not to deny that attention is a perceptual phenomenon in at least one important respect. Attention is a perceptual phenomenon at least in the sense that a full specification of what it is like for a perceiver must include a statement of which of the perceived objects, events, properties, or relations he is attending to in having that experience. The present point is just that a specification of whether the subject's attention is occupied in trying to do something may need also to be included in an account of what it is like for him.[5]

Corresponding to this relation between attention and action are certain divisions between imaginative possibilities. You can imagine seeing your hands and arms making certain movements in front of you, from your standpoint in the imagined world as the owner of the hands and arms. That is one thing, but it is another visually to imagine moving your hands and arms to make those motions. In characterizing imaginings, we can distinguish between what is suppositionally

---

[5] 'May', not 'must': nothing here rules out the possibility of unconscious goals and tryings.

imagined to hold in the imagined world and what it is imagined to be like for the subject in the imagined world. When you imagine seeing a suitcase with a cat wholly obscured behind it, you suppositionally imagine (S-imagine) that there is a cat behind the suitcase. Suppositionally imagining that there is a cat behind the suitcase is to be distinguished from imagining what it would be like for someone in the imagined world, i.e. imagining from the inside the subjective state of the person seeing the suitcase in the imagined world.[6] Now the distinctive contribution made to imagination by imagining doing something seems to fall on the side of what it is like subjectively, for the person in the imagined world, rather than merely on the side of what is suppositionally imagined. This is just what one would expect in advance, given the following two general principles: that to non-suppositionally imagine something is to imagine, possibly amongst other things, being in a subjective state of a certain kind; and that the fact the subject is doing something can contribute to the specification of his subjective state. The point that imagining doing something falls on the non-suppositional side also receives some confirmation when one reflects on the different requirements for suppositionally imagining that one is doing something, as opposed to imagining (not merely suppositionally) doing it. To imagine, non-suppositionally, doing something requires that one should know how do it. For this kind of imagining, only someone who knows how to play the *Appassionata* sonata can imagine, from the inside, playing it. This last species of imagining is distinct from imagining moving one's hands on the keyboard in any old fashion and hearing the sounds of the *Appassionata* come out. Merely to suppositionally imagine that one is playing that sonata does not require any knowledge of how to play it.

There is disagreement within psychology about the sub-personal mechanisms underlying perceptual attention at the personal level. There would, though, be less disagreement on the proposition that perceptual attention serves a function of selection. It selects particular objects, events, or particular properties and relations of objects and events, in such a way as to improve the perceiver's informational state concerning the selected items. The details of the nature of the improvement are a matter for empirical investigation. The improve-

---

[6] There is further discussion of the distinction in my paper 'Imagination, Possibility and Experience', in J. Foster and H. Robinson (eds.), *Essays on Berkeley* (Oxford: Oxford University Press, 1985).

ment might be a matter of more detailed, and new, kinds of informational content; or it might be a matter of the speed with which states of given informational content are attained. Whether this capacity for improved informational states for selected items is used effectively or wisely is another matter. Attention is a resource which may be drawn upon whatever the subject's purposes.

If what I have said about the occupation of attention by conscious thought is along the right lines, then the occupation of attention at least in directed thought also performs a function of selection. One can expect that the parallel cannot be precise, just because of the difference noted between the presence of objects of attention in the perceptual and sensational cases, and their absence in the case of conscious thought. None the less, when a thinker is engaged in directed thinking, he is in effect selecting a certain kind of path through the space of possible thoughts—thought contents—available to him. There is not selection for particular thoughts, of course: that would involve the rejected view that there are intentions to think certain particular thoughts. But there is selection of a certain kind of thought, given by the content of the thinker's aim in thought. Without such selection, human thought would be at the mercy of associational connections not necessarily at all pertinent to the reflective thinker's current goals. And as in the perceptual case, this capacity may be used wisely and effectively, or not.

Our ordinary, everyday notion of a conscious attitude does not apply only to occurrent attitudes. Each one of us has myriad conscious beliefs, intentions, desires, hopes, fears, suspicions, and the rest, and obviously these cannot all be contributing to what it is like for each one of us at any given time. Often when we talk of a conscious attitude we are concerned with an underlying state, producing on occasion manifestations in conscious occurrences which do contribute to a specification of what it is like for the subject. In the case of a conscious belief that *p*, some of these manifestations in consciousness—judgements and propositional impressions that *p*—may be prompted by an explicit question of whether or not it is the case that *p*. Much else may also trigger such a conscious state. It may be triggered by reflection on related subject matters, on other things learned in the same circumstances, or indeed on virtually anything that associative memory may link to the belief that *p*. In the case of belief, we will also want to distinguish what is already believed from beliefs formed when the issue arises. Length of time to conscious retrieval, and difficulty of retrieval or formation, which will itself be relative to the thinker's current intellectual and perceptual context, make these partially dispositional notions of a conscious but non-occurrent propositional attitude essentially a matter of degree along many dimensions.

5.2 FIRST STEPS TOWARDS A SOLUTION: RATIONAL SENSITIVITY WITHOUT INFERENCE

Conscious thoughts and occurrent attitudes, like other conscious mental events, can give the thinker reasons for action and judgement. They do so also in the special case in which they give the thinker a reason for self-ascribing an attitude to the content which occurs to the thinker, provided our thinker is conceptually equipped to make the self-ascription. On the position I am developing, we can, for instance, take at face value the statement that someone's reason for self-ascribing the belief that Dubček was Prime Minister of Czechoslovakia when the Soviet Union invaded is his just then judging that Dubček was Prime Minister at the time of the invasion. To spell it out in more detail, we can distinguish three stages a thinker may pass through when asked 'Whom do you believe was Prime Minister there when the Soviet Union invaded?'. First, after reflection, he may have

(1) an apparent propositional memory that Dubček was Prime Minister then.

Since he is, we may suppose, taking memory in these circumstances, and for this sort of subject matter, at face value, he moves to endorse the content of the apparent memory, and makes

(2) a judgement that Dubček was Prime Minister then.

This judgement makes it rational for him to make

(3) a self-ascription of the belief that Dubček was Prime Minister then.

To say that (2) is the thinker's reason for making the judgement in (3) is not to say that he infers the self-ascription from a premise that he has made such a first-order judgement. A mental event can be a thinker's reason for doing something (including the special case in which what is done is making a judgement), without the case being one of inference. An experience of pain can in ordinary circumstances be a thinker's reason for judging that he is in pain, a judgement which in those circumstances amounts to knowledge. To try to construe this as a case of judgement reached by inference would make it impossible to give an epistemology of the self-ascription of sensations. (Am I supposed to rationally reach the conclusion that I am in pain from the premise that I am in pain?) The pain case shows too that the model need not be that of perception, either. The conscious pain itself, and not some alleged perception of it, is reason-giving.

Let us call an ascription of an attitude with a certain content, by a subject to himself, made for the reason that he has an occurrent conscious attitude of a certain kind with that same content, a *consciously based self-ascription*. In the example as imagined, the self-ascription of the belief that Dubček was Prime Minister when the Soviet Union invaded is a consciously based self-ascription.[7] This characterization of a consciously based self-ascription also includes examples in which the self-ascription is made on the basis of the conscious occurrence of a mental event of the very kind ascribed, as when you judge 'It has just occurred to me that p' because indeed it has just occurred to you that p. Reaching a self-ascription of a belief by basing it upon a conscious state is of course only one of several means, each of them special to self-ascription, by which a thinker may knowledgeably come to self-ascribe a belief. It is a very important point that some knowledgeable self-ascriptions are not based on any intermediate conscious state at all. I will consider some of those cases and their significance later. Our immediate task is to try to understand the consciously based self-ascriptions better.

The description of a self-ascription made on a particular occasion as consciously based should not be regarded as in competition with the description of it as reached by Evans's procedure. In employing Evans's procedure, 'I get myself in a position to answer the question whether I believe that p by putting into operation whatever procedure I have for answering the question whether p'.[8] Searching your

---

[7] I should also emphasize that the procedure discussed in the example in the text is considered as a procedure for reaching beliefs, where belief is understood as a form of acceptance. We do, as Michael Martin emphasized to me, sometimes use 'belief' for a feeling of conviction; the above procedure is not meant to apply to those interesting cases, which need a different treatment.

[8] G. Evans, *The Varieties of Reference* (Oxford: Oxford University Press, 1982), ch. 7, sect. 4, p. 225.

memory to see if you have any information about who was Prime Minister when the Soviet Union invaded is precisely one of the methods you have for answering the first-order question of who was Prime Minister then. Coming to self-ascribe a belief on the basis of the deliverances of stored information is a special case of use of Evans's procedure, rather than any kind of rival to it.

The idea of consciously based self-ascriptions is sometimes regarded with great suspicion. In fact, in respect of the rational sensitivities required for consciously based self-ascription to proceed properly, these ascriptions are importantly similar to other, very different cases. Consider for a moment beliefs which are reached by inference. When a belief is reached by inference from certain premises, the contents of some of the thinker's states are taken by the thinker to support the inferred conclusion, and they do so in the case of valid inference. Now the thinker who successfully reaches new beliefs by inference has to be sensitive not only to the contents of his initial beliefs. He has also to be sensitive to the fact that his initial states are *beliefs*. He will not be forming beliefs by inference from the contents of his desires, hopes, or daydreams.

Another pertinent case is that of beliefs reached by endorsing the content of one of the thinker's perceptual experiences. Here too the thinker makes a transition—and this time not an inferential transition—from one state with a certain content to a belief with an overlapping, or an appropriately related, content (depending on your views about the nature of perceptual content). Again, the sensitivity does not involve merely some grasp of relations of content between the two states involved in the transition. The thinker is also sensitive to which kind of initial state it is that has the content. He will not be prepared to take the content of imaginings, for instance, at face value in the same way.

In cases of consciously based self-ascription of attitudes and experiences, a thinker similarly makes a transition not only from the content of some initial state, but also makes it because the initial state is of a certain kind. There is, though, also a difference from the cases of inference and perception mentioned in the last paragraph. In the case of consciously based self-ascription, the distinction between those events which are occurrent attitudes of the right kind to sustain the resulting judgement and those which are not is a distinction which is conceptualized by the thinker. The self-ascriber thinks of his state as belief, or as experience of a certain kind, or whatever it may be. He also thinks of himself as the state's subject. Possession of these important conceptual capacities goes far beyond the ability to make judgements rationally in response to one's own conscious states.

Taking short cuts in reaching knowledgeable judgements, without making explicit in conscious thought all the intermediate steps, is a ubiquitous phenomenon in human thought. Judgements in which a thinker self-ascribes a particular attitude with a particular content are no exception. For instance, many a thinker, when asked our earlier question about the Prime Minister of Czechoslovakia, will move straight from the apparent memory (1), in a context in which the deliverances of memory are taken at face value, to the self-ascription in (3). Such short cuts are permissible, and can still result in knowledgeable judgements, provided that they are taken only in circumstances in which the thinker could take the longer route, with each transition in the longer route made for the right sort of reasons. (In section 5.4 I return to the question of whether these cases support a purely reliabilist epistemology.)

It is worth noting a certain phenomenon when a short cut is taken. We can continue with the example of the short cut in the Dubček example. For the thinker who takes this short cut, the conscious apparent memory (1) is certainly causally and rationally influential in producing his self-ascription of the belief that Dubček was Prime Minister at the time. However, even in a context in which memory is taken at face value, an apparent propositional memory that Dubček was Prime Minister then is *not* a reason for self-ascribing the belief the Dubček was Prime Minister then. This can be puzzling: what is going on here?

What we have here can be called 'a failure of pseudo-transitivity'. The apparent memory gives a reason for judging that Dubček was Prime Minister then, and the occurrence of such a judgement gives a reason for self-ascribing the belief that he was; but the apparent memory does not give a reason for the self-ascription. More generally: from

(4) A conscious event of ϕ-ing gives a thinker reason to J that p

taken together with

(5) A conscious event of J-ing that p gives a thinker a reason to H that p

it does not follow that

(6) A conscious event of φ-ing gives a thinker a reason to H that *p*.

The Dubček example is an illustration of (6) not following from (4) and (5).

I call this only a failure of 'pseudo-transitivity', because what is rationalized in (4) is not literally the same as what does the rationalizing in (5). What is rationalized in (4) is the action-type of J-ing that *p*. What does the rationalizing in (5) is the occurrence of an actual event of J-ing that *p*. This indeed is the key to why pseudo-transitivity should fail. There must actually be an event of J-ing that *p* for the thinker to be given a reason to H that *p*. Premise (4) does not itself ensure that there is such an event, even if there is a conscious event of φ-ing. The thinker may not act on the reason which is given by the event of φ-ing (or may not respond to this reason by J-ing that *p*, for those who think that J-ings are not actions). We should, indeed, positively expect pseudo-transitivity to fail when what gives the reason is the occurrence of a conscious event of a certain kind.

By contrast, when the rationalizing is founded on a relation between the contents themselves, transitivity must hold when it is conclusive reasons which are in question. From the premises that

(7) *p* gives a conclusive reason for accepting *q*

and

(8) *q* gives a conclusive reason for accepting *r*

it does follow that

(9) *p* gives a conclusive reason for accepting *r*.

The conclusiveness of the reason stated in (8) does not require anyone to be in any particular state of consciously accepting that *q*. The relation of conclusive support holds between the contents themselves, independently of any psychological relations any particular thinker bears to them. What then would be a general characterization of the cases in which pseudo-transitivity fails? It fails in instances where the content of the rationalized judgement (or other attitude) mentioned in the second premise is fundamentally determined at least in part by the nature of the psychological state which does the rationalizing, and not just by the content relations of that state. In a case of pure logical inference, it would be fixed just by the content of that state, and transitivity would not fail.

Am I cheating by trading on the fact that I have chosen a relation of conclusive support to illustrate cases in which transitivity does hold? No cheating is occurring here. This is shown by the fact that even in cases where the reasons are conclusive, as long as the rationalizing of the content of the final judgement (or other attitude) is done by the nature of the rationalizing psychological state, and not just by underlying content-relations in which its content stands, pseudo-transitivity still fails. Thus we have both

(10) An experience of pain gives a thinker a reason to judge that he is in pain

and

(11) A judgement that he is in pain gives a thinker reason to self-ascribe the belief that he is in pain.

It still does not follow, however, that

(12) An experience of pain gives a thinker reason to self-ascribe the belief that he is in pain.

We can now bring these observations to bear on the main problem of this chapter. A necessary condition for our beliefs about our own thoughts and attitudes to be knowledge is the presence of a certain kind of sensitivity in our method of self-ascription to the content of our first-order attitudes. The thinker must believe that he believes that p because it is p which he believes; or at least the first-order and second-order beliefs have a common cause which ensure that they have the same embedded content p. That is, other things equal, and using the same method, if it had been q, rather than p, which the thinker had believed, then he would have believed that he believes q. In particular, if the thinker's environment were sufficiently different so that the intentional content of his first-order attitudes were different, then in those circumstances, if he were using the same method, the contents of his second-order beliefs about his first-order attitudes would be correspondingly different too. We require, for instance, the truth of this counterfactual: had it been twater (Putnam's well-known substance XYZ) in the thinker's environment, so that he had the first-order belief that twater quenches thirst, then, if he were using his actual method, and other things equal, his second-order belief would correspondingly be that he believes that twater quenches thirst. We can call this required sensitivity 'level-linking sensitivity', since it links variation in first-level contents to variations in second-order contents. As I say, this is only a necessary condition for the second-order beliefs to be knowledge. There are plenty of examples in the theory of knowledge which show that such sensitivity, by itself, does not suffice for knowledge. But there would be widespread agreement that if a thinker is, in making self-ascriptions, using a method of such a kind that in using it he would judge that he believes that he believes that p, even in circumstances in which he has a different belief with the content that q, then his actual judgement that he believes p would not be knowledge. One step towards accounting for the status as knowledge of our beliefs about our own attitudes must be devoted to explaining why the required level-linking sensitivity is present when we use our normal methods of self-ascription.

When a self-ascription of a belief is consciously based, the content of the first-order belief so ascribed may be as externally individuated as you please. It may be the belief that water quenches thirst, it may be the perceptual-demonstrative belief that that (perceptually presented) man is dangerous, it may be the belief that you have arthritis in your thigh. A consciously based self-ascription of any of these beliefs can lead to knowledge that you have the first-order belief. I suggest that when the content is externally individuated, the very nature of the procedure by which a consciously based self-ascription is reached ensures the fulfilment of the level-linking counterfactual. When, for instance, on the basis of an apparent memory, you eventually come to self-ascribe the belief that Dubček was the Czech Prime Minister when the Soviet Union invaded, in making the self-ascription you deploy exactly the same concepts, and the same intentional content built from them, as your memory represents as correct. One content rather than another features as the content of the belief self-ascribed because that content is the same as that of the conscious memory state endorsed as correct. Because of this identity, the necessary level-linking counterfactual is sustained. If the history and environment of the thinker were sufficiently different that a different first-order content were represented as correct by memory, then in those circumstances the second-order self-ascription would be of a belief with a different content in cases of this first kind. It is the redeployment of the same concepts in the second-order self-ascription that ensures the truth of the level-linking counterfactual.

The preceding paragraph is formulated on the supposition that the 'very close relation' which I spoke of as holding between the concept *summer* as it occurs in the first-order belief that summers are becoming warmer, and in the second-order belief when someone thinks of his own belief as the belief that summers are becoming warmer, is that of identity. This supposition of identity will be discussed further below. Though I think this supposition of identity is defensible, it is also slightly stronger than is required for the explanation of the holding of the level-linking sensitivity in the case of consciously based self-ascription. It suffices for the explanation that, even if the relation is not one of identity, but some other especially close relation, the following remains true: that if the thinker's environment had been sufficiently different that his first-order belief would have had in its content a different concept C, then the corresponding consciously based self-ascription would have had a content containing a different concept, one which stands in the especially close relation to that different concept C. Henceforth, I will omit this qualification, and speak just about identity of concepts in the first- and second-order ascriptions; readers who think the specially close relation is not identity can supply the qualification.

In several papers, Tyler Burge has emphasized the contextually self-verifying self-ascriptions such as 'I judge, hereby, that there are physical objects'.[9] In these cases, making the judgement with a certain first-order content is what makes true the self-ascription. So in environments in which the embedded first-order content is different, so too is thought I ascribe to myself when I make a judgement of this contextually self-verifying form. Burge notes—to put the point in the present terminology—that for contextually self-verifying self-ascriptions, the level-linking sensitivity is guaranteed. As Burge also states, many knowledgeable psychological self-ascriptions are not contextually self-verifying (and they can certainly still contain externally individuated intentional contents). The point I have been making is that redeployment, in consciously based self-ascriptions, can ensure level-linking sensitivity as effectively as in the self-verifying examples.

Not every knowledgeable self-ascription of an attitude is consciously based, not even amongst those self-ascriptions the agent comes to make in ways which are available only for his own attitudes. If you are asked your name, your address, your phone numbers, your occupation, you can often answer without waiting for a conscious

---

[9] T. Burge, 'Individualism and Self-Knowledge'; 'Our Entitlement to Self-Knowledge', *Proceedings of the Aristotelian Society* 96 (1996), 91–116.

memory representation. The same is true of corresponding self-ascriptions of knowledge of that information. If in some meeting a practical need emerges to find the phone number of my university department, I may think, and/or say, 'I know that the phone number of the philosophy department is such-and-such'. This self-ascription can itself be knowledgeable, but it is not true that it has to be based first on a conscious subjective memory to the effect that the department has a certain phone number. We can call these 'no-intermediate-conscious-state' (NICS) cases. They too are clearly not contextually self-verifying cases.

What then ensures level-linking sensitivity in the NICS cases? There is still here a form of redeployment of first-order concepts and contents. We have an underlying state with a first-order representational content that p producing in its subject the judgement that he knows that p, without the causation proceeding by way of an intermediate conscious state. We have here a kind of short cut. If such short cuts emerge in a person's thinking, one would expect them to persist and even be selected for, provided that the content of the self-ascribed knowledge, when reached in this way, is the same as would be produced if the underlying state had led in the appropriate way to a conscious state, and thereby to a self-ascription. When this identity of intentional content is part of the explanation of the existence and persistence of this method of reaching a self-ascription, once again we have a type of redeployment. The level-linking counterfactual required for environmentally neutral entitlements is again ensured. For it remains true that if the underlying informational state had had a different content, so too would the self-ascribed belief reached by this method.

In a third kind of case, there is neither an intermediate conscious state whose content is endorsed, nor a pre-existing underlying state. Rather, the process leading up to the self-ascription is one of making up your mind on the matter. When you are asked 'Do you intend to go to the philosophy conference next year?', you may be considering that question for the first time. You can answer the question by putting into operation whatever procedure you have for deciding whether to go to the conference in question, and answering 'I do intend to go' if and only if you do then decide to go. If the self-ascription is made by following that procedure, it is ensured that the content of the decision will be the same as the content of any intention self-ascribed by means of that procedure. So, again, there is level-linking sensitivity. This third kind of case also includes some in which you follow the procedure of Evans which we mentioned earlier—that of answering the question of whether you believe that p by putting into operation whatever procedure you have for answering the question whether p. Evans's procedure can be applied even when you have not, prior to the question's being raised, formed any beliefs as to whether or not p. The level-linking sensitivity is still present when that procedure is followed. If, as a result of environmental or societal differences, the procedures you use for answering the first-order question were to be procedures for answering the question of whether q, rather than the question of whether p, then you would in using the procedure correspondingly be self-ascribing the belief that q (or not, as the case may be), rather than the belief that p.[10]

So, in all three kinds of distinctively first-personal ways of coming to self-ascribe a propositional attitude, level-linking sensitivity is ensured. Such sensitivity is, however, only a necessary condition for the self-ascriptions to amount to knowledge. We need a much fuller explanation of why they are knowledge, and the issue remains on the agenda for a later section (5.4).

5.3 BETWEEN INTERNAL INTROSPECTIONISM AND 'NO-REASONS' ACCOUNTS

What I have said about consciously based self-ascription occupies an intermediate stance between two more extreme positions, elements of which can be found in some recent discussions. One of these two more extreme positions can be called the 'no-reasons' account of self-ascription of attitudes. At the other extreme is a form of internalist introspection. Those who have leant towards these more extreme positions may not have intended them to apply to consciously based self-ascriptions. In any case, it will provide us with a better understanding of such self-ascriptions if we consider how neither extreme can be applicable to them.

The spirit of the 'no-reasons' account can be introduced by quoting

---

[10] For more discussion of the nature and significance of the case in which you are making up your mind, see R. Moran, 'Making up your Mind: Self-Interpretation and Self-Constitution', *Ratio* NS 1 (1988), 135–51.

a paragraph from Sydney Shoemaker. Shoemaker is discussing the self-ascription of belief:

Compare another sort of case in which mental states 'automatically' give rise to other mental states—that in which a set of beliefs, *B*, give rise to a further belief, *C*, whose content is an obvious consequence (deductive or inductive) of their contents. No doubt there is a microstory (as yet unknown) about how this takes place. But one sort of microstory seems out of the question. It would be wrong-headed to suppose that having identified the underlying mechanisms or structures in which the possession of the various beliefs (and the various concepts they involve) is implemented, one must postulate *additional* mechanisms, completely independent of these, to explain how it is that *B* gives rise to *C*. Given a neural or other sub-personal mechanism, nothing could justify regarding that mechanism as an implementation of a given belief if the nature of the mechanism is not such that the microstory of its existence and operation involves an implementation of the inferential role of that belief (and so involves relations to a larger system). It is equally wrong, I think, to suppose that having identified the underlying mechanisms in which beliefs, thoughts, sensations, and so on, are implemented, and those in which the possession of concepts of these is implemented, one must postulate yet other mechanisms, independent of these, that explain how it is that these states give rise to introspective beliefs about themselves.[11]

It should be uncontroversial that it is an error to postulate mechanisms 'completely independent of' the mechanisms linking the sub-personal realizing states. Such complete independence would lead to familiar problems about overdetermination. But complete independence is not the issue I want to focus on. I want to consider the position of someone who says there never is a personal-level, causal, and reason-giving explanation of why a thinker has the belief that she has a certain belief, in normal cases. There is, according to this 'no-reasons' position, a genuine explanation at the sub-personal level, but that is not at the personal, reason-giving level. It is, according to this position, written into the functional role of the concept of belief that normally when someone has a first-order belief, he is willing to self-ascribe that first-order belief (if he has the concepts of himself and of belief, and if he considers the question). This, according to the 'no-reasons' position I am considering, is a definitional remark. It is

[11] S. Shoemaker, 'Special Access Lies Down with Theory-Theory', *Behavioral and Brain Sciences* 16 (1993), 78–9.

like the remark that valves allow only a one-way flow. It should not be confused with a causal explanation.

The epistemology which naturally accompanies the no-reasons theory is that of reliabilism. A reliabilist epistemology in this area is summarized by Shoemaker:

Our minds are so constituted, or our brains are so wired, that, for a wide range of mental states, one's being in a certain mental state produces in one, under certain conditions, the belief that one is in that mental state. This is what our own introspective access to our own mental states consists in. . . . The beliefs thus produced will count as knowledge, not because of the quantity or quality of evidence on which they are based (for they are based on no evidence), but because of the reliability of the mechanism by which they are produced.[12]

Reliabilism in this area may be elaborated in various different ways. Shoemaker's own view is that 'believing that one believes that P can be just believing that P plus having a certain level of rationality, intelligence and so on'.[13] On that version of the approach, it would, as Shoemaker immediately notes, be wrong to regard the second-order belief as caused by the first-order belief. But equally, someone who holds that the first-order belief causes the second-order self-ascription, in ordinary cases, could endorse the reliabilist epistemology. What will be common to all variants of the no-reasons theory is the claim that there are no reasons in the offing of the sort which would be required for the second-order beliefs to be knowledge on any more reason-based approach to epistemology.[14]

The no-reasons theory is, then, one of the two extreme positions I want to identify. The other extreme position is occupied by the internalist introspectionist, exemplified by Alvin Goldman in some of his recent writings.[15] The internalist introspectionist holds not only that

[12] S. Shoemaker, *The First-Person Perspective and Other Essays* (Cambridge: Cambridge University Press, 1996), 222. [13] Ibid. 244.

[14] I have drawn elements of the no-reasons theory from Shoemaker's writings, but I should note explicitly that I have not found an endorsement of it by him in so many words. I should also note, without developing the point, that if introspection involves the occupation of attention, and the treatment of the occupation of attention in sect. 5.1 above is roughly correct, then it is less tempting to elucidate introspection simply in terms of the production, in some specified way, of a certain kind of *belief* (as one of the sentences quoted from Shoemaker in the preceding paragraph suggests it can be).

[15] A. Goldman, 'The Psychology of Folk Psychology', *Behavioral and Brain Sciences* 16 (1993), 15–28.

conscious attitudes are subjective states, are such that there is something it is like to have them. The internalist introspectionist believes,
further, in an internalist theory of content: he holds that there is some
level of intentional content of which we have knowledge, and which
is not individuated by anything outside the thinker's head, neither his
perceptual nor his social environment. For this internalist introspectionist, any externally individuated features of a state—any such feature of its content or of its role—are not available in consciousness
itself.

It seems to me that each of these two extreme positions is correct
in the criticisms available to it of the position at the other extreme;
and that each of them is wrong in its own positive account. Suppose
it consciously occurs to someone that that liquid (presented in perception) is water. The content here has many externalist features,
even for someone who does not endorse Evans's and McDowell's
'object-dependent' view of senses.[16] The content of the perceptual
demonstrative involves the liquid being presented as occupying a certain region of space relative to the thinker, and such contents can only
be elucidated in externalist ways.[17] The concept *water* is itself the
topic of one of the most famous externalist discussions.[18] When it
occurs to you that that liquid is water, or you hear someone else
asserting that it is so, it seems that these very externally individuated
conceptual contents enter the content of your consciousness. We do
not have a full description of your subjective state if we omit what
you are thinking, or what you hear the other person as saying.

Actually, infidelity to the phenomenology would be the least of it.
It would be an epistemological disaster to suppose that, in having a
conscious belief, or indeed in understanding someone else's utterance, a person is aware only of something weaker than an externally
individuated intentional content. For it is a datum that we do know
the full, ordinary, externally individuated intentional content of our
own thoughts, and of other people's utterances, without reliance on
inferences from, or presuppositions about, something weaker which
is all, in some alleged stricter sense, we would be aware of on the

---

[16] Evans, *The Varieties of Reference*, chs. 1–3, 6; J. McDowell, '*De Re* Senses',
Philosophical Quarterly 34 (1984), 283–94.
[17] See my 'Externalist Explanation'.
[18] H. Putnam, 'The Meaning of "Meaning"', repr. in his *Mind, Language and
Reality: Philosophical Papers*, vol. ii (Cambridge: Cambridge University Press, 1975).

internalist introspectionist's view. How this ordinary non-inferential awareness and knowledge of one's own thoughts, and of the meaning of others' utterances, is possible at all would remain a mystery on the internalist introspectionist's view.

The problem would not be confined to knowledge of the content of one's own thoughts, and of the meaning of others' utterances. Let us take it as granted that the content of non-occurrent beliefs, desires, and intentions is externally individuated, and likewise for the representational content of perceptual states. To deny then that conscious occurrent attitudes have an externally individuated content would lead to trouble on the following three fronts.

(a) It is a truism that conscious thinking can lead rationally to the formation of beliefs which constitute knowledge. How could such belief-formation have the status of knowledge if the content of the formed belief is externally individuated, but that of the rational thinking leading to it is not? The belief formed would require that the thinker should stand in certain environmental relations which, on the internalist introspectionist's account, are not ensured by the contents of the conscious thoughts which rationally produce the belief.[19]

(b) Conscious thought can provide the rational explanation of an action under one of its environmental descriptions, such as reaching in one direction rather than another. Yet it seems that an action, under the given environmental, relational description, cannot be rationalized by conscious thoughts which are not relationally individuated. There would be a gap between the content of the thoughts and the pertinent relational property of the action which is, to all appearances, the property explained by the thought.

(c) If the content of perceptual experiences is, at least in part, externally individuated, then conscious judgements made rational by perceptual experience would involve a massive loss of information and specificity if the content of the conscious

---

[19] This argument has certain affinities to that given in C. Peacocke, 'Content, Computation, and Externalism', *Mind and Language* 9 (1994), 303–35, in support of the conclusion that if a sub-personal psychology is to be capable of explaining externally individuated propositional attitudes, the explanatory states introduced by the psychology must also be externally individuated.

judgement were not externally individuated. I see no reason in principle why this information must be thrown away in rational thought. As a fully rational intermediary between perception on the one side and belief, desire, intention and action on the other, it seems that conscious thought must retain the externalist character of what rationalizes it, and of what in turn it rationalizes.

It would be possible to continue in this vein, but the general problems which are emerging are enough to motivate a question. Why should anyone feel forced into a position in which they deny that conscious, occurrent states with externally individuated contents can give reasons for thought and action, including—amongst others—knowledgeable self-ascriptions?

There seem to be at least three substantial influences on those who make the denial. The first is the idea that the nature of knowledgeable self-ascription of intentional states is inconsistent with externalism about content. This was certainly influencing Goldman, who supports his view by observing that 'Cognizers seem able to discern their mental contents—what they believe, plan or desire to do—without consulting their environment'.[20] This whole chapter is devoted to developing a reconciliation of the agreed fact that cognizers are able to do this with externalism about content.

A second factor influencing those who reject the conception I have been outlining is reflection on particular examples. Even an objector who believes in the consistency of externalism with a range of authoritative intentional self-knowledge may still have a more specific concern. He may worry that it is subjectively exactly the same for someone on earth who has the occurrent thought that water is wet as it is for his twin on twin-earth who has the occurrent thought that twater is wet. A natural way of elaborating this second source of concern runs as follows. When John thinks that water is wet, and twin-John thinks that twater is wet, they are thinking of different liquids in exactly the same way—only their contexts differ.[21] According to this second objection, the subjective character of the occurrent thought that water is wet is fully captured by this way—'W' we can

---

[20] 'The Psychology of Folk Psychology', 25.
[21] Their thoughts are *relationally similar* in the sense discussed in sect. V of my 'Entitlement, Self-Knowlege and Conceptual Redeployment', *Proceedings of the Aristotelian Society* 96 (1996), 117–58, at 150–1.

call it—in which water is thought of, together with the way—⟨is wet⟩, let us say—in which the property of being wet is thought of. These ways, the objection continues, are common to the thought that water is wet and the thought that twater is wet. So according to this objector,

> John thinks that water is wet

will receive some analysis with the initial structure

> Thinks(John, water, W∧⟨is wet⟩)

while

> Twin-John thinks that twater is wet

will receive some analysis with the initial structure

> Thinks(Twin-John, twater, W∧⟨is wet⟩).

Our objector's point can then be formulated concisely. His point is that only the third term of this relation contributes to the subjective character of the occurrent thought.

The objector who presses this point need not be disagreeing with the main thrust of the argument I have been presenting. The objector can agree that the fact that it occurs to a thinker that water is wet can contribute to fixing what it is like for him then. He is just offering a particular view about the way in which the first-order content of this occurrent thought is to be analysed. Equally, this objector can be hospitable to the idea that a self-ascription of an attitude can be rationally based on a subjective state or event with a certain content.

Suppose we were to grant that there is some component of intentional content which cannot vary between twin-earthly counterparts, and that only that component contributes constitutively to the specification of subjective phenomenology. (I am not sure it is right to grant this, but let us do so for the sake of argument.) Granting that by no means implies that all subjective similarities involving intentional content are internally individuated. Suppose John has the perceptual-demonstrative thought, of a liquid he sees in a glass, that that liquid is drinkable; and that twin-John, similarly situated on twin-earth, equally has the perceptual-demonstrative thought, of a liquid *he* sees in a glass, that that liquid is drinkable. We can fill out the example so that the liquids are thought of in the same perceptual-demonstrative way, in the objector's use of this term. This way must involve the liquid's being presented as in a certain direction and distance from the subject. It is overwhelmingly plausible that this way can be individuated only in external terms. One who has a perception, or thought, whose content includes it, stands in certain complex, potentially explanatory relations to a place a certain distance and direction from him.[22] But this perceptual-demonstrative way certainly contributes to what it is like for one who has an occurrent thought 'That liquid is drinkable'. I would also say the same of the perception itself which makes available the perceptual-demonstrative way of thinking of that liquid in the subject's vicinity. The perception has an externally individuated content, and contributes to the nature of the thinker's subjective state. Both the occurrent thought and the perception can give reasons for the thinker to make knowledgeable self-ascriptions of attitudes with externally individuated intentional contents. The upshot is that insisting that there are no subjective differences between an earthly person and his twin-earth replica is by no means to eliminate the phenomenon of conscious states with externally individuated attitudes giving reasons for knowledgeable self-ascription of those very states.

There is also a third influence, of a rather different kind, upon those who think that conscious events with externally individuated contents cannot give reasons for thought and action. The factor is well identified—though not, I hasten to add, endorsed—in Paul Boghossian's discussion of a paradox. He writes: 'We sometimes know our thoughts directly, without the benefit of inference from other beliefs. . . . This implies that we know our thoughts either on the basis of some form of inner observation, or on the basis of nothing.'[23] Later he continues: 'Ordinarily, to know some contingent proposition you need either to make some observation, or to perform some inference based on observation. In this sense, we may say that ordinary empirical knowledge is always a *cognitive achievement* and its epistemology always *substantial*.'[24] Similarly, Crispin Wright suggests that if we are to have 'a substantial epistemology of intentional states', then 'it seems that the only relevant possibilities—since one does not know a priori of one's own beliefs, desires, etc.—are observation and inference'.[25]

---

[22] Peacocke, 'Externalist Explanation'.

[23] P. Boghossian, 'Content and Self-Knowledge', *Philosophical Topics* 17 (1989), 5–26, at 5.   [24] Ibid. 17.

[25] C. Wright, 'Wittgenstein's Later Philosophy of Mind: Sensations, Privacy and Intention', *Journal of Philosophy* 76 (1989), 622–34, at 631.

Now if the categories 'by observation; or by inference; or by nothing' were exhaustive, then one can see how pressure against the position I have been advocating would increase. As Boghossian says, observation of a coin cannot tell us about its relational properties, such as its place of minting. Yet it is apparently relational properties of a mental state that we know in knowing its content. Nor are conscious attitudes known only by inference. If those three categories were exhaustive, we would already be moving on to the freeway which leads to the conclusion that psychological self-ascriptions are judgement-dependent. But the three categories are not exhaustive. Consider your knowledge of some feature of the content of your current visual perception. You do not observe your perceptual states; nor do you know about them only by inference; and there is certainly a good case to be made that many, if not all, of the contents featuring in perceptual experience are in part externally individuated. There is no evident obstacle to holding that a perceptual experience's having a certain content makes reasonable, for one conceptually equipped to think it, the first-person judgement that she is having an experience with a certain content. The reasonableness of such a judgement does not at all rely upon some level of internalist content which the experience has, and for which the transition to a judgement about the experience is unproblematic. On the contrary, for perceptual experience we seem to have externalism about representational content all the way down. I would make corresponding points for self-ascriptions of thoughts with particular contents, when they are consciously based.[26]

On the other hand, the internalist introspectionist is right at least to the extent that he emphasizes the subjective aspect of conscious attitudes, their ability to contribute to a specification of what it is like for the thinker. Such conscious states can give reasons, and there is equally no evident reason to deny that, for a conceptually equipped thinker, they give reasons for a self-ascription of the attitudes that they are, with the contents they have. If one state gives a thinker's reason for a second state, they must be distinct states, and the reason-giving character of this explanation places it at the personal, not the sub-personal, level. These points rule out the no-reasons theory.

[26] If the no-reason theorist were so extreme as to declare that only a belief can give a reason for forming a belief, he would be committed to saying that even ordinary perceptual beliefs are not formed for reasons. This would be to use 'reason' in a way which loses touch with the rationality of belief formation.

If each of the extreme views' criticisms of the other is sound, as I suggest, then indeed neither of the extreme views can be correct. We need to recognize conscious propositional attitudes as a non-perceptual, non-sensational category of subjective, conscious states in their own right, with their externally individuated contents contributing ineliminably to the particular conscious states they are.

We have discussed the reasons which appear to, but do not in fact, support internalist introspectionism; but what of the considerations which lead to the no-reasons view? Of course, the spurious trilemma 'by observation; by inference; or by nothing' could be influential here too. But Shoemaker also offered some more specific analogies with other kinds of case.

The parallel with logical inference mentioned in the quoted paragraph from Shoemaker actually seems to me to count against, rather than in favour of, a no-reasons theory. Consider a belief with a content containing a logical constant, where the belief is reached by inference from another conscious belief. Suppose the logical transition in question is one the willingness to make which, without further inference, is partially constitutive of grasp of the logical concept in question. Acceptance of the premise of this transition does give the thinker a *reason* for acceptance of the conclusion, and, in standard cases, the premise will be the thinker's reason for accepting the conclusion. Like any other statement about reasons, this is a statement about the personal, not the sub-personal, level. In fact, the proper way of individuating the logical concept would itself entail that acceptance of certain contents containing it is, in certain very central cases, the thinker's reason for accepting the corresponding conclusions. The crucial point is this: the fact that certain transitions are involved in the very identity of a concept is entirely consistent with the fact that the thinker's reason for being in the second state of the transition is that he is in the state which is, in fact, the first state of the transition. The consistency of this combination is a commitment of anyone who holds the plausible view that concepts are individuated in part by what are good reasons for making judgements involving them, or by which contents involving them give good reasons for judging other contents.

An ordinary thinker's mastery of the concept of belief can then equally include as one component his readiness to self-ascribe the belief that *p* when he makes a conscious judgement that *p* (for the reason that he had made the judgement, and in circumstances in which the question arises). Such a component of ordinary mastery adverts to an explanation of the self-ascription which is neither wholly sub-personal, nor definitional in a way which excludes reason-involving explanation of one state by another. Nor, as we emphasized, does recognition of such explanations involve a reversion to perceptual models of self-knowledge. Once such explanations are acknowledged, we would also expect the short-cut mechanisms mentioned at the end of section 5.2 to come into play: states which would lead to a judgement that p can come to produce a self-ascription of the belief that p without proceeding through the middle stage of the first-order judgement.

The intermediate position I have been advocating for the case of consciously based self-ascriptions would actually be in agreement with Shoemaker when he writes that second-order belief about one's own beliefs 'supervenes on the first-order state plus human intelligence, rationality, and conceptual capacity'.[27] The truth of this supervenience claim cannot be used to decide the issue between a no-reasons theory and the intermediate position. Suppose it is indeed so that having the concept of belief involves taking certain conscious judgements as reasons for self-ascribing the corresponding belief, and that first-order beliefs produce such reason-giving conscious judgements. Then failure of the supervenience claim Shoemaker makes would be as impossible on the intermediate view as it is on the no-reasons view. The intermediate view will hold that the first-order beliefs produced judgements which, in someone with minimal rationality and suitable conceptual capacity, will rationalize the self-ascription of the first-order state. Correlatively, the holding of the supervenience claim cannot be used as evidence for the view that second-order beliefs about one's own first-order beliefs are not distinct existences from the first-order beliefs they are about.

Neat and simple as this exposition of the intermediate position for consciously based self-ascriptions may sound, I think it would be oversimple unless we draw a further important distinction. Within the class of conscious states, we can distinguish a proper subclass of states each member of which has the following property: it is either individuated in terms of what are good epistemic reasons for being in the state, or its individuation has consequences for what are good epistemic reasons for being in the state. A paradigm example of a

[27] 'Special Access Lies Down with Theory-Theory', 79.

state in this proper subclass is that of having a belief with a given content. This is a state which is either individuated by what are good reasons for being in it, or its individuation has consequences for what are good reasons for being in it. Paradigm examples of states outside the proper subclass are those of having an experience with a given representational content, and the state of having a certain kind of sensation. These are states which are outside the immediate control of reason.

This classification is a classification of states themselves, rather than anything to do with the aetiology of a thinker's coming to be in one of the states on a particular occasion. There may be no good reasons at all producing the paranoid's belief that others are out to get him. But the individuation of the belief does have consequences for what would be good (non-instrumental) reasons for being in that belief state. States in our distinguished class are not necessarily responsive to reason, but they are respons*ible* to reason. I call states in the distinguished class *reason-led* states. (An acknowledged leader may be disobeyed, but it is disobedience which is in question, rather than a weaker relation of not doing what fulfilment of the content of the command would require.) There is some rough overlap between class of states which are not reason-led and those which are exercises of a faculty of receptivity, rather than of spontaneity, in the sense used by Kant and revived by McDowell.[28] Some overlap is to be expected, since states in which one receives information about the world by perceptual contact are not ones the thinker is in because he has certain reasons.[29]

To be in a reason-led state is to be committed to something: to a certain content's being the case, or to one's doing something, or to something's being good in a certain respect (in the case of reason-led desires). Because of this element of commitment, there is always the possibility of a thinker's raising a question of whether he should, rationally, be in a given reason-led state—whether he should accept that *p*, or form a certain intention.[30] To enter one of these states is

---

[28] J. McDowell, *Mind and World* (Cambridge, Mass.: Harvard University Press, 1994).

[29] The coincidence of the classifications is not exact, though. For instance, states of visual imagination are not states of receptivity in the Kantian sense. But I also do not think (though this might take some argument) that they are individuated by, or that their individuation has consequences for, what are good, non-instrumental, reasons for being in them.

[30] Compare Moran, 'Making up your Mind'.

something which is subject to standards of rational assessment. Here what I have in mind, in the case of belief, is the assessment of the likelihood of the truth of the content believed—epistemic reasons for acceptance—rather than practical reasons for having the belief based on any extrinsic benefits (encouragement, optimism) derived from having the belief.

With all this in mind, let us go back to the case of a person who self-ascribes the belief that Dubček was the Czech Prime Minister at the time of the Soviet Union's invasion, and does so because he has a conscious propositional memory which represents Dubček as having that office then. The self-ascription of the belief on this basis goes beyond a mere report of oneself as having an apparent memory with that content. One makes the self-ascription in part because one is *endorsing* the content of the apparent memory. The self-ascription of the belief would after all not be correct if one were suspending judgement on the content of the apparent memory. So when a self-ascription of a reason-led state is made on the basis of the occurrence of a conscious state in this way, it is not a *mere* report of that state. It involves the same kind of endorsement and commitment as would be made in entering the first-order, reason-led state itself. This is a major difference from consciously based self-ascriptions of experiences, sensations, or mental images. The distinction can give one some limited sympathy with those who say that self-ascriptions of belief and certain other states are not just descriptions of mental states. To say that the self-ascriptions are not consciously based at all, however, would overstep the limits of legitimate sympathy.

5.4 WHY DO THESE SELF-ASCRIPTIONS AMOUNT TO KNOWLEDGE?

I argued that consciously based self-ascriptions will be ones for which the level-linking sensitivity is present. Though this sensitivity goes some distance to reconcile externalism and with a thinker's own knowledge of his intentional mental states, it also falls short of explaining why the consciously based self-ascriptions amount to knowledge. A fuller epistemological account must explain why the thinker is entitled to make consciously based self-ascriptions, and how such ascriptions track the truth. I will say something about tracking the truth first, since I will be arguing that a fuller elaboration of that helps with an account of entitlement in these cases.

For any concept with certain features, it is always illuminating to try to answer this question: what is the relation between proper applications of the concept with those features, and the capacity of those applications to track instances of the property picked out by the concept?[31] In the case of an observational concept, we have at least the rudiments of an answer to this question. The possession condition for the concept would mention the role of a particular kind of perceptual experience in possessing the concept. We would begin to answer the question, as applied to a perceptual concept, by explaining how ordinary perceptual experience involves a sensitivity of the perceiver to instantiation of the property picked out by the concept. It is clear, in outline at least, how other theories of the concept of belief would aim to answer the same question as posed for the concept of belief. A no-reasons theorist would speak simply of a reliable sensitivity of a thinker's self-ascriptions of beliefs to instances of the property of believing the relevant contents, a sensitivity built into the account he would offer of possession of the concept of belief. Equally, a theorist such as Wright, who treats the correctness of belief-ascriptions as constitutively partially dependent upon a subject's willingness to self-ascribe them, will also have his own answer to the question. For such a judgement-dependent theorist, the correctness of an ordinary self-ascription of a belief will not be independent of the thinker's willingness to make the self-ascription. This is a very different explanation of how the offered account of mastery connects with the truth of the self-ascriptions of belief. It may not be plausible; but at least it addresses the question. I, however, have rejected the pure no-reasons view, and I have not endorsed any judgement-dependent theory. So how do *I* answer the question of how proper applications of the concept of belief succeed in tracking instances of the property it picks out?

There are at least two sub-questions to be distinguished here.

> Sub-question (a). What account, if any, is available in the present framework of the nature of the first-order property of believing a given intentional content, the property whose instances in the thinker are to be tracked by properly made self-ascriptions?

---

[31] On the distinction between properties and concepts thereof, see Putnam, 'On Properties'.

One approach to this question would draw on *A Study of Concepts*. In the framework of that book, the nature of the property of believing that *p*, for a given content *p*, is fixed by the possession conditions for the various concepts which comprise the content *p*, together with their mode of composition. Each such possession condition for a concept contributes, at a point determined by the mode of composition, a requirement on a state's being a belief with a content containing that concept. The totality of such requirements fixes the condition for a state to be a belief with the given content *p*. This condition fixes a property whose instances may or may not be tracked. One does not, however, have to submit to the rather demanding constraints of *A Study of Concepts* to give a somewhat similar answer to this first sub-question about the nature of the property. Perhaps conditions for possessing a concept cannot be non-circularly specified, and we need rather to use a given concept within the scope of a thinker's attitudes in specifying the role we would expect a given concept to play in a thinker's cognitive economy when he possesses it.[32] That is still a specification of a role, and the totality of such roles for all the concepts comprising a given content *p* will, together with their mode of combination, fix a complex condition for some state to be a belief that *p*.

Whether the condition is fixed in the more or the less demanding way, there is in either case no plausibility that this way—which involves a detailed statement of conditions for possessing the concepts involved—is a route employed at the personal level when a subject knowledgeably self-ascribes a belief. Ordinary thinkers need not have any personal-level conscious knowledge of the conditions for possessing the concepts they employ, whether the constraints on these conditions are demanding or not. So this answer to the first sub-question takes us only as far as a fixing of the property about which the question of tracking can be raised. It is not an answer to that question, for it does not explain how any tracking takes place. It merely specifies the property which might be tracked.

> Sub-question (b). How do the earlier points in this chapter, about the nature of conscious, occurrent propositional attitudes, and their availability as reasons in their own right, contribute to answering the question of how properly made self-applications of the concept of belief track instances of the

---

[32] For more discussion of such cases, see my 'Implicit Conceptions, Understanding and Rationality'.

property of believing a given content? If they are irrelevant to answering the question, should they not be omitted from an account of ordinary mastery of the concept of belief? If they are relevant, how do they contribute to tracking the property?

To address the cluster of issues in sub-question (b), I suggest that we need to step back a little and consider the nature of belief. If we were asked about the nature of belief, we would very plausibly include the following principles:

(I)   To make a judgement is the fundamental way to form a belief (or to endorse it when it is being reassessed). Judgement is a conscious rational activity, done for reasons, where these reasons are answerable to a fundamental goal of judgement, that it aims at truth. As I said back in Chapter 2, my own view is that judgements are in fact *actions*, a species of mental action. Judgements are made for reasons. Perhaps they are not intentional under any description. I do not regard that as sufficient for them not to be actions. Forming an intention to do something seems equally to me to be an action (and can also be done for reasons). But in the sense in which judgements are not intentional under some description, forming an intention is not intentional under some description either. However, as also promised in Chapter 2, I observe that for those who insist that judgements are not actions, it will suffice for the points I want to make that judgements are made for reasons, and are answerable to reason.

(II) Beliefs normally store the contents of judgements previously made as correct contents, and these stored contents can be accessed so as to result in a conscious, subjective state of the thinker which represents the stored content as true. The contents will often need to be adjusted as the spatio-temporal location of the thinker varies. This is why a cognitive dynamics, in Kaplan's sense, is essential in the description of the mental life of any creature with beliefs.[33]

(III) Beliefs equally aim at the truth, rather than being a mere record of what was once judged. Hence their contents are always potentially open to revision by later judgements, per-

---

[33] Kaplan, 'Demonstratives', 537 ff.

ceptions, memories and reconsiderations of reasoning and evidence.

There is vast amount more to be said about the nature of belief and judgement, but it seems that features (I)–(III) of belief are core characteristics which will be retained in any more extensive elaboration.

Now we can bring this to bear on our second set of questions (b) above. I claim that our distinctive ways of coming to make consciously based self-ascriptions of beliefs are correct methods in part because of the nature of belief given in characteristics (I)–(III). It is important for this claim that the characteristics (I)–(III) do not themselves mention knowledgeable self-ascription. It also matters for the claim that these are relatively a priori and constitutive characteristics of belief. They are not a posteriori in the way in which, as a true principle about its nature, the statement 'Water is H_2O' is a posteriori.

Consider the procedure of making a self-ascription of a belief that p for the reason that one has just consciously judged that p. By characteristic (I) of belief, the first-order judgement will, when all is working properly, be an initiation (or continuation) of a belief that p. So the self-ascription will be correct.

Consider also the case in which someone has a propositional memory representation of its being the case that p, is taking these representations at face value, and rationally moves, directly or indirectly, from this particular memory to the self-ascription of the belief that p. Again, when all is working properly, the memory representation will be a manifestation of an underlying stored belief that p, the kind of representation which, according to characteristic (II), stored beliefs will generate. So the self-ascription will be correct. Equally, when there is new evidence which means that the memory must be re-evaluated, characteristic (III) of beliefs explains why a rational self-ascription cannot just consist in re-endorsement of the stored information (or misinformation).

In summary, when all is working properly, knowledgeable self-ascriptions track the property of belief for this reason: the very means by which they are reached are ones whose availability involves the thinker's having the relevant belief. When all is working properly, these means would not be available were he not to have the relevant first-order belief.

On this approach, representations in conscious thought of contents as true can be produced by underlying beliefs; can contribute to what it is like subjectively for the thinker; and can be involved in reasonable self-ascription, of a kind involved in ordinary mastery of the concept of belief. All of this is consistent with knowledgeable self-ascriptions tracking the instantiation of the property of belief in the appropriate content. The position I have been developing seems to me to endorse all those propositions simultaneously.

The position also seems to me to contain the seeds of an explanation of why a thinker is entitled to make consciously based self-ascriptions, and thus to help to account for their status as knowledge. A thinker is entitled to make consciously based self-ascriptions of belief because the rationality of making such ascriptions is grounded in a constitutive, and relatively a priori, account of the nature of belief itself. In particular, it is grounded in features (I)–(III). Such grounding goes far beyond the conditions counted as sufficient for knowledge in purely reliabilist accounts.[34]

It is worth noting the special link—whose existence one would well expect in advance—between the means for coming to make knowledgeable self-ascriptions and the first person. A conscious memory representation, and equally a conscious judgement, can give a reason for making a self-ascription (or indeed for doing anything else) only to the person who has that memory, or who is making that judgement. So these rational means are restricted to *self*-ascriptions of beliefs and other mental states and events. Certainly, a premise that someone else has a certain memory, or is making a judgement, can give a thinker reason to ascribe beliefs to someone else. But I have emphasized that consciously based self-ascription is not a case of inference, and a fortiori not a case of moving inferentially from premises about one's own mental states to a conclusion. The mental event itself, rather than acceptance of some premise about the event, gives the thinker a reason for making the judgement.

So far, I have been considering issues of knowledge and tracking

[34] Broadly analogous points seem to me to hold for the knowledgeable status of pain ascriptions made on the basis of the occurrence of pain to the thinker, and for self-ascriptions of seeing made on the basis of the subject's own visual experience. A thinker who self-ascribes a pain when he is not in fact in pain, or a blind person who sincerely denies he is blind (Anton's Syndrome) may still have some reason for making the erroneous self-ascription. Such a thinker could have a strong, belief-independent impression that the content is correct, without being in pain/really seeing. So these beliefs need not be wholly unjustified. These sorts of reasons do not, however, give knowledge, for they do not have the right relations to being in pain, or to really seeing.

for consciously based self-ascriptions. What of the no-intermediate-conscious-state cases (NICS cases), which I mentioned back in section 5.2? There are general reasons for thinking that there must be some alternative to a reliabilist treatment of the NICS self-ascriptions. For the objections to pure reliabilism—its omission of any rationality or entitlement requirement—are well known, and have not, so it seems to me, been overcome.[35] It would be very puzzling if reliabilism were right about just one kind of psychological self-ascription, but wrong elsewhere. It seems to me that there is in fact an alternative account which treats the NICS self-ascriptions as knowledge, but which is not a purely reliabilist account. This alternative account says that an NICS self-ascription of (say) a belief that *p* is knowledge only if it is made in circumstances in which the thinker is also willing to make the first-order judgement that *p*. We can call the requirement appealed to in this alternative account the requirement of first-order ratifiability.[36] There is considerable plausibility in the claim that it is the holding of first-order ratifiability which makes an NICS second-order self-ascription of belief a case of knowledge (makes the ascriber entitled to his second-order judgement, if you will). Suppose a thinker were to make an NICS self-ascription of a belief, but that first-order ratifiability failed—when he reflects on it, the thinker is not prepared to make the first-order judgement that *p*. In these circumstances, the second-order judgement would, other things equal, be unstable. The second-order judgement would in those circumstances normally be withdrawn. If it were the case that our subject had been told that his NICS self-ascriptions were a way of tapping into his unconscious beliefs, perhaps the second-order self-ascription would not be withdrawn. That would, though, then clearly be a case of inferential knowledge, very different from the normal case in which NICS self-ascriptions constitute non-inferential self-knowledge.

A requirement of first-order ratifiability can also help to explain the evident rationality of the Evans procedure for self-ascription. Necessarily, someone self-ascribing a belief by Evans's procedure meets the condition that he self-ascribes the belief that *p* in circum-

---

[35] See for instance, L. Bonjour, *The Structure of Empirical Knowledge* (Cambridge, Mass.: Harvard University Press, 1985), 37–57.

[36] One may want to strengthen the requirement somewhat, so that it does not merely talk of 'the circumstances' in which one would be willing to make the corresponding first-order judgement. A plausible stronger requirement is that the mechanism which produces the second-order judgement in the NICS case must persist because it has the property of first-order ratifiability.

stances in which he is also willing to make the first-order judgement that *p*.

If first-order ratifiability is the correct explanation of how NICS self-ascriptions can constitute knowledge, then in order of philosophical explanation—as opposed to frequency of examples—the intermediate-conscious-state cases are philosophically more fundamental than their NICS counterparts. If first-order ratifiability is required for these case to be knowledge, as I am inclined to believe, then NICS cases count as knowledge (when they do) because of the relation in which they stand to conscious first-order attitudes, and to the rational basis those conscious first-order attitudes provide for self-ascribing attitudes. On this approach, then, the existence of NICS self-ascriptions which constitute knowledge can be squarely acknowledged without embracing a purely reliabilist epistemology.[37]

In discussing consciously based self-ascriptions, I said that the nature of belief and judgement is part of the explanation of their correctness. It is not the full explanation, and my exposition was peppered with occurrences of the qualifying phrase 'when all is working properly'. There are several ways in which things may not be working properly, some familiar, some more exotic.

Amongst the familiar ways are those in which the condition which is said 'normally' to hold in (II) fails. Someone can make a judgement, and for good reasons, but it not have the effects that judgements normally do—in particular, it may not result in a stored belief which has the proper influence on other judgements and on action. A combination of prejudice and self-deception, amongst many other possibilities, can produce this state of affairs. Someone may judge that undergraduate degrees from countries other than her own are of an equal standard to her own, and excellent reasons may be operative in her assertions to that effect. All the same, it may be quite clear, in decisions she makes on hiring, or in making recommendations, that she does not really have this belief at all. In making a self-ascription of a belief on the basis of a conscious judgement, one is relying on the holding of the normal relations between judgement and belief which

[37] The points of this section also tell against the view that a full account of how self-ascriptions of belief are knowledge is given as follows: whenever a sentence *s* is stored in someone's 'belief-box', the sentence *I believe that s* is also stored in his belief-box. Some such sub-personal mechanism may—perhaps must—exist. But some additional account has to be given if we are to explain why the belief realized by storing the sentence *I believe that s* in the belief-box is knowledge.

are not guaranteed to hold. The methods of coming to make self-ascriptions which I have been discussing are by no means infallible.

There appear also to be more exotic ways in which things may not work properly. Suppose a thought occurs to a thinker, but he is not conscious of it as produced by himself. Suppose in fact subjectively it seems to him that the thought has been produced in him by someone else. This may strike one as impossible. It is, however, the experience reported by some sufferers of schizophrenia. Some subjects report these thoughts as being 'inserted' by someone else, and have illusions of control by others. For a long time, it was thought that these alleged experiences were delusions—false beliefs—rather than genuine experiences of the kind described by the subjects. More recently, an important trend in cognitive neuropsychology, including the writings of Christopher Frith, regards the reports as correct descriptions of the subjective experiences in question.[38] These thoughts occur in the subject's consciousness, but they do not seem to be the subject's own in the stronger sense of seeming also to be initiated by the subject himself. According to Frith's theory, these thoughts result from a failure of self-monitoring. Thoughts which do not seem to be the subject's own occur when sub-personal processes fail to monitor which events are self-initiated, and which are not. When a self-initiated thought occurs which is not sub-personally monitored as having been self-initiated, the result in consciousness is: subjective consciousness of a thought which is also consciously given as not self-originated.

Suppose that such conscious events really do occur. Their existence would have many consequences for the philosophy of mind. Here I will just be considering their bearing on consciously based self-ascriptions. If a thought which represents it as being the case that *p* occurs to the thinker, but the thinker has a consciousness in which this thought seems not to be self-originated, how could it possibly be that he is, if the question arises, rationally required to judge that *he* believes that *p*? Is it not only for thoughts of which he is conscious that they are self-produced that there is any plausibility in such a requirement?

One 'no-problem' response to this phenomenon would be to insist that in making a consciously based self-ascription, all that is rationally

---

[38] C. Frith, *The Cognitive Neuropsychology of Schizophrenia* (Hove, Sussex: Laurence Erlbaum, 1992), esp. ch. 5, 'Positive Symptoms, Abnormal Experiences'.

required is that the subject be subjectively conscious of the thought which represents it as being the case that p; it does not matter if the thought is consciously given as not one's own. This 'no-problem' response is vulnerable on two fronts.

First, it completely ignores the causal elements present in a range of the concepts we use in psychological self-ascriptions. When you think 'I am reasoning from these premises to that conclusion', your self-ascription will be true only if your conclusion is a causal result of your estimation of the implications of the premises. I would say that even the self-ascription 'I am judging that p', made in an everyday case on the basis of a conscious judging that p, requires that the first-order judgement be one of one's own actions (or belief-formings).

Second, even a thinker who uses the thinner notion of ownership involved in this 'no-problem' response will need to use the thicker and more committal notion in the more exotic cases. Consider someone who has the schizophrenic-like consciousness and comes to suspect (reasonably or unreasonably) that he is the victim of an intervening neurophysiologist who is 'inserting' not just tryings but also thoughts. This person will have to decide which of his conscious thoughts he is going to take as a basis for further reasoning, belief-formation, and action, and which not. He will want to take as a basis only those which are *his*, not just in the sense of being in his consciousness (for they all are), but in the sense of being self-initiated. Only these result from his own beliefs, and further his own projects, desires, and goals. A conception of ownership which involves origination is thus crucial for rational thought and action. The very thin notion involved in the 'no-problem' response cannot provide such a conception of ownership.

If this is right, then an important class of consciously based self-ascriptions is made rational only by conscious attitudes which the thinker is subjectively conscious of *as* his own, in the thicker, stronger sense. This has consequences for the epistemology of such self-knowledge. For is it not also metaphysically possible that an intervening neurophysiologist should produce the conscious impression that a thought originates with the subject himself, when in fact it does not? If that is possible, then, in the presence of the schizophrenic cases, we have a two-way independence of a thought's being the subject's own from his having a seeming consciousness that it is his own. There is then a reliance, in everyday conscious self-ascriptions, on these dissociations not actually obtaining. The ordinary self-ascriber is entitled to such presuppositions. But the philosophical lesson is that although there are many deep respects in which self-knowledge cannot be assimilated to perceptual knowledge, there is, even in consciously based self-ascription, reliance on a network of causal relations whose obtaining is by no means necessary.

There is a corresponding feature of the way in which the concept of belief is epistemically individuated. We can say that a normal thinker has the concept of belief only if he is willing to judge, and thereby judge knowledgeably, that he believes that p when (for instance) he has just consciously judged that p. The normal thinker is of course one who experiences what are in fact his own conscious judgements as his own. The phenomena of schizophrenia suggest that the normal case relies upon contingencies. Even when we are thinking about our own thoughts, and in ways made available by our having those thoughts, the possibility of knowledgeable self-ascription rests upon conditions of which infallible knowledge is impossible.[39]

5.5 CONCEPTUAL REDEPLOYMENT: SUPPORTING THE CLAIM

I have placed some weight on the claim that when a thinker self-ascribes an attitude with the content that summers are becoming hotter,

---

[39] In this chapter my concern has been with epistemological problems and the possibility of a thinker's distinctive type of knowledge of the intentional content of his own mental states. It is, however, well known that if such self-knowledge and externalism are reconcilable, then there is what Martin Davies calls the consequence problem. This is the problem of explaining, or explaining away, the possibility of a priori inferences about the world from the content of one's own mental states. For some discussions, see M. McKinsey, 'Anti-Individualism and Privileged Access', *Analysis* 51 (1991), 9–16; M. Davies, 'Externalism, Architecturalism, and Epistemic Warrant', in C. McDonald, B. Smith, and C. Wright (eds.), *Knowing Our Own Minds: Essays on Self-Knowledge* (Oxford: Oxford University Press, 1998); P. Boghossian, 'What the Externalist can Know A Priori', *Proceedings of the Aristotelian Society* 97 (1997), 161–75 ; B. Brewer, 'Externalism and A Priori Knowledge of Empirical Facts', forthcoming in a collection on the a priori edited by P. Boghossian and myself. It would take us too far afield to engage in details with this issue here. Here I would just note (i) that the present chapter commits me to endorsing some externalist resolution of the issue; (ii) that many of the arguments in the literature critical of externalism presuppose that it is a priori which concepts are externally individuated, something I would question; and (iii) many of the formulations need a sharper characterization of the a priori before their conclusions are challenging.

he apparently redeploys the very same concepts *summer*, *hotter*, and the like as he would employ in having a thought about the world, to the effect that summers are becoming hotter. This apparent redeployment of the same concepts was crucial in the explanation of why the level-linking sensitivity is present. Redeployment was also presupposed throughout the discussion of the status of consciously based self-ascriptions as knowledge. If it were not the same (or at least an a priori very closely related) content *p* which featured both in first-order judgements that *p*, and in self-ascriptions of the belief that *p*, the metaphysics of believing that *p* would fall short of providing any kind of account of how consciously based self-ascriptions can amount to knowledge.

The reasons for believing the Redeployment Claim need examination, and so do the consequences of the claim. This may seem to be an issue in the philosophy of language and thought; and so of course it is, in part. But the claim also has a wider significance. To mention but one example: the Redeployment Claim is, in the nature of the case, inextricably intertwined with the question of how a subject's ability to think about the world can help to make available some of the conceptual resources for his ability to think about the attitudes of others. This is one of the issues I will consider when I turn, in the following section, to the consequences of the Redeployment Claim.

The Redeployment Claim can be formulated for the case of thought thus:

> The concepts (senses, modes of presentation) that feature in first-level thoughts not involving propositional attitudes are the very same concepts which feature in thoughts about someone's propositional attitudes.

In its linguistic version, the Redeployment Claim states that:

> The sense of a word occurring in contexts not involving propositional-attitude constructions is the same sense which is redeployed when the word occurs within the scope of propositional-attitude verbs.

The Redeployment Claim is a thesis about any propositional-attitude ascriptions, of whatever order, whether first, second, or any arbitrary higher order. In effect it says that the sense of an expression in 'direct', non-oblique contexts is elevated through the hierarchy of orders of propositional attitudes as the one sense of that expression, which remains the same however far up the hierarchy of orders we travel. The Redeployment Claim is put forward as correct regardless of how the ascribee of the attitudes is picked out, whether it be it by a first-person or a third-person sense. The claim is not just that the concepts (understood here as senses) featuring in first-order contents also occur as components of the Fregean Thoughts to which thinkers stand in propositional-attitude relations. That was Frege's claim, and in its linguistic version it is a claim about the reference of expressions within oblique contexts. The Redeployment Claim is saying something different. It is rather a claim about the *sense* of expressions in oblique contexts.

Something like the Redeployment Claim is accepted by widely diverse thinkers in the philosophy of language who use either the notion of sense, or some surrogate for it. Almost fifty years ago, in *Meaning and Necessity*, Carnap modestly wrote: 'It does not appear, at least not to me, that it would be unnatural or implausible to ascribe its ordinary sense to a name in an oblique context.'[40] One quickly reaches something very close to the Redeployment Claim if one reflects on the consequences of a semantic theory which insists on an infinite hierarchy not just of objects and senses, but of distinct senses of senses, senses of senses of senses, . . . and so on, if it is supposed that there is no a priori determination of a canonical sense of a sense by that latter sense itself. Donald Davidson was surely right in saying that the truth conditions for the sentences of a language following this reading of Frege's model would not be generated by a finite set of semantic rules for the atomic expressions, with the consequence that the language would be unlearnable.[41] If the Redeployment Claim is right, there is no such failure of finite generation of the truth conditions of all the sentences of a language which can describe propositional attitudes.[42] There is, then, certainly a general motiva-

---

[40] Carnap, *Meaning and Necessity*, sect. 30, p. 129.

[41] 'Theories of Meaning and Learnable Languages'.

[42] On Davidson's own paratactic analysis, a form of the Redeployment Claim is especially plausible. According to that analysis, the embedded sentence within the 'that'-clause is mentioned in the attribution (see his 'On Saying That', repr. in *Inquiries into Truth and Interpretation* (Oxford: Oxford University Press, 1984)). Understanding the embedded sentence seems sufficient for knowing not only how the ascribee is said to be thinking of certain objects and properties, but also for knowing how the ascriber is thinking of the ascribee's thoughts (or sayings). This could be so only if the senses one grasps in understanding the embedded sentence somehow determine ways of thinking of those same senses.

tion in the philosophy of language for accepting something like the Redeployment Claim. Michael Dummett, for one, has been moved to accept it on closely related grounds in the philosophy of language.[43] These various considerations seem to me sound in themselves, but they omit the positive, direct grounds for accepting the Redeployment Claim.

Suppose you and your friend are walking at dusk along a narrow city street. You both see a man further down the street, and your friend says to you 'That man is dangerous'. As a result of his saying that, you come to have a belief about your friend's beliefs, namely,

My friend believes that that man is dangerous.

The belief you attribute to your friend is one which has a perceptual-demonstrative mode of presentation of the perceived man in its intentional content. But how do you, the ascriber of the belief, think of the content of your friend's belief? It falls far short to say merely that you believe that your friend has a belief of the person down the street that he is dangerous (a case of Quine's relational belief). As is very familiar, that would be true if the person down the street happened, unknown to your friend, to be Saddam Hussein, whom your friend certainly believes to be dangerous. What we want to capture is your knowledge that your friend believes that that man is dangerous, a belief which, unlike the mere belief that Saddam Hussein is dangerous, will make you turn around and walk the other way.

It would equally fall short to enrich the relational characterization of the belief to 'My friend believes of the person down the street that he is dangerous and is coming towards him', and to offer that as equivalent to the content 'My friend believes that that man is dangerous'. This is not equivalent either. The former would be true if your friend had learned from a message over his mobile phone that Saddam Hussein is coming towards him. We would begin to capture the required content if we added 'and believes of him that he is *over there*'. But this use of *over there* is redeploying the demonstrative your friend would also use, so far from being an alternative theory, the suggestion supports the Redeployment Claim.

There is no doubt waiting to be developed a substantive theory of what it is to be employing a perceptual demonstrative in thought or language. This theory would in some way link thoughts with

[43] M. Dummett, *Frege: Philosophy of Language* (London: Duckworth, 1973), 267–9.

perceptual-demonstrative contents to features of the subject's perceptual experience which make such thoughts available to him. The theory would have to talk of certain canonical ground for accepting or rejecting perceptual-demonstrative thoughts, amongst much else. If we had such a theory, its materials could be used to specify the demonstrative mode of presentation which features in your friend's thought. A certain role would be distinctive of perceptual demonstratives, and we could specify your friend's thought by saying that it is a thought containing a concept with such-and-such role (as specified in the theory), and made available by such-and-such perceptual experience on this very occasion of walking down the street at dusk. You do not, however, have to have any personal-level knowledge of such a theory in order to ascribe the perceptual-demonstrative belief to your friend.

Let me emphasize that I am talking about a case in which you are capable of using in thought the very same mode of presentation as your friend, to think about the very same object. Very often in attributing attitudes to another, we do not and could not use the very same modes of presentation as the other person, because we do not stand in the right relations to the objects of their thought to use the very same modes of presentation as they do. In such cases, we can *refer* identifyingly to the modes of presentation the other person is employing, even if we cannot ourselves *employ* them to think about the same objects. Such is always the case with attributions of first-person beliefs to others, to present-tense beliefs attributed now to others at other times, to *here*-beliefs attributed to those at other places.[44] The same can apply to perceptual-demonstrative beliefs. Even if you and I are located very differently in relation to an object, if I know how it is presented to you, I can refer to the perceptual-demonstrative way of thinking of the object which is available to you, even though that perceptual-demonstrative way is not one I could use to think about the same object. In our present example, however, in thinking 'That man is dangerous', you and your friend are thinking of the same man in the same way. The question I am asking, of how you are thinking of the mode of presentation your friend employs,

---

[44] C. Peacocke, 'Demonstrative Thought and Psychological Explanation', *Synthese* 49 (1981), 187–217; W. Künne, 'First Person Propositions: A Fregean Account', in W. Künne, A. Newen, and M. Anduschus (eds.), *Direct Reference, Indexicality, and Propositional Attitudes* (CSLI Lecture Notes no. 70) (Stanford, Calif.: CSLI Publications, 1997).

cannot be fully answered by a response which has you merely referring to that mode of presentation in a way which does not make it clear that, in the circumstances, it is the same one you would be employing in thinking 'That man is dangerous'.

It begins to be very plausible, as the Redeployment Claim proposes, that the only account of the way in which you think of the intentional content of your friend's belief is by using the very same perceptual mode of presentation again, *that man* (modulo minor differences in the angle of viewing). In the case of perceptual demonstratives, this has the independently plausible consequence that there is a way of thinking of the intentional content of your friend's belief which is available only to those who are situated, and perceptually equipped, as he is, at the time he has the belief.

The little argument that we have just given for the case of demonstratives is that, in thinking about a person's demonstrative propositional attitudes, we employ a way of thinking of their intentional content which is captured neither by purely relational attributions, nor by thought-theoretical characterizations of intentional contents, nor by indirect ways of referring to modes of presentation. As far as I can see, this argument is generalizable from demonstratives to any other intentional content which is available in thought both to ascriber and ascribee. For any such intentional content, the only way which is both correct and generally available for the ascriber to capture the content of the ascribee's attitudes is for him simply to reuse, to redeploy, the intentional content in question. (It is this which makes it possible for an intentional content in a contextually self-verifying self-ascription to be, as Burge says, both thought and thought about in a single performance.)

If the ascribee uses the first person in a thought, such as 'I am hungry', naturally the ascriber cannot redeploy that very mode of presentation in describing the ascribee's thought. The ascriber cannot use the mode of presentation employed by the ascribee at all, in fact, since if he uses the first person, it will refer to himself, not the ascribee. A corresponding point applies to *now*, *here*, and their ilk. Actually, if we are strict, we ought to say that such cases do not form a counterexample to the linguistic form of the Redeployment Claim, since the words employed in ascribing a first-person or present-tense belief to another are not 'I' and 'now', but 'he' or 'he himself' and 'then'. But that they are not counterexamples is no cause for rejoicing. The linguistic version of the Redeployment Claim is simply remaining silent about what happens in these cases, and to leave matters there would hardly be satisfactory.

In fact, there is more of a positive nature to be said about the cases in which the ascriber is not in a position to use the very same concept as the ascribee. Consider the first-person beliefs of the ascribee. As is widely agreed in the literature, the ascriber can know what the ascribee believes, because he can know that the ascribee is thinking a thought of the first-person type. It is, further, true that when you know that another person is thinking a thought of the first-person type, the way in which you are yourself thinking of that type has the following property: that it is, for you, a priori that your own first-person thoughts are of that same type. Some of the consequences of the Redeployment Claim which I will be elaborating below apply not only to the case in which we have strict identity of concept employed by ascriber and ascribee, but hold also when the ascriber knows himself to be employing an indexical concept of the same type as that employed by the ascribee. I will flag one such point later on.

5.6 THREE CONSEQUENCES OF REDEPLOYMENT

I have already argued that the Redeployment Claim contributes to an explanation of how second-order self-ascriptions can be sensitive to the externally individuated contents of first-order attitudes without the thinker having to rely on evidence about his environment. The other consequences of the Redeployment Claim I will be tracing out are, as one might expect, cases in which either we find relations characteristic of concepts as they feature in first-level contents being lifted in certain ways to the level of the ascription of attitudes; or in which we have cross-level interactions resulting from the identity of concepts stated in the Redeployment Claim.

(a) *Norms and the Ascription of Content*

There is a basic system of normative relations in which a content stands, a system of relations which a thinker will respect in his thinking, and basic in the sense that the thinker can respect these relations without yet employing concepts of propositional attitudes. These are the normative relations which specify what justifies acceptance of a content, what justifies its rejection, what partially confirms it; and so forth. These relations will include what, in *A Study of Concepts*, I called 'the normative liaisons' of a content. They are the relations which, as Sellars and McDowell would say, locate a content in the space of reasons.[45] It is very natural to take these normative relations of a given content as compositionally determined, as flowing from the identity of the concepts in the content together with their mode of combination.

Now consider a thinker who does advance to the stage of reflecting on what are good reasons for his beliefs, and what in turn the contents of his beliefs give good reasons for thinking. This thinker is in a position to know what (for instance) justifies a judgement with a certain content. There are certain justification relations that are not person-relative. The informational and perceptual circumstances of different thinkers may vary, and so may their epistemic daring. But the underlying normative relations will not vary from thinker to thinker. It is the circumstances in which thinkers find themselves that vary, along with their epistemic idiosyncracies. So, when other things really are equal, what, at this very basic level of justificational relations, justifies acceptance of a content for one thinker will justify it for others. Other things will almost always not be equal; some justificational relations will depend on collateral information and others (in my view) will not. But in any case, knowledge about what justifies a judgement of the given content, in given epistemic and perceptual circumstances, is available to our thinker as a principle he can draw upon in the ascription of content-involving attitudes to others. This is possible because, as the Redeployment Claim states, the very same concepts, comprising the content in question, feature both in the thinker's own base-level thoughts about the world, and in his attribution of attitudes to others.

It is worth thinking more about what is involved in this lifting of normative relations to the level of ascription. In reflecting on what it is rational for someone employing a given concept to think, you have to think about the *world*. In wondering what would justify another person's application or denial of the concept *square* to an object, you have to engage in such thoughts as 'Would such-and-such be sufficient to establish that it is square? Or for establishing that it is not?' This involves your use of the concept *square* in much the way that

---

[45] W. Sellars, 'Empiricism and the Philosophy of Mind', repr. in his *Science, Perception and Reality* (London: Routledge, 1963); and McDowell, *Mind and World*.

would be involved in deciding whether you yourself have sufficient grounds for concluding that the object is square, or for concluding that it is not. The principal difference between the two cases is just that in one of them you yourself are in the relevant evidential states, while in the other you are just thinking about them. In fact, this whole conception would be consistent with the view that in ascribing attitudes to others one draws on tacit knowledge of a normative theory of the justificatory relations in which contents stand.[46] In any case, we seem to have an intertwining of the ascription of content-involving states with both the normative and the externalist character of content.

This lifting of normative relations to the level of ascription is something which can also be present when we have identity only of the type of concept in question, as in the first-person uses by the ascribee which I mentioned above. The ascriber may first reflect that if he himself were in a situation of such-and-such a kind, he would have reason to form the belief, with a first-person content, that he himself is thus-and-so. Suppose he is then prepared to think of the ascribee as in a situation of the same sort as that about which he has just reflected, and that he also has the capacity to think of the first-person type. In these circumstances the ascriber can then, *ceteris paribus*, be in a position reasonably to attribute to the other a belief, of the first-person type, that he (the other) is thus-and-so. In such cases sameness of type of concept is sufficient in context to provide the bridge from, on the one side, thinking about the world and what would justify certain thoughts about it, to, on the other side, ascription of particular attitudes to the other person.

So much by way of the lifting of normative relations to the level of ascription.

(b) *Cross-Level Interactions: The Case of Inference*

If the same concepts (senses) feature, as used, in both first-order and higher-order contents, then we would expect there to be cross-level inferential interactions between the levels, inferences turning on this identity.

---

[46] See T. Stone and M. Davies, 'The Mental Simulation Debate: A Progress Report', in P. Carruthers and P. Smith (eds.), *Theories of Theories of Mind* (Cambridge: Cambridge University Press, 1996).

One species of cross-level interaction comes across most vividly in the first-person case. Consider someone who has the second-order, first-person belief

(1) I believe that that man over there is French.

Suppose she also believes, on the basis of what she currently sees and hears while in the airport, that

(2) That man over there is speaking with an American accent and is checking in with an American passport.

Our subject who has beliefs with the contents (1) and (2) is someone with a cognitive problem, a problem she can appreciate just from (1) and (2) alone. From the premises (1) and (2) she can rationally infer

(3) There is someone whom I both believe to be French and who is speaking with an American accent and is checking in with an American passport.

Statement (3) is to be understood in such a way that the scope of 'believe' concludes with the word 'French'; the immediately following 'and' has wider scope than 'believes'. The inference to (3) from (1) and (2) seems to be valid. But it is certainly valid only if the expressions 'that man over there' as used in (1) and 'that man over there' as used in (2) either have the same sense, or at least there is some a priori fixing, available to the thinker, of one of the senses by the other. If they do not express the same sense, or there is no such a priori fixing available to the thinker, there would be a fallacy of equivocation. It is not at all plausible that some suppressed additional premise of an a posteriori character needs to be made explicit and assumed for the move from (1) and (2) to be valid.

Nor does the validity of the inference turn solely on the identity of the normal, non-oblique references of the expressions in question. Suppose we replace (2) with (2a),

(2a) Bill Smith is speaking with an American accent and is checking in with an American passport,

so that we can then consider the inference from (1) and (2a) to the same conclusion (3). That is a transition which does not seem to me valid. To move from (1) and (2a) to (3) requires the additional a posteriori premise

(2b) That man over there is Bill Smith.

The overwhelmingly natural response to the original case is to hold that the demonstratives in the premises (1) and (2) have the same sense, so that the way of thinking the subject employs in thinking about the perceptually given man and the way of thinking she employs when thinking of the content of her first-order belief are one and the same. If we accept this identity, we have a smooth explanation of how second-order beliefs can rationally interact with first-order beliefs when a thinker is evaluating and revising her own propositional attitudes. This is just the kind of rational interaction which occurs in the case in which critical reasoning does involve a thinker's self-ascribing a belief.

Still, someone may object that this cannot be correct, because 'that man over there' in (1) and 'that man over there' in (2) actually have different references: the former refers to a mode of presentation (namely, itself), and the latter to a man. It will be said that we had better have constancy of reference in a given term if an inference is to be valid! And in any case, how can the modes of presentation be identical if one refers to itself, and the other to a man? Doesn't this just contradict Leibniz's Law?

The answer to this last point is that anyone who accepts the Redeployment Claim will have to use a relativized notion of reference. For both expressions and modes of presentation, the relation of reference will have to be relativized to a kind of context. For linguistic (or thought) contexts in which it does not occur within the scope of a propositional-attitude verb or concept, the mode of presentation has its normal reference. In other contexts, it refers to itself. This is a pair of rules which can be part of a finite set of rules which fully determine the truth conditions of the sentences of a language capable of expressing the propositional attitudes. On this approach, sense does determine reference, but only relative to a particular linguistic (or thought) context. On this, I am entirely at one with Dummett, who introduces just this relativization.[47]

It is worth emphasizing the general nature of this rule for propositional-attitude contexts. Consider someone who has mastered this rule, and who then acquires and understands a new expression true or false of things in the world. It is a prediction of this theory that

---

[47] *Frege: Philosophy of Language*, 267–9.

such a person does not need anything new to understand sentences in which the new expression occurs within propositional-attitude verbs already in his repertoire. This prediction seems to be correct: there is no question of having further to learn what concept of a concept is expressed by 'electron' as it occurs in 'Bohr believed there are electrons'. One's understanding of 'believes' and of 'electron' unembedded suffice. According to the Redeployment Claim, since the expression still has its normal sense when embedded, one is already in possession of all that is required for understanding such propositional-attitude sentences.

This treatment of the problem may seem to make the original objection—that difference of reference in different contexts will block inferences—all the more forceful. To address this, we can reconsider the inference from (1) and (2) to (3) with an intermediate step made explicit:

(1) I believe that that man over there is French.
(1') That man over there is such that I believe of him that he is French.
(2) That man over there is speaking with an American accent and is checking in with an American passport.

Hence,

(3) There is someone whom I believe to be French and who is speaking with an American accent and is checking in with an American passport.

Conclusion (3) follows from (1') and (2) by conjunction-introduction and existential generalization. (1') follows from (1) by exportation, which is valid for this demonstrative concept. The premise of an exportation inference involves a concept occurring in oblique position, and its conclusion involves the same occurrence occurring in a direct context, as simply specifying an object about which some relational attitude is ascribed. Exportation is then precisely a principle which crosses levels. In examples in which exportation is valid, the shift of reference does not involve any *non sequitur*.

On this treatment of the transition from (1) and (2) to (3), nothing turns on the use of the first person. If all occurrences of 'I' are replaced uniformly by any other singular term or variable, the resulting inference is also valid.

I do not say the believer in a strict hierarchy of senses, senses of senses, and so forth, and who favours the use of that hierarchy in the treatment of propositional attitudes, could not account for the validity of the inference from (1) and (2) to (3), but it is worth considering what he would have to say to achieve this result. For this strict theorist, there will be a sense of a sense, and this sense of a sense will be expressed by 'that man over there' in (1). Suppose we follow the convention that pointed brackets around an expression designate that expression's sense, so that '⟨that man over there⟩' designates a first-level sense. The believer in a strict hierarchy and its application to propositional attitude contexts will then have to say that every first-level sense uniquely determines a second-level sense, and he will also have to say that it is a priori that the uniquely determined second-level sense refers to the first-level sense which determines it. For learnability of his language, he would also have to insist on corresponding axioms relating all other pairs of adjacent levels. With these resources in place, he can account for the validity of the inference, provided he is prepared to attribute tacit knowledge of these axioms to ordinary thinkers.

The resulting account does, though, stretch credibility. The fundamental problem is that it seems to be operating with more distinctions than there are differences. This comes out in three ways.

(i) The special properties attributed by the strict hierarchy theorist to his second-level sense would be explained if the first-level sense were simply to be used again, as the Redeployment Claim holds, in oblique contexts. If the advocate of a strict hierarchy means more than can be accounted for by the Redeployment Claim, I do not know what the additional unexplained material might be. If he does not, he may not have any substantive dispute with the Redeployment Claim.

(ii) In other examples in which we draw the distinction between an object and the various ways of thinking of it (as the Evening Star, as *that planet* given in perception, and so forth), the distinction is forced by reflection on the nature of the mental states which employ those various different ways of thinking, and by the semantic properties of the sentences in which we describe those states. Such motivations seem to be lacking in the distinction between a first-level thought and the proposed canonical sense of that thought which, according to the hierarchy theorist, is required in a theory of second-order ascriptions. In fact, that is to understate the case. Reflection on second-order cases suggests positively that we precisely must not draw the distinction in the second-order cases in question. This moral is implicit in the earlier discussion of particular modes of presentation, but it is also worth reflecting on complete thoughts. Let us take an example of a second-order attribution, drawn from Tyler Burge's important discussion of the hierarchy:[48]

(4) Igor believes Bela believes Opus 132 is a masterpiece.

According to the hierarchy theorist, in specifying Igor's belief in (4), we make reference to a certain mode of presentation of (if you like, to a means of ascribing) the belief content which Igor ascribes to Bela, and this is to be distinguished from the content *Opus 132 is a masterpiece* itself. This seems to me an unintuitive description of the ascription. It seems to me that for (4) to be true, Igor must be thinking that one of Bela's beliefs has the content *Opus 132 is a masterpiece*, and in thinking of this content, Igor is employing exactly the same content in thought as Bela would if he were to think that Opus 132 is a masterpiece. It is not at all as if Igor is thinking of the content in some indirect way as the first content asserted on such-and-such page of Joseph Kerman's book about the Beethoven string quartets. If we should distinguish senses only where facts about epistemic possibility or cognitive significance require it, then we should not in these examples postulate a canonical sense of the content *Opus 132 is a masterpiece*.

(iii) Correlatively, the theorist of a strict hierarchy will give an implausibly elaborate account of what certainly appear to be very straightforward inferences. The following certainly seems to be a valid inference:

(4) Igor believes Bela believes Opus 132 is a masterpiece.
(5) It is true that Opus 132 is a masterpiece.

Therefore,

(6) Something which Igor believes Bela believes is true.

On the Redeployment account, this is a straightforward inference by existential generalization, since one and the same content is mentioned, by the same means, in (4) and (5). If '*p*' is a variable over

---

[48] T. Burge, 'Frege and the Hierarchy', *Synthese* 40 (1979), 265–81.

Fregean contents, if we use pointed brackets as before, and use '∧' for predicational combination of senses, then on the Redeployment account, the inference in question can be regimented thus:

(7) believes (Igor, ⟨Bela⟩∧⟨believes⟩∧⟨Opus 132 is a masterpiece⟩)
(8) true (⟨Opus 132 is a masterpiece⟩)

Therefore,

(9) ∃p (believes (Igor, ⟨Bela⟩∧⟨believes⟩∧p) & true (p)).

The theorist of the strict hierarchy has to offer something much more complicated, since for him (4) involves reference to a mode of presentation of the content ⟨Opus 132 is a masterpiece⟩, rather than to the content itself. There would have to be additional principles which either state, or entail, a connection between the truth of the content as given under the proposed canonical mode of presentation and the holding of (8). When we are dealing with inferences analogous to (4)–(6), but with multiple embeddings, there will have to be even more additional principles. My own view is that the inference from (4) and (5) to (6) is what it seems to be: a simple application of existential generalization which does not need validation by special additional premises.[49]

In earlier expositions of these points, I have sometimes written as if the above considerations should make us reject any use of the notion of the canonical concept of a concept. That now seems to me too strong. The arguments I have given, if sound, do show that we do not need the hierarchy of senses for the treatment of ordinary propositional-attitude contexts with iteration. It does not follow that there is not some other good motivation for recognizing canonical concepts of concepts which are distinct from those concepts themselves. There seems to be a good motivation when the language contains expressions explicitly referring to concepts, and making predications of them. It is arguable that the very concepts *the concept that man*, *the concept square* are canonical concepts of the concepts to which they refer. These concepts of concepts contain the concept

---

[49] Tyler Burge, in 'Frege and the Hierarchy', also suggests that there are problems in giving a systematic theory of truth conditions if one uses a notion of denotation which is relative to linguistic context. The issues are somewhat technical, and I will not pursue them here. For one way of developing a truth theory for a language for which denotation is relative to linguistic context, see the Appendix of my 'Entitlement, Self-Knowledge and Conceptual Redeployment', 153–7.

of the definite description and the concept of a concept as constituents, unlike the concepts to which they refer. For any expression A, the reference of such a definite description is determined by the rule that 'the concept A' refers to the sense expressed by A. This is, evidently, a distinct rule from the rule which states the reference of the concept expressed by A. We do not need these definite descriptions just for the purposes of making attributions of attitudes, but we certainly need them in explicit theorizing about concepts. One should, then, sharply distinguish the question of the correctness of Redeployment Claim from the question of whether there are good reasons for recognizing canonical senses of senses, and indeed a hierarchy of such senses. Accepting the Redeployment Claim does not require total rejection of that hierarchy, and there are good reasons, independent of the treatment of propositional attitudes, to acknowledge canonical senses of senses.[50]

(c) *Powers of Relational Explanation*

A propositional attitude with a first-order content can, when the thinker is in suitable auxiliary states, explain some relational fact about the thinker. A person's having a belief that water is thus-and-so may explain her acting in such-and-such way in relation to quantities of water; a person's seeing that the exit is in *that* direction may explain his walking in that direction; and so on. What is explained in these cases is not just a bodily movement non-relationally characterized. What is explained is the occurrence of an action with certain relational, environmental properties. These explanations support counterfactuals formulated in environmental terms.

It is plausible that the ability to explain relational states of affairs involving the subject in suitable circumstances is a constitutive property of attitudes to first-order contents. It is also plausible that particular relational explananda are traceable back to the presence of particular conceptual constituents of first-order contents.[51] I will henceforth be taking it for granted that such links between relational explananda and first-order contents do indeed exist.

If the Redeployment Claim is correct, we would expect these pow-

[50] I am indebted to Tyler Burge and Timothy Williamson for comments influencing my change of mind towards this middle position.
[51] These are the themes I developed in 'Externalist Explanation'.

ers of relational explanation to be elevated to second-order attitudes; and this does seem to be the case. If you think that your friend believes that that (perceptually presented) man is dangerous, and have reason to avoid anyone your friend believes to be dangerous, then we have enough, given a normal background, to explain your avoiding the perceptually presented man.

In that example, your reasoning leading up to your avoidance of the man would run thus. From the premise that your friend believes that that man is dangerous, you export, and infer that that man is believed by your friend to be dangerous; and then he falls within your reasons which apply to anyone your friend believes to be dangerous. So in this case, the powers of relational explanation associated with the second-order belief about your friend's belief operate via your making an exportation inference, of the sort discussed in (b) above, from your second-order attitude. I conjecture that this phenomenon is quite general. That is, I conjecture that the powers of relational explanation associated with particular concepts are elevated to second-order attitudes by way of the thinker's making exportation inferences from second- to first-order attitudes. These first-order attitudes then display the powers of relational explanation already noted. If this conjecture is true, it has the following consequence. Once we have properly accounted for the powers of relational explanation distinctive of certain concepts in first-order attitudes, and have also properly accounted for the validity of the appropriate class of exportation inferences, then we have the powers of relational explanation of the same concepts in second-order attitudes as a by-product.

These points about relational explananda have a special bearing when the second-order attitude is a self-ascription. Suppose you self-ascribe the belief that the person over there is French. We can imagine that you are an official acting on the instruction 'Check again on the nationality of anyone you believe to be French'. In this context, your second-order belief can explain your going over to meet that person—a relational explanandum. On this approach, in having second-order knowledge about your own knowledge, you know which things and properties your knowledge is about *in as strong a sense* as that in which you know which person is speaking with an American accent, when you know that that person over there is speaking with an American accent. In manifesting that first-order knowledge about the world, you can identify the person in question by pointing to him, or by engaging in other actions which are explained as bearing

certain relations to that person, and no other. But the ability to identify in this sense is also present when the concept *that man over there*
features in second-order attitudes too. Everything that you can do in
the first-order case you can also do in the second-order case, when
you have to answer the question 'Which person around here is the
one whom you believe to be French?'. You can point to the person,
or generally engage in actions which are explained as bearing certain
relations to that person. It is a consequence of the present account
that there is no question of a thinker's knowing the material, external objects of his second-order attitudes only indirectly, or obliquely.

6

Self-Knowledge and Illusions of Transcendence

Philosophical problems about the self and the first person provide a salient illustration of the challenge of integrating the epistemology and the metaphysics of a domain. There has been a persistent impulse amongst thinkers about the self to postulate a transcendental subject of experience and thought. It is an impulse to which Kant, Schopenhauer, Husserl and the early Wittgenstein all yielded. The impulse results from a combination of genuine insight and genuine error. The insight consists in the appreciation that there is an Integration Challenge which calls for a philosophical solution. The error consists in trying, in this domain, to achieve integration by postulating an exotic domain of the transcendent, rather than by revising and deepening one's epistemology.

There is probably more agreement on the preceding description of the situation than there is on the correct positive solution to this instance of the Integration Challenge. The first task in this area is to identify adequately and precisely the distinctive feature of some first-person thoughts which has led to illusions of transcendence. Once the feature is properly identified, the next task is the explanation of existence of this feature, and some elaboration of its significance.

The call for a good account of the nature of first-person thought has drawn forth some of the most justly celebrated and dazzling contributions of philosophy. My own experience has been that some of these contributions are dazzling not only in the intensity of the light they cast, but also in their having made it hard to see the true nature of the especially distinctive feature of first-person thought that has produced the illusion of transcendence. The feature has often been mischaracterized in one way or another, and theories have been built on these mischaracterizations. Sometimes an appreciation that an earlier characterization is defective has been replaced by a new mischaracterization. Before I go any further, I had better say what I think the feature is.

6.1 REPRESENTATIONAL INDEPENDENCE

Consider first the everyday case in which an ordinary person forms a belief with the content 'I am in front of a door', and does so for the reason that he sees a door ahead of him. His visual experience represents the door as bearing a certain spatial relation to him. This is so even if he cannot see or otherwise experience his own body on this particular occasion. It would still be true that, taking his experience at face value, he would judge that he is in front of a door. The way the visual experience represents the world as being is one which justifies his acceptance of the first-person content endorsed in his belief 'I am in front of a door'. Here I assume he possesses the concepts in the content of this belief. More generally, when a person forms a perceptual belief 'I am F', he does so because his experience itself has the content 'I am F', or has some content which justifies the content 'I am F'. This point would be agreed by theorists who may otherwise disagree about what philosophical theory is to be given of an experience's having a first-person content. I will return to that last point.

We can more generally consider examples in which the thinker's reason for making his judgement 'I am F' is his being in some state, other than a belief state, which represents a certain content C as correct. In the class of examples I want to consider, the content C may, but need not, be the same as the content 'I am F'. Some theorists believe that perceptual states have non-conceptual contents which are distinct in kind from the contents which feature in beliefs.[1] What I have to say is orthogonal to that issue. In the class of examples on which I want to focus, it will be the case that the content C, even if it is distinct from the content 'I am F', is still one which stands in an implicational relation to the content 'I am F'.

In our opening example, it is a perceptual experience which is the content-possessing state which gives a reason for forming the first-person belief. But the general property I specified can be present in cases in which the reason-giving state is not an experience, and still is not a belief either. If you are sitting at your desk in the night, and

---

[1] Evans, *The Varieties of Reference*; Peacocke, *A Study of Concepts*.

a power cut turns out all lighting, you may still in the dark be able to keep track of your movements relative to the room you are in. You may walk across the room, and then form the belief 'I am in front of a door'. You have a faculty which allows you to keep track of your location, and the exercise of the faculty on this occasion results in its seeming to you that you are in front of the door. This seeming is not a perceptual experience. Nor is it to be identified with a belief. You may know that your tracking faculty misfunctions in a specific way. In those circumstances, your judgements may overrule the deliverances of your inaccurate faculty, and you may form the belief that the door is probably two feet to the left of you. When, however, you are in the dark and you are taking the spatial faculty's deliverances at their face value, your reason for forming your belief 'I am in front of the door' is a belief-independent state, and one which represents it as being the case that you are in front of the door.

We can say that a use of the first person, in a particular belief with the content 'I am F', is *representationally dependent* if

(i) 'I am F' is the content of one of the thinker's current mental states, a state which represents that content as correct; and

(ii) the thinker forms the belief 'I am F' by taking the mental state mentioned in (i) at face value, in respect of this content. That is, in the terminology of Chapter 2, the thinker is operating in a mode in which such states are taken at face value.

The uses of 'I' in the two beliefs 'I am in front of the door' in each of our two opening examples, based on visual perception in the one case and the deliverances of the spatial faculty on the other, are both representationally dependent uses. In the usual case of knowledge of one's bodily and spatial properties resulting from perception, clause (ii) will be fulfilled because in such cases the subject is taking the representational state at face value. In a huge range of cases, the content of a representationally dependent use of the first person is one which represents the subject as having some location in the spatio-temporal world.

The characterization (i)–(ii) says what it is for a use of the first person in thought to be representationally dependent. We could similarly give a characterization of what it is for an utterance, on a particular occasion, of the first-person pronoun to be representationally dependent.

From the standpoint of someone engaged in giving an account of mastery and understanding, representationally dependent uses form a theoretical natural kind. For these uses, there is the possibility of giving a partial account of mastery of these uses by describing the rational sensitivity of certain beliefs involving them to the content of the representational states with the same content.

Representational dependence is not a notion which is definitionally restricted to the first person. Quite generally, for any mode of presentation *m*, we can say that a use of *m*, in a particular belief '*m* is *F*', is representationally dependent if there is a content '*m* is *F*' having the properties which result from clauses (i)–(ii) above by substituting '*m*' for 'I'. That is, the content '*m* is *F*' must be the content of one of the thinker's current representational mental states; and the thinker must form the belief '*m* is *F*' because he is in the mode of taking such states at face value. A use of a perceptual-demonstrative such as 'that car', in an ordinary perceptual-demonstrative belief like 'That car is travelling fast', is representationally dependent.

A *representationally independent* use of the first person, in a belief 'I am *F*', is a use in a belief which the subject forms for a reason, but whose content 'I am *F*' does not meet the conditions (i) and (ii) in the definition of representational dependence. Representational independence is the crucial notion which I want to put to work in this chapter.

The uses of the first person in beliefs with the following contents can, in appropriate circumstances, be representationally independent:

> I am thinking about Pythagoras's Theorem.
> I see the phone is on the table.
> I remember attending the birthday party.
> I remember that Russell was born in 1872.
> I am beginning to dream.
> I fear that the motion will not be carried.

As the definition of representational independence should have made clear, to say that such uses are representationally independent is not to say that the beliefs in question are not held for reasons. On the contrary: the thinker's reason for believing 'I am thinking about Pythagoras's Theorem' are his recent thoughts about that theorem. There are also reasons in the other cases on this list: the thinker's reason for self-ascribing a seeing of the phone on the table is the occurrence of just such a visual perception; and so on. What matters for a representationally independent use of the first person is not at all absence of reasons. What matters is rather the nature of the reason, and in particular its relation to the content of the belief in question. When our thinker comes to judge 'I am thinking about Pythagoras's Theorem', his reason for his judgement is not a mental event or state whose representational content is that he is thinking about Pythagoras's Theorem. His reason is rather his particular occurrent thoughts about Pythagoras's Theorem. When our thinker judges 'I see the phone to be on the table', his reason for making his judgement is the occurrence of his visual perception. That perception is a seeing that the phone is on the table; but that perception is not one which has the representational content that he is seeing the phone. An experience in a given modality does not normally have the represen-tational content that the subject is having an experience in that modality.

A fortiori, then, what justifies the use of the first person in repre-sentationally independent beliefs is not its occurrence in the content of some representational state which the subject is taking at face value.

A theorist might be tempted—I have felt the temptation myself—to say that the contents of beliefs which involve representationally independent uses of the first person are not in general implied by the contents of the states which are the thinker's reason for forming the representationally independent belief. It seems evident that the con-tent of the visual experience, the perceptual-demonstrative content

> *that phone is on that table*

could be true without it being true that

> *I see that that phone is on that table.*

It is of course certainly true that that phone could be on that table without my seeing that that phone is on that table. But our question was whether the first content 'implies' the second, and 'implication' is here a term of art. The metaphysical necessity that if the first con-tent holds, the second content holds, is certainly not the only impor-tant notion of implication in the offing here. Suppose we use the notion of implication under which one content implies another if any context with respect to which the first content is true is a context with respect to which the second content is true. The first of the displayed contents above, if we take '*that phone*' and '*that table*' to be visual perceptual-demonstratives, could not be true in a given context unless the subject of that context were visually perceiving the phone and the table in question. But if the subject is visually perceiving them, then the second content will also be true with respect to that same context. This is entirely consistent with the failure of the metaphysical necessity of the conditional that if the first content is true, then so is the second content. The notion of implication as preservation of truth in any given context is of great epistemic importance. This notion of implication is in the spirit of the notion of logical validity as defined in Kaplan's logic of demonstratives.[2] We should by now have learned the point of his lesson that such notions come apart from those of metaphysical necessity.

One of the reasons that the epistemically oriented, rather than the metaphysical, notion of implication is important in these cases concerns the mastery of self-ascription of psychological states. It is very plausible that one of the fundamental elements in the capacity to self-ascribe psychological states in a way which amounts to knowledge is precisely the ability to make such transitions from, for instance, a visual experience with the first of the displayed contents to a judgement with the second of the displayed contents. The same applies to auditory experiences and the self-ascription of auditory experiences; and so forth. An account which treats this as a fundamental element in the capacity to self-ascribe has the attractive feature that it makes the ability to employ concepts in thinking about and experiencing the world a prerequisite for the ability to self-ascribe experiences. Now any account which proceeds along these lines needs to explain why self-ascriptions so reached are knowledge. To explain this, we need to make the point that the second content, the content of the self-ascription, is guaranteed to be true in any context in which the thinker has an experience with the first content. The epistemically oriented notion of implication is, then, going to be important for the theory of understanding and mastery, as it is for epistemology more generally. The notion obviously merits further discussion on some other occasion. For the present, the point is that there is indeed an important notion of implication on which, at least in perceptual cases, the content of an experience implies the content of the self-ascription in a representationally independent use of the first person. There is an epistemically important notion of implication on which

---

[2] Kaplan, 'Demonstratives'.

it is incorrect to characterize representationally independent uses as ones in which the content of the self-ascription does not follow from the content of the reason-giving state.

Four salient points about representationally independent uses of the first person emerge just from the introductory materials and distinctions we already have before us.

(a) Representational independence of a use of the first person is to be distinguished from immunity to error through misidentification, the phenomenon defined in the discussions of first-person thought in Wittgenstein, Shoemaker, and Evans.[3] To reactivate our memory traces about this distinction, I quote Shoemaker's characterization: '[T]o say that a statement "*a* is φ" is subject to error through misidentification relative to the term "*a*" means that the following is possible: the speaker knows some particular thing to be φ, but makes the mistake of asserting "*a* is ψ" because, and only because, he mistakenly thinks that the thing he knows to be φ is what "*a*" refers to'.[4] Actually, this formulation would include the quite irrelevant case in which the thinker makes an error because he fails to understand the term '*a*' correctly. So let us transform this definition to one concerning the level of thought, by replacing 'asserting' and 'statement' by 'believing' and 'belief'. The kind of mistake in question would then be that of believing that the thing he knows to be φ is identical with *a*. The variables are now used for modes of presentation, or thought constituents.

As the connoisseurs of this literature will remember, Shoemaker also draws two further distinctions within beliefs which are immune to error through misidentification. One is the distinction between the circumstantially immune and the absolutely immune. A judgement is circumstantially immune to error through misidentification relative to the first person if it is immune to such misidentification when the judgement is made on a certain basis.[5] When made on some other basis, it may be subject to errors of identification. The other distinction is that between *de facto* immunity to error through misidentification and stronger forms of immunity. A judgement 'I once played

---

[3] L. Wittgenstein, *The Blue and Brown Books*, 2nd edn. (Oxford: Blackwell, 1969); S. Shoemaker, 'Self-Reference and Self-Awareness', repr. in his *Identity, Cause and Mind: Philosophical Essays* (Cambridge: Cambridge University Press, 1984); Evans, *The Varieties of Reference*.

[4] 'Self-Reference and Self-Awareness', 7–8.   [5] Ibid. 8

in a concert' made on the basis of a memory, from the inside, as of playing an instrument in a concert, has only *de facto* immunity. In a world in which people have apparent, and appropriately causally related, memories of others' experiences, there would be no such immunity.[6]

Shoemaker himself, and later Evans in *The Varieties of Reference*, made a convincing case that the belief 'I am in front of a door', when judged on the basis of an experience of being in front of a door, is immune to error through misidentification. This is an example of Shoemaker's 'circumstantial' and *de facto* immunity. Belief in such a content is immune when made on the basis of perceptual experience, in the circumstances of the actual world. Yet this was our paradigm, initial example of a representationally *dependent* use in thought of the first person. So such immunity to error through misidentification of a first-person belief is not sufficient for it to be representationally independent.

A converse proposition is, though, very plausible, and supported by the account I will offer below. This is the proposition that all representationally independent uses of the first person in which the first-person belief is knowledge are also uses which are immune to error through misidentification. Certainly, a representationally independent use cannot be based on an identity-elimination inference from the contents of two other mental states. Such an inferential transition would require that the contents of the reason-giving states should give reasons for the first-person belief, and that is contrary to the definition of representational independence.

When we have rather more in front of us, I will return to address the question of whether absolute, 'logical' immunity to error through misidentification is sufficient for representational independence. I believe it is not sufficient.

(b) Is infallibility at least necessary for representational independence? Our list of contents which, believed in suitable circumstances, involve representationally independent uses of the first person included contents of the form 'I remember that p' and 'I see that p'. A thinker is not infallible about these contents.

It may be objected that such contents should not be on the list anyway. It may be said that in judging these fallible contents, the

---

[6] S. Shoemaker, 'Persons and their Pasts', also in *Identity, Cause and Mind*.

thinker takes for granted or presupposes the first-person content that he is perceiving properly (in the relevant modality), or the first-person content that his memory is functioning properly. I agree that these are taken for granted; but that does not imply that the examples should be excluded from the list of representationally independent uses. Perhaps the objector's point is that 'I see that p' is justified jointly by 'I have an experience as of its being the case that p' and 'I am perceiving properly'. Here the former content, 'I have an experience . . .' would have to be the content of a belief (it is not part of the content of normal visual experience). This raises the following question.

Can it ever be that a seeing justifies the one who sees in self-ascribing a *seeing*? Or is it always the case that what is justified is, in the first instance, only a self-ascription of an experience, from which one must infer, with the additional information that one is perceiving properly, that one is also genuinely seeing? It looks as if the latter will have to be the position of the person who insists that knowledgeable, representationally independent uses of the first person must be infallible. But the position is highly problematic. In particular, it is difficult to square with a plausible view of ordinary perceptual knowledge. There would be widespread agreement that ordinary perceptual knowledge, while justified by perceptual experience, does not have to result from inference from the thinker's current experiences. A seeing can, in suitable circumstances, justify the thinker's belief 'That tree has leaves'. Why can it not, in the same circumstances, equally justify the thinker's belief 'I see that tree has leaves'? It seems that any doubt that it can would equally spill over into a doubt as to whether non-inferential perceptual knowledge is possible either. So there is considerable plausibility in this conditional: if non-inferential perceptual knowledge of the world is possible, then so also must be knowledgeable, representationally independent uses of 'I see that p'. If this is right, then infallibility is not necessary for representational independence.

(c) To say that a use of the first person is representationally independent is not in any way to imply that it does not refer. The characterization of a use as representationally independent has to do with the absence of a certain kind of reason for forming the belief in which the first-person way of thinking is employed. The conclusion that representationally independent uses do not refer would follow if it were a necessary condition for a use of the first person to refer that the thinker's reasons for accepting it should be of the kind characterized in the definition of representational dependence. But I cannot see any reason for believing that, and many against. One reason against is that forms of reasoning involving the first person, and whose validity requires that the first person refers, seem valid regardless of whether the use of the first person in a premise is representationally dependent or not. Nor in my judgement do we have any satisfactory model for the semantic evaluation of first-person thoughts which does not employ the notion of reference. Representationally independent uses of the first person, like all other uses, conform to the principle that they refer to the thinker of the thought in which they occur. I will return later in this chapter to non-referential treatments of the first person.

(d) When a mental state provides a reason for a belief involving a representationally independent use of the first person, the *content* of that state cannot fully explain what makes the first-person belief rational (when it is so). This much is a consequence of the very definition of a representationally independent use. It follows that to find an account of mastery and understanding of these uses we must look elsewhere.

The phenomenon that I want to highlight is not merely that there are true beliefs which contain representationally independent uses of the first person. That contents of the sort listed in the examples above of representationally independent uses of the first person are on occasion true is not obviously something which should by itself prompt a search for a philosophical theory. The mere truth of these contents does not depend upon the uses of the first person being representationally independent. They will have the truth values they do regardless of how they come to be believed. The phenomenon I want to highlight is rather the fact that beliefs containing representationally independent uses of the first person can on occasion have the status of *knowledge*. What explains this fact?

6.2 DELTA THEORIES

I now turn to consider a class of theories which aim to explain how beliefs involving representationally independent uses of the first person can amount to knowledge. Theories in this class differ from one another in the way in which they elaborate important aspects of the explanation, but the broad structure of the answer they give is common to all of them. According to these approaches, when a person self-ascribes an experience (say), it is the occurrence of the experience itself which is part of the person's reason for making a judgement whose content contains the concept of experience. That it is an experience she judges herself to be having is rationally explained in part by the fact that she is having an experience. The case contrasts with a representationally dependent example, in which the content judged does not go beyond what is justified by the content of the experience.

Under this treatment of the representationally independent case, the thinker's reason for making her judgement that she has an experience of a certain kind is not some thought to the effect 'This experience is occurring, and is of such-and-such a kind'. The thinker's reason for making her judgement is not itself a thought about the experience. Any such thought is part of what is explained, rather than part of the explanation. The explanation is just the occurrence of the experience itself to its subject. Nor does any thought or representation of herself as the subject of the experience enter her reasons for her judgement. I think this is what is right in Shoemaker's remark that 'When one is introspectively aware of one's thoughts, feelings, beliefs and desires, one is not presented to oneself as a flesh-and-blood person, and one does not seem to be presented to oneself as an object at all'.[7] There is no reason to object to the formulation that the thinker judges the content because she has the experience, for this explanation posited does not thereby involve any thought or conception of herself as having the experience in the statement of her reason for making the judgement. It is worth noting that in that minimal sense, we can equally truly say of an observational judgement about the external world that the thinker makes it because she has an experience of a certain sort. But when a thinker makes an observational judgement, her reasons for making it do not need to include some thought to the effect that she has a certain type of experience.

Now the occurrence of an experience, or of any other particular conscious state, can give an immediate reason for forming a belief (or

---

[7] S. Shoemaker, 'Personal Identity: A Materialist's Account', in S. Shoemaker and R. Swinburne, *Personal Identity* (Oxford: Oxford University Press, 1984), 102.

doing anything else) only to the subject who has the experience or conscious state. Suppose a person has a visual experience as of the phone being on the table, and that the occurrence of this experience is her reason for forming the belief 'I have an experience as of the phone being on the table'. Then the owner of the experience will be the same as the subject referred to in the first-person component of the belief. The situation can be diagrammed as in Figure 6.1.

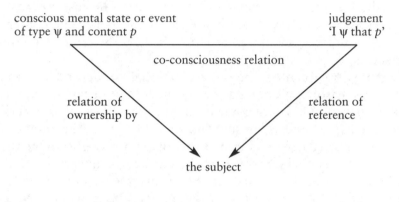

FIGURE 6.1

Because of the shape of this diagram, I call accounts of the general kind I have been outlining *delta accounts*. (The diagram should not be thought to beg the question against reductionist views of the self, 'the subject' of the diagram. All the diagram emphasizes is that, in the circumstances it depicts, the reference of 'I' will be identical with the owner of the relevant particular mental state of ψ-ing that *p*. That is consistent with the holding of reductionist theses about the owner; and consistent too with their rejection.) Delta accounts may differ over how it is that a conscious state can provide a reason for forming a belief, notably over conscious beliefs and other propositional attitudes, which have been found far more problematic than the self-ascription of experiences. I will return to these matters. Our present concern, though, is with the explanation offered by delta accounts of the representationally independent phenomena in question.

Why is a first-person belief formed in the way described in a delta account also a true belief? Part of the explanation must be the fact that when a belief is formed in this way, the owner of the conscious state will be the reference of the first-person component of the self-ascription. Another part of the explanation must say why the person is right about the kind of mental state she is enjoying. The explanation of the correctness of the belief formed does not need to involve the correctness of the first-person content of some other representational state. It may do so if the attitude in question is factive, as with self-ascriptions of genuine perception, knowledge, or memory (and in those cases the explanation must involve more, too). But it is only because these attitudes are factive that that element must be involved in the explanation of correctness of those particular kinds of self-ascription. The correctness of the content of the reason-giving state, if indeed it is correct, does not play any part in the explanation of the correctness of a self-ascription of a belief or of an experience based upon that reason-giving state.

This contrasts sharply with the explanation of the truth of a perceptually based belief containing a representationally dependent use of the first person. It would be impossible to explain why judging 'I am in front of a door' on the basis of a perception with that first-person content yields a true belief, in the ordinary circumstances in which it does, without alluding to the correctness of the first-person representational content of the perceptual experience (or to the correctness of that content's non-conceptual ground). A corresponding point holds for first-person beliefs formed as a result of use of the faculty we mentioned for keeping track of location in the dark, and for any other method of reaching representationally dependent first-person beliefs.

We need an explanation not merely of truth, but of the status of the resultant beliefs as knowledge, when they are formed in the way described by a delta account. Delta accounts have the resources to meet this demand, and to do so in a way which goes beyond mere reliability requirements, to meet the demand for a species of justification and rationality which can sustain the status of knowledge. Consider a thinker who makes the transition from a conscious state or event of type ψ with content p to the belief 'I ψ that p', where her reason for forming the belief is the occurrence of this very conscious state or event. It is an a priori truth that any use of the first-person concept in thought refers to the thinker of the thought. So we can conclude on a priori grounds that when the first-person belief about her mental state is formed for these reasons, it will be true. That is, from facts about the nature of the first-person concept, we can infer that transitions of this sort, when made for the specified reasons, will lead to true beliefs. This is somewhat analogous to the way in which we can infer from the nature of the logical concepts involved, and the way their semantic values are fixed, that certain logical transitions are valid. Certainly, in both the delta case and the logical case, what underwrites the rationality of the transitions, and what would be mentioned in a full account of why they are justified, goes well beyond what is involved in mere *de facto* reliability.[8]

We can highlight the point by contrasting such self-ascriptions of conscious psychological states with a self-ascription 'I have a malfunctioning kidney'. Even if having a malfunctioning kidney were to reliably cause the belief that one has a malfunctioning kidney, and even if it strikes the thinker as correct that he has a malfunctioning kidney, this by itself is not a way of coming to know that one has a malfunctioning kidney. The relevant difference from the case of pain is that having a malfunctioning kidney is not itself a conscious state (nor is it one which can become conscious), and cannot itself give reasons for making judgements. The thinker whom it strikes as true that he has a malfunctioning kidney may in some sense have a justification for his belief—at least he is different from someone who is just guessing; but this is not the kind of justification which can underwrite the status of knowledge. For a state to give a good, knowledge-sustaining reason for judging a content, it is not sufficient that the state reliably cause such judgements, not even when the content of the judgement is that the subject is in that very state. The delta theorist will emphasize the difference between the example of 'I have a malfunctioning kidney' and the judgement 'I am in pain', made knowledgeably, and for the reason that the thinker is in pain.

This is part of the way in which a delta theorist can discharge the obligation to show that the relevant self-ascriptive beliefs are knowledge. It is not meant to imply that we do not equally have justification and knowledge in the representationally dependent cases too. We do. The point is rather that an account of how the status of knowledge is achieved in the representationally dependent cases will be of a different kind. It must, in the representationally dependent cases, involve an account of how the thinker is entitled to take the content of the initial reason-giving state at face value.

---

[8] Though reliabilist elements may also be present: see, *inter alia*, the later paragraphs of section 5.2 in the preceding chapter on the case in which there is no intermediate conscious state.

Any delta account must be filled out with a detailed theory in the philosophy of mind and epistemology of how conscious states justify self-ascriptions. It would take us too far from representational independence to pursue this thoroughly here. But I do want to indicate a few aspects of the location of such a position in the space of possible positions, in a way intended to indicate that the idea is not a total non-starter.

Delta accounts are not required to assimilate conscious occurrent propositional attitudes to the different category of sensations and perceptual representational states. Conscious occurrent attitudes form a category of conscious states in their own right. A delta account is committed only to the modest view that a conscious occurrent propositional attitude is something which can give a thinker a reason for forming another attitude. I discussed in section 5.2 of the preceding chapter the way in which conscious occurrent states or events can give a thinker reasons for making judgements. The points made there apply here too. According to the delta accounts, a thinker's reason for judging (for instance) 'I remember attending the party' can be his prior conscious apparent personal memory of attending the party. The transition this involves from an event with a certain representational content to one with a corresponding content 'I remember doing so-and-so' should not be construed as an *inference* from the memory to the self-ascription, any more than the transition from a perceptual experience to a belief should be construed as inferential. Rather, there is a rational sensitivity to the distinction between those of one's states which are memories, and those which are not. This sensitivity is already employed in ordinary first-level conscious thought and practical inference. This pre-existent sensitivity is exploited by someone who has the concept of memory, and self-ascribes personal memories in the manner given in a delta account. Similar remarks apply to other conscious attitudes.

Two important disclaimers should be made on behalf of delta accounts. There is indeed a sense in which a delta account explains how a representationally independent 'I think' is capable of accompanying any of a thinker's conscious states. But a delta account cannot amount to an elucidation of the relation of ownership, nor of its close relative, the relation of co-consciousness. On the contrary, delta accounts simply presuppose those relations. The most that can be said is that if a delta account is correct, a good explication of these relations must leave room for a delta account.

The other disclaimer is that the delta account offers no positive support for 'no-subject' theories of mental states. By 'no-subject theories' I mean theories according to which mental phenomena have no subjects—and a fortiori no owners—at all. Perhaps Hume held a no-subject view in some moods; it is also suggested in some early and middle period writings of Wittgenstein; some Buddhist texts may also express it. (A theorist who holds that subjects are reducible to entities of other kinds, and to their properties and relations, is not propounding a no-subject theory in this sense: he is just offering a particular view of what subjects are.) A misconstrual of the phenomenon of representationally independent uses might encourage no-subject theorists, but it would take a misconstrual to do it. The phenomena as identified so far are at the level of sense, not reference. A delta account explains the status as knowledge of beliefs containing representationally independent uses of the first person, while agreeing that conscious states are owned. So, if anything, delta accounts are rather in the first instance ammunition for the opponent of the no-subject theorist. These highly distinctive phenomena can be explained without resort to a no-subject account.[9]

The no-subject theorist may in fact enter these discussions as an objector to what has so far been said. If the no-subject theorist were right in thinking that there is some important respect in which experiences and other conscious events do not have subjects and hence are not owned, then clearly there would be a need to say much more about the transition from a conscious event itself to a thought in which some mental property is self-ascribed. If the self-ascription is taken straightforwardly, as involving reference to a subject, the no-subject theorist may worry that the transition is unsound. He may say that delta accounts give a good explanation of why some beliefs containing representationally independent uses of the first person amount to knowledge, *if* it is taken for granted that conscious states have to have subjects. If there are subjects of conscious states, the thinker of the self-ascription must, for a priori reasons, be the same as the subject of the mental event providing his reason for the self-ascription. But this justification of an identity presupposes the existence of such a subject, and this is precisely what the no-subject theorist questions. There is certainly an issue to be addressed here,

---

[9] The delta account is also prima facie neutral on whether a reductionist view of the self is correct or not.

and I will return to it in section 6.5. First we need to understand representational independence and its consequences better.

6.3 REPRESENTATIONAL INDEPENDENCE OUTSIDE THE FIRST PERSON?

It is not obvious that the abstract structure exhibited by a delta account is restricted to judgements involving the first person. We can hope to learn more about the phenomenon of representational independence by considering whether the phenomenon extends beyond the first person. The natural place to look is amongst the other indexical modes of presentation.

The abstract structure of a delta account involves three relations and three terms. One term is an event of a certain kind, or a state of affairs, and the second is a judgement made rational by the first term. For each of these two terms, there are two different relations, corresponding to the lower sides of the inverted delta, in which they stand to the same thing, corresponding to the third, lowest node of the inverted delta. There is also a third relation between the first two terms. This triangular structure seems to be instantiated if we take, for instance, a particular event—say, a particular political demonstration—as the first term; a perceptual-demonstrative judgement 'That demonstration is happening now' as the second term; and the time *t* of the event as the third term. The corresponding relations are given in Figure 6.2.

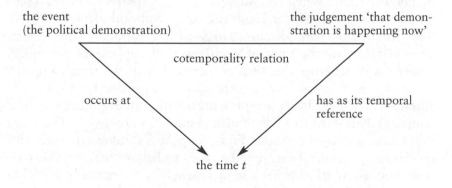

FIGURE 6.2

We could set up a similar example for a spatial judgement 'That demonstration is happening here', if the spatial demonstrative is sufficiently broadly understood. I will concentrate on the temporal example. Similar points will apply to the spatial case.

The temporal diagram instantiates the same abstract structure as that for the first-person case. But does the situation it depicts really result in a belief which is not merely knowledge, but also involves a representationally independent use of 'now'? A problem surfaces at the top left-hand vertex of the temporal diagram. It is not just the event of the demonstration itself, it is rather the thinker's perception of the event, which is his reason for making the present-tense judgement. But when we bring in the perception of the event, we must remember that the perceptual experience itself has a present-tense content. It represents to the perceiver the event as occurring *then*—at the time of the experience. It is because this is so that if we introduce a large time-lag in the production of someone's experiences, he is subject to a perceptual illusion. When there is a large time-lag, it looks as if things are occurring *then* to the subject of the experience, when in fact they are not. This present-tense component of perceptual experience undermines any claim of the use of the present-tense constituent in the judgement 'That demonstration is occurring now' to be representationally independent. In making this judgement, the thinker is simply endorsing part of the present-tense content of his perceptual experience. So this use of 'now' is after all representationally dependent.

We can envisage a subject who suffers huge time-delays in the operation of her perceptual mechanism, and who also knows this to be her situation. When this subject has an experience of representational kind T, she can still use the temporal demonstratives [that$_T$time] of the sort I discussed in *Sense and Content*. This demonstrative refers to the time of occurrence of the events perceived, regardless of whether this time is identical with the time of occurrence of the perceptual experience. But I do not see how these circumstances will yield us a representationally independent use of a temporal demonstrative which also results in knowledge. There are two kinds of case to consider. First, suppose a thinker who uses this special temporal demonstrative happens to believe that, on this particular occasion, [that$_T$time] is in fact now. If he forms the belief 'That event is happening now' in these complex circumstances, it will rest on the identity belief '[that$_T$time] = now'. The present-tense component of his belief 'That event is happening now' results not from the content of some representational state whose present-tense content he is taking at face value, but from the identity premise he also accepts. In the second case, we can consider the same person who knows of the real possibility of massive delay, and suppose he judges the content 'That demonstration is happening at [that$_T$time]'. Is this use of [that$_T$time] representationally independent? No, for in these circumstances, the perceptual experience does still represent the demonstration as occurring at [that$_T$time]. The position is structurally just the same as it is for the present-tense component 'now' in the normal situation.

An important difference between these temporal cases, then, and the first-person representationally independent uses is that when an experience, or some other conscious state, gives a thinker a reason for forming a belief about his own mental states, we do not—and for many independent reasons must not—regard the thinker as presented with that state or event only through perception. The relation between a thinker's judgements about some of his mental states and the states themselves differs in this respect from the relation between a thinker's judgements about external states of affairs and those states of affairs themselves.

This does not mean that representationally independent temporal indexicals cannot be involved in knowledge. On the contrary, when, for example, an experience is knowledgeably self-ascribed, and the use of the first person is representationally independent, the resulting judgement has a present-tense content: 'I have such-and-such kind of experience *now*'. This use of 'now' is representationally independent. But there do not seem to be autonomous examples wholly underived from the mental cases. Certainly, the existence of structural delta-like diagrams like Figure 6.2 above for the temporal case is not by itself sufficient to show that there are knowledgeable representationally independent uses outside the mental realm.

It begins to look as if two generalizations about representational independence are true. First, if a property is knowledgeably self-ascribed with a representationally independent use of the first person, the property is either a psychological property, or is inferred from such a self-ascription of a psychological property. Descartes's use of 'I' in 'I exist', as the conclusion of the *cogito* argument, is a knowledgeable self-ascription of a non-psychological property, but it manifestly meets the condition of having been inferred from such a self-ascription of a psychological property, namely, that of thinking (in Descartes's rather general sense). Psychological self-ascriptions seem to have an explanatorily prior role within the class of knowledgeable, representationally independent self-ascriptions. If this conjecture is true, it would be a vindication of the common intuition that there is a close connection between some mental phenomena and a certain distinctive use of the first person.

The second, and more general, conjecture, given the earlier reflections about representationally independent uses of other concepts, is that any knowledgeable, representationally independent use of a concept will be in a content which is either a psychological self-ascription, or is soundly inferred from one.

I have concentrated on knowledgeable, representationally independent uses of the first person in beliefs of a particular kind, namely, those which result from self-ascription of a psychological state or event which is rationally based upon an occurrence of a conscious state or event of the very same kind as is self-ascribed. This is partly because I think that such examples have been the most influential historically. I do not, however, want to leave the impression that all knowledgeable, representationally independent uses are of this kind. Evans, for instance, mentions an ascent procedure for the self-ascription of belief: the procedure of judging 'I believe that p' if, putting into operation whatever procedure he has for judging whether p, the subject comes to the conclusion that p.[10] Self-ascriptions of belief reached by this procedure will be knowledgeable, and the use of the first person in them will be representationally independent; and it can be true that the self-ascription involves reasons (though of course these will be reasons for thinking the world is a certain way). But it is also true that in these cases we can give the analogue of a delta account.

6.4 AN ILLUSION AND ITS SOURCE

The writings of Kant, Schopenhauer, Husserl, and the early Wittgenstein contain the claim that there is a 'transcendental' or 'metaphysical' subject of experience and thought. This transcenden-

---

[10] *The Varieties of Reference*, 225.

tal subject is said to be distinct from the ordinary person who has the experiences and thoughts. I want to argue that the notion of a transcendental subject of experience results from an unjustified and incorrect projection from the realm of sense to the realm of reference. Or equivalently: it results from mistaking an epistemological phenomenon for a metaphysical phenomenon. There is a genuinely distinctive representationally independent use of the first-person concept. It does not follow that such representationally independent uses of 'I' refer to a distinctive kind of thing, something not referred to in representationally dependent uses of the first person.

The transcendental subject in Kant's thought, to remind ourselves, is not what is denied in Kant's critique of 'rational psychology'. Rational psychology was said by Kant to have used unsound arguments for such properties as the simplicity and immortality of the soul, but the critique he gave of rational psychology does not involve denying the existence of the transcendental subject of experience. On the contrary, Kant's critique is written from the standpoint of one who endorses the existence of the transcendental subject, but disputes that the rational psychologist's methods are legitimate means of coming to know anything about it. It is also quite clear from the text elsewhere that Kant endorses the existence of the transcendental subject.[11] Even if its existence were not explicitly endorsed, the distinctive doctrines of Kantian transcendental idealism could hardly be formulated without commitment to the existence of a transcendental subject.

Now suppose someone thinks that representationally independent, knowledgeable uses of the first person do refer, but holds also that they refer to something which can be known about *only* in knowledge involving representationally independent uses of the first

---

[11] See *Critique of Pure Reason*, A355 (in the translation of Guyer and Wood): 'But it is obvious that the subject of inherence is designated only transcendentally through the I that is appended to thoughts, without noting the least property of it, or cognizing or knowing anything at all about it. It signifies only a Something in general (a transcendental subject).' See also Kant's footnote at A478–9/B506–7; and A492/B520. In a version of some of the present material published earlier in 'First-Person Reference, Representational Independence, and Self-Knowledge', in Künne, Newen, and Anduschus (eds.), *Direct Reference, Indexicality and Propositional Attitudes*, I also quite erroneously cite B426–7 in support of the point. At B426–7, Kant is expressing the transitions made by the rational psychologist, and not endorsing them himself.

person. What might one expect such a person to hold about the entity to which he takes such uses of 'I' to refer?

I suggest that he would hold just about what Kant in fact held of the transcendental subject. Kant wrote of the transcendental subject:

Through this I, or He, or It (the thing), which thinks, nothing further is represented than a transcendental subject of thoughts = x, which is recognized only through the thoughts that are its predicates, and about which, in abstraction, we can never have even the least concept; because of which we therefore turn in a constant circle, since we must always already avail ourselves of the representation of it at all times in order to judge anything about it; we cannot separate ourselves from this inconvenience, because the consciousness in itself is not even a representation distinguishing a particular object, but rather a form of representation in general, insofar as it is to be called a cognition; for of it alone can I say that through it I think anything. (A346/B404)

This is a brilliant but difficult passage. I think that we can understand it better using the distinctions and theses I have proposed. I suggested that all knowledgeable self-ascriptions which involve a representationally independent use of the first person rest ultimately on psychological self-ascriptions containing representationally independent uses of the first person. So if the idea of a transcendental subject of experience has its origins in the phenomenon of representational independence, it is understandable that one who believes in such a subject should say that it 'is recognized only through the thoughts that are its predicates'.

It is true that in this passage Kant mentions only thoughts, and not the other conscious states which can also be ascribed in representationally independent uses. But in other passages, 'thoughts, feelings, inclinations, or decisions' are all included amongst what Kant would call the 'predicates of inner sense' (A358, A359). This suggests that Kant would have been quite happy, if pressed, to replace 'recognized only through the thoughts' in the displayed passage by 'recognized only through the thoughts and other conscious states'.

The account of representationally independent use that I have been giving also allows us to see a ground in that phenomenon for the claim Kant makes in the second part of the displayed passage. This is the claim that the reason why the transcendental subject can be known only through its thoughts is that consciousness in itself is not a representation distinguishing a particular object, but a form of representation. Precisely what distinguishes a representationally independent use of 'I' when a thinker knowledgeably thinks 'I am *F*' is that the thinker's reason for self-applying the predicate *F* is *not* that one of his conscious states has the content 'I am *F*'. His reason is not given by a 'representation distinguishing a particular object' as *F*. It is rather the occurrence of a certain kind of conscious state itself which is his reason for making the judgement. It is the kind of state he is in, 'a form of representation in general', which gives his reason for the particular psychological predication which is being made in thought.

This general diagnosis of the inclination to postulate a transcendental subject of experience also bears upon Kant's view that the categories are inapplicable to this postulated subject. Kant wrote: '[T]he subject of the categories cannot, by thinking them, obtain a concept of itself as an object of the categories; for in order to think them, it must take its pure self-consciousness, which is just what is to be explained, as its ground' (B422). What is true is that in judging knowledgeably 'I am thinking about such-and-such object as having so-and-so properties (involving the categories)', or even 'I am thinking about the categories', the use of 'I' is representationally independent. In such knowledge, the subject is not thought of in a way which makes it manifest that it is subject to the categories. Equally, it is also true that any knowledge of a content '*m* is *F*', where *F* involves one of the categories, and where this knowledge is based on the perception that *m* is *F*, will be representationally dependent in respect of the use of the singular concept *m*.

It obviously does not follow that what a representationally independent use of 'I' refers to is something which is not subject to the categories. That would be a slide from truths about the level of uses of the first-person concept to very questionable claims about the level of reference. That slide does seem to be present in some passages in Kant. It is particularly striking in such phrases as this: 'all questions of the transcendental doctrine of the soul . . . have to do with the transcendental subject of all inner appearances, which is not itself an appearance and hence is not *given* as an object, and regarding which none of the categories (at which the question is really being aimed) encounter conditions of their application' (footnote, A 478–9, B506–7). From the fact that in certain self-ascriptions the reference of 'I' is not then given as an object, it does not follow that it is not subject to the categories.

On the present diagnosis, the critique of Kant's notion of the transcendental subject would at certain points be close to Kant's own highly effective critique of (certain aspects) of rational psychology. Kant wrote that 'the simplicity of the representation of a subject is not therefore a cognition of the simplicity of the subject itself' (A355). Equally, to attain knowledge about the subject from reason-giving states which do not themselves present the subject as located in the spatio-temporal world is not thereby to have knowledge that the subject is not located in the spatio-temporal world.

In effect, by appealing to a transcendental subject, Kant is saying that an exotic metaphysics can help to explain a genuine epistemological phenomenon: the existence of knowledgeable, representationally independent uses of the first person. As I said at the start of the chapter, it was a deep insight that these uses exist, and an insight too that, here as elsewhere, the epistemology and the metaphysics must be integrated. None the less, Kant's proposed solution makes things worse. The Integration Challenge for the domain of noumenal objects looks quite insoluble. Presumably we must attribute Kant's departure from the formidable standards he rightly applied against some aspects of rational psychology in part to his prior acceptance of transcendental idealism.[12]

The apparatus I have been introducing plausibly has other historical applications, but I will not pursue historical concerns further here. Instead I turn to address this question: what is the most fundamental explanation of the dual temptations to suppose that, in some of its uses, 'I' does not refer at all, or to suppose that it refers to something extraordinary, something other than a person?

In the *Blue Book*, Wittgenstein's later (or middle) self famously explained the temptation as resulting from a misconstrual of the genuine phenomenon of immunity to error through misidentification of certain first-person judgements.[13] This explanation was illuminatingly elaborated by Shoemaker, and further investigated by Evans. Immunity to error through misidentification is a necessary part of the explanation; but I want to argue that it is not the full explanation, nor is it fundamental.

Suppose a thinker makes a perceptual-demonstrative judgement

---

[12] There are readings of Kant on which the transcendental subject is an abstraction, something in a different category from that of an individual thinker. For an excellent discussion of such views, see Q. Cassam, *Self and World* (Oxford: Oxford University Press, 1997), 9–21.

[13] Wittgenstein, *The Blue and Brown Books*, 67.

'that [perceptually given] F is G', and in doing so applies an observational concept, on the basis of her current experience, to an object presented in the same experience. When such a judgement comes to be made in that way, it is immune to error through misidentification relative to the demonstrative component 'that F'. The judgement does not rest on any identity belief 'that F is identical with such-and-such', and so there is no room for error resulting from the falsity of such a belief. Such immunity from error through misidentification does not in these cases involve any temptation to regard the object demonstratively thought about as 'not in the spatio-temporal world'—on the contrary. So the source of any temptation in the first-person case cannot be immunity to error through misidentification alone. Something else must be involved.

Is the explanation, then, the combination of immunity to error through misidentification with the infallibility of the judgement made, given the reasons for which it is made? We already know this combination cannot be a necessary condition for the illusion to arise, if it is granted that self-attributions of memory and knowledge give rise to it. Those self-attributions are not infallible.

The combination of immunity to error through misidentification and infallibility is also not sufficient for this kind of illusion either. Consider the judgement 'This pain is acute', where the thinker's reason for making the judgement is the acuteness of the pain he experiences. This is both immune to error through misidentification relative to the demonstrative component 'this pain', and it is infallible if anything is. But there is not the same strength, or kind, of temptation that there has been in the first-person case to suppose that 'this pain' does not refer, or refers to something extraordinary. The same example also arguably shows that adding a third requirement to the explanation, to the effect that in the circumstances the term in question is guaranteed to have reference, is still not enough.

One feature differentiating those self-ascriptions which have led to problematic claims about the first person from those of the preceding three paragraphs is this. In the latter cases, a certain experience, either sensation or perception, is required for the demonstrative component 'that F'—the perceptual demonstrative—or 'this pain' to become available to the thinker. But in the cases which have led to the illusions, there is no experience, neither perception nor sensation, whose presence is required before the first person becomes available for such uses in thought. When a person makes a judgement of the form 'I am in mental state M', and does so for the reason that he is in the conscious mental state M, it is not that mental state M which makes available the first-person component of his thought. It could not be, since the very same first-person component is employed in the different circumstances when he judges, indeed knows, 'I am not in mental state M'. This characteristic differentiates the first person from both perceptual demonstratives and demonstrative thought about one's own sensations. We can label this characteristic by saying that 'I', unlike these other demonstratives, *is not made available by the particular course of conscious experience.*

Uses of 'I' in certain knowledgeable present-tense psychological self-ascriptions have then at least these three characteristics in the circumstances in which they are made:

(i) they have guaranteed reference;
(ii) they are immune to misidentification errors; and
(iii) they are not made available by the particular course of conscious experience.

Even with this threefold combination, however, it is hard to believe we have reached the source of the illusion that in some of its uses, 'I' either does not refer, or refers to something extraordinary. Properties (i) and (iii) on this list, i.e. guaranteed reference and being made available independently of the particular course of conscious experience, are present in any use of the first person in thought, in whatever circumstances and with whatever predicate the first person is combined. As we noted, the second property on this list is present, at least in the form of what Shoemaker calls 'circumstantial' immunity, for such perceptually based spatial thoughts as 'I am in front of a door', and these thoughts, *par excellence*, locate one in the objective order. It is not as if, when we confine our attention to the circumstances in which such spatial thoughts are immune to error through misidentification, we are more tempted by the illusion—we are not. In any case, it is not particularly transparent why the combination of properties (i) to (iii) should lead to this particular syndrome of illusions about the first person.

I suggest that a better explanation of the illusion is one which makes essential reference to the fact that the uses of the first person which produce the illusion are representationally independent. There is no pull towards the illusions in uses of the first person in judgements which are representationally dependent, and whose justifying mental states have a representational content which clearly represents the subject as an item in the objective spatio-temporal order. As we just noted, there is no such pull even if the resulting judgement is circumstantially immune to error through misidentification. In knowledge which involves a representationally independent use of the first person, on the other hand, the subject's reason for making the judgement is not one which involves the exercise of the conception of himself as located in the objective order. He must of course *be* an element in the objective order, for many an incoherence would result from the supposition that he is not. It may also be arguable that he must have some conception of himself as located in the objective order. None the less, no such conception is actually exercised by the thinker when he makes a knowledgeable, representationally independent judgement about himself, and a delta account makes clear how this is possible.[14]

6.5 SELF-KNOWLEDGE, SUBJECTLESSNESS, AND REDUCTIONIST VIEWS

I turn now to the task mentioned and postponed at the end of section 6.2. This is the task of constructing an account which addresses the objection we imagined coming from the theorist who holds that conscious mental events are fundamentally subjectless. This theorist was worried that the transition from the occurrence of a conscious mental state to an ascription to a subject may simply be unsound. So we have to develop an account which evaluates the soundness of the transition from the occurrence of a conscious event or state to the corresponding self-ascription. Only if the account's evaluation is favourable can the position I have outlined stand.

The account must have at least three strands. It will have to have a metaphysical strand, if it is to address the claims of the no-subject

---

[14] Thomas Nagel remarked to me that the view that a use of the first person cannot fail of reference may well be playing a part in the explanation of the illusion. I think that is true. If it were playing no such part, the question would arise of why recognition of the distinctive epistemological phenomena did not simply lead to a subjectless view of experience and thought. Acknowledging the possibility of such an element in the explanation does not, though, by any means make reference to representationally independent uses of the first person redundant. It is only when these specific phenomena are misconstrued that we can see why someone might be led to the erroneous conclusion that the subject is not in the spatio-temporal world.

theorist. It will have to have an epistemological strand, in its assess-ment of whether the transitions from psychological states to their self-ascription are justified transitions. Finally the account will have to have draw on part of a theory of content for thought and language, for a theory of content is what is needed to explain any links there may be between the metaphysics and the issue of justification.

We can distinguish at least three different kinds of account of the transition from a conscious state to its self-ascription.

(1) According to accounts of the first kind, the transition from a psy-chological state to its self-ascription is justified, but at some funda-mental level there is no genuine reference made with 'I' in thought or language in the self-ascription. In this latter respect, positions of the first kind are in agreement with the view expressed in Wittgenstein's *Philosophical Remarks*, when he wrote

One of the most misleading representational techniques in our language is the use of the word 'I', particularly when it is used in representing immedi-ate experience, as in 'I can see a red patch' . . . It would be instructive to replace this way of speaking by another in which immediate experience would be represented without using the personal pronoun; for then we'd be able to see that the previous representation wasn't essential to the facts . . . We could adopt the following way of representing matters: if I, L.W., have toothache, then that is expressed by means of the proposition 'There is toothache' . . . It's evident that this way of speaking is equivalent to ours when it comes to questions of intelligibility and freedom from ambi-guity.[15]

Of course the later Wittgenstein would almost certainly not be happy with a conception of conscious events under which they can be rea-sons for a thinker's doing something, including forming a belief. Positions of this first general kind are adopting only the quoted idea of the first person as non-referential, and need not accept either the middle or the later Wittgenstein's views on experience.

(2) Positions of the second kind hold that the function of the first per-son in thought and language is indeed to make reference. For just this reason, the second position continues, the transition from the occur-rence of a conscious event to a corresponding self-ascription is not

---

[15] L. Wittgenstein, *Philosophical Remarks*, trans. R. Hargreaves and R. White, ed. R. Rhees (Oxford: Blackwell, 1975), sects. 57–8.

justified. This is the position sometimes attributed to Lichtenberg in his criticism of Descartes's *cogito*, when he complained that Descartes was entitled only to the premise. 'There is thinking going on'.[16]

(3) While accounts of kind (1) aim to validate the relevant transitions to a self-ascription by reducing the content of the self-ascription, accounts of kind (2) do not reduce it. Accounts of both of these first two kinds are implicitly taking it that one cannot simultaneously have both the correctness of the transition and take it that the function of 'I' is to refer. The third species of position rejects this implicit assumption which is common to the first two positions. Positions of the third kind agree with the second position that the function of the first person is to refer, but agree with the first position that the transition is justified.

Accounts of this third kind subdivide into those which we can classify as concessive to the no-subject theorist, and those which are non-concessive.

The concessive accounts hold a reductionist thesis: that for a subject of a conscious mental event or state to exist is nothing more than for certain mental events and states to exist and to stand in certain relations to one another, where these events, states, and relations can be individuated in ways that do not involve the existence of subjects. The concessive reductionist accounts thus agree with the no-subject theorists in at least the following respect. They both hold that there is, in principle, a possible level of description of mental events and states which does not explicitly mention subjects. They differ in that the no-subject theorist holds that there are no subjects, while the reductionist holds that the existence of subjects consists in the holding of certain relations at this more fundamental level. The

---

[16] Rather more was going on in Lichtenberg's thought at this point than is commonly attributed to him. According to Günter Zöller, Lichtenberg 'inferred that something need not be spatially outside of us in order to be independent from us, thus allowing for the possibility that something might be in us which is yet independent from us. Lichtenberg encapsulated this line of thought in his most famous and influential philosophical aphorism, in which he proposes to replace the Kantian "I think" with the phrase, "it thinks", to be construed along the lines of the locution "it lightens", thus indicating that the I is not the producer but merely the observer of its own thoughts'. See Zöller's article on Lichtenberg in the *Routledge Encyclopedia of Philosophy*, ed. E. Craig (CD-ROM Version 1.0, London: Routledge, 1998).

reductionist will say that there is a reference for the first person, built from materials available at the more primitive level, and of such a kind that our transition is justified.

The non-concessive accounts deny the existence of any level of description in principle which does not speak of subjects. A non-concessive account aims to say why our transition is justified without presupposing the existence of any such level at which all the facts could be captured without explicit mention of subjects. I will be advocating a non-concessive form of this third kind of position.

The very idea of a conscious state or event involves the existence of a subject of the state or event. A conscious state, as Nagel said, is one such that there is something it is like to be in that state.[17] This must mean: something it is like for the subject. Reference to the subject of conscious states is essential in elucidating what it is for them to be conscious. The subject here cannot be dismissed as a mere intentional object. It is not just represented as being the case that there is something it is like for the subject. Rather, there really is something it is like for the subject, when enjoying a conscious state. This is a constitutive, metaphysical point about the nature of consciousness. The point is vividly expounded in Frege's famous essay 'Thoughts'.[18] It has been well stated recently by Galen Strawson.[19] When the point is properly formulated and appreciated, it becomes very difficult to understand how there could be an account of what it is for a state to be conscious if the account is to be stated in a wholly impersonal fashion.

If the consciousness of a state has to be elucidated in terms which require the existence of a subject of that state, certain kinds of Humean and neo-Humean reductionism about subjects (and, I would argue, persons) will be undercut. For certain extreme reductionists about the subject of experience and thought, conscious events and states are supposed to be the very building blocks in terms of which the existence of subjects is analysed. The metaphor of building blocks is meant to imply, for the extreme reductionist, that the materials

---

[17] T. Nagel, 'What Is It Like to be a Bat?', repr. in his *Mortal Questions* (Cambridge: Cambridge University Press).

[18] G. Frege, *Collected Papers on Mathematics, Logic and Philosophy*, ed. B. McGuiness (Oxford: Blackwell, 1984), esp. 360 ff.

[19] G. Strawson, *Mental Reality* (Cambridge, Mass.: MIT Press, 1994), ch. 5, sect. 10 (pp. 129–34).

employed by the reduction are individuated without any reference to what is constructed from them. If, however, consciousness itself has to be elucidated in terms which already require the existence of a subject, the materials drawn on by the proposed extreme reduction would be presupposing what the reduction purports to elucidate.[20]

In response to this objection, the extreme reductionist may pursue certain analogies. An academic society or a club may, and perhaps must, be involved in events of such a kind that only a society or club could be involved in them. This would hold for the admission of new members, changing its rules, and any other case of taking action as a society or club. This does not, it may be said, rule out the possibility of an ontological reductionist's attitude to these societies and clubs as sets of persons related to one another in complex ways. Structurally, however, this situation is very different from the challenge which the connection between consciousness and subjects poses for an extreme reductionist. The persons in terms of whom the reductionist wants to explain the existence of societies and clubs are not themselves plausibly analysed in terms of their relations to societies and clubs.

A more moderate species of reductionism may hold that it is still true that the existence of persons or subjects consists in the existence of certain mental events, interrelated in specifiable ways, without holding that the identity of those events can be explained independently of the subjects whose mental events they are. Whether such a position is appropriately labelled 'reductionism' is a substantive issue. It is a substantive issue because a relation given the label 'consists in' sounds as if it should be asymmetrical. But if particular mental events also fundamentally involve subjects' having certain properties, there must also be a constitutive ontological dependence

---

[20] The most celebrated modern statement of a reductionism about persons is Derek Parfit's, in his *Reasons and Persons* (Oxford: Oxford University Press, 1987 revised printing). Parfit is not, I should emphasize, an extreme reductionist. He is explicit in holding that there is a sense in which his species of reductionism is consistent with mental events being ontologically posterior to the subjects or persons who enjoy them. See the analogy between the branches and twigs of a tree, and the mental events enjoyed by a subject, in his paper 'Experiences, Subjects and Conceptual Scheme' (unpublished, forthcoming in a Festschrift for Sydney Shoemaker). (Parfit credits David Pears with help in making this point.) For a thorough critical discussion of Parfit's views, see Cassam's *Self and World*, ch. 5. Cassam's other general conclusions in that book are highly congenial to the conclusions and reasoning of the present chapter.

in the opposite direction from that proposed by the moderate reductionist. My own view is that it would be better here to claim mutual interdependence. What it is to be a conscious mental event cannot be elucidated without making reference to subjects of experience and thought. It is certainly also true that we cannot elucidate what it is for something to be a subject without mentioning conscious mental events. There do not seem to be any asymmetries of explanatory dependence in the offing here.

Bernard Williams has observed that from the holding of the two 'impersonal' conditions that there is a thinking that *p* and there is a thinking that *q*, it does not follow that there is a thinking that *p and q*.[21] For someone who accepts the link we described between consciousness and the existence of subject, this gap is just what one would expect. For there to be a conscious thinking that *p* is for there to be a conscious state or event such that there is something it is like for its subject; and for there to be a conscious thinking that *q* is for there to be a conscious state or event such that there is something it is like for *its* subject. It does not follow that these are the same subject, and so does not follow that there is a conscious thinking that *p and q*.

Reductionists, moderate or extreme, will naturally reply that the use of the existential quantifier in Williams's formulation improperly skews the case against them. Of course, the reductionist may say, two existential quantifications can be true without being instantiated by the same thing. The reductionist may insist that singular terms for particular events are used in the impersonal specifications. We have as premises 'Particular event *a* is a thinking that *p*', and 'Particular event *b* is a thinking that *q*'. If *a* and *b* are simultaneous and co-conscious, the reductionist may insist, then there is a complex mental event which is a thinking that *p and q*.[22] There is, however, a problem with this reductionist defence. The problem lies not in the reductionist's account of the transition, but in the meaning of his premises.

When a person consciously judges that *p*, this truth is not adequately captured by saying of this event *a* 'Particular event *a* is a judging that *p*'. Consider the schizophrenic experiences of thought insertion we discussed back in Chapter 5, section 5.4. A mental event

---

[21] Williams, *Descartes: The Project of Pure Enquiry*, 95–101.
[22] Compartmentalization aside: that has never been at issue in this dispute.

can be, and can be experienced as, a thinking (even a judging) that p, without being one in which the thinker is consciously judging that p. To characterize a mental event as a judging that p which is in consciousness is not to employ a characterization which implies that the subject of the mental event consciously judges that p. To characterize events of that latter kind, reference to the subject is unavoidable. The impersonal characterization omits this, even when it proceeds in terms of singular terms, and not just existential quantification. The problem is not one of accounting for the validity of the transition, but of expressive power—of the expressive resources available to the impersonal view. If the impersonal theorist says that the form of words 'particular event a is a judging that p' is to be understood as restricted to the case in which the subject is consciously judging, then reference to subjects is still involved in her characterizations. If no such restriction is intended, it will apply to the mental events involved in the experiences of thought insertion. Then the impersonal theorist will not have distinguished the schizophrenic from the normal case.

We should always have been alert to the possibility of some such essentially subject-involving phenomena, given the well-known symmetries between perception and action. In perceptual states, as conscious states, we have an ineliminable involvement of a subject, since there must be something it is like to be in that state, for the subject. In action too—which includes judging, if we recognize judgement as a mental action—the subject's producing a certain event can matter to the individuation of an event-type, and is omitted in impersonal characterizations.

It also seems to me highly problematic on other grounds whether there could be an impersonal characterization of mental phenomena, of the sort to which the no-subject theorist is committed, and to whose possibility the reductionist is committed (if the claim of reduction is not to suffer from vacuity). The model favoured for this impersonal level is one which hopes to regard seeings, thinkings, judgings, and the rest like events of thunder, which do not involve the existence of anything which thunders. But we cannot always subtract a subject, and be left with something intelligible. If someone says 'I'm talking about events which are collisions, but which do not involve things which collide, and about events which are strikings, but which do not involve anything which strikes or is struck', we would rightly think that he has not introduced any applicable notions at all here. It seems to me the same could be said of someone who tries to introduce a notion of events of seeing and hearing which do not presuppose that there is any subject who sees or hears.[23]

I also question whether 'It is raining', 'It is thundering', and the like can give the support or parallels needed to support the possibility of impersonal descriptions of mental phenomena. Proponents of the possibility of such impersonal descriptions often seek comfort from parallels with the existence of what Peter Strawson calls feature-placing utterances.[24] The points I have been making against the possibility of impersonal description are entirely consistent with the recognition of some genuinely feature-placing thoughts or sentences, and with acknowledgement that the 'it' in 'It is raining' does not refer to anything. One can no more make sense of the possibility of a locution which means that there is rain without presupposing the existence of a place, than one can make sense of a locution meaning that there is pain without presupposing that there is a subject.

The truth of this point does not require one to construe the 'it' in 'It is raining' as making reference to a place. The reference to a place is rather provided for by words and phrases following 'It is raining', like 'here', 'in Oxford'. It is also this position which accepts quantifiers, as in 'It is raining everywhere in Europe'. In psychological self-attributions, by contrast, it is the grammatical subject which occupies the slot that can equally be filled with other singular terms and with quantifiers.[25] The metaphysical truth that there is no rain without its place is entirely consistent with treating these appended terms and phrases, rather than the grammatical subject, as the referential devices. It would be quite wrong to conclude from the fact that 'it' in 'It is raining' is not a referential term, that one can somehow describe

---

[23] It may be said that a theorist who aims to replace talk about continuant objects with talk of processes can coherently say that there are collisions, but no objects which collide. If, however, this theorist still acknowledges material particles which persist over time, as elements which are involved in his processes, he will still be recognizing genuine collisions after all. If he aims to eliminate talk of continuant particulars altogether, he will not be recognizing genuine collisions. A collision is not just a certain kind of co-instantiation of physical properties at adjacent locations at a given time. For a quite different critique of the possibility of impersonal descriptions, see the important paper by Tyler Burge, 'Reason and the First Person', in C. McDonald, B. Smith, and C. Wright (eds.), *Knowing our Own Minds: Essays on Self-Knowledge* (Oxford: Oxford University Press, 1998).

[24] Strawson, *Individuals*, 202 ff.

[25] For further pertinent grammatical considerations towards the same conclusions as those reached in this chapter, see J. Katz, 'Descartes's *Cogito*', *Pacific Philosophical Quarterly* 68 (1987), 175–96.

the phenomenon of rain in a way which does not involve any pre-supposition of the existence of places and times. One could not.

To accept that the existence of subjects of experience and thought are not reducible to the existence of anything else is not to be committed to the view that every distinction we can describe involving subjects corresponds to a genuine difference. It is not to be committed to the view that in a case of perfect fission, if such a thing is possible, there is a genuine difference between the original person surviving as one but not the other of the two resulting people. In general, it is a *non sequitur* to move from irreducibility to the claim that all distinctions drawn using the unreduced ontology correspond to genuine differences. I have never seen, and doubt that there could be, a reduction of the ontology of places to anything else. From the irreducibility of the ontology of places, does it follow that absolute space in the sense in which Newton believed in it must be an intelligible possibility? This does not follow. There must be a coherent position according to which places are irreducible, but on which truths about them are linked to truths about other matters in such a way that we cannot make out a genuine difference between the whole universe being at rest with respect to (alleged) absolute space, and it being in uniform motion with respect to absolute space. Similarly, someone who is not a reductionist about subjects or persons need not be committed to saying that, in a case of perfect fission, it can be true that just one of the resulting persons is the original.

The general position I have been outlining supports Descartes on two points. First, Descartes did, just from his enjoyment of conscious states, have a right to the premise of the *cogito*. Second, the transition he made from the premise to the conclusion 'I exist' was a sound transition. My points to date obviously do not license all of Descartes's conclusions about the nature of the referent of the first person. The nature of the subject whose existence is entailed by the occurrence of conscious states is rather something for further investigation.

Some conclusions can be drawn, though, just from the austere description of the subject as the enjoyer of conscious states.

(a) If the subject is capable of remembering its own earlier states, it must be something capable of persisting through time. This follows just from the fact that correctness of a memory requires that the subject of the memory state—that is, the one who is remembering—be identical with the one who in the memory is represented, from the first-person viewpoint, as having been thus-and-so. Since the subject who has current experiences is identical with the subject who remembers, it follows that the subject who experiences must be capable of persisting through time. This subject must have the required complex capacities for memory storage, memory retrieval, and temporal representation.

(b) Some conscious states can give a subject reasons for making spatial judgements about itself, such as 'I am underneath this tree'. In suitable circumstances, the judgements so made amount to knowledge. When they are knowledge, it follows that the subject of experience must have a spatial location in the world. When the spatial judgement is knowledge, the perceptual experience which makes it rational does not merely support a weaker conclusion of the form 'Something bearing such-and-such relation to me is underneath this tree'. It supports a first-person content which locates the subject itself in the spatial world.

(c) It is the same subject who both experiences and acts (indeed some forms of thinking are actions). Since the subject of conscious states is also identical with the subject who acts, the conscious subject who is also an agent must have the complex of causal powers required for attempts and for actions based on reasons.

(d) There will be constitutive links between certain types of contents featuring in the mental states a subject may enjoy, and the subject's environmentally individuated relations and capacities. The explanation of perceptions and beliefs by external states of affairs, and the explanation of external states of affairs by the subject's mental states, play a constitutive role in the individuation of those states. This is the general thrust of externalist developments in the philosophy of mind and language.[26]

---

[26] See, as starting points amongst much else: Putnam, 'The Meaning of "Meaning"'; T. Burge, 'Individualism and the Mental', in P. A. French, T. E. Uehling, and H. Wettstein (eds.), *Midwest Studies in Philosophy 4: Studies in Metaphysics* (Minneapolis, Minn.: University of Minnesota Press, 1979), 73–121; M. Davies, 'Psychological Explanation, Externality and Narrow Content', *Proceedings of the*

In the theses (a)–(d) we have the starting point for an approach which proceeds from relatively Cartesian data about the properties of the subject of experience and, by way of various constitutive principles about those properties, draws substantial conclusions about the nature of the subject of experience. There is a great deal more to be said about all of (a)–(d), in particular about the idea of a person as a persisting object in the world. Further pursuit of this approach may also illuminate the issue of why there is an internal connection between consciousness and the existence of subjects. At this late stage of the chapter, however, instead of pursuing that, I return to the main question of the moment—the bearing of these reflections upon the transition from a conscious state to its self-ascription, and upon the kinds of position (1)–(3) we distinguished above.

These reflections seem to me to support the non-concessive form of the third of the three kinds of position we distinguished, that is, the position on which the transition in question is justified, and there is genuine reference with the use of the first person in these self-ascriptions. The transition is justified in part because if these reflections are correct, conscious states already involve the existence of a subject of the conscious states. The non-concessive form of the position is supported because there is no subjectless level of conscious phenomena from which a constructed reference for the first person might be built up.

Finally, it follows from two other truths we noted that it is the subject of conscious states to which the first person refers, when used in the self-ascriptions. One of the truths is once again the a priori principle of the theory of reference and content, that any use of the first person in thought refers to the thinker of the thought. The other truth is that the subject of conscious states and experiences which give immediate non-inferential reasons for self-ascriptions is the thinker. From these two principles it follows that any use of the first person in a self-ascription of a conscious state, rationally made because such a conscious state occurs, must be a use which refers to the subject of the conscious state. This is the fuller account of why the transition is justified.

We might conceive of an objector who complains that though the considerations to date show there must be a subject of conscious states, the first person in thought and language does not refer to it.

Aristotelian Society, supp. vol. 60 (1986), 263–83; Peacocke, 'Externalist Explanation'.

Given the reasoning we have employed to reach our conclusion, this objector will have either to deny that the first person in thought refers to the thinker of the thought, or to deny that the subject of conscious states is also the thinker. Neither option is attractive.

The same considerations tell equally against positions of the first kind, the positions which agree that the transition is justified, but say that there is no genuine reference made with 'I'. The arguments have already been given, but it is worth reflecting on how they get a grip against the positive proposal that is likely to accompany positions of the first kind. Defenders of the first kind of position will be tempted by apparently subjectless formulations, such as the principle that a particular thought, on a particular occasion, with the content 'I am in pain' is true just in case there is a pain co-conscious with that thought. Since co-consciousness presupposes consciousness, and consciousness according to the present reflections presupposes a subject, the objection would be that this is indeed only apparently a subjectless formulation. What is required for such a particular thought 'I am in pain' to be true involves the existence of a subject of the pain. These points are all on the side of the truth condition of 'I am in pain'. They enter again when we consider the justification of the transition to a thought 'I am in pain', for it must involve the occurrence of the pain, and this, according to these reflections, must involve a subject, the same subject as the thinker of the thought.

The second kind of position on the transition was the Lichtenbergian stance that 'I'-thoughts are true only if 'I' refers, and the transition is unjustified. It is equally undermined by the considerations I have offered. From the standpoint I have been developing in this paper, it is natural to suspect that the Lichtenbergian position results from an illegitimate slide. There are two different relations in which a thinker may stand to a given mental state which provides the reason for a particular thinker's psychological self-ascription. For the thinker who is *in* the conscious state, that state can give a reason for judgements and other actions without his having to identify the owner of the state in advance at all (not even in a first-personal way), and without his having to think about the relations in which he stands to it. All the same, the state is his, it can provide reasons for him only because it is so, and it will commonly be thought of as possessed by a particular thinker when other people think about the state. It may also be thought about in indirect ways which differ even more from the way in which it is given to its owner. The *non sequitur* is to move from these very different agreed relations in which its owner and other thinkers stand to a given conscious state, to the conclusion that there are two different states of affairs here, 'one more substantial than the other', in Williams's phrase[27]—one of them involving a thinker, and the other not. An appreciation of the way in which a subject's conscious states do not themselves involve his thought of himself as having them should not be pumped up into the claim that a conscious state could occur without irreducibly having an owner. The delta accounts of section 6.2 above themselves show how the transition from simply being in a conscious state to the judgement that one is in it is warranted, and they do so without commitment to any level of unowned thoughts and mental states.

The positions (1)–(3) are all at least in part about the level of reference. It should be acknowledged, though, that not every writer who has insisted upon the 'subjectless' character of certain psychological self-ascriptions has been making a claim about the level of reference. Some have been making claims primarily about the level of sense. The claim has been that in the first-person self-ascription, no concept of oneself is or need be deployed, or perhaps no concept of a certain kind, or again no concept that involves thinking of oneself as one object amongst potentially many others. John Perry develops one such position.[28] Such theorists need not have any quarrel with the theses of this chapter. It is open to at least some of them to accept a delta account. Their claims about concepts should not, though, be seen as simply orthogonal to the direction in which I have been proceeding. A psychological self-ascription made for the reason that the thinker is in a certain conscious state requires the thinker to have the concept of the psychological state in question. It is a substantive and important philosophical question, and one of pertinence also to psychology, what kind of thing a person must think of himself as being if he is to be able to ascribe psychological states to himself. It is not at all clear that a positive account of mastery of psychological notions can leave any room for 'no-concept' treatments of the first-person element in psychological self-ascriptions. The issue should be on our agenda.

---

[27] *Descartes: The Project of Pure Enquiry*, 95.

[28] J. Perry, 'Self-Notions', *Logos* 11 (1990), 17–31, and 'Thought Without Representation', repr. in his collection *The Problem of the Essential Indexical and Other Essays* (New York: Oxford University Press, 1993).

7

Freedom

7.1 THE CLASSICAL PROBLEM AND THE
INTEGRATION CHALLENGE

The classical problem of free will involves a problem of reconciliation and integration. The problem of freedom presents itself in part as the challenge of reconciling our impression and our seeming first-person knowledge of our freedom in thought and action with a description of what is really going on in the world as characterized in terms of causation, determination, and causal possibility.

Reflection on the problem rapidly brings the metaphysical aspect to the centre of attention. A large part of the problem lies in saying what an impression of freedom is an impression of. We have the greatest difficulty even in saying how the world would have to be for a particular action to be free, let alone whether the world is actually that way. The philosophically prior problem in this area is to say what such truths involve. If that can be done, it is then a later question to elaborate an epistemology which integrates properly with that truth condition for 'that action was free'.

I would not go so far as to say that once the metaphysical problem is resolved, the epistemological problem is trivial. Perhaps a similar remark on the case of metaphysical necessity, given the treatment in Chapter 3, would be fair comment. There the epistemology slipped relatively easily into place given the principle-based truth conditions for modal statements. By contrast, non-trivial epistemological challenges persist after the attempt I will make to offer truth conditions for ascriptions of freedom. I will consider the epistemology of free will at the end of this chapter. The core of the problem, however, remains the metaphysical aspect.

Back in Chapter 1, we divided possible responses to the Integration Challenge in a given area into two groups, the conservative and the radical. The conservative options were those of revising the metaphysics, the epistemology, or our conception of the relations between them. The radical options, in their various ways, rejected the very idea that there are truth conditions which fully capture the intuitive meaning of the statements in question, and for which the integration problem is soluble. The problem of free will has proved so recalcitrant that the topic is perhaps the only one on which even the more radical revisionary options have each been endorsed by one or another recent thinker. The views of Peter Strawson and Christine Korsgaard on free will exemplify the option according to which the explanation of discourse about freedom and responsibility is not to be given in terms of truth conditions at all.[1] Even the most radical option, of declaring the whole apparent domain spurious and irretrievably entangled in contradiction, has been endorsed in print by Thomas Nagel and Galen Strawson, and in conversation by several others.[2]

My plan in this chapter is first to articulate some aspects of our intuitive notion of freedom in decision, actions, and thoughts. Then I will attempt to give an account of what 'could have done otherwise' means which is satisfiable, and which does not make the Integration Challenge in this area insoluble. The account I will offer attempts to build a theory which is either conservative, or at worst indeterminate as between conservatism and the case in which some truth conditions are offered which capture much of what we mean (option (4) in our classification of options back in Chapter 1). I will try to respond to those arguments which have pressured others, in the case of free will, into the revisionary options (5) or (6), or into competing conservative conceptions. In terms of the traditional labels, the conservative conception I will be advocating is compatibilist. G. E. Moore made famous a species of compatibilism according to which 'when we say that we *could* have done a thing which we did not do, we *often* mean merely that we *should* have done it, *if* we had chosen'.[3] The variety of compatibilism which I shall be defending is rather different from Moore's.

My own view is that we should aim, if at all possible, for an account which gives a genuine and satisfiable truth condition for an attribution of freedom. Though the point would be disputed by some

[1] Strawson, 'Freedom and Resentment', and Korsgaard, 'Creating the Kingdom of Ends'.

[2] T. Nagel, *The View from Nowhere* (New York: Oxford University Press, 1986), ch. 7, sect. 2; Strawson, 'The Impossibility of Moral Responsibility'.

[3] G. E. Moore, *Ethics* (London: Oxford University Press, 1966), ch. 6, pp. 112–13.

distinguished writers—to whose views I will turn later—it seems to me implausible that an attribution of freedom involves no factual as opposed to practical commitments; or that it involves on the factual side nothing going beyond the immediate phenomenology of decision-taking. Consider one of Penfield's experiments, in which he inserts an electrode into patient's brain, and fires it. As a result, the patient says he has spontaneously taken the decision to do something.[4] I doubt anyone would happily classify this as a free decision, even though it may have the phenomenology of one. In more ordinary cases, we can make sense of the suggestion that our decisions in some area are really the result of some neurosis, and that our decisions are thus not freely made. It needs empirical investigation to confirm or refute any such hypothesis. It cannot be ruled out just by the subjective character of the first-person perspective of the decision-taker.

It may be said the existence of factual commitments in an attribution of freedom is consistent with a non-truth-conditional view (that is, with option (5)). There are, it may be said, certain conditions—manipulation by others, neuroses—which are on a list sufficient for legitimate assertion that the agent is not freely thinking, deciding, or acting. It seems to me, however, implausible that our understanding of a predication '*x* is deciding freely' involves tacit knowledge of a mere list, and nothing more. We seem to have an open-ended ability to classify new examples as free or unfree, in a way going beyond anything which could be captured by a list of cases. We had a general conception of free decision prior to any theory of neuroses, and then applied that conception in classifying a new case, once neurosis had been identified. I doubt whether something so important to us as freedom could ever be captured by a list of conditions which do not have some deeper unifying characteristic.

I am, therefore, aiming to give a metaphysical account of freedom, in the belief that this is the first step we need to take if we are ever to meet the Integration Challenge for attributions of freedom. It is impossible within the ambit of a chapter to address all of the issues which could be raised for the position I will be developing, nor of

---

[4] W. Penfield and T. Rasmussen, *The Cerebral Cortex of Man: A Clinical Study of Localization of Function* (New York: Macmillan, 1950), 111–14. The significance of these cases was recognized by D. Pears: see his *Motivated Irrationality* (Oxford: Oxford University Press, 1984), 198.

course to address all of the voluminous and often very interesting literature on the subject. To identify a potentially occupiable position in logical space will be my main task. Of some of those who attempted to give metaphysical accounts, Nietzsche wrote:

The desire for 'freedom of the will' in the superlative, metaphysical sense, such as still holds sway, unfortunately, in the minds of the half-educated, the desire to bear the entire and ultimate responsibility for one's actions oneself, and to absolve God, the world, ancestors, chance, and society therefrom, involves nothing less than to be precisely this *causa sui*, and, with more than Munchausen daring, to pull oneself up into existence by the hair, out of the slough of nothingness.[5]

The metaphysical account I will be offering will be less than a 'superlative, metaphysical sense' of the sort Nietzsche has in his sights. Something less than the superlative may suffice, however, consistently with recognition of those truths Nietzsche is emphasizing.

7.2 AN INTUITIVE CHARACTERIZATION OF FREEDOM

The concept of freedom is organized around the notion of a person being free with respect to a factor. Such a factor might be either a prima facie reason for decision one way rather than another; or it might be some other factor which may influence one's decision in some wholly non-rational fashion. To be free with respect to a factor is to have the capacity to reflect on that factor and to decide effectively whether or not to let that factor influence one, and if so in what way. The claim that the heroin addict is not free, without assistance, not to act on his desire for the substance is the claim that he does not, unaided, have the capacity not to act on that desire.

There are non-rational influences on choices which cannot be regarded as the operation of any kind of prima facie reason. Consider an agent who has to appoint one out of several candidates to some post. When comparing two candidates for a position, one of whom has been interviewed and who has left a favourable impression, and the other of whom is known only from his c.v., many people give, and indeed are aware that they give, undue weight to the favourable

---

[5] F. Nietzsche, *Beyond Good and Evil*, trans. H. Zimmern (Buffalo, NY: Prometheus Books, 1989), sect. 21.

impression left by the interviewed candidate. It is an empirical question whether the appointing person has the capacity to overcome this tendency. That is, it is an empirical question whether he is free with respect to this tendency. When it is operative, this tendency will not of course be operating as any kind of prima facie reason within the agent's deliberation.

Given this characterization of freedom with respect to a factor, we can go on to say that a person is free with respect to a range of factors if he is free with respect to each one of them. Similarly, one person is more free than a second person if the range of factors with respect to which the first is free properly includes those with respect to which the second is free.

One feature of this initial, intuitive characterization of freedom with respect to a factor is that it makes clear one of the links between conceptualization and freedom. We can deliberate only about what we can think about. A thinker must conceptualize some factor before it can enter his rational, or irrational, deliberations about whether it should influence him, and if so in which way. New theoretical knowledge, framed in concepts which are also new, may identify new factors which influence our decision-taking. It will again be an empirical question which of these newly identified factors are ones with respect to which we are free. In some cases the new theory may entail that we are not free in some range of our activities. But only when we have properly conceptualized the factors influencing us will there be any chance of our being, or becoming, free with respect to them.

Another feature of the characterization of freedom with respect to a factor is that it applies to thought too. On this characterization, a thinker can be free with respect to the factors which may be influential when he is making up his mind what to think or judge. The capacity effectively to give weight to some prima facie reasons, and none to others, or to block otherwise influential non-rational factors, is one that can be present in making judgements just as it is present in taking practical decisions. My own view is that this is no accident, for back in Chapter 2 I argued that judging is a species of action, a mental action.

There are necessarily certain limits to freedom in the case of thought. The rational thinker who accepts that all Fs are Gs is not free to judge that something is both F and not-G while continuing to accept that all Fs are Gs. This point cannot be dismissed by the observation that we should distinguish causal from rational determination.

We should indeed distinguish them. Many theorists of concepts would, however, insist that a proper theory of possession of logical concepts entails that certain states of acceptance stand in causal relations to other content-involving states, including relations of production and exclusion. Such treatments are likely to say that it is partially constitutive of a concept's being that of universal quantification that, if the question arises, a thinker rejects the thought that all *F*s are *G*s when he comes to accept that something is both *F* and not-*G*. The apparent loss of freedom such theories entail should not, however, be thought of as something to be regretted. If certain combinations of thoughts cannot be simultaneously accepted, as a consequence of a philosophical account of the possession of the very concepts involved, then there is, on a priori philosophical grounds, no possibility of still employing those concepts whilst not being subject to those constraints. Losing the capacity to think certain thoughts is not a way of increasing freedom. In fact one paragraph back we were noting just the contrary.

It is a consequence of this intuitive characterization of freedom with respect to a factor that an animal without the capacity to think of itself as influenced by a range of factors will not be free with respect to them. Nor does the definition make it suffice for freedom with respect to a range of factors that the agent has higher-order attitudes about those factors, or about his own attitudes to them. An agent may have second-order attitudes which influence his actions. Such is the case of the Puritan who has a second-order desire not to act on certain of his first-order desires. If our Puritan is not capable of preventing those second-order attitudes from influencing him, he is not free with respect to them.

To have, for any given factor that may influence one, the capacity to decide effectively whether to let it influence one is to be distinguished from the following capacity: the capacity to decide, for all the factors which may influence one, whether to let all of them influence one. To suppose that the first capacity requires the second is analogous to moving from the premise that one has, for each book in the British Library, time to read it before one dies, to the conclusion that one has time to read them all before one dies. Actually, it is worse than that transition. The conclusion, in the case of factors that may influence one, is incoherent, and not merely, in Russell's phrase, a medical impossibility. Whatever process takes place of scrutinizing and weighing factors which may influence one, once a decision is made there is always something left unscrutinized, on pain of the task being uncompletable. Such scrutiny is, in the phrase Ryle memorably used to describe the impossibility of a certain kind of self-prediction, 'logically condemned to eternal penultimacy'.[6] The point applies also to non-rational factors influencing the choice of which of several prima facie reasons is to be operative with one, if there is some explanation of why the agent makes the decision she does. Whatever the non-rational factors that affect that final choice, they will not themselves have been the subject of a decision on whether they should be influential or not.

A fully rational and free thinker does not need to aim at the incoherent goal of scrutinizing everything that may influence a decision. If a thinker is entitled to believe that further adequately informed scrutiny of rational and non-rational factors will not affect the direction of her decision—if she is entitled to believe that her decision is *stable*, as we may call it—then she can rationally cease the process of scrutiny.

The intuitive account of freedom with respect to a factor which I have just given is less distant than it may seem from some others. In the extended discussion of freedom in her book *Freedom: A Coherence Theory*, Christine Swanton writes: 'The freedom phenomena are characterized by the absence of various flaws, breakdowns and restrictions on human practical activity, namely, those which limit the *potential* of human beings as agents'.[7] A sympathetic reading of the reference to human beings in this statement would not take it as a sign of advocacy of the view that the very concept of freedom is species-specific. A sympathetic reading would rather take the statement as committed to the view that human freedom involves the absence of certain kinds of limitations on the potential of humans as agents. Correspondingly one could claim that the freedom of some other actual or possible intelligent organism involves the absence of certain kinds of limitations on their potential as agents. It would, however, be incorrect to revise the characterization down simply to the claim: 'The freedom phenomena are characterized by the absence of various flaws, breakdowns, and restrictions on activity which limit the potential of a creature as an agent.' A properly functioning,

---

[6] G. Ryle, *The Concept of Mind* (London: Penguin, 1963), 186

[7] C. Swanton, *Freedom: A Coherence Theory* (Indianapolis, Ind.: Hackett, 1992), 33.

healthy animal may be suffering no flaws or breakdowns; but, as I noted, it may not be free. It is not free if it is not capable of reflecting on the factors influencing its actions, of deciding effectively whether or not to let them influence its actions. Appealing to the 'absence of restrictions' clause to capture this point would be placing a weight on it which it cannot bear without explicit characterization of the restrictions in question. The ability to reflect on influential factors, and to act effectively as a result of such reflection, needs to be added to the characterization. This revision would be wholly within the spirit of Swanton's account. Her view is that the perceived value of freedom 'lies in the value of realizing the various aspects of individual human potential in agency, for the actualization of potential in this area contributes to individual flourishing'.[8] The 'actualization of human potential in this area' must involve reflection on the factors which influence an agent's own actions, and must involve effective decisions about those influences taken as a rational result of such reflection. The natural development of Swanton's position would draw upon the resources used in the intuitive elaboration of freedom with respect to a factor.

7.3 'COULD HAVE DONE OTHERWISE': THE CLOSENESS ACCOUNT

When the intuitive description of being free with respect to a particular factor applies to a person, it will be true that the subject could have let the factor influence him, and could equally have made it not influence him. Whatever he decided, he could have decided and done otherwise. Accounts of the nature of the modality in 'he could have done otherwise' offered hitherto by compatibilists, and in particular the account offered by Moore which I mentioned earlier, have been found very unconvincing by incompatibilists. I find them unconvincing too. Some have tended to move from this point in the discussion, together with the non-negotiability of some form of modal requirement in our ordinary conception of freedom, to an incompatibilist conclusion. That was certainly how I myself thought for many years. But I have come to think that there is a compatibilist option which has been overlooked, and this section is devoted to developing it.

[8] Ibid. 38.

Suppose you travel on a train through the Channel Tunnel, and there is a fire in the engine. Suppose also that the only reason that the fire does not spread poisonous smoke through the ventilation system is that some baggage, which could easily have been placed in a different configuration, happens to set up a draught which diverts the smoke from the ventilation system. It is true to say of this situation that there could easily have been a fatal accident. This is the kind of 'could have' with which we are concerned when assessing safety. It also seems that this species of possibility is compatible with determinism. If it were determined, on this particular occasion, that the baggage is stored in that configuration, perhaps because of the particular practices of the individual baggage-handlers on duty that day, that is not enough to establish that that particular journey was safe— to establish that, in the particular sense with which we are concerned, there could not easily have been an accident. Intuitively, only small variations from the actual conditions just before the trip, small variations which there is no occasion-independent mechanism preventing, would have resulted in an accident. Happily favourable initial conditions are not sufficient for safety. Nor do they imply that there is no kind of possibility under which an accident was possible.

The relevant kind of possibility is one under which something's being not possible means that in a certain way one can *rely* on its not obtaining. Another area in which we employ this kind of modality is epistemology. I use a time-worn but effective example.[9] It would be widely agreed that if someone is in a region where there are, unbeknownst to him, many convincing barn façades scattered through the countryside, he cannot learn that something is a barn just by looking at it. This correct verdict on the case is unaltered if we lived in a deterministic, Newtonian universe, so that it is determined that it is a barn, and not a barn façade, that he is now seeing. The method of taking such perceptual experiences at face value still cannot be relied upon in those circumstances. If conditions had been only slightly different—for instance, if our subject had turned left rather than right at the last junction—he would have been confronted with a barn façade rather than a barn. The method would have led him into error. We can hear some species of possibility in the statement 'The method

---

[9] The case is Alvin Goldman's: see his 'Discrimination and Perceptual Knowledge', *Journal of Philosophy* 73 (1976), 771–91, at 772–3.

could have led him into error' on which it is true, even in a deterministic world.[10]

Let us call the kind of possibility involved in the safety and in the knowledge examples 'closeness possibility'. Closeness evidently needs elucidation, but a great deal of what I have to suggest involves only the existence of such a kind of possibility, and is independent of particular analyses. So for the present, let us just specify that we are concerned with the kind of possibility involved in those examples, whatever its proper elucidation may be.

A closeness elucidation of this modal element of freedom could then be offered. It states that a person, whom we take also to meet the reflective conditions on being free with respect to any factors which might make him φ, is free to φ just in case

(a) he could (closeness possibility) try to φ, and
(b) he would φ if he tried to.

The point of clause (a) lies in its assimilation of the modality involved in freedom to a kind which is also found in the safety and the barn examples. On this approach, there is not a 'could' of a kind which is unique to free action. 'He could have acted differently', 'There could easily have been a fire', and 'He could easily have encountered a barn façade' all involve the same species of modality.

Clause (b) may be negotiable down to 'He might φ, if he were to try to'. There are some arguments for the stronger version. It may be said that when only the weaker condition is met, it is true only that the agent is free to try. There might also be some indeterminacy in the ordinary meaning; in any case, the difference will not be crucial to the issues I will be discussing. The position I will propose could equally be developed using the weaker version.

So, according to the closeness elucidation, I am free to act on (free with respect to) a prima facie reason on which I do not in fact act, if (a) it could easily have been the case that I try to act on it, and (b) if I had tried to act on it, I would have succeeded in bringing about that for which it is a prima facie reason. The friend of the closeness

---

[10] Mark Sainsbury has outlined a similar conception of close possibilities, and indeed has both applied it in epistemology, and also insisted on its consistency with determinism. For his highly congenial discussion, see R. M. Sainsbury, 'Easy Possibilities', *Philosophy and Phenomenological Research* 57 (1997), 907–19. I am grateful for Timothy Williamson for drawing this paper to my attention.

elucidation will say that it is because we take it that this condition is fulfilled with respect to a particular factor that we count a particular person as free with respect to it. By contrast, it is not true of the kleptomaniac wandering in the department store that it could easily be the case that she does not steal some object within her grasp. Our conception of kleptomania is that of a state which, when someone is in it, it is a prima facie law that the person will steal when the opportunity arises, and this state is not one of which, when in the department store at least, she could easily rid herself.[11]

I said that (a) and (b) are sufficient for freedom to φ in the context of someone who is free with respect to the other factors which might make him φ. Outside that context, (a) and (b) together are certainly not sufficient for freedom. They do not even require the ability to reflect on the factors in favour or against φ-ing. A dog could meet the conditions (a) and (b). The reflective element in the notion of freedom and the modal element in the notion of freedom are both essential to it. Failure of either one is sufficient for absence of freedom. The two elements must also be related in the right way. Someone who is capable of impressive reflection on the factors supporting various courses of action, and who could also act differently, but whose reflection is quite ineffective in making him act differently, is far from our paradigm of a free agent. I will be concentrating on the modal element in the next few sections, but we should not forget that the reflective requirements, and their required relation to the modal element in freedom, are still there in the background.

I take it that a person is free to do what she actually and intentionally does. That she is free to do what she actually and intentionally does is also implied by the closeness account consisting of clauses (a) and (b). We should, though, distinguish between being free to do something, and doing it freely. Someone does something freely only if they are free not to do it. The fact that someone actually and inten-

---

[11] The analysis (a) and (b) could be much simplified if there are cases in which trying does not even make sense. Clause (b) could be omitted, and clause (a) simplifed to the statement that there is a close possibility in which the agent φs. The substance of the theory would then lie entirely in its assimilation of the possibility involved in freedom to the closeness possibilities in the safety and the knowledge examples. However, I am not sure whether there are any types of case in which it never makes sense to speak of the agent's trying. Even for the action of belief formation it can make sense. Rudyard Kipling could not accept that his son had been killed in the First World War. Someone could have said to him: 'Try to accept that your son is no longer alive.'

tionally does something, and so is free to do it, does not imply that she is free not to do it. Nor does the closeness account imply that she is free not to do it.

There is one last preliminary, before we move to more substantive issues about the closeness account. Conditions (a) and (b) are not necessary, without qualification, for even a reflective agent to be free to φ. An agent can be free to φ without (a) and (b) holding, in cases in which the agent does not know how to φ. Suppose you are in a locked room. You have the key to the door, but you mistakenly identify as the relevant keyhole one which is in fact obsolete. You do not notice the keyhole which must be used to unlock the door. There is certainly a close world in which you try to leave the room, something you will do by inserting the key in the obsolete keyhole. But doing that will not lead to success in your attempts to leave, nor will it do so in close worlds. None the less, it seems to me that you are free to leave. It quite intuitive to say that freedom to φ is of value only to those who know how to φ. It is ignorance, not lack of freedom, which prevents you leaving, should you so wish. I will not encumber the later formulations with the qualifications this type of example motivates, but ask the reader to supply them when required. The briefer formulations I will use are applicable to agents who know how to φ.[12]

The closeness account is a compatibilist account. There are, though, three points on which it actually agrees with the criticisms which incompatibilists have levelled against other compatibilist attempts at elucidation.

(1) Successive generations of thinkers have objected to the early Moore-style compatibilist accounts of freedom to which I alluded earlier, according to which 'He was free to φ' means only 'If he had tried to φ, he would have' (or perhaps with 'choose' instead of 'try'). The entirely compelling objection, voiced by successive generations of thinkers, and accepted by Moore himself later in life, is that one is not free to φ if one is not free to try to φ, or is not free to choose to φ.[13] Far from

---

[12] The longer formulation would run roughly along the following lines. For a reflective agent to be free to φ, it has to be that there is some way W of φ-ing such that: (a1) there is a close possibility in which the agent tries to φ in that way W, and (b1) the agent would φ if he tried to φ in that way W.

[13] 'A Reply to my Critics', in P. Schilpp (ed.), *The Philosophy of G. E. Moore*, 2nd edn. (New York: Tudor Publishing Company, 1952), 623–7.

being an objection to the closeness elucidation, however, the point on which all these thinkers rightly insisted is entailed by the closeness elucidation. The closeness elucidation entails that if there is no close world in which the subject tries to φ, then he is not free to φ. The point that one must be free to try to φ if one is to be free to φ is not the exclusive property of incompatibilist positions. Its soundness can equally be explained on a properly marshalled compatibilist position which appeals to closeness.

(2) There is another point on which the closeness theorist will agree with a classical incompatibilist criticism of other compatibilist positions. Excusing conditions, the closeness theorist will insist, do not have to reduce merely to an unexplained list, with no underlying principle of unification. One class of excusing conditions will be unified by the condition that each is one whose obtaining implies that there is no close world in which the agent tries to act in the relevant way. On this approach, one will, for instance, distinguish between those cases in which the excuse really does involve a lack of freedom, from those in which the subject is free to act, but the costs of acting are too high.[14]

(3) The modality involved in freedom, on the closeness account, is not merely epistemic. It is metaphysical. Closeness possibilities do not have to align in any straightforward way with epistemic possibilities. It may seem, from the best available information, that something could easily have been the case, when in fact because of some hitherto undiscovered scientific principles and other conditions which could not easily have been different, it could not easily have been the case. The converse is possible too. It may be that, unbeknownst to us, the earth could easily have been destroyed by a passing asteroid a century ago. Similarly, chaos theory in effect shows that many conditions which one might have thought could not easily have obtained in fact could have come about with only tiny changes from the way the actual world is. So, when incompatibilists object to

---

[14] Here I am in agreement with B. Williams, 'How Free does the Will Need to Be?', in his *Making Sense of Humanity and Other Philosophical Papers* (Cambridge: Cambridge University Press, 1995), at p. 4.

those compatibilists who offer merely epistemic elucidations of 'could have done otherwise', our closeness compatibilist will agree.

What is the relation between the notion of a close possibility which I have been using, and the *closer than* relation which is used in some possible-worlds semantics for counterfactuals? (Those unmoved by this question can skip to the next section.) It should not be assumed that the notion of closeness I have been using is simply the positive form of some concept whose comparative is the *closer than* relation used in some possible-worlds semantics, not even under the supposition that some such semantics is correct. Suppose for present purposes that Lewis's semantics for counterfactuals is correct.[15] We could equally make the corresponding points under Stalnaker's original treatment.[16] So that we have a notation which does not encourage any begging of the question, let us indicate the three-place relation used in Lewis's semantics with the expression 'world u is L-closer to world w than is world v'. Lewis's semantics states that an arbitrary counterfactual 'If A were to be the case, then C would be the case' is true at w iff some (accessible) world in which A and C are true is L-closer to w than any world in which A and ¬C are true. (A person could agree to this without accepting Lewis's own philosophical theory of the nature of the three-place relation $L\text{-}closer(u,v,w)$. I also ignore the vacuous case.) Now let us return to consider the unsafe, but causally determined, train trip. Suppose that we also hold the following principles, which may be found tempting: first, that backtracking counterfactuals ('If I were to strike the match now, something in the past would have been different') are false; and second, that close worlds contain no violations of laws of nature. If we agree that there is a close possibility that there is a fire on the train, then any world history in which this close possibility is embedded must have at some point a different past from that of our actual world, given the supposition of determinism, and no violations of the laws. If this world were an L-close world, there is a danger that some backtracking counterfactuals will then be counted as true in cases in which they are not true. One way out of this is to distinguish sharply between the closeness property I have been discussing, and any

---

[15] D. Lewis, *Counterfactuals* (Oxford: Blackwell, 1973).

[16] R. Stalnaker, 'A Theory of Conditionals', in N. Rescher (ed.), *Studies in Logical Theory* (Oxford: Blackwell, 1968).

positive form derived from the relation of L-closeness. The matter could be given extensive separate discussion, and I will consider the notion of closeness below. At any rate, the important point for present purposes is that the notion of closeness I am using is introduced by way of the examples of our apparent use of it. Any connections between the notion so introduced and the relation *L-closer(u,v,w)* and others needed in modal semantics have to be established by further argument.

7.4 A PUZZLING INFERENCE

We can elaborate the closeness conception by considering a puzzle. The puzzle concerns a certain form of inference. Suppose someone is not free not to be *F*. Suppose too that it is causally (nomologically) necessary that if he is *F* then he is also *G*. Does it follow that he is not free not to be *G*? We can abbreviate the inference in question thus:

(1) ¬free¬*F*
(2) causally necessary(if *F*, then *G*)

——————————————————————— (L)

(3) ¬free¬*G*.

The puzzle emerges if we raise the question: is this inference (L) valid on the closeness conception of freedom? It may strike one as valid. It may also appear that there is a sound argument from the semantics of 'is free to' on the closeness conception to the validity of (L). The argument would run thus. It seems reasonable to suppose that laws of the actual world are also laws of close worlds. If that is so, then premise (2) of argument (L) implies that in any close world in which our agent is *F*, he is also *G*. Now suppose, contrary to the conclusion (3), that our agent were free to be ¬*G*. It would certainly be puzzling if, under this approach to freedom, none of the close worlds in which he tries to be ¬*G* is one in which he succeeds. By (2), any close world in which he so tries and succeeds in being ¬*G* will also be one in which he is ¬*F*. Won't he then be free to be ¬*F*, simply by trying to be ¬*F* by in turn trying to be ¬*G*? This then contradicts (1). So, it may seem from the semantics, the argument schema (L) must be valid.

So far, no puzzle. The puzzle emerges only when we add that (L) closely resembles, indeed has as an instance, the argument classically used by libertarians, and by incompatibilists, in attempts to establish that freedom conflicts with determinism.[17] Libertarians say that under the supposition of determinism, there are properties you had at a certain time in the past, and for which the following is a sound argument. You are not free now not to have had that property then; it is causally necessary that if you had that property then, you act in a certain way now; hence you are not free not to act in that way now. Yet the closeness conception was put forward as a compatibilist elucidation of freedom. So somewhere on the short journey made in this and the preceding paragraph, a mistake must have been made, maybe more than one. What is it, or what are they?

An analogue of (L) is indeed valid for some intuitive notion of determination. If we substitute 'determined' for '¬free¬', then I have no quarrel with the validity of the resulting schema. The same applies if we substitute a specifically determinism-related 'open' for 'free'. However, in offering a compatibilist elucidation of freedom, we will be developing an approach on which those substituted notions are distinguished from what they are replacing. We will be in agreement with David Lewis's point that not all ways of being determined not to do something on a given occasion are ways which amount to inability to do it on that occasion;[18] or, I would add, to lack of freedom to do it on that occasion. And in fact, the original form of (L), a schema involving the notion of freedom, is invalid.

Consider an instance of (L), as incompatibilists commonly do, in which 'F' is replaced by some predicate about some time t; in which 'G' is replaced by some predicate about some later time $t+n$; and in which the time index of the the operator 'is free to' is in both (1) and (3) understood as being the later time $t+n$. That is, we are considering the case:

(1a) He is not free at $t+n$ to be $\neg F$ at t

(2a) Causally necessary(if he is F at t, then he is G at $t+n$)

(3a) He is not free at $t+n$ to be $\neg G$ at $t+n$.

[17] P. van Inwagen, 'A Formal Approach to the Problem of Free Will and Determinism', *Theoria* 40 (1974), 9–22, and 'The Incompatibility of Free Will and Determinism', *Philosophical Studies* 27 (1975), 185–99; D. Wiggins, 'Towards a Reasonable Libertarianism', repr. in his *Needs, Values and Truth* (Oxford: Blackwell, 1987).

[18] D. Lewis, 'Are We Free to Break the Laws?', in his *Philosophical Papers*, vol. ii (New York: Oxford University Press, 1986), at 292.

An agent is not free to change the past. That is uncontroversial on the intuitive understanding of freedom. It is also the verdict of the closeness elucidation. On that elucidation, an agent's being free to change the past would require it to be true that if the agent tried to, he would—and of course he would not. No doubt the agent is free in some sense to have had a different past, but this just means that in the past, he was free to have acted differently. So (1a) is true. We can suppose G chosen so that (2a) is also true. Conclusion (3a) may none the less still be false. It is false if there is a close world in which he tries to be $\neg G$ at $t+n$, and if it is also true that were he to try to be $\neg G$ at $t+n$, he would succeed. Nothing in the premises (1a) and (2a) rules out the holding of those two conditions. A close world in which he is G at $t+n$, and which has the same laws as the actual world, may of course have a different past from the actual world, and must do so if determinism holds. But nothing in the premises (1a) and (2a) rules out the existence of such a world, and nor do the other requirements on close worlds.

The fallacy in the semantic argument occurred when it said 'Won't [the agent] then be free to be $\neg F$, simply by trying to be $\neg F$ by in turn trying to be $\neg G$?'. The answer to this question is negative in the particular case in which trying to be $\neg G$ involves the agent's trying to bring about the truth of some proposition about a time earlier than that of his attempt, where the proposition is false of that earlier time.

I am developing a treatment of the case on which it matters that some close worlds are worlds in which the past is different from the way it actually is. The intuitive examples by which we introduced closeness possibilities should make us recognize that state of affairs. We said that the following combination is coherent: the train trip is not safe, even when it is determined from fortunate initial conditions that there will not be an accident. If lack of safety consists in the closeness of a world in which there is an accident, then that close world must be one whose initial conditions are also different from those of the actual world, if it has the same laws as the actual world and no violations of those laws. We could make a corresponding point about lack of reliability in the knowledge example.

So, on this treatment, the holding of

(4) The agent is not free at $t+n$ to be $\neg F$ at t.

does not imply that

(5) There is at $t+n$ no world close at $t+n$ at which he is F at t.

There may be such a close world. The closeness account is, then, providing for at least two different ways in which a statement of lack of freedom may be true. First, it may be true because there simply is at $t+n$ no close world in which he tries to do the thing and succeeds (or perhaps he cannot even try). This is the case which includes my current, and no doubt permanent, inability to jump eight feet high. The second way a statement of lack of freedom may be true is as follows. Although there are close worlds in which the agent has the property in question, the counterfactual 'If he were to try to have the property, he would have it' is false. This applies, at least as things actually are, to any case in which the property concerns a time prior to $t+n$, and is one the agent did not in fact have at $t+n$. I return at the end of section 7.5 to address those incompatibilists who think this sort of defence weakens the compatibilist's position.

A less general form of inference (L+) is valid on the closeness conception. The less general valid form is that in which the time indices for F and G are the same. This instance of (L+) is a valid argument:

(1b) He is not free at $t+n$ not to keep the air pressure in the cabin constant.

(2b) It is causally necessary that if he keeps the air pressure constant, the temperature stays constant.

(3b) He is not free to vary the temperature in the cabin.

Suppose, once again, that (3b) were false—that our agent is free to vary the temperature. Then we ask the question 'Won't he then be free not to keep the air pressure constant simply by trying to make it vary by varying the temperature?'. Here the answer to the quoted question is affirmative. A close world in which he tries to vary the temperature and succeeds will also be one in which he varies the pressure, if the world has the same laws as the actual world. (Premise (2b) assumes that we are outside the range in which the cabin blows up with increasing pressure. I also assume, in accordance with the announcement in section 7.3, that our agent knows how to vary the temperature.) The form (L+), unlike the more general (L), is valid. Its validity may help to explain the attraction of (L) to some incompatibilists. On the present theory, though, it cannot justify that attraction.

7.5 THE CLOSENESS CONCEPTION ELABORATED

Kant claims that '[W]e must necessarily attribute to every rational being who has a will also the idea of freedom, under which only can such a being act'.[19] Does a rational being also act under the idea of freedom as the closeness conception elucidates freedom? It seems that we do act under the idea that in engaging in ordinary practical deliberation, the options we are considering are ones that we could try or decide to act on, and be effective in so acting or deciding. The 'could' in this claim seems to me to be the 'could' with a closeness elucidation. Suppose there is no close possibility in which we realize options other than the one actually chosen. I noted earlier that for the closeness 'could have', there is a correlative 'reliably', of such a kind that 'there is a close possibility that p' is equivalent to 'not reliably not-p'. If there is no close possibility in which we realize options other than the one actually chosen, that is equivalent to its reliably being the case that we do not realize those other options. (This of course does not mean that the actual deliberation is not causally effective.) It seems to me that ordinary rational deliberation about a range of options presupposes that those options are ones the deliberator could realize, where this is the 'could' of closeness possibility. A rational deliberator who became convinced that a certain subset of his apparent options are ones which he could not, in any close possible world, realize cannot rationally continue to include them in the range of options about which he is deliberating. We can rationally deliberate between options when we believe, correctly or incorrectly, that they may be close possibilities. However, as soon as we judge that something is not a close possibility, we cannot rationally include it in our deliberations.

It may be objected that this argument proves too much. Is it not equally true that as soon as you know something is not actually going to be realized, you cannot rationally include it as a relevant possibility your deliberations? True: but of options open to the agent, which one is going to be realized depends on the decision the agent makes. In the case of a possibility whose realization depends on what the agent decides, the non-realization of that possibility cannot be used in the rational deliberations of the agent without question-begging in respect of her final decision. Its actual non-realization cannot be a presupposition of her deliberations in the way in which its closeness is.

19 I. Kant, *Ethical Philosophy*, trans. J. Ellington (Indianapolis, Ind.: Hackett, 1994), 50 (p. 448 of the Akademie edition of the *Grundlegung*).

It also seems to me that we want it to be the case that, over a certain range, we could try to act on desires or values other than those which were in fact operative with us on a particular occasion, and would be effective in so trying. Freedom with respect to a factor can be something worth having. The qualification 'over a certain range' here matters. I would rather be of a psychological make-up of such a sort that there is no close world in which I can even bring myself to try to act cruelly, for instance. Being free to ϕ for arbitrary ϕ is not a desirable capacity.

What is involved in properly assessing which worlds are close to a given world? What is the right way to assess whether there is a close possibility that a person, object or system of things be other than it actually is? Three kinds of factor should enter the assessment.

(A) The *ceteris paribus* laws of a given world w are preserved at worlds which are close to w. That is, they are preserved as *ceteris paribus* laws. In worlds close to the actual world, it is also true that, *ceteris paribus*, a rise in interest rates in a country produces an inflow of capital to that country; true that, *ceteris paribus*, meandering rivers erode their outer banks; and so forth. There is no close possibility of something which involves violation of a *ceteris paribus* law. There can be a close possibility in which some event falls under the antecedent, but not under the consequent, of a prima facie law, provided there is some independent reason, of a sort which would apply equally in the actual world, for declaring that other things are not equal. That would not strictly be a violation, and can equally occur in the actual world, given that the law has merely a prima facie status.

(B) We have a conception of some properties and relations of a given system of objects at a given time being much more robust than others. These robust properties and relations are also preserved, *ceteris paribus*, as properties and relations of that system, at that time, in close worlds. Precisely what we aim to put in place in making the train safe are devices which, for instance, detect smoke, insulate from heat, or will not shatter dangerously, in a wide variety of conditions.[20]

[20] This is closely related to Nancy Cartwright's notion of an object's having a certain capacity: see her *Nature's Capacities and their Measurement* (Oxford: Oxford University Press, 1989), ch. 4.

(C) Assessment of which possibilities are close depends not only on the factors (A) and (B), but also on what, contingently, is the case outside the system for which close possibilities are in question. Consider again, for instance, whether the earth could easily have been destroyed in the last century by some collision with some other massive object in space. This question cannot be answered just by considering the *ceteris paribus* laws describing the stability of orbits in the solar system and the robustness of the arrangement of most solar systems into planets and a sun. Whether a collision is a close possibility depends also on whether comets or asteroids far away in time and space from the earth in the nineteenth century could easily have traced a somewhat different course, and eventually have collided with the earth in that century. If there were no such heavenly bodies anywhere near the regions they would have to have occupied for a collision to occur, and there could not easily have been, then our intuitive verdict would be that there could not easily have been a collision.

One proper way, then, to make it plausible that there is a close possibility in which a given object is *F* at *t* is to make it plausible (a) that a little before *t*, some small difference from the actual world could obtain, a variation which some *ceteris paribus* law implies is sufficient for the object's being *F*, and (b) that there would in those circumstances be no changes in the robust conditions which undermine the applicability of the *ceteris paribus* law. There are negative existentials in these conditions, so a certain open-endedness is present. In general such claims of close possibilities will be potentially open to undermining by the discovery that some unobvious, robust conditions were preventing the earlier condition from holding. Equally they could be undermined by the discovery that it is much easier than was previously thought for the conditions to obtain under which things are no longer equal.

It is important in evaluating statements about close possibilities at a time *t* to consider what could be the case a little before *t*. There is a close world in which you buy a different newspaper this morning. There is not, now, a close world in which you have a different genetic makeup. Yet consider the sperm and egg cell from which you developed. There is a time at which the egg cell could easily have had a different genetic content, as a result of mistranscription, random errors, and the like. The same applies to the sperm cell. Hence it is not sufficient for there to be a close possibility at t in which x is F at t that there is some time t_0 earlier than t such that at t_0 it is a close possibility that p, and in that possibility, x would (or might) have been F at t. Rather, it has to be the case that just before t, there is some proposition p such that it is then a close possibility that p, and in that possibility, x would (or might) have been F.

Whether an object which is not actually F could easily have been F can vary with time. Such time-dependent variation is precisely what we are aiming to achieve when we try to make our trains safe, try to cure kleptomaniacs, or try to make our belief-forming methods more reliable means of reaching the truth. Correspondingly, a notion of 'could have chosen otherwise' explained in terms of closeness will be significantly time-relative. What could easily happen to a train may vary over time; what a person is capable of choosing may change over time. The notion of freedom identified by the closeness conception is genuinely historical, a function of the agent's situation at the time. There is also a relativity to circumstances: the full form is the four-place *x is free to ϕ in circumstances C at time t*. It is a further reason for the insufficiency of the proposal discussed in the preceding paragraph that it provides for relativity neither to circumstances, nor to times, in a sufficiently strong form.

Since closeness is evidently a matter of degree, the closeness elucidation makes freedom a matter of degree. Is this a problem? Freedom is commonly thought to be a matter of degree, and we use the comparative and superlative forms in talking about it. Abraham Pais, in his celebrated biography of Einstein, writes: 'Were I asked for a one-sentence biography of Einstein, I would say, "He was the freest man I have ever known." '[21] However, the common conception of freedom as a matter of degree, to which comparatives and superlatives can legitimately be applied, is arguably concerned just with the *range* of factors with respect to which a person is free. The freer person is free with respect to a wider range of factors. It is not so clear that the ordinary conception allows that freedom with respect to a given factor can be a matter of degree, or may have borderline cases, or can admit of an intelligible comparative. Yet the closeness account is committed to all of these.

---

[21] A. Pais, *'Subtle is the Lord . . .': The Science and Life of Albert Einstein* (Oxford: Oxford University Press, 1982), p. vii.

The closeness theorist should reply that it can sometimes come as a surprise which concepts admit of degree, and correspondingly exhibit a certain sort of borderline case. Let us take one of our parallel cases again. The factors which underlie knowledge of a given proposition, as opposed to how knowledgeable someone is, may seem initially not to be a matter of degree. Yet one can be forced to soften such a position by examples. There is a spectrum of cases, perhaps many spectra, which show that the factors which underlie knowledge are matters of degree. Consider our subject who believes 'That's a barn', when taking his visual experience at face value. He does not know it to be a barn, even when he is seeing a barn, if there are barn façades scattered around nearby. But of course the barn façades might not have been installed, and he still not know, if there had merely been a delay in installing them, so that he could easily at that time not have been in a façade-free environment. Or we can consider the case in which they were installed somewhere else altogether, but the film director had still been considering our believer's location as a filming site; or the case in which he was still choosing between installing barn façades and real barns, not yet having selected a site; or the case in which he was deliberating between filming only in a studio, and filming in some countryside somewhere or other . . . and so forth. As we know from much reflection on vagueness, we cannot avoid this element of degree by moving from a requirement 'no close worlds of such-and-such a kind' to 'no *definitely* close worlds of such-and-such a kind'. 'Definitely close' seems to display the same problematic phenomena, the borderline cases and the like. I think that, contrary to first appearances, the factors which underlie knowledge of a given proposition are to be classified with other predicates which are, apparently, matters of degree. The closeness theorist will say the same of being free with respect to a given factor. Further on, I will offer some independent evidence for this position.

Alternatively it may be objected that the closeness possibilities I have been identifying may be real enough, but that I have not shown that they are under the agent's control. What might be meant by this, and what does the objector want? The complaint should not be that on the closeness conception, which of various close possibilities is realized does not depend on the agent's choice or decision. That would be false. On the closeness conception, what the agent does causally depends upon his decision (a standard compatibilist remark). The closeness possibilities which the present position identifies as crucial to freedom have the feature that the agent could try to realize them, and would succeed if he were to try. What more could be required for the possibilities to be under the agent's control? The objector may rather be concerned that there is nothing in the closeness conception which entails that it is indeterminate, prior to the agent's making a choice, which course of action he will pursue. The closeness conception is at least in the target area of that remark, for indeed it has been put forward as a compatibilist view. This last construal of the objection is just a classic statement of the incompatibilist intuition, and I will consider it in section 7.7.

How does the closeness conception compare with some other recent compatibilist elaborations of freedom? By addressing this question, we can reach a better articulation of what distinguishes the closeness conception. David Lewis presented a classic compatibilist position in his 'Are We Free to Break the Laws?'. Suppose I am free to go to the meeting, but do not in fact go. Lewis highlights the distinction between (a) my doing something such that, were I to do it, either it or one of its effects would be a breaking of an actual law, and (b) my doing something such that, were I to do it, some or other earlier small miracle would have occurred. Lewis's points are that it is (a) which would have to be involved in a freedom to break the laws, and that nothing in his position commits him to (a). On Lewis's own theory of counterfactuals, it is only (b) which is entailed by my freedom to go to the meeting. On that theory, if I were to go to the meeting, some or other small 'divergence' miracle would have occurred earlier. I think that Lewis's response to van Inwagen-style incompatibilism is the right one for someone who accepts all of the Lewisian approach to counterfactuals—the full Lewisian, as we can call him.

There is a position in logical space which combines the full Lewisian view with the closeness analysis of freedom which I have been presenting. Under this combination, the role of the closeness analysis is to state the conditions which some event, in a non-actual possible world, of my going to the meeting must satisfy in order for it to be true in the actual world that I am free to go to the meeting. It is, however, important that the closeness analysis is quite independent of any commitment to the full Lewisian treatment of counterfactuals, with its reliance on his particular theory of the counterfactually significant similarity relations between worlds.

In particular, the closeness elucidation can also be accepted in combination with Frank Jackson's theory of counterfactuals.[22] On Jackson's approach, a sequential counterfactual 'If it were to be the case that p at t, then it would be the case that q at $t+n$' is true iff q is true at $t+n$ in all worlds in which p is true and which also meet the following three conditions. First, their causal laws at and after t are the same as those of the actual world. Second, their time-slices at t are most similar in matters of particular fact to ours. Third, they are identical in matters of particular fact to the actual world prior to t. Jackson emphasizes that on his theory, non-vacuous and empirical sequential counterfactuals are true only if there are appropriately sustaining laws. Similarity not based on laws cannot sustain such counterfactuals.

Still, even the combination of the closeness conception of freedom and the Jacksonian treatment of counterfactuals may be thought to have unacceptable consequences. Must it not still be involved with miracles in the worlds that verify the counterfactuals? In particular, if I do not in fact leave for the meeting at 8.00 p.m., must not this combination count the following counterfactual as true: 'If I were to leave for the meeting at 8.00 p.m., then some miracle would have occurred in the period of time up to 8.00 p.m.'? Must not something have gone wrong in a compatibilist account of freedom which, if freedom exists, is committed to the nearby possibility of small miracles?

I argue that there is no such commitment, provided the case for the closeness elucidation of freedom is properly marshalled. We should distinguish very sharply between counterfactuals of the form

> If it were to be the case that p at $t+n$, then it would have been the case that q at the earlier time t

and conditionals of the form

> If it were to be the case that p at $t+n$, then that could only be because q was the case at the earlier time t

or of the form

> If it had been the case that p at $t+n$, then it would have had to be the case that q at the earlier time t.

Counterfactuals of the first of these three forms—the backtrackers—

---

[22] 'A Causal Theory of Counterfactuals', *Australasian Journal of Philosophy* 55 (1977), 3–21.

are sometimes regarded as mere terminological variants of the latter 'could only' and 'would have to have' conditionals. It seems to me that they have a quite different meaning.[23] Let us call a non-vacuous, empirical backtracking counterfactual with a consequent which is false with respect to the actual world a *threatening* backtracker. It seems to me that the defender of the combination I am advocating should say that threatening backtrackers are true only if there is backwards causal influence, provided that it is distinct events which are mentioned in the antecedent and consequent. That is what assertion of the threatening backtrackers would ordinarily be used to express, pre-emption and the like aside.

The defender of the present combination can and should agree with the truth of such conditionals as 'If I were to leave for the meeting at 8.00 p.m. (which I will not), then that could only be because [or: then it would have to have been the case that] some conditions earlier were different from those which actually obtain'. The worlds which verify these conditionals do not involve the occurrence of any miracles, however small.

This combination differs also from the positions offered to the compatibilist in other recent discussions. In his valuable book *The Metaphysics of Free Will*, John Martin Fischer considers how the compatibilist might respond to the challenge that an agent cannot do something of which it is true that were he to do it, the past would have been different.[24] Fischer offers the compatibilist a position on which in certain examples both a 'can' claim is true, and so too are certain backtrackers. He considers a seadog who would never go sailing at noon unless the weather forecast earlier in the morning had been favourable. Fischer says the compatibilist can say, even after an unfavourable weather forecast, both that the seadog can go sailing, and that 'if the seadog were to go sailing at noon, the past would have been different from what it actually is'.[25] On the combination I am proposing, though, since there is no real possibility of backward causal influence, such backtrackers as the one just quoted from Fischer are never true. No correct position can require their truth. It is rather the 'could only have been because . . .' and 'would have to

[23] For a defence of the contrary view, see J. Bennett, 'Counterfactuals and Temporal Direction', *Philosophical Review* 93 (1984), 57–91.

[24] J. Fischer, *The Metaphysics of Free Will: An Essay on Control* (Oxford: Blackwell, 1994): see in particular the principle he calls '(FPnc)', p. 79.

[25] Ibid. 91.

have been because . . .' conditionals which are true in the Fischerian examples. Their truth does not involve any denial of the fixity of the past.[26]

How then does the combination I am favouring respond to Fischer's 'Basic Version' of incompatibilism, which he captures in the principle that 'an agent can do X only if his doing X can be an extension of the actual past, holding the laws fixed'?[27] On one intuitive understanding of the phrase, the closeness account does give an account of what is involved in an agent, with her actual past, being free to do X. Her actual past is highly relevant, since it determines whether she is in a state which prevents there from being any close world in which she tries to do X (or any close world in which she tries and succeeds). Fischer would protest, though, that that intuitive construal is not what he means. What he means by the Basic Version is that an agent can at t do X only if there is a possible world coinciding at all times prior to t with the actual world, with the same laws as the actual world, and in which the agent at t does X. This, though, seems to be too strong as a necessary condition of close possibility at t, even outside cases of agency. In our example of the deterministic world in which at t our subject sees a barn, we emphasized that there is still a close possibility that at t our subject is seeing a barn façade. In that example, there is no possible world coinciding at all times prior to t with the world there envisaged as actual, with the same laws envisaged as actual there, and in which the agent is not seeing a barn. None the less, it seems that there is some sense in which our subject could have been seeing a barn façade. That is why he does not count as knowing that there is a barn in front of him. On the way I have been developing the closeness conception, corresponding points hold for the 'could have' involved in freedom.

7.6 NON-THEORETICAL CONSTRUALS OF FREEDOM

I now turn to consider some options that I have implicitly rejected in putting forward the closeness conception. I will consider in a little more detail those views that construe ascriptions of freedom or

---

[26] In effect, this is to suggest that Fischer's (FPnc) principle, in which the 'nc' indicates the claim that it is a non-causal principle, is in fact causal after all.

[27] *The Metaphysics of Free Will*, 87–94. In his discussion, Fischer also cites C. Ginet's *On Action* (Cambridge: Cambridge University Press, 1990).

responsibility as a manifestation, perhaps an expression, of a practical attitude, rather than of a theoretical belief which might be false. This is the kind of position famously associated with Peter Strawson, but a position of this general character is developed in detail, with great resourcefulness, by Christine Korsgaard in the title essay of her collection *Creating the Kingdom of Ends*. She writes: 'Responsibility is construed practically by those who think that holding someone responsible is adopting an attitude towards her, or, much better, placing yourself in a relationship with her' (198). She contrasts the practical construal she favours with one on which 'deciding whether to hold someone responsible is a matter of assessing the facts; it is a matter of arriving at a belief about her' (197). Korsgaard's view is that the practical rather than the theoretical construal of responsibility 'is implicit in our actual practices' (197). I want to consider briefly the phenomena she cites in support of that, and to argue that those phenomena can be explained on a theoretical conception of freedom and responsibility.

(a) On Korsgaard's practical conception, there is, she notes, some distance between the practical issue of whether to hold someone responsible and the question of whether he acted voluntarily. She writes: '[T]here is neither need nor reason to . . . say that people under severe emotional stress *cannot* control themselves. We do not need to understand a form of debilitation as a form of impossibility in order to make allowances for it; we need only to know what it is like' (198). This seems to me intuitively correct. But it is also to be counted as correct on the closeness view. It will, on that view, be a matter of degree how easy it is to overcome some factor which, unless one makes some effort, will cause one's actions. It may be easy, somewhat hard, hard, . . . through to extremely difficult to overcome it. These distinctions in degree correspond to differences in how close are the worlds in which one does overcome it, the more difficult cases being less close (though still close enough for the agent to be free to overcome it). A theoretical construal of freedom with respect to a factor does not need to, and should not, take it as an all-or-nothing matter. In short, what we earlier raised as an objection to the closeness account, its recognition of degrees of freedom with respect to a factor, should properly be counted as a virtue of the approach.

(b) Korsgaard also very acutely notices that 'it may be perfectly reasonable for me to hold someone responsible for an attitude or an action, while at the same time acknowledging that it is just as reasonable for someone else not to hold the same person responsible for the very same attitude or action. Perhaps it is reasonable for *you* to forgive or overlook our friend's distrustful behavior on the grounds that he has suffered so much heartbreak, but not for me, *not* because I fail to appreciate how hurt he has been, but because I am the woman whose loving conduct is always met with distrust' (199). Korsgaard gives this as an example of a possibility 'that would not make sense if responsibility were a fact about the person' (199). But it seems to me that the theoretical view can accommodate this phenomenon too, provided that it recognizes differences in degree of difficulty in carrying through an action the agent is free to perform. In Korsgaard's example, there are two relations in which the two people stand to the agent. The one person is an outside observer of the situation, the other engages in loving conduct towards the agent. These different relations generate different entitlements or legitimate expectations in the degree of effort subjects standing in the different relations can properly demand of the agent in overcoming difficulties in pursuing a course of action, before they forgive or overlook some of the agent's behaviour. It seems to me that Korsgaard is right to say that the loving woman has a right to require more than the disinterested observer of the situation may reasonably expect. What I cannot see is that the phenomenon is inexplicable on the theoretical conception of freedom, once we acknowledge that the different relations to the agent are generating the differences in legitimate expectations. The example does not force us to say inconsistent things about the factual issue of the freedom of the agent.

(c) I am much less sure than Korsgaard that there is so tight a connection between one's placing oneself in a relationship with someone, and attributions of responsibility and freedom. She discusses the reciprocity and openness involved in close friendship, and ways in which this may be abused. As she notes, we may eventually 'write someone off', and in extreme cases cease to have reactive attitudes to them altogether (200). Yet it is not at all clear to me that this must involve thinking of this other person as unfree or as not responsible, as opposed to just being awful, manipulative or utterly egocentric. These latter characteristics seem to me, unfortunately, to be compatible with freedom.

7.7 LIBERTARIANISM

Russell at one point wrote:

Perhaps in the brain the unstable equilibrium is so delicate that the difference between two possible occurrences in one atom suffices to produce macroscopic differences in the movements of muscles. And since, according to quantum physics, there are no physical laws to determine which of several possible transitions an atom will undergo, we may imagine that, in a brain, the choice between possible transitions is determined by a psychological cause called 'volition'. All this is possible, but no more than possible.[28]

I want to introduce a cluster of issues by starting with the comment made on this passage from Russell by the prominent libertarian David Wiggins, who wonders: 'Could not the incidence of human acts of "volition" upon quantum phenomena upset the probability distributions postulated by the quantum theory?'[29] Wiggins also observes that if the volitions were postulated to have some immaterially realized source (perhaps to connect them with the agent's character), the theory would be unacceptably Cartesian. He writes that 'We need not trace free actions back to volitions construed as little pushes aimed from outside the physical world'.[30]

It seems to me, however, that if Wiggins's argument about the incidence of 'volitions' on quantum phenomena is sound, there is also a problem lurking here for the libertarian conception of freedom. It is a problem which can be formulated in a way quite independent of any commitment to Cartesian mythology. The assumption required for formulation of the problem is rather the non-Cartesian principle that mental events and states supervene on physical states and events. The states and events on which they supervene are not necessarily restricted to physical states of the brain. (In fact they are necessarily not restricted to physical states of the brain, but must include a more or less extensive section of the environment, given externalist theories of content.) Now suppose an agent has a choice between an action-type A and an action-type B, and suppose that he cannot do both. Let S_A be the set of physical states and event-types on which his

---

[28] B. Russell, *Human Knowledge: Its Scope and Limits* (London: Routledge, 1992 reprinting), Part I, ch. 5, pp. 55–6.

[29] 'Towards a Reasonable Libertarianism', 292.

[30] Ibid.

choosing A would supervene, and let S_B be the set of physical states and event-types on which his choosing B would supervene. Just before the moment of choice, his being in some or other state in S_A and his being in some or other state in S_B each have certain probabilities. (The probabilities cannot be calculated in practice.) If the libertarian theory is that the subject's complete freedom to choose either A or B implies that it is completely indeterminate which he will choose, won't the libertarian theory imply that an agent with this freedom can make either choice with whatever frequency he pleases? Cannot a collection of agents, similarly situated, make either choice with whatever frequency they please? *If* Wiggins's objection to Russell is sound, then we might equally argue that this would eventually conflict with the probabilities implied by quantum mechanics. This means that the original point, raised by Wiggins against the conception Russell described, would if correct equally count against a range of libertarian views. It would not be only volitional theories and Cartesian variants thereof which are vulnerable to the objection. It is worth noting that only supervenience has been employed in this argument. There has been no commitment to token-identity theories, nor even to the existence of realization or constitution relations between mental events and physical events.

But is Wiggins's original objection to Russell sound? The matter is shrouded in some obscurity. Quantum theory postulates probabilities, not actual frequencies. We would also need to know more about the libertarian theory to assess whether its conception of freedom is incompatible with there being a determinate probability of the agent being in state S_A and a determinate probability of the agent being in state S_B. We would also need to consider separately the case in which many agents make separate, uncoordinated decisions, from that in which they are genuinely independent. A case could be made that only the case of genuine independence is a potential threat to the position Russell outlines. But in that case it is not clear that even the frequencies will diverge from those one would reasonably expect from a probabilistic microtheory. There are many other issues here too. Perhaps these points are enough to establish that the soundness of the argument is moot.[31]

---

[31] I am indebted for the point about genuine independence to remarks by Timothy Williamson. This paragraph represents a change of mind from pp. 372–3 of my paper 'The Modality of Freedom', in A. O'Hear (ed.), *Current Issues in*

There is, though, another problem for the libertarian who accepts the supervenience of the mental on the physical. That libertarian is committed to saying that an actual decision is freely made because there is a microstate, not actually instantiated, and on which his making a different decision supervenes, a microstate which is not determined by earlier conditions. What is distinctive of the libertarian's position is not that neither the actual nor this alternative microstate is determined by earlier conditions. Everyone should accept that, if determinism is in fact false. What is distinctive of his position is rather that this indeterminism of the microstates is involved in *making* the decision a free one. Now there is a problem here for the libertarian in accommodating a further intuitive feature of our ordinary conception of a free decision. On that conception, if an agent who decides freely were to have made a different decision, in accordance with his freedom to do so, the reasons in favour of that different decision would then have been operative in producing that decision. But how is the libertarian who believes in supervenience to accommodate that feature? When a probabilistic and indeterministic theory of microstates is correct, and two outcome-types are possible given the initial conditions, one cannot truly say of the outcome-type which is not realized that had it been so, different factors would have been operative in its production than were operative in the production of the actual outcome. But it is not clear to me how the libertarian can avoid commitment to that conclusion, given his conception of a free action, and the existence of the intuitive feature of free actions.

There is no corresponding problem for the form of compatibilism I have been suggesting. That form of compatibilism is not committed, under the assumption of a true indeterministic microtheory, to saying that different factors would have been operative had a probabilistic outcome been different from the actual course of events. Rather, on that compatibilist theory, the freedom of the decision consists in the existence of a close possibility of a different state of affairs in which the subject decides differently, but in which some other initial conditions may also be different. On this view, a world in which other reasons are operative is a world which is different in

Philosophy of Mind, Royal Institute of Philosophy Supplement 43 (Cambridge: Cambridge University Press, 1998), which not only formulates the parallel with Wiggins's argument, but endorses it. I am continuing to maintain that there is a parallel argument, but am now refraining from the endorsement.

other respects too. The problematic commitments of the libertarian are avoided.

I am inclined to draw three conclusions from these reflections. The first is that a probabilistic microtheory is just as threatening as classical determinism to the existence of freedom as conceived by libertarians.

Second, these reflections also make me wonder whether a libertarian theory will not have to be non-naturalistic to a degree that its proponents may not have envisaged.

Third, if neither deterministic nor indeterministic physical theories of the sort we currently have can be squared with the libertarian elucidation of freedom, it must follow that either we are not free, or the libertarian elucidation is incorrect.

This is a kind of modern fork against the libertarian, though it does not involve quite the same conclusions and commitments as Hume's fork. What I have said does suggest that any form of physical theory will be problematic for the libertarian, at least given supervenience. But, unlike Hume, I do not conclude that freedom requires determinism. (All to the good, since there is evidence that determinism is false.) My own view is that, even on a non-deterministic conception of causal explanation, when it comes to free choices, the choice may or may not be fully rationally caused and explained. Sometimes a free choice is rationally caused and fully rationally explained, of course. But sometimes it is part of the nature of the case that it is not. Consider, for instance, someone in the position of Buridan's ass, making a choice between two exactly equally attractive options, with no reason to choose one over the other. Unlike Buridan's ass, we do succeed in choosing; but the rational agent may in such a case have no reason for opting for the one he actually selects. The choice between it and its equivalent alternative is not one which falls within the ambit of rational psychological explanation. Any explanation there is will be, at best, sub-personal. But the choice can nevertheless be a free one. My view, in short, is that freedom does not require determinism, and it does not require indeterminism either.

What then produces the illusion, if it is an illusion, that freedom requires indeterminism? One source is the genuine recognition that there is a 'could have done otherwise' requirement, when that recognition is combined with the belief that only an indeterministic construal of the modality can be given. I have tried to give an alternative construal of the modality. I think, though, that part of the explanation of the illusion may also be the fact that when an agent is presented with various prima facie reasons for different courses of action, there is apparently no *ceteris paribus* psychological law of common-sense psychology about which she will choose, not even when she has deliberated and found one of the courses best all things considered. All kinds of impulsive, and/or weak-willed, but nevertheless free, choices may be made by the agent. Since there is no such psychological law, and we also consider the alternatives between which the agent is deliberating to be genuinely open to her, it may be tempting to conclude that there is no law at all explaining her choice. Put like that, though, any such conclusion would be a *non sequitur*. It would be entirely consistent with those premises that there is some other kind of *ceteris paribus*, and perhaps probabilistic, law which, in the circumstances in which the agent is placed, explains the choice under its intentional description. It may be anything ranging from the sub-personal computational, or the psychoanalytic, to the sociological or the economic. All our premises said is that there is no *ceteris paribus* psychological law of common-sense psychology.

7.8 THE EPISTEMOLOGY OF FREEDOM

When we confine our attention to judgements about another person's freedom, there is a relatively straightforward and plausible way of integrating the metaphysics and epistemology of freedom. According to the truth conditions of the closeness account which we gave in section 7.3 above, someone who meets the background conditions on effective reflection is free to ϕ if (a) there is a close possibility in which he tries to ϕ, and (b) he would ϕ were he to try to. According to the relatively straightforward approach to integration in the third-person case, one who possesses the concept of freedom has tacit knowledge—an implicit conception of freedom—whose content is precisely the truth conditions given by the closeness account. This approach can also endorse the Linking Thesis of Chapter 2 for the subject matter of freedom. Someone whose judgements about the freedom of another person are appropriately made as a result of using this tacit knowledge, and whose judgements are made on the basis of information about the other person which also has the status of knowledge, will come to make judgements about the other person's freedom, or unfreedom, which also have the epistemic status of knowledge.

That approach to integration for the third-person case does not, however, even begin to speak to the Integration Challenge as it arises for freedom in the first-person case. In ordinary practical and theoretical deliberation, various possibilities are apparently open to us. We ordinarily have the subjective impression that we are free to pursue any of several options. This is the impression which William James described as 'the consciousness of the alternative also being possible'.[32] This impression is part of the phenomenology of ordinary deliberation. It was probably his taking this impression at face value which made Dr. Johnson say 'We *know* our will is free, and *there's* an end on't'.[33] These impressions which are present in the first-person case have no analogue in our judgements about the freedom of someone thought about in a third-personal way. Since it is plausible that these impressions ordinarily play both a causal and a rational role in a thinker's self-ascriptions of freedom, the shape of any attempt to meet the Integration Challenge in the first-person case must accommodate them, and explain their role, or else explain why it rejects them.

Accommodation and explanation which justify all our pretheoretical beliefs in this area would involve carrying out at least the following two tasks. First, we would have to account for the apparent combination of impressions of freedom being both inconclusive (as in the Penfield example given at the beginning of this chapter), and yet on some occasions, with a suitable background, being capable apparently, on our pretheoretical beliefs, of leading to knowledge of the subject's own freedom. Second, we would have to give some philosophical explanation of how impressions of freedom might play a role in leading to first-person knowledge of freedom.

Can a causal theory explain these epistemic phenomena? There is an initial obstacle which needs to be overcome in stating a causal

---

[32] *The Principles of Psychology*, with an Introduction by George Miller (Cambridge, Mass.: Harvard University Press, 1983), 1176. James's discussion makes it clear that he holds that the content of this 'consciousness' can be erroneous. For a more extensive discussion of subjective elements in our conception of freedom, combined with a more sceptical view about its reality than I have been advocating, see G. Strawson, *Freedom and Belief* (Oxford: Oxford University Press, 1986).

[33] J. Boswell, *Life of Johnson*, ed. R. Chapman (Oxford: Oxford University Press, 1980), 10 October 1769.

theory, an obstacle to stating a causal theory of knowledge of freedom in as straightforward a form as one finds in causal theories of perceptual knowledge. The apparent availability of alternative courses of action—the impression of freedom—is an actual phenomenon. Only what is actual can causally explain the actual. The closeness of a possibility in which one acts differently is, however, not in itself something actual. The modal truth that with only small differences in initial conditions, one would have tried to do something different, cannot itself causally explain any actual events. The point worried J. S. Mill: 'Consciousness tells me what I do or feel. But what I am able to do, is not a subject of consciousness. . . . [W]e are conscious of what is, not of what will or can be. We never know that we are able to do a thing, except from having done it, or something equal and similar to it.'[34]

It may help to consider some other cases of modal knowledge. We do know on some occasions that something different could easily have happened. Consider the case of a vase at the edge of a table. We know it could easily fall off. We know this because, given its actual location relative to the table's edge, only slightly different initial conditions just before that time, conditions there is or would have been nothing robust to prevent coming about, would have led to the vase being knocked off (by vibrations, breezes, passers-by). Here the actual position of the vase on the table is capable of interacting with us causally. We know that with such a position, a range of initial conditions will lead to the vase falling. This intuitive mechanics we have either acquired, or inherited. In this example, there is a role for causality in explaining our knowledge of the spatial arrangement. It is also plausible that if objects in that sort of arrangement would not easily fall, we would not believe it. Selection processes, either in the life of the individual or the species, will filter out much erroneous intuitive mechanics (though, as is well known, not all). If the spatial arrangement is of a sort for which the thinker's intuitive mechanics is correct, and persists because it is correct, then the thinker can know that the vase could easily fall.

Can such examples provide a model for knowledge of one's own freedom? They instantiate a structure which explains the possibility of such modal knowledge, but there are some differences. In the case

---

[34] J. S. Mill, *An Examination of Sir William Hamilton's Philosophy* (London: Longmans, Green & Co., 1889), ch. 26, p. 50.

of intuitive mechanics, it is open to dispute whether the modals about mechanics enter the very content of the thinker's subjective experience, as opposed to entering merely the content of the subject's beliefs about the perceived objects. Let us then switch to a slightly different example, that of impressions of causation, of the sort famously investigated by the psychologist Michotte.[35] We sometimes have the experiential impression, of one perceived particular event, that it caused another particular event, where that second event is also given in perception. These impressions may, like the other contents of an experience, be either endorsed or overruled by the perceiver's judgements.

In addition to being genuinely part of the content of experience, impressions of causation have two features which make for a pertinent comparison with the case of freedom. First, what an impression of causation is an impression *of* is something which, in normal circumstances, has counterfactual consequences. Second, the impression is clearly fallible. Indeed, in Michotte's own experimental setup the impressions induced were incorrect. These first two features are analogues of agreed characteristics of the impression of freedom. There is also a plausible selection argument that impressions of causation, though certainly subject on occasion to error, will not be wildly erroneous in circumstances important to an organism's survival and success.

When I addressed the Integration Challenge for the topics of the previous chapters—metaphysical necessity, the past, and various properties of the self—I attempted to make a case that, on the metaphysics and epistemology I defended, knowledge of the sort we ordinarily take ourselves to have in the area in question is not merely possible, but actual. It is unclear whether it is possible to go that far in the case of freedom. There is no doubt common-sense prima facie evidence that we are free with respect to certain factors. There may even be a sound selectionist argument that the impressions of freedom enjoyed by a mature individual of a well-evolved species will be approximately correct in a core of cases. It would be wasteful of time and energy to deliberate about options which are not realizable by that individual in any close possibility. Yet there are equally general arguments threatening to freedom on the other side. One of the most powerful is that our subjective impression of freedom comes from an illegitimate transfer. The impression we have that our own decisions

---

[35] A. Michotte, *The Perception of Causality* (New York: Basic Books, 1963).

are made by us, without conclusive determination by factors at the personal level, is, the sceptic may say, pumped up into the impression that there are nearby worlds in which we could have done differently. For the content of this pumped-up impression, the sceptic may say, there is no justification on the notion as I have characterized it.

I doubt that the case for or against our actual freedom in any given area—as opposed to its possibility—can be decided simply on the basis of obvious truths and philosophical theory, however resourceful. Freedom is neither a mere practical commitment, nor something incoherent and unachievable. To suppose that we can establish or refute claims about our freedom in a given area from a combination of obvious truths and a priori theory is to fail to do justice to the strength of the notion of freedom. I have been trying to say what that notion is, and thus what we would need to know of its instantiation.

7.9 NEITHER TOO MUCH NOR TOO LITTLE?

As the reader might expect, I am inclined to present the closeness account as a form of the very first of the seven theoretical possibilities I distinguished when there is trouble in squaring the metaphysics and the epistemology in a given domain. The closeness account of freedom seems to be an account of the metaphysics of freedom which makes freedom an intelligible possibility, and makes the distinction between the cases in which an agent is free to do something, and those in which he is not, an empirical matter.

To this, it may be objected that some intrinsically problematic conception of freedom is inextricably entwined in our normal thought and practices, and that because this is so, the closeness account must rather be revisionary. The objection is that the closeness conception is rather an example of the fourth of the seven options I identified back in Chapter 1, that is, the option in which we offer a surrogate rather than a full-width truth condition for statements of the problematic kind.

My immediate reaction to this objection is one which, despite our disagreement on the correct positive account, I share with Peter Strawson, when he writes that 'the idea that an entire range of emotions which pervade our personal and social lives as thoroughly as those in question should be thus linked to a condition which cannot be coherently described has a degree of implausibility which it would be difficult to rival'.[36] It may help to consider a parallel. Suppose we had a benighted community which believed in an extreme form of absolute space, and with it a distinction between absolute rest and absolute motion. This would certainly be a case in which the integration of the metaphysics and the epistemology would present severe—I would say insuperable—problems. Suppose we point out to members of this community that cases in which they speak of absolute rest really involve rest relative to some specified object or array of objects, and that is how the truth conditions of their statements about absolute rest and motion should be given. Would it be right for members of this community to object that the truth conditions we propose would really be revisionary, would be an example of the fourth option rather than the first, and thus would not really capture what they meant? Well, our proposal would certainly be revisionary of a misconception of the nature of what they call rest, or motion, *sans phrase*. Maybe the misconception is indeed so inextricably involved in their thought that they would not know what to say in their old vocabulary once the situation is pointed out to them. What is clear, however, is that it would be futile in the spatial case to hope for a *better* solution than that we have offered them.

Now no one could honestly say that the case of freedom is as clear as that of absolute location. Whatever one's favoured solution, philosophical humility is the only appropriate mode in which to present it, in the face of the tremendous difficulty and recalcitrance of the problem of freedom. I do, though, want to suggest one similarity between the case of freedom and this spatial example. I suspect that we cannot coherently have more than the closeness account offers; while to settle for less seems to leave us in the queasy position of engaging in practices without entitlement. If that is so, then the closeness account is something with which it would be reasonable to rest content.

---

[36] P. Strawson, 'Replies', in Z. van Straaten (ed.), *Philosophical Subjects: Essays Presented to P. F. Strawson* (Oxford: Oxford University Press, 1980), 265.

8

Concluding Remarks

I have tried to meet the Integration Challenge in a few salient areas, sometimes by offering a revised metaphysics, sometimes by offering a different epistemology, and sometimes by suggesting a reconception of the relations between an extant metaphysics and an extant epistemology. The treatment of metaphysical necessity exemplifes the case in which we revise the metaphysics. The treatment of thought about the past exemplifies the case in which we revise the epistemology; and the treatment of a thinker's knowledge of the content of her own mental states involves some reconception of the relations between metaphysics and epistemology. Though the solutions offered have been of several varieties, some general principles emerge from them. These general principles may or may not have been attractive to readers prior to the discussion of the Integration Challenge. It is, however, arguable that they receive new sources of support from the discussion in this book.

(1) It is often possible to acknowledge the objectivity of some area of thought, and its distinctive features, without postulating an exotic metaphysics. I suggested a middle way which avoids the metaphysics of Lewisian possible worlds in the treatment of metaphysical necessity, and a middle way which avoids the metaphysics of transcendental subjects in the treatment of distinctive features of first-person thought.

(2) Statements which may seem like the merest truisms involved in our ordinary grasp of some family of concepts may turn out to have previously hidden metaphysical or epistemological significance. Take the statement that any present thought 'Yesterday it rained' is true if and only if yesterday had the same property today has to have for 'It is raining today' to be true. I argued in Chapter 3 that, in combination with other plausible principles, this truistic-sounding principle rules out all verificationist and constructivist treatments of thought

about the past. Tracing out the consequences of a family of truisms is sometimes essential to meeting the Integration Challenge in an intuitively acceptable way.

(3) No conclusions about the mind-dependence of a subject matter can be drawn from biconditionals stating that in certain circumstances, a thinker will be right in his judgements about that subject matter. This point holds even if the biconditionals are necessary and a priori; and even if there is no question of the thinker's judgements being causally explained by facts about the subject matter. A thinker with tacit knowledge of the principles of possibility will be right in a core of cases about modal matters, his errors being explicable by his erroneous beliefs about non-modal matters. This point is entirely consistent with modal truth being fixed by the principles of possibility, in a way which is mind-independent.

(4) The notion of an implicit conception with a certain content, and which is involved in understanding, has loomed large in the discussion of many of the topics in this book. It is a notion with significant rationalist dimensions, and with ramifications many of which remain unexplored. It is reasonable to expect the notion to loom equally large in the discussion of other areas in which the Integration Challenge is pressing.

Finally, it seems to me that if some of the discussions of this book are approximately correct, there is a more general conclusion to be drawn about metaphysics and epistemology themselves. We can learn more about each of metaphysics and epistemology, and be stimulated to develop new approaches to each of them in a given domain, when we are required to consider them not in isolation, but in the light of the relations they must bear to one another.

BIBLIOGRAPHY

ADAMS, R. 'Theories of Actuality', *Noûs* 8 (1974), 211–31.

ANSCOMBE, G. E. M. 'Causality and Extensionality', *Journal of Philosophy* 66 (1969), 152–9.

BENACERAFF, P. 'Mathematical Truth', repr. in Benaceraff and Putnam (eds.), *Philosophy of Mathematics* (q.v.).

—— and PUTNAM, H. (eds.). *Philosophy of Mathematics: Selected Readings*, 2nd edn. (Cambridge: Cambridge University Press, 1983).

BENNETT, J. 'Counterfactuals and Temporal Direction', *Philosophical Review* 93 (1984), 57–91.

BERLIN, I. 'Empirical Propositions and Hypothetical Statements', *Mind* 59 (1950), 289–312; repr. in his *Concepts and Categories: Philosophical Essays*, ed. H. Hardy (Oxford: Oxford University Press, 1980).

—— 'Verification', *Proceedings of the Aristotelian Society* 39 (1938–9), 225–48; repr. in his *Concepts and Categories* (q.v.).

BLACKBURN, S. *Essays in Quasi-Realism* (New York: Oxford University Press, 1993).

—— 'Morals and Modals', repr. in his *Essays in Quasi-Realism* (q.v.).

BOGHOSSIAN, P. 'Content and Self-Knowledge', *Philosophical Topics* 17 (1989), 5–26.

—— 'What the Externalist can Know A Priori', *Proceedings of the Aristotelian Society* 97 (1997), 161–75.

BONJOUR, L. *The Structure of Empirical Knowledge* (Cambridge, Mass.: Harvard University Press, 1985).

BOOLOS, G. *The Unprovability of Consistency* (Cambridge: Cambridge University Press, 1979).

BOSWELL, J. *Life of Johnson*, ed. R. Chapman (Oxford: Oxford University Press, 1980).

BREWER, B. 'Externalism and A Priori Knowledge of Empirical Facts', forthcoming in a collection on the a priori edited by P. Boghossian and C. Peacocke.

BURGE, T. 'Content Preservation', *Philosophical Review* 102 (1993), 457–88.

—— 'Frege and the Hierarchy', *Synthese* 40 (1979), 265–81.

—— 'Individualism and Self-Knowledge', *Journal of Philosophy* 85 (1988), 649–63.

BURGE, T. 'Individualism and the Mental', in P. A. French, T. E. Uehling, and H. Wettstein (eds.), *Midwest Studies in Philosophy* 4: *Studies in Metaphysics* (Minneapolis, Minn.: University of Minnesota Press, 1979), 72–121.

—— 'Our Entitlement to Self-Knowledge', *Proceedings of the Aristotelian Society* 96 (1996), 91–116.

—— 'Reason and the First Person', in McDonald, Smith, and Wright (eds.), *Knowing Our Own Minds* (q.v.).

CAMPBELL, J. *Past, Space and Self* (Cambridge, Mass.: MIT Press, 1994).

CARNAP, R. *Meaning and Necessity: A Study in Semantics and Modal Logic*, 2nd edn. (Chicago, Ill.: Chicago University Press, 1956).

CARTWRIGHT, N. *Nature's Capacities and their Measurement* (Oxford: Oxford University Press, 1989).

CASSAM, Q. *Self and World* (Oxford: Oxford University Press, 1997).

CHISHOLM, R. 'Human Freedom and the Self', repr. in G. Watson (ed.), *Free Will* (Oxford: Oxford University Press, 1982).

CRAIG, E. 'Arithmetic and Fact', in I. Hacking (ed.), *Exercises in Analysis* (Cambridge: Cambridge University Press, 1985).

—— *Knowledge and the State of Nature: An Essay in Conceptual Synthesis* (Oxford: Oxford University Press, 1990).

DAVIDSON, D. 'On Saying That', repr. in his *Inquiries into Truth and Interpretation* (Oxford: Oxford University Press, 1984).

—— 'Theories of Meaning and Learnable Languages', repr. in his *Inquiries into Truth and Interpretation* (q.v.).

DAVIES, M., 'Externalism, Architecturalism, and Epistemic Warrant', in McDonald, Smith, and Wright (eds.), *Knowing Our Own Minds* (q.v.).

—— 'Psychological Explanation, Externality, and Narrow Content', *Proceedings of the Aristotelian Society*, supp. vol. 60 (1986), 263–83.

—— 'Singular Terms, Quantification and Modality', B.Phil. Thesis, Oxford University, 1975.

—— 'Weak Necessity and Truth Theories', *Journal of Philosophical Logic* 7 (1978), 415–39.

—— and HUMBERSTONE, L. 'Two Notions of Necessity', *Philosophical Studies* 38 (1980), 1–30.

DUMMETT, M. 'A Defence of McTaggart's Proof of the Unreality of Time', repr. in his *Truth and Other Enigmas* (q.v.).

—— *Frege: Philosophy of Language* (London: Duckworth, 1973).

—— *The Logical Basis of Metaphysics* (Cambridge, Mass.: Harvard University Press, 1991).

—— *Origins of Analytical Philosophy* (Cambridge, Mass.: Harvard University Press, 1993).

—— 'The Philosophical Basis of Intuitionistic Logic', repr. in his *Truth and Other Enigmas* (q.v.).

—— 'The Reality of the Past', repr. in his *Truth and Other Enigmas* (q.v.).

—— *Truth and Other Enigmas* (London: Duckworth, 1978).

—— 'What is a Theory of Meaning? (II)', in G. Evans and J. McDowell (eds.), *Truth and Meaning: Essays in Semantics* (Oxford: Oxford University Press, 1976).

Encyclopaedia Britannica, 'Olbers' Paradox' (1998 CD-ROM).

EVANS, G. *The Varieties of Reference* (Oxford: Oxford University Press, 1982).

FIELD, H. 'Quine and the Correspondence Theory', *Philosophical Review* 85 (1974), 200–28.

—— *Realism, Mathematics and Modality* (Oxford: Blackwell, 1989).

—— *Science Without Numbers: A Defence of Nominalism* (Oxford: Blackwell, 1980).

FINE, K., 'Essence and Modality', in J. Tomberlin (ed.), *Philosophical Perspectives, 8: Logic and Language* (Atascadero, Calif.: Ridgeview, 1994), 1–16.

FISCHER, J. *The Metaphysics of Free Will: An Essay on Control* (Oxford: Blackwell, 1994)

FLANAGAN, O. *Consciousness Regained* (Cambridge, Mass.: MIT Press, 1992).

FORBES, G. 'Melia on Modalism', *Philosophical Studies* 68 (1992), pp. 57–63.

—— *The Metaphysics of Modality* (Oxford: Oxford University Press, 1985).

FREGE, G. *Collected Papers on Mathematics, Logic and Philosophy*, ed. B. McGuinness (Oxford: Blackwell, 1984).

FRITH, C. *The Cognitive Neuropsychology of Schizophrenia* (Hove, Sussex: Laurence Erlbaum, 1992).

GALLISTEL, C. *The Organization of Learning* (Cambridge, Mass.: MIT Press, 1990).

GEACH, P. *Mental Acts* (London: Routledge & Kegan Paul, 1957).

GINET, C. *On Action* (Cambridge: Cambridge University Press, 1990).

GOLDMAN, A. 'Discrimination and Perceptual Knowledge', *Journal of Philosophy* 73 (1976), 771–91.

—— 'The Psychology of Folk Psychology', *Behavioral and Brain Sciences* 16 (1993) 15–28.

GOODMAN, N. *Fact, Fiction and Forecast*, 2nd edn. (Indianapolis: Bobbs-Merrill, 1965).

GUPTA, A. 'Modal Logic and Truth', *Journal of Philosophical Logic* 7 (1978), 441–72.

HAHN, M., and RAMBERG, B. (eds.). Festschrift for Tyler Burge (Cambridge, Mass.: MIT Press, forthcoming).

HARMAN, G., and THOMSON, J. *Moral Relativism and Moral Objectivity* (Oxford: Blackwell, 1996).

HILBERT, D. 'On the Infinite', trans. E. Putnam and G. Massey, repr. in Benacerraf and Putnam (eds.), *Philosophy of Mathematics* (q.v.).

HINTIKKA, J. *Models for Modalities* (Dordrecht: Reidel, 1969).

HUGHES, G., and CRESSWELL, M. *A New Introduction to Modal Logic* (London: Routledge, 1996).

HUMBERSTONE, I. 'From Worlds to Possibilities', *Journal of Philosophical Logic* 10 (1981), 313–39.

INWAGEN, P. van. 'A Formal Approach to the Problem of Free Will and Determinism', *Theoria* 40 (1974), 9–22.

—— 'The Incompatilibility of Free Will and Determinism', *Philosophical Studies* 27 (1975), 185–99.

JACKSON, F. 'A Causal Theory of Counterfactuals', *Australasian Journal of Philosophy* 55 (1977), 3–21.

JAMES, W. *The Principles of Psychology*, with an introduction by George Miller (Cambridge, Mass.: Harvard University Press, 1983).

KANT, I. *Critique of Pure Reason*, trans. P. Guyer and A. Wood (Cambridge: Cambridge University Press, 1998).

—— *Ethical Philosophy*, trans. J. Ellington (Indianapolis, Ind.: Hackett, 1994).

KAPLAN, D. 'Demonstratives: An Essay on the Semantics, Logic, Metaphysics, and Epistemology of Demonstratives and Other Indexicals', in J. Almog, J. Perry, and H. Wettstein (eds.), *Themes From Kaplan* (New York: Oxford University Press, 1989).

—— 'Dthat', in P. Cole (ed.), *Syntax and Semantics* (New York: Academic Press, 1978).

KATZ, J. 'Descartes's *Cogito*', *Pacific Philosophical Quarterly* 68 (1987), 175–96.

KORSGAARD, C. 'Creating the Kingdom of Ends: Reciprocity and Responsibility in Personal Relations', in her *Creating the Kingdom of Ends* (Cambridge: Cambridge University Press, 1996).

KRIPKE, S. *Naming and Necessity* (Oxford: Blackwell, 1980).

—— 'Semantical Considerations on Modal Logic', repr. in L. Linsky (ed.), *Reference and Modality* (Oxford: Oxford University Press, 1971).

KÜNNE, W. 'First Person Propositions: A Fregean Account', in Künne, Newen, and Anduschus (eds.), *Direct Reference, Indexicality, and Propositional Attitudes* (q.v.).

—— NEWEN, A., and ANDUSCHUS, M. (eds.). *Direct Reference, Indexicality and Propositional Attitudes* (CSLI Lecture Notes no. 70) (Stanford, Calif.: CSLI Publications, 1997).

LEIBNIZ, G. W. *New Essays on Human Understanding*, trans. and ed. P. Remanant and J. Bennett (Cambridge: Cambridge University Press, 1981).

LEWIS, D. 'Are We Free to Break the Laws?', repr. in his *Philosophical Papers*, vol. ii (q.v.).

—— *Counterfactuals* (Oxford: Blackwell, 1973).

—— 'Counterfactuals and Comparative Possibility', repr. in his *Philosophical Papers*, vol. ii (q.v.).

—— *On the Plurality of Worlds* (Oxford: Blackwell, 1986).

—— *Philosophical Papers*, vol. ii (New York: Oxford University Press, 1986).

LUCAS, J. *The Future: An Essay on God, Temporality and Truth* (Oxford: Blackwell, 1989).

McDONALD, C., SMITH, B., and WRIGHT, C. (eds.). *Knowing Our Own Minds: Essays on Self-Knowledge* (Oxford: Oxford University Press, 1998).

McDOWELL, J. '*De Re* Senses', *Philosophical Quarterly* 34 (1984), 283–94.

—— 'Knowledge and the Internal', *Philosophy and Phenomenological Research* 55 (1995), 877–93.

—— *Mind and World* (Cambridge, Mass.: Harvard University Press, 1994).

—— 'On "The Reality of the Past"', in C. Hookway and P. Pettit (eds.), *Action and Interpretation* (Cambridge: Cambridge University Press, 1978).

McGINN, C. 'Rigid Designation and Semantical Value', *Philosophical Quarterly* 32 (1982), 97–115.

McKINSEY, M. 'Anti-Individualism and Privileged Access', *Analysis* 51 (1991), 9–16.

MELIA, J. 'Against Modalism', *Philosophical Studies* 68 (1992), 35–56.

MICHOTTE, A. *The Perception of Causality* (New York: Basic Books, 1963).

MILL, J. S. *An Examination of Sir William Hamilton's Philosophy* (London: Longmans, Green & Co., 1889).

MOORE, A. *The Infinite* (London: Routledge, 1990)

—— 'A Note on Kant's First Antinomy', *Philosophical Quarterly* 42 (1992), 480–85.

MOORE, G. E. *Ethics* (London: Oxford University Press, 1966).

—— 'A Reply to my Critics', in P. Schilpp (ed.), *The Philosophy of G. E. Moore*, 2nd edn. (New York: Tudor Publishing Company, 1952).

MORAN, R. 'Making up your Mind: Self-Interpretation and Self-Constitution', *Ratio* NS 1 (1988), 135–51.

NAGEL, T. *The View from Nowhere* (New York: Oxford University Press, 1986).

—— 'What Is It Like to be a Bat?', repr. in his *Mortal Questions* (Cambridge: Cambridge University Press, 1979).

NIETZSCHE, F. *Beyond Good and Evil*, trans. H. Zimmern (Buffalo, NY: Prometheus Books, 1989).

NOZICK, R. *Philosophical Explanations* (Cambridge, Mass.: Harvard University Press, 1981).

PAIS, A. '*Subtle is the Lord . . .*': *The Science and Life of Albert Einstein* (Oxford: Oxford University Press, 1982).

PARFIT, D. 'Experiences, Subjects and Conceptual Scheme', forthcoming in a Festschrift for Sydney Shoemaker.

PARFIT, D. *Reasons and Persons* (Oxford: Oxford University Press, 1987 revised printing).

PEACOCKE, C. 'Conscious Attitudes, Attention and Self-Knowledge', in McDonald, Smith, and Wright (eds.), *Knowing Our Own Minds* (q.v.).

—— 'Content, Computation, and Externalism', *Mind and Language* 9 (1994), 303–35.

PEACOCKE, C. 'Demonstrative Thought and Psychological Explanation', *Synthese* 49 (1981), 187–217.

—— 'Entitlement, Self-Knowledge and Conceptual Redeployment', *Proceedings of the Aristotelian Society* 96 (1996), 117–58.

—— 'Externalist Explanation', *Proceedings of the Aristotelian Society* 93 (1993), 203–30.

—— 'First-Person Reference, Representational Independence, and Self-Knowledge', in Künne, Newen, and Anduschus (eds.), *Direct Reference, Indexicality, and Propositional Attitudes* (q.v.).

—— 'How are A Priori Truths Possible?' *European Journal of Philosophy* 1 (1993), 175–99.

—— 'Imagination, Possibility and Experience', in J. Foster and H. Robinson (eds.), *Essays on Berkeley* (Oxford: Oxford University Press, 1985).

—— 'Implicit Conceptions, Understanding and Rationality', in E. Villaneuva (ed.), *Philosophical Issues, 8: Concepts* (Atascadero, Calif.: Ridgeview, 1998), with comments by E. Margolis, G. Rey, S. Schiffer, and J. Toribio; and, with comments by T. Burge, in a Festschrift for Tyler Burge ed. M. Hahn and B. Ramberg (Cambridge, Mass.: MIT Press, forthcoming).

—— 'Metaphysical Necessity: Understanding, Truth and Epistemology', *Mind* 106 (1997), 521–74.

—— 'The Modality of Freedom', in A. O'Hear (ed.), *Current Issues in Philosophy of Mind* (Royal Institute of Philosophy Supplement 43) (Cambridge: Cambridge University Press, 1998).

—— 'Necessity and Truth Theories', *Journal of Philosophical Logic* 7 (1978), 473–500.

—— 'Proof and Truth', in J. Haldane and C. Wright (eds.), *Reality, Representation and Projection* (New York: Oxford University Press, 1993).

—— *Sense and Content: Thought and their Relations* (Oxford: Oxford University Press, 1983).

—— 'Sense and Justification', *Mind* 101 (1992), 793–816.

—— 'Sense, Truth and Understanding', in J. Higginbotham (ed.), *Language and Cognition* (Oxford: Blackwell, forthcoming).

—— *A Study of Concepts* (Cambridge, Mass.: MIT Press, 1992).

—— *Thoughts: An Essay on Content* (Oxford: Blackwell, 1986).

—— 'Understanding Logical Constants: A Realist's Account', *Proceedings of the British Academy* 73 (1987), 153–200.

PEARS, D. *Motivated Irrationality* (Oxford: Oxford University Press, 1984).

PENFIELD, W., and RASMUSSEN, T. *The Cerebral Cortex of Man: A Clinical Study of Localization of Function* (New York: Macmillan, 1950).

PERRY, J. 'Self-Notions', *Logos* 11 (1990), 17–31.

—— 'Thought Without Representation', repr. in his *The Problem of the Essential Indexical and Other Essays* (New York: Oxford University Press, 1993).

PRIOR, A. 'The Notion of the Present', *Studium Generale* 23 (1970), 245–8.

—— *Papers on Time and Tense* (Oxford: Oxford University Press, 1968).

PUTNAM, H. *Mathematics, Matter and Method: Philosophical Papers*, vol. i (Cambridge: Cambridge University Press, 1975).

—— 'The Meaning of "Meaning"', repr. in his *Mind, Language and Reality* (q.v.).

—— *Mind, Language and Reality: Philosophical Papers*, vol. ii (Cambridge: Cambridge University Press, 1975).

—— 'On Properties', repr. in his *Mathematics, Matter and Method* (q.v.).

ROSEN, G. 'Modal Fictionalism', *Mind* 90 (1990), 327–54.

RUSSELL, B. *The Analysis of Mind* (London: George Allen & Unwin, 1968).

—— *Human Knowledge: Its Scope and Limits* (London: Routledge, 1992).

RYLE, G. *The Concept of Mind* (London: Penguin, 1963).

—— 'A Puzzling Element in the Notion of Thinking', repr. in his *Collected Papers*, vol. ii: *Collected Essays 1929–1968* (London: Hutchinson, 1971).

SAINSBURY, M. 'Easy Possibilities', *Philosophy and Phenomenological Research* 57 (1997), 907–19.

SALMON, N. 'The Logic of What Might Have Been', *Philosophical Review* 98 (1989), 3–34.

—— 'Modal Paradox', in P. A. French, T. E. Uehling, and H. Wettstein (eds.), *Midwest Studies in Philosophy* 11 (1986), 75–120.

—— *Reference and Essence* (Princeton, NJ: Princeton University Press, 1981).

SELLARS, W. 'Empiricism and the Philosophy of Mind', repr. in his *Science, Perception and Reality* (London: Routledge, 1963).

SHOEMAKER, S. 'Causality and Properties', repr. in his *Identity, Cause and Mind* (q.v.).

—— *The First-Person Perspective and Other Essays* (Cambridge: Cambridge University Press, 1996).

—— *Identity, Cause and Mind: Philosophical Essays* (Cambridge: Cambridge University Press, 1984).

—— 'Identity, Properties and Causality', repr. in his *Identity, Cause and Mind* (q.v.).

—— 'Personal Identity: A Materalist's Account', in S. Shoemaker and R. Swinburne, *Personal Identity* (Oxford: Blackwell, 1984).

—— 'Persons and their Pasts', repr. in his *Identity, Cause and Mind* (q.v.).

SHOEMAKER, S. 'Self-Reference and Self-Awareness', repr. in his *Identity, Cause and Mind* (q.v.).

—— 'Special Access Lies Down with Theory-Theory', *Behavioral and Brain Sciences* 16 (1993), 78–9.

SOAMES, S. 'The Modal Argument: Wide Scope and Rigidified Descriptions', *Noûs* 32 (1998), 1–22.

STALNAKER, R. Critical Notice of David Lewis, *On the Plurality of Worlds, Mind* 97 (1988), 117–28.

—— 'Possible Worlds', *Noûs* 10 (1976), 65–75.

—— 'A Theory of Conditionals', in N. Rescher (ed.), *Studies in Logical Theory* (Oxford: Blackwell, 1968).

STONE, T., and DAVIES, M. 'The Mental Simulation Debate: A Progress Report', in P. Carruthers and P. Smith (eds.), *Theories of Theories of Mind* (Cambridge: Cambridge University Press, 1996).

STRAWSON, G. *Freedom and Belief* (Oxford: Oxford University Press, 1986).

—— 'The Impossibility of Moral Responsibility', *Philosophical Studies* 75 (1994), 5–24.

—— *Mental Reality* (Cambridge, Mass.: MIT Press, 1994).

STRAWSON, P. 'Freedom and Resentment', repr. in his *Freedom and Resentment and Other Essays* (London: Methuen, 1974).

—— *Individuals: An Essay in Descriptive Metaphysics* (London: Methuen, 1959).

—— 'Replies', in Z. van Straaten (ed.), *Philosophical Subjects: Essays Presented to P. F. Strawson* (Oxford: Oxford University Press, 1980).

SWANTON, C. *Freedom: A Coherence Theory* (Indianapolis, Ind.: Hackett, 1992).

TARSKI, A. *Logic, Semantics, Metamathematics: Papers from 1923 to 1938*, 2nd edn. (Indianapolis, Ind: Hackett, 1983).

THOMSON, J. J. 'Reply to Critics', *Philosophy and Phenomenological Research* 58 (1998), 215–22.

UNGER, P. *Ignorance: A Case for Scepticism* (Oxford: Oxford University Press, 1975).

WIGGINS, D. *Sameness and Substance* (Oxford: Blackwell, 1980).

—— 'Towards a Reasonable Libertarianism', repr. in his *Needs, Values and Truth* (Oxford: Blackwell, 1987).

WILLIAMS, B. *Descartes: The Project of Pure Enquiry* (Harmondsworth: Penguin, 1978).

—— 'How Free does the Will Need to Be?' in his *Making Sense of Humanity and Other Philosophical Papers* (Cambridge: Cambridge University Press, 1995).

WILLIAMSON, T. 'Is Knowing a State of Mind?', *Mind* 104 (1995), 533–65.

—— 'Knowing and Asserting', *Philosophical Review* 105 (1996), 489–523.

WITTGENSTEIN, L. *The Blue and Brown Books*, 2nd edn. (Oxford: Blackwell, 1969).

—— *Philosophical Investigations*, trans. G. E. M. Anscombe, 2nd edn. (Oxford: Blackwell, 1958).

—— *Philosophical Remarks*, trans. R. Hargreaves and R. White, ed. R. Rhees (Oxford: Blackwell, 1975).

—— *Remarks on the Foundations of Mathematics*, trans. G. E. M. Anscombe, 3rd edn. (Oxford: Blackwell, 1978).

WRIGHT, C., 'Anti-Realism, Timeless Truth and *Nineteen Eighty-Four*', repr. in his *Realism, Meaning and Truth* (q.v.).

—— 'Necessity, Caution and Scepticism,' *Proceedings of the Aristotelian Society*, supp. vol. 63 (1989), 203–38.

—— *Realism, Meaning and Truth*, 2nd edn. (Oxford: Blackwell, 1993).

—— 'Realism, Truth-Value Links, Other Minds and the Past', repr. in his *Realism, Meaning and Truth* (q.v.).

—— 'Second Thoughts about Criteria', repr. in his *Realism, Meaning and Truth* (q.v.).

—— 'Strict Finitism', repr. in his *Realism, Meaning and Truth* (q.v.).

—— *Truth and Objectivity* (Cambridge, Mass.: Harvard University Press, 1992).

—— *Wittgenstein on the Foundations of Mathematics* (London: Duckworth, 1980).

—— 'Wittgenstein's Later Philosophy of Mind: Sensations, Privacy and Intention', *Journal of Philosophy* 26 (1989), 622–34.

WRIGHT, G. H. VON. *An Essay in Modal Logic* (Amsterdam: North-Holland, 1951).

ZÖLLER, G. 'Lichtenberg', in E. Craig (ed.), *Routledge Encyclopedia of Philosophy* (CD-ROM Version 1.0, London: Routledge, 1998).

INDEX